A Disorderly Compendium *of* Golf

A Disorderly Compendium *of* Golf

Lorne Rubenstein and Jeff Neuman

WORKMAN PUBLISHING, NEW YORK

Published simultaneously in Canada by McClelland & Stewart.

Library of Congress Cataloging-in-Publication Data is available.

ISBN-13: 978-0-7611-4084-9
ISBN-10: 0-7611-4084-0

Cover design by Paul Hanson
Interior design by Paul Hanson and Patrick Borelli

Workman books are available at special discounts when purchased in bulk for premiums and sales promotions as well as for fund-raising or educational use. Special editions or book excerpts can also be created to specification. For details, contact the Special Sales Director at the address below.

Workman Publishing Company, Inc.
225 Varick Street
New York, NY 10014-4381
www.workman.com

Printed in the United States of America

First Printing August 2006
10 9 8 7 6 5 4

To Herb Wind, for his writing and encouragement.

—LR

To Hans and Billie, who knew I had it in me.

—JN

"Tumultuous and disorderly golf never is; interesting it can be; good it seldom is. . . ."

—Seamus Mallon

INTRODUCTION

Did you ever wonder about the ways tour pros have it easier than the rest of us, or, alternately, how they have it harder than we do? Want to hear the things that nobody ever tells you about Augusta National, Pine Valley, and Shinnecock Hills? Maybe you've been curious about whether Bob Dylan plays golf, or what the poet T. S. Eliot might have said if he had been a television golf analyst. Do you know that the putting woes called "the yips" fall into the class of movement problems known as *focal dysonias,* and that there's another strange condition called *atupsia* that affects the full swing? Don't worry—reading about it won't give it to you.

Perhaps more than any other sport, golf is in the details. That might seem a surprising assertion, because, after all, the score is all that matters. Clichés prove as much: "It's not how, but how many." Or, "There are no pictures on the scorecard," meaning that nobody really cares how you made that par four on a hole—when you drove your ball into a lake, took the required one-stroke penalty (honest golfer that you are), then rattled your next shot off a tree to within 40 feet of the hole, and made your putt, which was going so fast it would have run eight feet by if it hadn't hit the back of the hole, jumped in the air and dropped back in. Nope, there's only the number. As they say on the University of Houston golf team, "Don't give me the weather report; just tell me the temperature."

But golf is really about much more than the numbers. It's about the games golfers play, like Wolf or Twenty-One, and it's about the places, like Pebble Beach (which will set you back $450 just to put your tee in the ground). It's about getting a ticket to a practice round for the Masters, and buying a commemorative plate or a Golden Bell candle (the most popular item during the 2006 Masters). It's about Jack Nicklaus and Ben Hogan and Tiger Woods, whose epic careers have earned them spots on the game's mythical Mount Rushmore. But it's also about Marty Fleckman, Mike Donald, Jenny Chuasiriporn, and other golfers who nearly won a major championship and then were never heard from again. We honor these golfers in a section called Footnotes to History, and we scatter their stories throughout this book in a random and disorderly fashion. Open the book anywhere and you'll find stories and items and facts and figures of interest.

Flick through these pages, and you'll come across the things every golfer should do in his or her lifetime—The Golfer's Life List. William Wordsworth observed that "Golf is a day spent in a round of strenuous idleness," and we agree, except that we prefer to think of golf as a game, a sport, an activity, a lifetime spent in pursuit of strenuous and not-so-strenuous, but always enjoyable, engagement. We have misspent our lives in thrall to golf, an odd and beguiling pastime. We've traveled the world in search of the extraordinary in golf, and in celebration of the ordinary, and if you took out of our lives everything except our experiences in St. Andrews, we'd not quite be satisfied but we'd still feel pretty good.

We've teed it up on manicured grounds that God might envy for Heaven, and on pastures tended by sheep. We've spent months in the Scottish Highlands at a latitude equal to that of Juneau, Alaska, and journeyed to Oregon in February for pleasures of a royal and ancient nature. We've scaled Klondyke and traversed the Valley of Sin; carried Stillwater Cove and trekked through Hell's Half Acre; hoisted pints of Guinness at the Dunvegan pub around the corner from the Old Course and eaten pimento-cheese sandwiches at Augusta National. None of our vast body of knowledge has kept us from three-jacking, chili-dipping, duck-hooking, sculling, or putting off the green and into a bunker.

We do, however, share a fascination for the minutiae of the game, a fact you'll discover shortly. We can tell you why James II of Scotland is important (his order that "Golfe be utterly cryed down" in 1457 is the first written reference to the game). We can tell you who played in both the Masters and in baseball's World Series; detail the correct ways to tend a flag and rake a bunker, suggest some betting games to liven your weekly foursome's next outing; and describe the most famous shot hit with each club in the bag, from Arnold Palmer's opening drive that launched his charge at Cherry Hills to Bernhard Langer's missed final putt in the 1991 Ryder Cup.

Most of all, we enjoy the absurd and the random in the game, and highlight these here. The left-handed golfers who won major championships, but were really right-handed; the hustler who would bet you at night that he could make a forty-foot putt on his first try the next morning, and how he made sure he'd pocket your money; some suggestions on how you might become an R&A member; an excerpt from Apollo 14's Lunar Surface Journal that relates the story of Alan Shepherd's moon shot. (The third time an earthling sets foot on the moon, he tries to play golf on it. We wonder what took us so long.)

We've taken our own shots as we range widely through the world of golf. Come on along for the journey, to Hog's Back, Bottle, Ginger Beer, Miss Grainger's Bosoms, the Harvey Masters, the Church Pews, and Wawashkamo, which means Walk a Crooked Path. But that's another story. And it's in here, too.

—Lorne Rubenstein
Jeff Neuman

THE ORIGINAL RULES *of* GOLF

The oldest surviving written Rules of Golf were set down in 1744 by the Gentlemen Golfers of Leith, later known as the Honourable Company of Edinburgh Golfers. (All spelling as in the original.)

1. You must tee your ball within a club's length of the hole.

2. Your tee must be on the ground.

3. You are not to change the ball which you strike off the tee.

4. You are not to remove stones, bones, or any break club for the sake of playing your ball, except upon the fair green, and that only within a club's length of the ball.

5. If your ball comes among watter, or any wattery filth, you are at liberty to take out your ball and bringing it behind the hazard and teeing it, you may play it with any club and allow your adversary a stroke for so getting out your ball.

6. If your balls be found anywhere touching one another you are to lift the first ball till you play the last.

7. At holling you are to play your ball honestly at the hole, and not to play upon your adversary's ball, not lying in your way to the hole.

8. If you should lose your ball, by its being taken up, or any other way, you are to go back to the spot where you struck last and drop another ball and allow your adversary a stroke for the misfortune.

9. No man at holling his ball is to be allowed to mark his way to the hole with his club or anything else.

10. If a ball be stopp'd by any person, horse, dog, or any thing else, the ball so stopp'd must be played where it lyes.

11. If you draw your club in order to strike and proceed so far in the stroke as to be bringing down your club, if then your club should break in any way, it is to be accounted a stroke.

12. He whose ball lyes farthest from the hole is obliged to play first.

13. Neither trench, ditch, or dyke made for the preservation of the links, nor the Scholar's Holes or the soldier's lines shall be accounted a hazard but the ball is to be taken out, teed and play'd with any iron club.

FIVE WAYS THE PROS HAVE IT EASIER THAN WE DO

Those pampered players out there on the pro tours, they have lost all touch with how tough the game can be. They don't have to suffer through five-hour rounds, chewed-up teeing areas, hardpan lies in the fairway, bunkers strewn with pebbles and leaves, shaggy greens, or unevenly cut cups. And look at the millions they make for playing a game we *pay* to play! Yes, the pros have it easy; let me count the ways:

1. Buffered targets. Around every green and fairway there's at least a single line of spectators, sometimes a thick mass that makes the target look like a catcher's mitt. The spectators provide both a backdrop and a backstop; an errant shot might give a fan a bruise, but the resulting ricochet will keep the player from getting into too much trouble. In the unlikely event that he hits the ball wildly past the stands or bleachers, he's provided with a drop area that's in the clear instead of having to hit from the next county like we would. No wonder they don't rack up the triple bogeys!

2. No lost balls. Between fans and marshals, there's almost always someone around to spot the location of an errant shot and save the player that long walk back to the tee (or the two extra strokes on the provisional ball). This might not always be beneficial, as Phil Mickelson learned in the San Diego playoff in 2001; once spectators found his drive in the barranca at Torrey Pines, he could no longer use his provisional drive in the fairway and had to declare an unplayable ball and go back to the tee. Fortunately for him, his double bogey still won the hole—a result that we can definitely relate to.

3. The latest and greatest. You know the feeling: You've just ponied up a couple hundred bucks for the biggest-newest-latest-and-longest club you've ever seen. A few rounds after you bought it, your buddy gets an even bigger-newer-later-longer club that promises to put every shot in the fairway and will also balance his checkbook, wash away the gray, protect his car from thieves, and add six years to his life. You know you want it. What do you do?

The pros have no such dilemmas. They don't pay for their clubs, *they get paid to use them.* They have access to the newest technologies before they come onto the market, and they get whatever they want delivered the next day. They can spend hours, days, even weeks tinkering with something new, deciding if they want it, if they like it, and then the equipment trailers and reps on-site will see that it gets tweaked to fit their exact specifications, mood, or biorhythmic stage. How can this not help?

4. Manicured sand. Bunkers are supposed to be a hazard. So why do the pros wish for their imperfect approaches to land in the sand? It's not just because of the hundreds of hours they've spent practicing those shots (hours we could spend, too, if we didn't have, you know, *jobs*). It's because those so-called traps have been raked and smoothed and groomed and curried as if by monks creating a sand mandala. The pros don't know the joys of trying to hit a sand shot when the ball is in the trough of an unraked footprint. They also aren't worried about whether the sand will be like Aspen powder or more like Moroccan couscous, because the Tour seeks consistent conditions from week to week. When we see our ball heading toward the sand, we have no idea what we'll face when we get there; the pros know it's most likely the best lie they'll find around the green.

5. Partner and companion. Remember the best caddie you ever had? Maybe it was on your once-in-a-lifetime trip to Scotland, or a visit to a friend's country club, or a group outing at Bandon Dunes. Maybe it was the time your club's best player decided to skip the member-member, and you snagged his usual looper. Remember the confidence you felt, the way he planted the ideal swing thought with the way he told you to "smooth the six right in there," and led you through the round like a sherpa through the Himalayas? The pros have that guy on their bag every week, every round, even every practice session. Sure, there's only one guy who does the actual swinging, but the round is very much a joint event, and the guy at the player's side has done a lot to create the conditions for success.

FIVE WAYS THE PROS HAVE IT *HARDER* THAN WE DO

A couple of good rounds with your friends, and you're starting to feel you're getting it together. A good run in the club championship, and you're entertaining Champions Tour dreams. You know the game, your swing's pretty good, if you only had the time. . . . Well, forget it. Those proud rounds on your home course that are the heart of your résumé probably wouldn't get you under 80 out on Tour. Bobby Jones said, "There is just plain golf, and there is tournament golf. The two are in no way the same." Here's why:

1. Long, longer, longest. The game played from the blue tees is a far simpler affair than the one played from the tournament tips. How do you like 480-yard par fours? When was the last time you saw a par three of less than 190 yards on Tour, unless it was surrounded by water and the green was contoured like Anna Nicole Smith? Maybe you're comfortable playing a 7,200-yard course, but it's a different matter when it's also got 25-yard-wide fairways and four-inch rough. And if your game is built around your skill with the scoring clubs, how often are you going to get to use them when a 420-yard hole is considered a breather?

2. Fast greens/hard greens. You might hear a pro say that putting is actually easier on Tour because the greens are so true. Don't believe him. The difference between your home greens at their fastest and the average tournament green is greater than you can imagine. Every flaw in your putting stroke is magnified by the speed, and your awareness of this can eat away at your confidence. The greens themselves present problems you've never encountered before. How often do you have to play for ten feet of break? Or stroke a putt that will break more than 180 degrees? Or plumb-bob a two-footer? And it's not just the speed of the greens; they're also playing firmer than ever, so your approach shots from unaccustomed distances are tougher to hit and stick the way you're used to. Yes, the pros can do it; they're *really* good.

3. Tucked pins. Unless they start putting the flagsticks in the bunkers, the holes are about as close to the fringe as they can get. Three paces from the edge is nearly standard, assuming the contours of the green allow such a placement. That doesn't leave much margin for error, and with the speed and firmness of the greens (see number 2, above) you don't want to be chipping out of the rough or from a downhill lie onto these surfaces. You can always go for the middle of the green, but a diet of pars will leave you with a lot of free time on the weekend.

4. Lead poisoning. That's the term that legendary amateur golfer and player agent Vinny Giles uses to describe what happens to a golfer when there's a pencil in his pocket. Stroke play, especially under tournament conditions, is a whole different game than the matches you're used to at home. One really bad hole can ruin your entire day, something that's sure to tighten your sphincter when you're facing a forced carry to a flagstick placed right by the water. Those two-foot downhillers that you rake away while muttering, "That's good, right?"—they're an entirely different proposition when a miss can leave you eight feet past the hole. And that four-footer for double bogey that you picked up because you'd already lost the hole is every bit as hard as any other four-footer, only the pressure's even greater when you need it to avoid a triple. Any low-handicapper will tell you he'll happily give average players a few extra strokes if they'll agree to make the wager a stroke-play Nassau. Same thing for the pros against the good club player.

You don't feel pressure with people watching, do you?

5. First tee jitters on every tee. Does your heart get a little frisky on the opening tee shot when you're being watched not just by your friends, but by the next few groups, the starter, a marshal, and the cart girl? Try hitting it in front of a thousand strangers, most of whom are hoping you'll succeed, but some of whom have bet that you'll doink it into the sandbox. There won't be quite as many at the next tee, but some'll be there too, and at the next one, and the next. Watching that twenty-yard pitch over the bunker to that tight pin, too. Moving around a little while you're grinding over that bogey putt. Oh, and pay no attention to the roar that comes from the green two holes back, even if it comes in the middle of your downswing. Or the sound of the guy slamming the port-o-let door. None of this is going to mess with your steely powers of concentration, right?

ALISTER MACKENZIE'S ESSENTIAL FEATURES *of* AN IDEAL GOLF COURSE

Alister Mackenzie's architecture is considered the apotheosis of classical, strategic design, in which the player is provided options. His holes invite and even demand that the player choose from a variety of possible ways to play them. Before turning to course design, he was a physician, and in World War I served as an expert in camouflage—a skill he applied to the creation of memorable and challenging golf holes. Three of his courses are perennially ranked among the ten best in the world: the Cypress Point Club on the Monterey Peninsula in northern California; Augusta National Golf Club (co-designed with Bobby Jones); and Royal Melbourne's composite course.

The 18th green at Cypress Point, where Mackenzie designed golf's most unspoiled walk.

1. The course, where possible, should be arranged in two loops of nine holes.

2. There should be a large proportion of good two-shot holes, two or three drive-and-pitch holes, and at least four one-shot holes.

3. There should be little walking between the greens and tees, and the course should be arranged so that in the first instance there is always a slight walk forwards from the green to the next tee; then the holes are sufficiently elastic to be lengthened in the future if necessary.

4. The greens and fairways should be sufficiently undulating, but there should be no hill climbing.

5. Every hole should have a different character.

6. There should be a minimum of blindness for the approach shots.

7. The course should have beautiful surroundings, and all the artificial features should have so natural an appearance that a stranger is unable to distinguish them from nature itself.

8. There should be a sufficient number of heroic carries from the tee, but the course should be arranged so that the weaker player with the loss of a stroke or portion of a stroke shall always have an alternative route open to him.

9. There should be infinite variety in the strokes required to play the various holes—viz., interesting brassy shots [*fairway woods*], iron shots, pitch and run-up shots.

10. There should be a complete absence of the annoyance and irritation caused by the necessity of searching for lost balls.

11. The course should be so interesting that even the plus man *[scratch golfer or better]* is constantly stimulated to improve his game in attempting shots he has hitherto been unable to play.

12. The course should be so arranged that the long handicap player, or even the absolute beginner, should be able to enjoy his round in spite of the fact that he is piling up a big score.

13. The course should be equally good during winter and summer, the texture of the greens and fairways should be perfect, and the approaches should have the same consistency as the greens.

PROFESSIONAL MAJORS

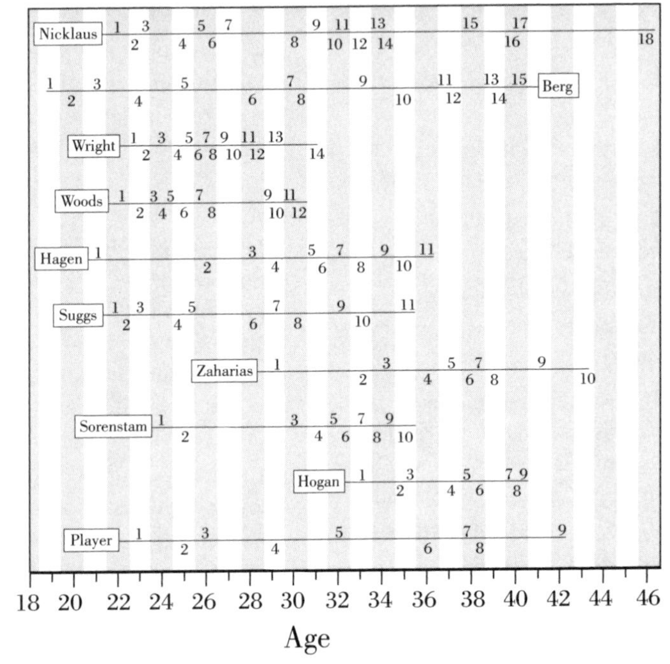

WAS SHAKESPEARE A GOLFER?

He understood the drama of the game:

"This green plot shall be our stage."

—*A MIDSUMMER-NIGHT'S DREAM*, III, i

He played with blades:

"I will wink and hold out mine iron. It is a simple one . . ."

—*HENRY V*, II, i

He had trouble keeping his swing on plane:

"The shaft confounds."

—*TROILUS AND CRESSIDA*, III, i

He caddied at the 17th of the Old Course:

"I train'd thy brethren to that guileful hole."

—*TITUS ANDRONICUS*, V, i

He always went for the green in two . . .

"Forego the way which promises assurance, and give up yourself merely to chance and hazard."

—*ANTONY AND CLEOPATRA*, III, viii

. . . even to a back-left pin guarded on both sides by water:

"My bended hook shall pierce their slimy jaws."

—*ANTONY AND CLEOPATRA*, II, v

He admired Jack Nicklaus:

"Bear-like, I must fight the course."

—*MACBETH*, V, vii

He was a cautious bettor:

"Be wise as thou art cruel; do not press . . ."

—SONNET 140

The Bard of Stratford-upon-Avon C.C.

He agreed with Scott Hoch about St. Andrews (see page 343):

"Uneven is the course; I like it not."

—*ROMEO AND JULIET*, IV, i

He sympathized with Ian Woosnam's caddie at Royal Lytham & St. Annes (see page 53):

"What trick, what device, what starting hole canst thou now find to hide thee from this Open and apparent shame?"

—*HENRY IV, PART I*, II, iv

He even played golf at night:

"Be happy! Let all the number of the stars give light to thy fair way."

—*ANTONY AND CLEOPATRA*, III, ii

HOW TO RAKE A BUNKER LIKE A PROFESSIONAL CADDIE

Always enter and exit the bunker at its lowest point to prevent damage to the sides. This will also avoid any possible injury, because it's easy to take a bad step if coming in or exiting at too steep an angle. That's one way to twist an ankle or break a leg.

The main principle is to leave the bunker as you found it—assuming you found it in good order. The best way to do that is to have a light touch. Here's how to rake a bunker the proper way, according to Don Thom, a retired police officer who has caddied for ten years on the PGA Tour—the last six for Craig Barlow:

"First, make sure you fill in any holes that the ball made when it landed in the bunker and any areas where the player stood. The easiest way to do the job is to rake away from you as you leave the bunker. You won't leave rake marks this way. Rake away from you until you get to the edge of the bunker.

"If the sand is firm, I rake in what looks like a herringbone pattern, forty-five degrees to the left and forty-five degrees to the right. The pattern looks like a fishbone, and doesn't leave any marks.

"The most difficult job is when the ball is up against the face of the bunker and the player has to dig in deep to get his balance. Rake up against the face where it's deep, and again, rake away from you as you walk back. You always want to be raking up the slope."

The Golf Course Superintendents Association of America offers some further advice: "Greenside bunkers are usually raked in the direction of play or toward the center of the green. Fairway bunkers are raked parallel to play from tee to green."

And what about the rake? Do you leave it in or out? If you leave it inside the bunker, a ball might come to rest against it. The Rules of Golf allow you to remove that rake, but demand that you recreate the original lie as nearly as possible and place the ball there. That's not always possible, and it can also be impossible to find a spot that's not nearer the hole. Leaving a rake outside the bunker creates the possibility that it might stop a ball from going into a bunker or deflect a ball into it. Some golfers debate this question endlessly. For what it's worth, the USGA believes that fewer complications arise when a rake is left outside a bunker.

HOW TO PLUMB-BOB

1. First, determine which is your dominant eye. (See below.) Do not assume that it's the same as your dominant hand.

2. Stand behind the location of your ball, looking directly toward the hole.

3. Hold your putter loosely from the top so that it hangs freely and the line of the shaft runs through the middle of your ball (or ball marker).

4. Look at the shaft and the hole with your dominant eye *only*. If the hole appears to the right of the shaft, the putt will break to the right; if it appears to the left, the putt will break left.

Determining your dominant eye

Hold your arms outstretched and form a triangle with your thumbs and forefingers. With both eyes open, look through this triangle at an object in the distance. Now, without moving your arms, close each eye alternately, and notice which eye keeps the object inside the triangle. This is your dominant eye.

WHAT NOBODY EVER TELLS YOU ABOUT . . .

Augusta's 13th green—it looks flatter on television.

Augusta National: Because television tends to flatten out topography, nearly all first-time visitors to Augusta National are amazed by how hilly the course is. The 18th hole plays straight uphill; the 10th hole can comfortably play as a 500-yard par four because it runs so steeply down the same hill. On the dogleg par-five 13th, the landing area slopes significantly from right to left, so the approach shot over Rae's Creek is undertaken with the ball well above a right-hander's feet. And laying up on the 15th hole is no bargain, because there's no flat place to aim for; if you decide not to go for the green in two, you're facing a short wedge pitch over the pond from a steeply downhill lie to a shallow green with a shaved bank in front.

One striking aspect of the course when it isn't thronged by Masters patrons is how open it is. For all its tree-lined splendor, there are wide vistas where many holes can be taken in at once, and the trees between holes are almost always sparse enough to allow for recovery shots. While it's hard to imagine a course whose reputation is less linkslike than Augusta National's, the green surrounds make the bump-and-run a vital shot on a surprising number of holes, because of the tightness of the turf.

Another feature unique to Augusta National is the nature of the sand in the bunkers. The "sand," which consists of finely ground feldspar, is so powdery that a ball rolling through a bunker can leave the impression of its dimples in its wake.

Pine Valley: Large stretches of scrub and sand make Pine Valley the most visually intimidating course in the world. Yet if you look back at the tees from the fairways, you will wonder what you were so worried about. The fairways are among the widest in golf, beyond merely generous; the carries are generally about 180 to190 yards or so—they'll punish the bad shot, but are comfortably avoided by most average hitters. Of course, the more you want to bite off in search of birdies, the incrementally more difficult the shot will be. But if you consider parring a hole a good score—and on this track, who doesn't?—it is somewhat attainable, if not remotely easy.

PEBBLE BEACH: Two of the most dramatic shots in golf history were hit at Pebble Beach's par-three 17th hole: Jack Nicklaus's one-iron that struck the flagstick and landed inches away to cement the 1972 U.S. Open title, and Tom Watson's chip-in from the left greenside rough to beat Nicklaus a decade later. This famous hole, with its hourglass green and gaping bunkers, has a hazard that is rarely mentioned but tends to affect things in a major way: the sun. The hole, at nearly any time you're likely to play it, runs directly into the glare of the sun on the Pacific. *Blinding* glare: it is all but impossible, as you come through the ball, to avoid flinching from the assault on your retinas.

There is no more exhilarating stretch of holes in the world than numbers 4 through 10 on Pebble Beach, where the course hugs the coastline and the ocean's danger is just a loose swing away. But Pebble also has a surprising number of ordinary holes: the first three, 12 and 13, 15 and 16. This, combined with the otherworldly cost of a round, is why some amateurs admit quietly that they prefer nearby Spyglass Hill once they've put Pebble on their lifetime list.

THE OLYMPIC CLUB: San Francisco's unusual climate owes much to the marine layer of fog that sits just off the coast and is drawn in whenever the weather threatens to get and stay too warm. This cool, damp air has a significant effect on play at the Olympic Club, keeping the grass moist and the fairways from running. As a result, the course plays distinctly longer than its listed yardage. It's generally a good idea to go up a club on nearly every approach.

SHINNECOCK HILLS: If Augusta National plays more linkslike than you would imagine from its looks, Shinnecock Hills plays *less* like a links than you would think. While the sweeping views, low trees that do little to block the wind, and waves of long fescue give the impression of a links, Shinnecock has few holes where playing the ball along the ground rather than through the air is an option. Most greens are raised and won't accept a run-up. This contributed to the dissatisfaction with the setup at the 2004 U.S. Open; with the greens rock-hard, there was no reasonable way to play the course, because it does not offer linksy alternatives. (If you want a true links experience, pretend to be confused by the routing and wander over mid-round to the contiguous National Golf Links.)

THE OLD COURSE, ST. ANDREWS: On your first visit, you'll start out overwhelmed, and will soon wind up confused. Standing in front of the clubhouse of the R&A and then striking your tee shot to the unmissable fairway of the first hole is one of the great thrills in golf. Whether you negotiate the Swilcan Burn successfully or not (the pin will be up; the pin is always up), you'll take the short walk to the second tee feeling thrilled. You'll play the second hole still intoxicated by the aura. Then comes the third hole . . . and the fourth . . . and the fifth . . . and the sixth . . . hole after hole with tee shots hit blindly over scrubby gorse, varying only by the exact positioning and depth of the bunkers that wait, unseen, to swallow your ball. By the time you reach #8, Short Hole Out—oh, you won't see the putting surface on this par three either—you will be ready to curse the creator of this bizarre concoction. But then you'll remember who the Creator truly was, and you'll hold your tongue.

One tip about the impossibly oversized double-greens: According to historian and links connoisseur James W. Finegan, who has played the Old Course approximately one hundred times, roughly 80 percent of the putts are straight, whether they're from four feet or forty. Unless you're facing a putt with a totally obvious slope in front of you, aim at the hole. He asserts that the twists and turns will even out. Yes, really.

WINGED FOOT: The West Course has hosted many memorable championships, from Bobby Jones's curling twenty-footer on the 18th green in the 1929 U.S. Open to Hale Irwin's seven-over-par triumph in the 1974 Open "massacre" to Phil Mickelson's misadventure. It is one tough course. Hole after hole, relentlessly long par four after relentlessly long par four, the West Course will wear you out. If you have the opportunity, you will derive much more pleasure from a round on the East Course, the "weaker" course that is ranked a mere 34 in *Golf Digest*'s 2005 ratings (to the West Course's 8). Oh, by the way, the USGA has assigned the East Course a higher Slope Rating from

On Winged Foot West's 17th green, you can re-create Geoff Ogilvy's clutch chip-in for par. Or you can play the East course, and enjoy yourself.

Royal Melbourne. If the sand doesn't get you, the sand flies will.

its middle tees than the West. More fun, and as great a challenge—a tough pair to beat.

Lahinch Golf Club: Here be monsters. Check your expectations at the gate and give in to the outlandish charms of the quirkiest golf course in the world. Any old course can have blind tee shots; Lahinch offers you a blind second shot on a hole that is crossed by another fairway! A fairway may terminate at a huge and seemingly bottomless pit, though there must be a bottom because some lunatic has stuck a sand bunker there. Your caddie might advise you to forget about hitting a delicate pitch to a green running away from you and instead slam the ball hard into the sandhill behind the green; the ball will trickle down the hill and feed toward the hole, winding up closer than you'd have gotten it any other way. In short, bucko, you're not in Kansas any more, and if you come to Lahinch expecting a normal round of golf, you might wind up frustrated and disappointed. But if you yield to her, you'll find yourself laughing out loud at the sheer pleasure of the place.

Royal Melbourne Golf Club: In the Sandbelt south of Melbourne, Australia, are several courses of extraordinary quality, capped by this Alister Mackenzie gem that hosted the 1998 Presidents Cup. The course is delightful and playable and a triumph of design. The sandy soil is an ideal base for golf, and so firm that players are even permitted to roll their pull-carts across the greens. The sandy base is also, alas, ideal for breeding flies. Fortunately, these sand flies don't bite, but they buzz, relentlessly, and it is almost inevitable that as you walk along at some point you will swallow one that's flown into your mouth. The courses are worth it, but vegans might want to think twice before planning a trip.

THREE-HANKY GOLF

The Squire, Skip, and the 1932 Open

Although he had won the 1922 U.S. Open and the 1922 and 1923 PGA Championships, Gene Sarazen had yet to win the one major he most coveted: the British Open. (There was no Masters yet.) Sarazen had had his problems in the British Open, and after he failed to qualify for the championship back in 1923, he started searching for ways to improve his technique. Formerly not one to get too technical about the game, he hurt himself with this approach. Gradually he worked himself into form, though, and he finished second to Walter Hagen in the 1928 British Open at Royal St. George's Golf Club in Sandwich, England. He didn't take his Scottish caddie Skip Daniels's advice on the 14th hole the second day, which cost him two strokes—Hagen's final margin of victory.

It can't be concluded that he lost the championship because of his errors on that hole, because they happened during the second round. But Sarazen was bothered that he had gone against Daniels's counsel. He told Daniels that he felt his callous disregard for his advice had cost them the title.

"We'll try it again, sir, won't we?" Daniels asked, or said, to Sarazen with tears in his eyes. "Before I die, I'm going to win an Open Championship for you."

The British Open wouldn't return to Sandwich until 1932, this time at the Prince's Club adjacent to Royal St. George's. Sarazen wasn't certain he wanted to play, even if Daniels were available. In the end he did go, but he decided to work with a younger caddie than Daniels, who was by then in his 60s.

Daniels hadn't heard of the change in plans, though, and met Sarazen at the gate to Prince's. Daniels had weakened considerably in the intervening years and the limp he had long suffered was more pronounced. Nonetheless, he was ready to caddie for his player. But Sarazen told Daniels that he felt the bag was too heavy for him, and that he didn't want to burden him with carrying it for seventy-two holes.

In his customary dignified manner, Daniels simply said, "Righto, sir, if you feel that way about it." Sarazen felt like a worm, but he told himself business was business. Still, his heart ached. He'd hurt a decent man.

Sarazen went out for his practice rounds with the younger caddie, but it didn't take long for him to sense they weren't right for each other. The fellow didn't discuss club selection with Sarazen, but instead yanked a club from the bag and handed it to him.

The caddie told Sarazen after giving him the wrong club and seeing the ball come up short that he hadn't hit the shot well. Sarazen began to feel anxious as the first round drew near. He also was uneasy every time he saw Daniels in the gallery during the practice rounds. Daniels was there to caddie for Sarazen and only Sarazen; if he couldn't caddie for him, he would watch him.

Daniels, observing that Sarazen wasn't getting along well with his caddie, felt he could help. The same thought had crossed Sarazen's mind. He instructed that a message be sent to the caddiemaster advising Daniels to meet him at his hotel at seven the next morning.

The chemistry between Sarazen and Daniels was still there. Daniels told Sarazen he had improved since 1928 at Sandwich. He noticed that Sarazen's sand play was much sharper. Sarazen had invented the sand wedge in 1931 and told Daniels not to show it to anybody. He also asked Daniels if he remembered the mishap at the 14th hole a few years back. "Do I! Why, it's haunted me," Daniels said, his hand across his eyes. Sarazen told him they had to avoid such a hole and that the plan was to never play a hole more than one over par. He also told Daniels that he would accept his advice.

"You'll be calling them and I'll be playing them," Sarazen told Daniels.

Sarazen got through the qualifying rounds easily. He was in three bunkers during the first nine holes of the championship and came out with his sand wedge each time to within a few inches of the hole. Soon everybody was aware of the new club. Sarazen shot 70 that first round, and his 69 and 70 in the second and third rounds gave him a five-shot lead over Arthur Havers heading into the final round. Daniels was still fresh after the morning round on the last day and full of his usual encouragement and gentle prodding. Sarazen was well in the lead when he bogeyed the 16th hole. He was moving quickly, a bit too quickly for Daniels. "We're going to win this championship, sir," Daniels told him on the 17th tee as a means of softening his pace. "I have no worries on that score. But let's make our pars on these last two holes. You always play them well."

Sarazen did, too. He got his pars, shot even-par 74 and came in with a total of 13-under-par 283 to win by five shots over Mac Smith, the fine Carnoustie-born golfer who never won the U.S. or British Open although he finished within three shots of the winner nine times. Sarazen's score was two shots lower than the record 285 Bobby Jones had shot to win the 1927 British Open at the Old Course. He hadn't made worse than a bogey on a single hole, as per the prescription he and Daniels had settled on.

Sarazen asked officials if Daniels could stand beside him during the trophy presentation, but the officials of the Royal and Ancient Golf Club of St. Andrews refused to budge from their policy and said that wouldn't be possible. Still, Sarazen tried to delay the ceremony as long as he could, so that Daniels could at least attend. Finally he saw the old gentleman coming up the road on his bicycle, with a grandson on each handlebar.

Gene Sarazen—nattily dressed and always in balance.

Following the ceremony, Sarazen gave Daniels—he called him Dan—his polo coat and said he looked forward to seeing him the next year in St. Andrews for the Open. But Sarazen learned a few months later that Daniels had died after a brief illness. He was told that Daniels wore his polo coat wherever he went, "even inside the pubs, as he told the golf fans of three generations the story of 'how Sarazen and I did it at Prince's.'" Sarazen, who had started his life in golf as a caddie at the Apawamis Club in Rye, New York, had won the Open with the right man at his side. It was the only British Open he would win.

FAMOUS COLLAPSES IN MAJORS

Sam Snead, 1939 U.S. Open, Philadelphia Country Club

Snead came to the final hole of Philadelphia Country Club's Spring Mill course needing only a bogey to tie for the championship and go into a playoff the next day. In that era before ubiquitous scoreboards, he did not realize his position and thought he needed a birdie. He hooked his drive into the left rough on the 558-yard par five; played a wood from the trampled lie and pulled it into a bunker a hundred yards short of the green; tried to hit out of a semiburied lie with an eight-iron and drove the ball into the collar of the trap; slashed the ball out of the lip and into another bunker; pitched onto the green; three-putted from forty feet for a triple-bogey eight. It was while he was walking to his fifth shot that he was informed that all he'd needed was a bogey to tie Byron Nelson, who had finished, and Craig Wood and Denny Shute, who were to arrive presently at the final green.

"That night I was ready to go out with a gun and pay somebody to shoot me," Snead wrote in his autobiography, *Slammin' Sam.* "It weighed on my mind so much that I dropped 10 pounds, lost more hair, and began to choke up even on practice rounds. . . . My doctor said I was headed for a nervous breakdown."

Writer Trent Frayne was only twenty years old when he attended the 1939 U.S. Open. He wrote the following for the

Winnipeg Tribune, recalling what Snead's golfing colleague Ralph Guldahl said then:

"It's just like Bobby Jones once remarked," Guldahl said. "The Open isn't won. It's lost. I've seen a lot of blowups in my time but none as complete as Sam's. I doubt if Sam will ever regain his true form. The recollection of that 18th hole will always be a mental hazard to him. He'll be punch-drunk a long time."

Despite Guldahl's dire prediction, Snead managed to struggle his way to seven major championships in the next fifteen years. He never did win the Open, however.

WILLIE'S RULES

Every course has its local rules, usually printed on the scorecard. At Pedernales Cut-N-Putt in Spicewood, Texas—better known as Willie Nelson's course—the rules are a little different from the ordinary:

1. When another is shooting, no player should talk, whistle, hum, clink coins, or pass gas.

2. Excessive displays of affection are discouraged. Violators must replace divots and will be penalized five strokes.

3. Replace divots, smooth footprints in bunkers, brush backtrail with branches, park car under brush, and have the office tell your spouse you're in conference.

4. "Freebies" are not recommended for players with short putts.

5. No more than twelve in your foursome.

6. Gambling is forbidden, of course, unless you're stuck or you need a legal deduction for charitable or professional expenses.

7. No bikinis, miniskirts, or skimpy see-through attire. Except on women.

8. Please leave the course in the condition you'd like to be found.

NAMES OF THE HOLES *at the* OLD COURSE

1. Burn. Named for the Swilcan (rhymes with "silken") Burn, the creek that guards the front of the green.

2. Dyke. The wall that separates the Old Course Hotel from the 17th fairway. So why isn't the 17th hole called "Dyke"? You'd think a wall along the fairway would be as significant as a road behind the green.

3. Cartgate (Out). The first of four names duplicated on the outward and inward nines. The crescent-shaped Cartgate bunker guards the front left of the third green and is named for the cart track that used to cross this fairway.

Hole #3. Now that's a bunker.

4. Ginger Beer. Freelance concessionaire Old Daw Anderson used to have his mobile refreshment stall at this hole in the nineteenth century. Anderson's son, James, was the first to win three consecutive Open Championships on three different courses (Musselburgh, 1877; Prestwick, 1878; St. Andrews, 1879).

5. Hole O' Cross (Out). There are two competing versions of the origin of this name: Some say it came about because players had to cross the chasm short of the green; others say a cross once stood on this spot. It might be a better name for the 7th and 11th holes, which actually do cross each other.

6. Heathery (Out). While there is more than enough heather to justify the name anywhere on the course, here it refers to the original condition of the green shared by numbers 6 and 12, which consisted of heather, dirt, and shell fragments.

7. High (Out). The green provides a vantage point for a view of the Eden Estuary. On a course with so little elevation change, this is almost literally making a mountain of a molehill.

8. Short. The first of only two par threes, at 166 yards it is marginally shorter than the 11th hole.

9. End. The point at which you turn and begin your second nine, though in fact the next two holes will take you farther away from town. The farthest point from the clubhouse is actually the 11th green.

10. Bobby Jones. Named for the great American amateur champion in 1972, the year after Jones died. Curiously, this was the last hole Jones completed before withdrawing in frustration during the third round of the 1921 Open Championship after a front-nine 46, a double-bogey on 10, a tee shot into Hill Bunker on 11, and several more futile shots.

11. High (In). Same reason as number 7, with which it shares a green. A better name might be If I Put The Ball In Strath Bunker One More Time I'll Give Up This %*&%@! Game, but that wouldn't fit on the scorecard.

12. Heathery (In). Same green as number 6, same condition in its earlier days. The holes that share double greens on the Old Course always total eighteen; only numbers 1, 9, 17, and 18 have their own greens.

13. Hole O' Cross (In). Same reasons as number 5. Also, you might feel you're crossing several time zones as you traverse the hundred-yard-deep green.

14. Long. The second of two par fives (number 5 was the first). As simply and appropriately named as its most famous feature, Hell Bunker.

At #14, heaven and Hell await the pilgrim.

15. Cartgate (In). See number 3. Americans believing the name describes a scandal involving pilfered revenue from electric vehicles are advised that such carts are generally called "damned buggies" over here.

16. Corner of the Dyke. Describes the location of the green, which is tucked into a corner of the wall that gives the second hole its name.

17. Road. The old turnpike road behind the green is no longer used for transport, but it is most definitely in play, as many unhappy golfers have learned.

18. Tom Morris. The professional whose shop on Links Road overlooked this hole also built the green here, with its distinctive Valley of Sin guarding the front left portion.

THE GOLFER'S LIFE LIST

Follow Tiger Woods for an Entire Round

All golfers know that so much can happen during a round; the score in the end is all that matters, but a round proceeds. Watch a golfer for eighteen holes and you're part of the proceedings. You know the golfer in a way that doesn't happen if you see him hit only a shot or two. There's nothing wrong with sitting by a green and watching group after group come through, but the truth of a player's round is in its entirety.

It's not easy to watch Tiger Woods at any time, to be sure. But make the effort, even for a practice round. Woods plays his practice rounds early. He's often out just as dawn is breaking. Watch him warm up and then walk the course as he plays. It's easy to hear his chatter with his caddie Steve Williams, and fun to watch as he hits different shots from a variety of places around the greens. Hundreds more spectators will have gathered by the time he finishes, but it's still possible to follow him. Tiger usually plays his practice round in three hours.

As interesting as it is to watch Woods play a practice round, it's more entertaining and enlightening to follow him for an entire tournament round. You won't see every shot because of the size of the crowd, but you can see a surprising amount by moving around quickly and finding good vantage points; you just might see him hit one of his "miracle" shots. Take a pair of binoculars. Try to get behind him on a tee if possible, to hear the sound of his driver meeting the ball. You're looking for a moment like that, and you'll find it out on the course if you put in the time. Something is guaranteed to happen. Most likely, it will be something you won't forget.

GREAT CAREER AMATEURS

Bobby Jones was clearly the most accomplished amateur of them all. No one will ever match his record of success in open championships while competing against the play-for-pay crowd. At least partially because of Jones, there will always be a place in golf for the talented amateur. Throughout this volume, we pay tribute to those who have played high-level golf all their lives without making it their livelihood.

CHICK EVANS, B. INDIANAPOLIS, 1890, D. CHICAGO, 1979

Evans learned the game while caddying at the Edgewater Country Club in Chicago. He won the 1916 U.S. Amateur at the Merion Golf Club and the 1916 U.S. Open at Minikahda near Minneapolis, becoming the first player to win both in the same year. Evans coined the phrase "the white faces of Merion" in reference to its bunkers. He carried only seven hickory-shafted clubs while winning at Minikahda, where his two-under par 286 was the first time anybody won the championship with a subpar total. All told, Evans won fifty-four tournaments, including five Western Amateurs. He competed in forty-nine U.S. Amateurs, winning in 1920, and played in the 1967 Western Open when he was seventy-seven years old.

Off the course, Evans made an important and lasting contribution. He was able to spend only one year at Northwestern University in Chicago because of a lack of money and knew that it was likely that other caddies were also short of funds needed to attend college. He established the Charles Evans Jr. Trust in 1928, which eventually turned into the Chick Evans Caddie Scholarship Program and spread to a number of states. Some 800 grants are provided every year, including 140 to women. Nearly 80,000 Evans scholars have graduated.

BIG JOHN'S BIG NUMBERS

There has never been a figure in professional golf quite like John Daly. From the moment he emerged on the scene with his Cinderella victory in the 1991 PGA, he has awed pros and fans alike with his prodigious drives, rollercoaster lifestyle, and intermittent bursts of greatness. While most professional golfers strive for steadiness, Daly shares the high-handicapper's thirst for glory. He's been in the spotlight since that 1991 PGA Championship and not only for his play on the course. Daly's been married four times. He wrote a song called "All My Exes Wear Rolexes." Sherrie Daly, one of his wives, was convicted and sentenced in December 2004 to five months in prison for her role in a money-laundering scheme. He's had serious gambling and drinking problems and has been in rehab twice. He travels in a motor home because he fears flying, and he hawks merchandise such as beer mugs, caps, and T-shirts out of the trailer, which he parks near tournament sites. He withdraws from tournaments frequently, and the PGA Tour has suspended him for his behavior. His life may be a country song, but his game is operatic: He tries big, he succeeds big, and he fails big and often. Here are some of the big numbers he's posted in his pro career.

10: July 17, 1998, Open Championship, Royal Birkdale Golf Club, Southport, England, second round: Needs a bogey on 18 to make the cut. Drives into a fairway bunker on the right side of the hole, then hits his second shot into another bunker. Flails away in there five times; finally gets out on his fifth try, into a greenside bunker, comes out to ten feet, then two-putts. Daly isn't sure of how many shots he took. Payne Stewart, marking Daly's card, says, "John, I've got to put a number in here that's right. I can't just go, yes, on what you're saying." Daly: "It doesn't matter. Give me a ten." Stewart and Bernhard Langer, the other player in the group, agree that's what Daly made, a sextuple bogey. Shoots 78. Stewart: "He was not a happy camper when he left here."

10: June 3, 1999, Memorial Tournament, Muirfield Village Golf Club, Dublin, Ohio, first round: Playing his sixth consecutive tournament, Daly is four over par when he reaches the par-four 18th hole. He reaches the green on his fourth shot and has an eight-foot uphill putt for bogey. He runs that putt eight feet by the hole, and then moves into high-speed golf. Back and forth he goes, taking six putts in the end for a six-over-par 10.

11: June 20, 1999, U.S. Open, Pinehurst No. 2, Pinehurst, North Carolina, second round: Hits a 340-yard drive on the par-four eighth hole, then hits approach over green into a closely cropped swale. Tries to putt back up the swale to the green. Ball comes back to his feet. Tries same shot. Same result. Doesn't wait until ball comes to a stop, tries same shot, and hits moving ball with some oomph. Ball picks up speed when it hits the green and rolls all the way off the front edge. Chips back and comes up twenty feet short of the hole. Putts ten feet past. Next putt near hole. Taps in. Records an 11, which includes a two-shot penalty for hitting a moving ball. Shoots 83 after opening with a 69, only a shot out of the lead. Says that he no longer considers the U.S. Open a major and that he won't play another.

14: June 15, 2000, U.S. Open, Pebble Beach Golf Links, Pebble Beach, California, first round: Having decided after all to play the next U.S. Open, Daly makes a 14 on the par-five 18th in the first round. He hits his drive out-of-bounds to the right, and then pumps two tee shots into the ocean, hitting wild, hot hooks. Now hitting seven from the tee, he chooses an iron and keeps that inside the golf course. His eighth is a layup, and then his ninth goes across the long bunker to the left and short of the green, and into the hazard. He takes his drop beside the sea wall and, now hitting 11, left-handed, leaves the shot in the sand. He plays his twelfth onto the green and two-putts for 14. Daly signs his scorecard for 83, withdraws, and, emerging from the scoring trailer, says, "Get me to the airport fast."

18: March 22, 1998, Bay Hill Invitational, Bay Hill Club, Orlando, Florida, final round: After a good drive on the par-five sixth hole on the last day of the Bay Hill, tries to go for the green 270 yards away across a lake and hits a three-wood into the water six straight times. Makes an 18 and shoots 85. Makes a birdie two on the next hole, for the unusual run of 18–2 on consecutive holes.

FOOTNOTES TO HISTORY

For better and for worse—mostly for worse—some golfers are remembered more for what they didn't do, sometimes what they nearly did, than for what they accomplished. The players labeled Footnotes to History came tantalizingly close to winning a major, and some played beautifully to put themselves in that position. None ever did win one, but some of them are better remembered than those who did.

DAVE HILL, 1970 U.S. OPEN, HAZELTINE GOLF CLUB, CHASKA, MINNESOTA

Dave Hill, the U.S. Open's unhappiest contender.

Robert Trent Jones designed the Hazeltine Golf Club on a piece of ground that was less than promising. The course was full of doglegs—Jones felt that they compelled players to think about what they were doing from the tees, rather than simply hitting the ball as far as possible. Jones was being crafty here. He went too far, however, with another idea, at least according to most of the players: They didn't like the many blind shots.

Jack Nicklaus pointed out that eleven of fourteen tee shots were blind. Nicklaus shot 81 in the first round, Gary Player shot 80, and Arnold Palmer shot 79, in high winds. The 1969 British Open champion, Tony Jacklin, managed 71 and led after thirty-six holes with a score of three-under par 141, while Dave Hill was in second place, two shots behind the Englishman.

Hill's criticisms made Nicklaus's observation seem mere commentary. Asked his opinion of the course after the second

Hazeltine's flat, open landscape had to be wrestled into a championship course.

round, Hill said, "They ruined a good farm." That was the start. Following the second round, Hill was asked, "How did you find the course?" He replied, "How did I find the golf course? I've been trying to find it since I came to Minneapolis. Just because you cut the grass and put up flags, it doesn't mean you have a golf course."

Hill was also asked what the course lacked. "What does it lack? Eighty acres of corn and a few cows." That comment has become one of the most fondly remembered in the annals, although neither the Hazeltine members nor the United States Golf Association were at the time enamored of Hill's views. Meanwhile, there's a story that Bob Rosburg said it first, but in the locker room rather than before the press.

Notwithstanding Hill's ill will towards Hazeltine, he shot even-par 288 to finish second behind Jacklin, who was seven shots better. And his remarks had a positive effect. The course was revised a couple of times. Hazeltine hosted the 1991 U.S. Open and the 2002 PGA Championship, with few complaints.

THE GOLFER'S LIFE LIST

Play Worst-Ball

There's no more effective way of practicing than this. The only condition is that you need a few empty holes behind or ahead of you, so a summer's evening will probably be the best time to play worst-ball. You might find a time when you can play a full round of worst-ball, but that's not likely. It's also not crucial, because you'll benefit from three or four holes.

The idea is simple: You use two balls on every shot, and play the worse of the two shots. For example, you hit your first drive into the middle of the fairway. You hit your second ball off the tee into a deep fairway bunker. Too bad: You now have to play two balls from the bunker.

Worst-ball teaches you to handle pressure. You've just hit a six-iron five feet from the hole. Wonderful. But you still must play your second ball, and you're over the ball knowing there's water to the right of the green. You don't care if you hit this second ball to five feet, but you'd like to find the green. Focus, focus. Target, target. There, you've hit the green. You've coped with the pressure. Well done. Now you know you can back up one good swing with another when the heat's on.

The pressure mounts on the green. You make a tricky downhill three-footer. Can you do it again? Your next putt lips out and spins hard to the right, finishing eight feet away on the slick green. Now your next two putts are from there.

Ben Hogan often played worst-ball to prepare for majors. George Knudson used to say that anybody who could shoot 75 or better playing worst-ball at the National Golf Club of Canada, outside Toronto, had the game to play the Tour. Lanny Wadkins liked to play worst-ball around Preston Trail in Dallas, and said that par was a superb score. Tiger Woods played worst-ball during a friendly match in July 2001 at the Limerick Golf Club in Ireland against businessman J. P. McManus. Woods gave him shots and let McManus play a scramble. McManus beat Woods in a close match. Sergio Garcia introduced Justin Rose to worst-ball at the Lake Nona Golf Club in Orlando, Florida, in March 2004, and they played a match under that format. Rose took $180 from Garcia.

Have a go at worst-ball. Your next round of conventional golf will seem easy by comparison.

NAMES *of the* HOLES *at* AUGUSTA NATIONAL GOLF CLUB

Each hole is named for a tree or plant that is predominant along its fringes, a practice that recalls the property's prior life as a commercial nursery.

1. Tea Olive
2. Pink Dogwood
3. Flowering Peach
4. Flowering Crabapple
5. Magnolia
6. Juniper
7. Pampas
8. Yellow Jasmine
9. Carolina Cherry
10. Camellia
11. White Dogwood
12. Golden Bell
13. Azalea
14. Chinese Fir
15. Fire Thorn
16. Red Bud
17. Nandina
18. Holly

Camellias flower on command at the Masters.

OTHER RULES OF GOLF

In the eighteenth and nineteenth centuries, the Rules of Golf were made not by a centralized governing body but rather by individual clubs. Codes were issued by the Honourable Company of Edinburgh Golfers, the Society of St. Andrews Golfers (later the R&A), the Edinburgh Burgess Golfing Society (later the Royal Burgess), the Aberdeen Society of Golfers, the Musselburgh Golf Club, and many others. Eventually, the various clubs joined with the St. Andreans to develop generally accepted rules, and the first set of agreements from this Rules of Golf Committee of the R&A was issued in 1899.

Kenneth G. Chapman's invaluable book, *The Rules of the Green,* provides examples of rules that have not survived the winnowing and revision process. Here are some of our favorites, with our comments (apologies to Dan Jenkins):

FROM THE RULES OF THE BLACKHEATH GOLF CLUB, 1828: "If the Player by mistake strikes his Opponent's Ball in playing through the Green, the stroke shall not be reckoned against either, and the Ball must be played as it may chance to lie." *So, Charlie, how come every time you make a "mistake" you hit the ball into a bunker?*

SOCIETY OF GOLFERS OF ABERDEEN, 1783: "It is understood that Partners may consult with, and give verbal Directions to one another; how to play; but nothing further." *So keep your stock tips to yourself, buddy.*

SOCIETY OF GOLFERS, IN AND ABOUT EDINBURGH, AT BRUNTSFIELD LINKS (ROYAL BURGESS GOLFING SOCIETY), 1773: "No golfer shall under any pretense whatever give any old Balls to the Cadies, if they do, they shall for every such Ball given away forfeit sixpence to the Treasurer." *But, Jimmie, I've been trying to save on tips by giving my old worn featheries to my caddie . . .*

NEXT RULE, SAME CODE: "That no member of this Society pay the Cadies more than one penny [per] round." *Oh. Never mind. That I can live with.*

ROYAL AND ANCIENT GOLF CLUB OF ST. ANDREWS, CODE OF 1851: "Unplayable Balls: When the ball lies in a hole or in any place that the player considers it not playable, he shall, with the consent of his adversary, lift the ball, drop it behind the hazard, and lose a stroke. Should the adversary say, however, that he thinks the ball playable, then he (the adversary) plays the ball; if he gets the ball out of the place in two strokes, these two strokes count as if the player had played the ball; the player then plays the ball as if he himself had played it out; but, if the adversary does not get the ball out at two strokes, then, as stated above, it is lifted and dropped, a stroke being lost."

Never mind the Rules; how did they swing wearing those clothes?

Wouldn't this be fun? Who could resist taking those two free whacks, knowing you have nothing to lose? For this very reason, the Liverpool Golf Club adopted a variation of this procedure in 1870: When an adversary challenges a declaration of an unplayable ball, the adversary has three strokes to knock it clear; if he succeeds, the player is charged the number of strokes his adversary took, but if he fails, the adversary is charged the three strokes he has taken. The R&A abandoned the challenge provision in 1856; Liverpool gave it up in 1875.

R&A, 1842: "The party losing a ball on a medal day shall, after five minutes search, go back and lose three strokes and the distance as penalty." *Three-strokes-and-distance is strong incentive to keep your ball in play—though paying $56 for a dozen balls works pretty well, too.*

THREE-HANKY GOLF

The Harvey Masters

Somewhere in a cave in Tibet there may be a holy man who dispenses simple wisdom to all who come, speaking of their trek to his mountain as though it were life itself. In a small town in France, perhaps, lives a parish priest whose green thumb is known to all and whose advice about tending one's garden is in equal parts horticultural and metaphoric. When these worthies pass on to their eternal reward, they will surely encounter a man whose chosen vehicle was golf and whose pulpit ran from tee to green: the sage of Austin, Texas, Harvey Penick.

In 1990 I was working at Simon & Schuster in New York when a letter came to us through the powerhouse literary agent Esther Newberg. The letter was handwritten by Bud Shrake, and it described him sitting under a tree at the Austin Country Club and being approached by Penick, who was carrying (as he so often did) a red leather-bound Scribbletext notebook in which Harvey had jotted down a lifetime's worth of thoughts. "You're about to get a real privilege," Tom Kite told Shrake. "I've never seen what's inside that notebook." Harvey had been ailing, and before he passed away he wanted to preserve in some form the notes and anecdotes he'd been keeping during his nearly eighty years' association with the club.

I doubt there were three editors in book publishing who'd heard of Harvey Penick, but I certainly had. I knew he had taught both Tom Kite and Ben Crenshaw from an early age and that he had worked at one time or another with virtually every golfer who ever came out of Texas. We acquired the rights to the book for a modest five-figure sum, and the rest is, if not history, then at least legend and lore. (One such legend is that when Shrake informed Harvey that Simon & Schuster was willing to publish the book for the sum we had offered, Harvey replied, "But I can't raise that kind of money.")

The publication had a profound effect on Harvey's outlook. He was very ill while the text was being prepared and was not necessarily expected to live to see it come out. But as the accolades spread and as grateful readers came to see him or wrote him letters expressing their thanks, he grew stronger, drawing purpose from the knowledge that his teachings were helping people. The relief from financial concerns must have been a blessing as well. (In the time after the book hit the bestseller lists but before the first royalty payments were to be made, I received a call from Esther Newberg asking if Simon & Schuster might be willing to make an early payment to the Penicks. That first royalty check would be several hundred thousand dollars; the requested early amount was five thousand dollars, "because Helen Penick wants to buy a new sofa and some drapes." Even the accountants at S&S asked, "Are you *sure* she doesn't want more?")

Among those most delighted by the change in his mentor's fortunes was Ben Crenshaw. Gentle Ben, handsome, charismatic, and one of golf's great naturals, was first brought to Harvey at age eight. Harvey gave him a cut-down seven-iron, and asked him to hit a ball off a tee onto a green that sat seventy-five yards away. Ben did so, and Harvey said, "Now let's go to the green and putt the ball into the hole." Crenshaw replied, "If you wanted it in the hole, why didn't you tell me the first time?" Harvey coached Crenshaw and his contemporary Tom Kite all through high school and college, and he maintained a close relationship with both throughout their professional careers.

By the winter of 1995, Harvey was growing progressively weaker. At the beginning of April, the Austin Country Club honored him by unveiling a statue behind the clubhouse that showed Harvey observing Tom Kite's swing. Harvey was too sick to attend the proceedings. A week before, Crenshaw visited and took a putting lesson from Harvey on the carpet in his modest home. On Sunday, April 2, Kite drove the two miles from the ceremony at Austin CC to see Harvey and, he no doubt knew, to say goodbye. On a television in the living room, Davis Love III, son of yet another pupil of Harvey's, was trying to win the PGA Tour's New Orleans event, knowing he needed to win in order to qualify for the following week's Masters. Shortly after Kite's visit, Harvey was informed that Love had in fact won in a playoff and would make it to Augusta after all. Harvey brought his hands together in a single clapping motion, then lay his arms down. Minutes later, he slipped away.

Harvey Penick, the little red Sage.

The golf world mourned Harvey's death; he had become America's best-loved golf teacher, a combination of words so unusual that the distinction has lain vacant since his passing. On Wednesday, April 5, his funeral was held in Austin, Texas. Bud Shrake spoke at the service; Kite and Crenshaw were among the pallbearers, having flown in on a private plane from Augusta. Both seemed solemn and shaken. I rode with Shrake that day, and after the ceremony at the gravesite, he talked about the conversations he'd had with Tom and Ben; then, out of nowhere he added, "You know, I think either they're both going to miss the cut [in the Masters] or one of them's going to win it."

Carl Jackson comforts Ben Crenshaw as the week's emotions hit home.

One of them did indeed miss the cut. And one of them, having incorporated a tip from his long-time Augusta caddie Carl Jackson, opened with rounds of 70 and 67, then continued with a 69 to tie for the fifty-four-hole lead, and birdied two of the last three holes to finish with a 68 to win his second green jacket. How unlikely was this victory? Crenshaw had only two top-ten finishes in his last twenty majors. After this win, he would make only two more cuts at the Masters. On the 14th hole on Sunday, when his drive appeared to graze a tree before being directed back into the fairway, the CBS commentators spoke for everyone in seeing Harvey's guiding hand in the carom.

Ben arrived at the 72nd hole needing only to make bogey to win the tournament (over runner-up Davis Love III); when the final putt was holed, he bent at the waist and wept, at last giving vent to feelings he had been controlling all week. The sight of Crenshaw doubled over and of Carl Jackson standing by him and consoling him in his moment of victory remains one of the most indelible images in the history of Augusta National's 18th green.

Back in Austin, as Crenshaw sealed his unlikely yet inevitable win, Helen Penick uncorked a magnum of champagne that had been sent by a book editor to celebrate Harvey's ninetieth birthday that previous autumn. The wine flowed, eyes brimmed, and once again a sporting event surpassed the wildest imaginings of the creators of sentimental fiction.

—*JN*

COMPETITIVE FIRE: SEEING WITH THE EYE OF A TIGER

In June 2000, Tiger Woods took an eight-shot lead into the final round of the U.S. Open at Pebble Beach. Clearly, he was going to win. But how would he motivate himself?

Bill Bradley, the former U.S. senator and gifted basketball player who starred for Princeton University and then the New York Knicks, has written of the importance of getting what he calls the "chills" for an upcoming game. He described a game that the U.S. Olympic team was about to play against Russia in 1964, when Cold War relations were still fairly tense. Bradley had an interest in Russian history and had made a point of getting to know some of the Russian players. He was the key member of the U.S. team, but he found it hard to summon the requisite motivation to excel against them on the court; instead, he convinced himself that he was playing for Princeton against its archrival Yale University and led the U.S. team to a 73–59 win.

With an eight-shot lead and eighteen holes to play, Woods had to be feeling comfortable with his situation, but comfort is the ultimate danger for an athlete. Ken Venturi blew an eight-shot advantage over Jackie Burke Jr. in the final round of the 1956 Masters by thinking about two-putting every green, which, he later explained, "is the easiest way to three-putt." Nick Faldo picked

Venturi at the '56 Masters, before the fall.

up eleven shots on Greg Norman in the last round of the 1996 Masters. Woods needed to find a way to get the chills in the final round at Pebble Beach, and his strategy was to set a personal goal of playing a bogey-free final round at Pebble, one of the game's most storied courses. No one had ever played the final round of a U.S. Open without a bogey.

He parred the first nine holes, then birdied four of the next five. By the time Woods stood over his approach shot on the par-four, 403-yard 16th hole, he was two and a half holes from reaching his objective. He hadn't made a bogey, and he was fifteen shots ahead of Ernie Els, who was in second place. He and Els were playing in the final twosome.

Woods's shot to the 16th green, with a nine-iron from the first cut of shorter rough, flew right at the flag. The hole was cut in the rear left portion of the green. But the ball sailed over the top of the flag and the green before settling into typically deep and gnarly U.S. Open rough. Woods needed to make sure he would put the ball on the green, so that he could leave himself a putt for par. He couldn't risk one-hopping the ball through the high rough, lest it stay there. He couldn't risk landing the ball just over the rough, at the edge of the green, because there was so little margin for error in that shot.

Woods took a convincing cut at the ball, which popped out of the rough and rolled fifteen feet by the hole. He made the par putt and gave his trusted caddie, Steve Williams, a look that said, "How about that, bud? Saved my par." The shot was hardly the most dramatic or remarkable shot in Woods's career to that point—a career that had seen no end of such shots. But it was remarkable for the energy Woods invested in it. He had the tournament won. He could have triple-bogeyed his way in and still won, or even quadruple-bogeyed the last three holes.

But he had something else in mind: that bogey-free final round at the U.S. Open. To see Woods make that putt was to see a golfer who had the chills.

But he still had two holes to play. Woods hit his tee shot into a bunker left of the green on the par-three 17th hole where Carmel Bay provides the background. He wanted to get the ball up and down to save par, and that's all he was focused on. It was as if he weren't even playing the U.S. Open; he was engaged in a battle with himself. He'd set a goal, and that's all there was to it. He might as well have been a kid playing alone in the late afternoon and fantasizing about being where he in fact was; all that mattered was the match in his mind. Woods was having fun on the course the way he likes to have fun: He was pushing himself. He was sinking into the experience, which is what it's all about for a champion. Winning is a by-product.

Woods planted his feet to stabilize himself on the sidehill, downhill lie. He splashed his ball out so that it landed softly on the green and watched as it rolled toward the hole, sliding a couple of inches past the right side. He parred the hole, hit a four-iron safely into the fairway from the tee of the par-five 18th, hit a wedge on the green, just missed his birdie putt, and tapped in to meet his goal of playing a bogey-free final round at the U.S. Open.

He got the job done.

BEDEVILED EGGS (SOME REAL BRAND NAMES OF GOLF BALLS)

Baby Dimple
Blue Flash
Bramble
British King
Bunny
Callaway HX Tour
Diamond Chip
Dunlop 65
Eagle
Eclipse
Eyeball
Faultless
First Flight
Flipoot
Flying Lady
Flying Scotsman
Glory Dimple
Glory Floater
Gold Flash
Golden Girl
Golden Ram
Hawk
Homer
Hunter's Ball
Jack Rabbit
Jolly Junior
Kite
MacGregor Tourney
Molitor
Musselburgh
Nobby
Oneup
Ortogo Singer
Radio
Raw Distance
Silver King
Silvertown
Smart Core
Spalding Dot
Spalding Executive
Spalding Midget
St. Mungo Water Core
Sweet Shot
Swift
Tiger
Tit-Bit
Titleist Pro V1X
Top Notch
Vardon Flyer
Wizard
Zodiac

FAMOUS COLLAPSES IN MAJORS

Tom Watson, 1974 U.S. Open, Winged Foot Golf Club

With one round to play, Watson led the U.S. Open by a shot over Hale Irwin and three shots over Arnold Palmer. Watson, twenty-four, had yet to win a PGA Tour event, let alone a major championship. But he'd shot one-under-par 69 in the third round at Winged Foot, which was playing about as tough as a course could. He was at three-over-par 213 and had been playing solid golf to lead the championship.

But Watson was relatively inexperienced and not full of confidence. After leaving the 18th green in the third round, he noticed Sandy Tatum, the USGA's championship committee chairman. Tatum had been asked during the week if the USGA was trying to embarrass the best players in the world, considering the course's difficulty. "No, we're trying to identify them," he said—a comment that would endure.

Watson, upon seeing Tatum, asked, "Do you think I can do it?" Tatum, like Watson a graduate of Stanford University in Palo Alto, California, and a lawyer who didn't mince words, came back with a question of his own. "Do you think you can do it?"

"Yes, I do," Watson said.

Watson played with Irwin in the final round. They were tied for the lead through eight holes, at six over par for the tournament. Watson was three over for the day. He three-putted the glassy 10th green for bogey, and continued to drop shots. Watson eventually shot 79, and tied for fifth with Palmer and others at 12-over-par 292. Irwin won with a score of 287, seven over.

Watson learned from his experience. He soon won his first PGA Tour event, the 1974 Western Open near Chicago. The next year, in 1975, he won the British Open in a playoff at Carnoustie against Jack Newton.

TEN MOST MEMORABLE LINES *from CADDYSHACK*

Ty Webb

1. *The Zen philosopher Basho once wrote, "A flute with no holes is not a flute, and a donut with no holes is a Danish."*

2. *I don't think the heavy stuff is going to come down for quite a while.*

3. *He hauls off and whacks one. Big hitter, the Lama. Long!*

4. *This is a hybrid, a cross—bluegrass, Kentucky bluegrass, featherbed bent, and northern California sinsemilla. The amazing thing about this is, you can play thirty-six holes on it in the afternoon, then take it home and get stoned to the bejesus on it.*

5. *How about a Fresca?*

6. *Don't put yourself down, Al. You're not . . . you're not good. You stink.*

7. *Wonderful boy. Oh, he's a good boy. (Now I know why tigers eat their young.)*

8. *Don't worry about this one. If you miss it, we lose.*

9. *Well, the world needs ditchdiggers, too.*

10. *What you've got to do with Smails is, you cut the hamstring on the back of his leg right at the bottom. He'll never play golf again. Because when he goes back, his weight displacement goes back, and his weight stays on his right foot, and he'll be pushing everything off to the right. He'll give up the game.*

Al Czervik

AWARDS PRESENTED TO JACK NICKLAUS

- Gold Tee Award, Metropolitan Golf Association of New York, 1968
- Honorary Doctorate, Ohio State University, 1972
- Inductee, World Golf Hall of Fame, 1974
- Bob Jones Award, 1975, United States Golf Association
- Athlete of the Decade, 1970s, National Sports Writers
- Golfer of the 1970s, *Golf Magazine*
- William Richardson Award, 1978, Golf Writers Association of America, recognizing an individual who has consistently made an outstanding contribution to golf. Richardson wrote for *The New York Times* and was instrumental in founding the GWAA in 1946.
- Sportsman of the Year, 1978, *Sports Illustrated*
- BBC Overseas Sports Personality of the Year, 1980
- Honorary Doctorate, St. Andrews University, 1984
- Providencia Award, 1992, Palm Beach County, to an individual who or organization which has made a significant contribution to the tourism industry
- Inductee, Canadian Golf Hall of Fame, 1995
- Payne Stewart Award, 2000, PGA Tour
- Memorial Tournament Honoree, 2000, Captains Club
- Distinguished Service Award, 2000, PGA of America
- Donald Ross Award, 2001, American Society of Golf Course Architects
- Vince Lombardi Award of Excellence, 2001
- ESPY Lifetime Achievement Award, 2001, ESPN
- Don A. Rossi Award, 2001, Golf Course Builders' Association of America
- Florida Athlete of the Century, Florida Sports Awards
- Best Individual Male Athlete of the Twentieth Century, *Sports Illustrated*
- Golfer of the Century, *Golf Magazine, Golf Digest, Golf World,* BBC

- Muhammad Ali Sports Legend Award, 2003
- International Association of Golf Tourism Award, 2004
- Orthopaedic Hospital Paul Runyan Recognition Award, Los Angeles, 2005
- Listener of the Year, International Listening Association, 2005
- Old Tom Morris Award, 2005, Golf Course Superintendents Association of America
- Japan's Foreign Minister's Commendation in Commemoration of the 150th Anniversary of the U.S.-Japan Relationship, 2005
- Royal Bank of Scotland Five-Pound Note, 2005
- Michael Williams Award, 2005, Association of Golf Writers, for cooperation with and support of British golf writers
- Presidential Medal of Freedom, 2005. This is the highest civilian award in the United States.
- ASAP Sports/Jim Murray Award, 2006, Golf Writers Association of America, for cooperation with the media

Nicklaus hoists one of the many trophies he won, which begat all the awards he was given.

GOLF IN THE TOP TEN: DAVID LETTERMAN *and the* LINKS

From "Top Ten Signs Your Golf Partner is a Killer," February 6, 1997:

Gets really jumpy whenever anyone goes near his golf bag.

His last partner was found hanging off the little windmill at the local putt-putt.

From "Top Ten Ways to Make Golf More Exciting," April 10, 1997, and April 8, 1999:

Have a minister, a priest, and a rabbi play—that always turns out hilarious.

New rule: Miss a putt, swallow a tee.

Replace Tiger Woods with an actual tiger.

Each foursome must include at least one man wrongly acquitted of double homicide.

From "Top Ten Signs Tiger Woods is Overconfident," April 7, 2000:

On his tax return, lists his occupation as "Best Damn Golfer on Planet."

When asked, "What do you think of the competition?" laughs his ass off for 20 minutes.

From "Top Ten Tiger Woods Pet Peeves," August 21, 2000:

Have to hire three maids for the trophy-polishing alone.

At press conference, not allowed to admit, "I kicked everyone's ass because I'm much, much better than they are."

From "Top Ten Tiger Woods Excuses," July 22, 2002:

"I was up late the night before celebrating my inevitable victory."

Too much haggis.

From "Top Ten Surprising Facts About Rich Beem," August 19, 2002 (following Beem's win in the PGA Championship):

For a brief period in 1997, called himself "Richie."

Even he has never heard of him.

From "Top Ten Messages Left on Mike Weir's Answering Machine," April 14, 2003 (following Weir's win in the Masters):

"This is the Canadian Golf Hall of Fame. Want to be our first member?"

DEFENDING MAJOR CHAMPIONSHIP WINNERS WHO MISSED THE CUT (SINCE 1960, MEN'S MAJORS)

- Bob Rosburg, 1960 PGA Championship
- Jerry Barber, 1962 PGA Championship
- Jack Nicklaus, 1963 U.S. Open
- Julius Boros, 1964 U.S. Open
- Ken Venturi, 1965 U.S. Open
- Jack Nicklaus, 1967 Masters
- Lee Trevino, 1969 U.S. Open
- Orville Moody, 1970 U.S. Open
- Tommy Aaron, 1974 Masters
- Tom Watson, 1976 British Open
- Seve Ballesteros, 1981 Masters
- Larry Nelson, 1982 PGA Championship
- Seve Ballesteros, 1984 Masters
- Sandy Lyle, 1989 Masters
- Mark Calcavecchia, 1990 British Open
- Tom Kite, 1993 U.S. Open
- Lee Janzen, 1994 U.S. Open
- Paul Azinger, 1994 PGA Championship
- Ernie Els, 1995 U.S. Open
- Ben Crenshaw, 1996 Masters
- Nick Faldo, 1997 Masters
- Mark Brooks, 1997 PGA Championship
- Mark O'Meara, 1999 British Open
- José Maria Olazabal, 2000 Masters
- Paul Lawrie, 2000 British Open
- Retief Goosen, 2002 U.S. Open
- David Toms, 2002 PGA Championship
- Rich Beem, 2003 PGA Championship
- Mike Weir, 2004 Masters
- Ben Curtis, 2004 British Open
- Todd Hamilton, 2005 British Open
- Michael Campbell, 2006 U.S. Open

Mark O'Meara with the Claret Jug.

THE PLAYOFF THAT NEVER WAS

In the second Open Championship held at St. Andrews, in 1876, there was a controversy and a finish unique in the annals of golf history.

The Championship was played during the same week as the fall meeting of the R&A. The Championship committee hadn't realized it would have to reserve starting times for the competitors, and the course was crowded with golfers, some playing their own games, some playing in the Open. Bob Martin and David Strath were tied for the lead after the morning round, four shots ahead of the field. Martin went out first and was finished by the time Strath reached 17.

The home of golf, but not of David Strath after the playoff snafu.

On the 14th hole, Strath's drive hit a St. Andrean upholsterer who was coming up the fifth; this Mr. Hutton was struck on the forehead and knocked down, though he recovered and was able to walk home on his own. Strath, shaken by the incident, dropped a stroke compared to level fives ("par" was still a few years in the future) on 14 and 15 before righting himself on 16.

On the 17th tee he learned that he needed two fives to win the event. He got the first of them on the Road Hole, hitting his third shot to the green and getting down in two putts. His approach shot, however, had struck the twosome in front of him, who were still on the green; there are conflicting accounts as to how much this might have helped him, and he did require two putts. Strath took six shots on the 18th, and he finished the day's play tied with Martin for the Championship, seven shots ahead of their nearest competitor.

Martin's supporters claimed that Strath should have been disqualified for hitting into the pair on 17 before they left the green. The point wasn't covered in the rules, and there was no umpire appointed to settle disputes as there had been in the Opens held previously at Prestwick. (Under today's rules, and any that have contemplated this situation, hitting an "outside agency" falls under "rub of the green," and the ball is played as it lies without penalty.) The tournament committee did not reach a decision after the day's play, and with the next day being Sunday, no meeting or round would take place until Monday. They declared that Strath and Martin should play off for the title then and that the committee would issue a ruling on the possible disqualification after that replay.

Strath felt this was absurd, since a ruling against him would mean that no playoff was necessary in the first place. He refused to participate, so Martin won in a "walkover"—and, like a racehorse in a walkover after every other horse has scratched, he walked the course on his own, without striking a shot, before being declared the victor. (The call for disqualification was apparently dropped, because Strath received the second-place prize money of £5, half the amount brought home by Martin. Still, Strath was stung by the events, and he soon departed St. Andrews to move across the Firth of Forth, becoming the greenkeeper of North Berwick. His expansion of the course there included creating the original and much-imitated Redan hole.)

FOOTNOTES TO HISTORY

Jean Van de Velde, 1999 British Open, Carnoustie

The par-four 18th hole at the Carnoustie Golf Club was playing 487 yards when Jean Van de Velde stepped onto the tee on the last day of the 1999 British Open. Van de Velde, a Frenchman who played the European Tour regularly, held a three-shot lead over the field. He was in the last group, and the engraver had nearly finished etching his name onto the Open Championship Trophy.

Van de Velde chose to hit a driver and pushed his ball well right and into the 17th fairway. He had an excellent lie on the crisp, short turf and decided to hit a two-iron. Ahead of him and short of the green was the Barry Burn, whose serpentine shape makes it one of Carnoustie's most feared hazards.

His second shot, while clearing the burn, also strayed to the right. Van de Velde's ball hit the front of a grandstand and, amazingly, bounced back across Barry Burn, settling into high grass thirty yards short of the green. Van de Velde's ball was well down in the grass, which covered him up to his knees. He took a cut at the ball, which wobbled and fell into the burn.

Lying three, Van de Velde took off his shoes and socks, rolled up his slacks, and scrambled down into the water. Hands on hips, he surveyed the situation. A concrete wall was very near him, and he would have to loft his ball over it to reach the green. His ball was in the water. Craig Parry, with whom he was playing, wondered silently whether Van de Velde should wait until the tide went out.

Van de Velde decided to take a penalty stroke and drop outside the hazard. Now playing his fifth shot, he came up short into a greenside bunker. His sixth shot finished six feet from the hole. After being ahead by three on the tee, Van de Velde needed to make the putt for triple bogey just to get into a playoff with Paul Lawrie and Justin Leonard. The putt went down.

Jean Van de Velde, badly Burned.

The Royal and Ancient Golf Club of St. Andrews uses a four-hole playoff to break ties at the British Open. Leonard had bogeyed the final hole and was sure he had no chance to make a playoff. Lawrie, a Scot, had shot 67 the last round, but since he'd trailed Van de Velde by ten shots at the start of the day, he too assumed his score would not be good enough. But Van de Velde changed all that.

Lawrie won the playoff, playing even-par golf for the four holes. In a sense, he became the real footnote to the story of this championship. Everybody remembers Van de Velde's collapse, a series of events that bordered on farce.

"It's a game," Van de Velde told the golf media a few minutes after the debacle concluded. "There are worse things in life." A few years later he said, "That's what sport is all about. It's about emotion, whether good or bad. Until you are there with the trophy, it's not over."

SOME FAMOUS PENALTIES

1941 U.S. Open

Ed "Porky" Oliver

Apparently tied for the lead after seventy-two holes, Oliver was disqualified (along with five others) for beginning his round ahead of his starting time. The six, concerned about an impending storm, ignored a marshal's instruction that they had to wait.

1957 U.S. Women's Open

Jackie Pung

Disqualified after apparently winning the tournament by a stroke, for signing a scorecard with a 5 entered by playing partner Betty Jameson for the fourth hole instead of her actual 6. (Her total for the round was listed correctly.) Curiously, Pung made the same mistake on Jameson's scorecard, Jameson signed it, and was disqualified as well.

1968 Masters

Roberto de Vicenzo

Missed out on a playoff with Bob Goalby after tying for the seventy-two-hole lead, but signing a scorecard on which his playing partner Tommy Aaron had written a 4 instead of a birdie 3 on the 17th hole. Since the score was higher than the actual score, the higher score became the official result, and Goalby won by a stroke.

1987 Andy Williams/ San Diego Open

Craig Stadler

In the third round, Stadler played a shot on his knees from a muddy lie near a pine tree. To protect his light-colored slacks, he placed a towel on the wet ground. After finishing his fourth round in second place, he was informed that he'd violated the rule against building a stance, and since he'd failed to include that penalty in his third-round score, he was being disqualified. The rules officials at the tournament missed the infraction, but a television viewer called it in.

1996 Greater Hartford Open

Greg Norman

Norman was the defending champion and held the first-round lead when he noticed that the ball he was using was improperly stamped and thus was not on the approved list of permissible balls. He reported the violation and was disqualified.

1996 Disney World Classic

Taylor Smith

Disqualified for using a long putter with an illegal grip after apparently having tied for the tournament lead at the end of the final round. (A putter may have more than one grip, but both must be circular; Smith's club had a split grip with one portion flat-sided.)

1997 PLAYERS CHAMPIONSHIP

Davis Love III

Putting on the 17th hole of the final round, Love inadvertently nudged his ball with a practice stroke. Instead of replacing the ball at a penalty of one stroke, Love putted out from the new position, incurring a two-stroke penalty. He signed a scorecard charging himself with a one-stroke penalty and was disqualified for giving himself a lower score than he had earned. The disqualification cost him $105,437.

2001 BRITISH OPEN

Ian Woosnam

Received a two-shot penalty while tied for the lead at the start of the final round, for having fifteen clubs in his bag as he played the first hole. (Woosnam was unlucky to be playing at Royal Lytham & St. Annes, the only British Open course that opens with a par three. The offending club was a second driver, and he or his caddie would surely have noticed it at any other opening hole.)

2003 MASTERS

Jeff Maggert

Earned a two-shot penalty on the third hole of the final round, after a fairway bunker shot hit the lip of the hazard and rebounded to hit him in the chest. The resulting triple-bogey seven knocked Maggert out of the lead, and he finished in fifth place.

2003 BRITISH OPEN

Jesper Parnevik and Mark Roe

Disqualified following the third round, when it was discovered they had neglected to exchange scorecards before the round, and each had mistakenly entered each other's scores, including some that were lower than their actual scores. Roe was only two shots out of the lead at the time. (Under the Rules changes announced by the R&A and the USGA for 2006, this error can be corrected so long as the scores are right.)

2005 SAMSUNG WORLD CHAMPIONSHIP

Michelle Wie

During the third round of her first professional tournament, Wie took a drop for an unplayable lie. *Sports Illustrated* reporter Michael Bamberger believed that Wie had dropped the ball closer to the hole; he reported the problem to a rules official the following day. After Wie completed her fourth round, it was determined that she had dropped improperly. Since she should have assessed herself a two-shot penalty but didn't, she was disqualified, costing her $53,126—an amount she makes every four days under her Nike contract.

THE MAJORS AND HOW THEY GOT THAT WAY

In the beginning, it was simple: There was only one Grand Slam, and it belonged to Bobby Jones. The Slam was invented by sportswriters in 1930 who wanted to set a goal for the Georgian amateur. (George Trevor of the *New York Sun* called it "the impregnable quadrilateral," setting a standard for excessive grandiloquence matched only by Jones's own description of golfers as "dogged victims of inexorable fate.") It required winning the Open and Amateur Championships of the United States and Great Britain in a single year. The definition suited Jones, because it was suited to him; no professionals need apply.

As the professional game grew, the Slam became obsolete. When Ben Hogan completed an unprecedented triple in 1953 by winning the Masters, the U.S. Open, and the British Open (or Open Championship, as it is known everywhere but the United States), Isaac Grainger, vice president of the USGA, hailed the achievement by commenting, "That's wonderful. If Hogan could become an amateur, he might even go after [Jones's] record and score another Grand Slam." Grainger was joking, but the statement shows that no one had thought up the professional Grand Slam yet. The PGA Championship, today the fourth leg, was a match-play event, with all the quirks match play entails. When Hogan announced his plans to play in the British Open for the first and only time in 1953, no one mentioned that its qualifying rounds would coincide with the last two days of that year's PGA; there was no linkage between the two in the public's or press's imagination.

In 1960, Arnold Palmer won the Masters and the U.S. Open, and according to Palmer's autobiography *A Golfer's Life,* he and his sportswriter friend Bob Drum had a little discussion while flying across the Atlantic for that year's Open Championship. Palmer was one of the few American professionals to head over to the Open in those days; the purses were so meager that a top-five finish might not cover a player's expenses. Drum was lamenting the fact that the Grand Slam had become a virtual impossibility; no amateur had won the U.S. Open since 1933, or the British since Jones in 1930.

"Then why don't we create a new grand slam?" asked Palmer. "What would be wrong with a professional Grand Slam involving the Masters, both Open championships, and the PGA Championship?"

The idea took hold, and the Associated Press account of Palmer's second-place finish in the 1960 British made reference to the end of his bid for the "modern Grand Slam." Historians have since treated these four tournaments as majors and as constituting a unified set retroactively; today we credit Walter Hagen with winning three legs of a career "Grand Slam" that he never knew existed.

On the women's side, the designation of "majors" is a bit more involved. The LPGA has explicitly named specific tournaments from specific periods as majors in women's golf history. These tournaments are as follows:

- Western Open, 1930–67
- Titleholders Championship, 1937–42, 1946–66, 1972
- U.S. Women's Open, 1950–present
- LPGA Championship, 1955–present
- *Kraft Nabisco Championship, 1983–present
- duMaurier Classic, 1979–2000
- Women's British Open, 2001–present

*originally known as the Dinah Shore, with various corporate sponsors, 1983–99

There may be a bit of retroactive elevation here, as there is on the men's side, in the LPGA's first decades. The LPGA Championship and the U.S. Women's Open are indisputable; the Titleholders was certainly considered an important tournament, as was the Western Open, but it's not clear that they were thought of on the same level as the other two. In 1964, Mickey Wright finished second in the Titleholders, second in the Open, and won the LPGA Championship—but didn't play in the Western. Similarly, in 1966, she was second in the LPGA, third in the Open, and won the Western—but didn't play in the Titleholders. "Majors" did not always mean the same thing we mean when we speak of them today.

Complicating the issue, in some years there were two majors, in some there were three, and in some there was just one. Has someone who won the only two majors in a season won a "Grand Slam"? Sorry, Sandra Haynie, but winning the LPGA and the U.S. Women's Open in 1974 isn't enough; impregnable or not, a true Slam requires a quadrilateral. (Babe Didrikson Zaharias fell short by the same measure in 1950, when she won all three available titles.) If this seems unfair, we can compensate by giving extra honor to Karrie Webb, who is so far the only player to win *five* different professional major championships, having won both the duMaurier and the Weetabix Women's British Open that took its place on the major roster in 2001. (The LPGA treats the duMaurier and Weetabix as one championship for Grand Slam purposes.) This remarkable accomplishment is called the Super Career Grand Slam by the LPGA, and among active players, Juli Inkster alone is within one victory of matching Webb, needing only the Women's British title.

MAJOR CHAMPIONSHIPS (INCLUDING U.S. AND BRITISH AMATEUR)

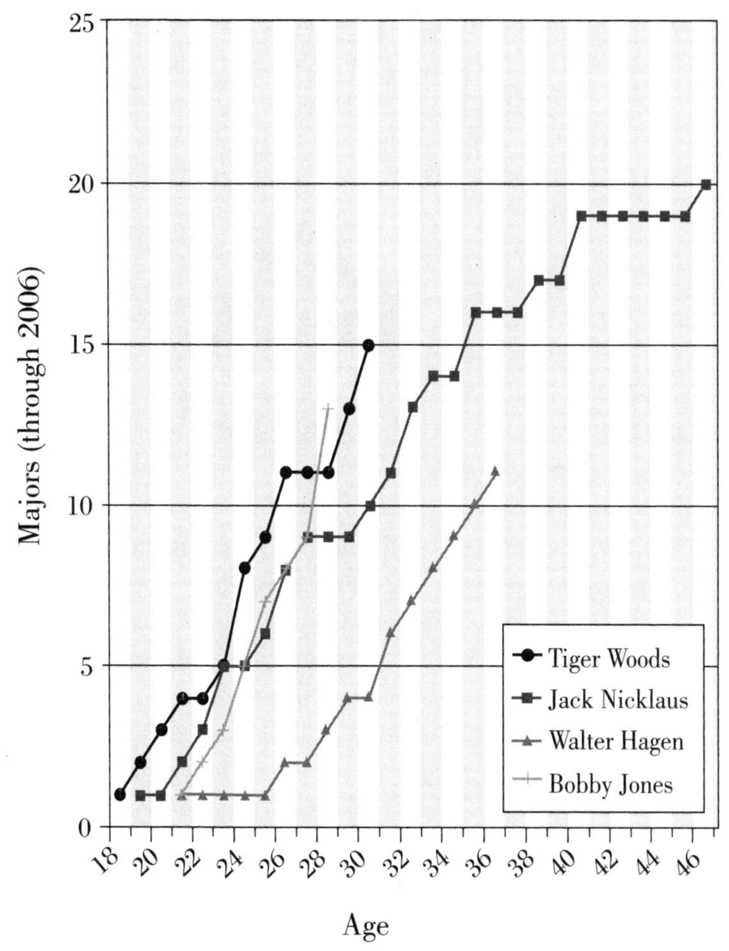

THE GOLFER'S LIFE LIST

Attend the Masters

You've probably heard that the Masters is the best-run sporting event in the country. You've undoubtedly heard that tickets ("badges") are impossible to come by, that they're passed down from generation to generation on a tightly held subscription list. You've always longed to gaze down Magnolia Lane, to take in Amen Corner, to sit on the hillside next to the pond on 16, to see just how scary downhill putts on 9 can be—but you've always figured that it was either impossible or hideously expensive.

Large crowds ("many patrons") gather, but Augusta's hills provide excellent vantage points.

In fact, practice-round tickets are not that hard to come by on the so-called secondary market (a lovely term for scalpers, and one appropriate to a place that calls bleachers "observation stands" and fans "patrons"). If you're willing to run the gauntlet of fast-food joints and chain stores on Washington Road, you'll find semi-competitive sellers with inventory to unload, knowing that their real money will come in when the tournament begins.

Once you're inside the gates, take your time and soak in the experience. Don't expect to see Tiger—he'll have finished his round early in the a.m.—but find some of the former champions who treat April in Augusta as a reunion of an elite and fortunate fraternity. Walk the entire course, making note of the hills where you didn't expect them. Watch players try to figure out the lines on the impossibly tricky seventh green. Have a pimento cheese sandwich that costs $1.50, much less than you expected. Spend your savings (and a lot more) in the crowded, yet surprisingly orderly merchandise building—no mere tent for this retail operation, with its Disneyland-style switchback lines that can mean a forty-five-minute wait just to get inside. Chat with the people around you, some of whom will be at their first Masters, some at their thirtieth. Don't miss the chance to see the par-three course, a subsidiary gem that some older members prefer to the "big course." Just *try* to litter, and note how quickly one of the jump-suited volunteers spears your refuse and deposits it in a green sack. And when you're back home, watch the TV coverage with fresh knowledge of the real conditions, and marvel at the polite efficiency possible in a controlled environment run by a benevolent dictatorship.

MOST YEARS BETWEEN TOUR VICTORIES

Men

- Robert Gamez, fifteen years and six months between 1990 Nestle Invitational at Bay Hill Club in Orlando and 2005 Valero Texas Open in San Antonio
- Butch Baird, fifteen years, five months, and ten days between 1961 Waco Turner Open and 1976 San Antonio Texas Open
- Tommy Armour III, thirteen years and eight months between 1990 Phoenix Open and 2003 Valero Texas Open in San Antonio

Women

- Dale Eggeling, fourteen years, eleven months, and four days between 1980 Boston Five Classic and 1995 Oldsmobile Classic
- Shelly Hamlin, thirteen years, five months, and thirteen days between 1978 Patty Berg Classic and 1992 Phar-Mor at Inverrary

MOE NORMAN: THE GREATEST GOLFER YOU NEVER SAW

Who is Moe Norman, and what was so special about him? Why did Lee Trevino call him "a living legend, a genius when it comes to playing the game of golf"?

Perhaps no golfer has ever hit the ball with more precision, or a more unusual swing, than Moe Norman. Born in 1929 in Kitchener, Ontario, a city of a couple hundred thousand people seventy miles west of Toronto, Norman had a winter accident when he was five years old that may well have influenced the rest of his life. He was tobogganing down a hill when a car that was pulling out of a driveway hit him. Norman was dragged a hundred yards before freeing himself. He seemed okay and wasn't taken to the hospital. Soon, however, his teachers and his parents noticed that he was behaving differently. His speech sped up, and he started to repeat himself. His mother said many years later that she regretted not taking her son for neurological tests.

Norman wasn't much of a student, except in mathematics. He multiplied figures rapidly, and in sports, he had a keen eye for the movement of a ball in flight. Norman batted .610 in a softball league and seemed able to hit the ball to specific locations. He was also a loner. His twin sister Marie noticed that he didn't take kindly to criticism and that he chose activities he could do on his own. Golf fit perfectly, and after Norman left school in the ninth grade, he filled his time with the game. He caddied at a local public course and played as often as possible. He loved to hit balls, all day and into the night when he could, 800 balls, 1,000 balls. He'd found his calling.

Pros would gather to watch Moe Norman practice, well into his seventies.

Soon Norman was winning amateur tournaments all around southern Ontario. His family wasn't poor but by no means was it anywhere near wealthy. Norman brought home winnings such as wristwatches, kitchen appliances, and stereos. Sometimes he sold them. He worked as a pinsetter at a bowling alley, earning a reputation as the fastest kid with the pins. He also played golf fast, very fast. Later Norman would say, "I'm the 747 of golf, I'm the 747 of golf, one look and I hit it, one look and I hit it." He never took a practice swing in his life.

Norman won the 1955 and 1956 Canadian Amateurs, but he was excruciatingly shy and couldn't speak at the presentation ceremonies. He was invited to the 1956 Masters and took a bus to Augusta, Georgia. He was hitting balls on the practice range when Sam Snead approached him to give some advice. Norman didn't need to learn anything about the swing, because his worked beautifully, but it was very different from anybody else's. Norman stood far from the ball, arms outstretched, legs spread wide. He appeared ungainly while taking the club back, far back, from the ball, and then stretched far past it after impact. But the ball went where he aimed it. Still, when the great Sam Snead offered a tip, Norman heard him out and then hit balls until dark, hundreds of balls. His hands were raw the next day, and he could hardly hold the club. Norman withdrew in pain from the Masters in the middle of the second round.

Norman played most of his golf in Canada and did clinics, always entertaining, for the Canadian PGA. Speaking about the backswing, Moe would say, "Long and low, stretch it. Shake hands with the flagstick. I want the right arm bent and the left arm a rod at impact." He'd watch golfers hitting ball after ball on the range without paying attention to what they were doing. Moe would stop them and say, "Come on now, let's not be a ball beater, let's be a mind beater." Or, playing a round with friends, he'd notice how they became tense and say, "Hope and fear, hope and fear, that's what people see when they play golf. Not me. I see happiness." Or, he'd define the game for others: "Golf is hitting an object to a defined area with the least amount of effort and an alert attitude of indifference."

Moe played one winter on the American tour after turning pro, but didn't last. Some pros laughed at him. They didn't like the way he looked or dressed, what with his snaggled teeth, his red pants inches too short, his rainbow sweaters. While Norman couldn't cope with the social side of the game, he could still hit the ball accurately time after time after time. He won provincial Opens across Canada and Canadian PGA Championships. He became a cult figure, with crowds gathering when he hit balls. He could hit for hours and hours, but, he liked to say, "I'm not ball-oriented. I'm divot-oriented. I swing past the ball."

Paul Azinger's teacher John Redman called Norman "the best ball-striker that ever lived." Lee Trevino said, "I don't know of any person that I've ever seen who could strike a golf ball like Moe Norman as far as hitting it solid, knowing where it's going, knowing the mechanics of the game, and knowing what he wants to do with the golf ball."

Norman won everything in Canada but the Canadian Open. He was in contention in the final round of the 1963 Canadian Open, but became anxious when he thought about having to speak at the prize ceremony. He three-putted his way in and lost the tournament to Doug Ford. He was inducted into the Canadian Golf Hall of Fame in 1995.

Finally, late in life, Norman became more comfortable with public speaking. Even then, he usually spoke in practiced ways using material he'd memorized. He could be counted on to recite a poem he learned from Paul Bertholy, a teacher and friend he saw when he stopped in to Pinehurst, North Carolina, on his drive north from Florida every spring. Norman died in September 2004, on the weekend prior to the Canadian Open at the Glen Abbey Golf Club in Oakville, Ontario. The Canadian flag flew at half-mast all week. One long-time Norman fan said his death left "a hole in the world." There was certainly a hole on the range. Norman used to hit balls on the range every Tuesday at every Canadian Open. The tour pros wanted him there, so he'd amble out, and was soon mesmerizing them. They all stopped to watch him hit balls, with their clubs, in his street shoes. Moe liked nothing better than to hit balls, to watch the ball fly to his target.

Here's the poem that Moe recited when he spoke. It's called "What is Happiness?" It's not exactly Wordsworth, but it meant a lot to Moe.

Golf is happiness, for happiness is achievement
The Mother is encouragement
The fine golf swing is truly achievement
Man may lie, cheat and steal for gain but these will never gain
The golf swing
To gain the golf swing, man must work
Yet it is work without toil
It is exercise without the boredom
It is intoxication without the hangover
It is stimulation without the pills
It is failure, yet its successes shine even more brightly
It is frustration, yet it nourishes patience
It irritates, yet its soothing is far greater
It is futility, yet it nurtures hope
It is defeating, yet it generates courage
It is humbling, yet it ennobles the human spirit
It is dignity, yet it rejects arrogance
Its price is high, yet its rewards are richer
Some say it is a boy's pastime, yet it builds men
It is a buffer for the stresses of today's living
It cleans the mind and rejuvenates the body
It is these things and many more for those of us who know it
and love it
Golf is truly happiness.

GREAT CAREER AMATEURS

Marvin "Vinny" Giles, b. Richmond, Virginia, 1943

Giles was twenty-nine when he came to the 1972 U.S. Amateur at the Charlotte Country Club. He was on the cusp of what he thought would be a career in investment banking and was tired after a summer of competitive golf. But he'd come so close in previous U.S. Amateurs; perhaps his time would come. He'd missed a playoff when Bob Dickson holed from fifteen feet on the last hole of the 1967 championship at the Broadmoor Country Club to win. Bruce Fleisher had drilled a three-iron fifteen feet from the hole in 1968 to beat him on a day when he'd shot 65 at the Scioto Country Club in Columbus, Ohio. Still, it was obvious that Giles had an affinity for courses that Donald Ross had designed; Ross did both Broadmoor and Scioto, and he'd designed the Charlotte Country Club.

Giles at the '72 Amateur; Tiger did not invent the gesture.

This time Giles did win, by three shots over Ben Crenshaw and Mark Hayes. Two summers later he won the British Amateur, defeating Mark James 8 & 7 in their final match. Giles went on to a successful career as an agent for professional golfers, including Tom Kite, Davis Love III, and Justin Leonard. He played on four Walker Cup teams and was captain of the U.S. side in 1993 at the Interlachen Country Club near Minneapolis. The Americans won 19–5 over the Great Britain and Ireland side.

HOW TO GET ON BETHPAGE BLACK

The most famous municipal course in America hosted the U.S. Open in 2002, and it was such a smashing success that the USGA decided to return there for the 2009 Open. The Black Course is one of five eighteen-hole layouts at Bethpage State Park in Farmingdale, New York. A sign by the first tee warns, "The Black Course is an extremely difficult course and is recommended only for highly skilled players." Before the mid-1990s, this sign was taken very seriously, and as a result the waits were shorter to play the Black Course than any of the four others. (This may also be attributed to the walking-only policy on this very hilly course.) Today golfers flock to the track that tested Tiger and Phil and Sergio and all the rest, and tee times are difficult to come by, but not impossible. Here are a few tips:

1. Camp out. Tee times for the first hour of every day (generally beginning at 7 A.M., earlier in the summer), and one foursome per hour thereafter, are allocated on a first-come first-served basis. This has led to the legendary night patrol, those hearty golfers who sleep in their cars for the chance to get beaten up by the famously deep bunkers and impressive carries. (At least today those bunkers have probably been raked in the last few weeks; that was not the case in the old days.) If you're willing to sacrifice a comfortable night, and have the physical flexibility to work out the kinks quickly the next morning, simply arrive by seven or eight o'clock the night before and join the line; you will get on. Less hearty souls, keep reading.

2. Call in. New York State residents may make a phone reservation on Bethpage Black (516-249-0707) up to a week in advance. You will be required to provide your driver's license number, and you may make no more than one reservation per month. You'll also need a quick dialer and a lot of luck; the lines open at 7 P.M., and the times disappear in a matter of minutes. Nonresidents can call two days in advance—Tuesday night for a Thursday time, say. If you don't get through, check back a day before you'd like to play; there are occasional cancellations, which must be made forty-eight hours in advance to avoid a fee.

3. Show up. If you're a single on a weekday, even in midsummer, your chances of getting out are close to 100 percent. On the weekend it's much lower, but as compensation there are the four other courses; the Red Course has hosted many state and regional events, and is an excellent test of anybody's game at 7,000 yards and par 70 from the back tees. If you do get out on Black, you'll find a course that requires you to play every club in the bag, outstanding condition for a public course of any kind, and the greatest bargain in golf even at the 2006 post-Open rates ($41 weekday/$51 weekend for New York residents, $82 weekday/ $102 weekend for nonresidents; a $4 reservation fee if you've booked a time).

Bethpage's 8th hole—open to all.

TOP TEN FINISHES IN ALL FOUR MEN'S MAJORS IN ONE YEAR

(since 1958, when the PGA changed to stroke play; sorted by "ranking points")

NAME	MASTERS	U.S. OPEN	BRITISH	PGA	POINTS
Tiger Woods, 2000	5	1	1	1	8
Tiger Woods, 2005	1	2	1	4T	8
Jack Nicklaus, 1971	2T	2*	5T	1	10
Arnold Palmer, 1960	1	1	2	7T	11
Jack Nicklaus, 1973	3T	4T	4	1	12
Jack Nicklaus, 1975	1	7T	3T	1	12
Phil Mickelson, 2004	1	2	3	6T	12
Tom Watson, 1977	1	7T	1	6T	15
Tom Watson, 1982	5T	1	1	9T	16
Gary Player, 1974	1	8T	1	7	17
Jack Nicklaus, 1977	2	10T	2	3	17
Ernie Els, 2004	2	9T	2*	4T	17
Jack Nicklaus, 1974	4T	10T	3	2	19
Ben Crenshaw, 1987	4T	4T	4T	7T	19
Arnold Palmer, 1966	4T	2*	8T	6T	20
Doug Sanders, 1966	4T	8T	2T	6T	20
Hale Irwin, 1975	4T	3T	9	5T	21
Vijay Singh, 2005	5T	6T	5T	10T	26
Tom Watson, 1975	8T	9T	1	9	27
Miller Barber, 1969	7	6T	10	5T	28
Sergio Garcia, 2002	8	4	8T	10T	30

*tied for first after seventy-two holes, lost in a playoff

TOP TEN FINISHES IN ALL FOUR WOMEN'S MAJORS IN ONE YEAR (SINCE 1983)

(As detailed on page 55, there were four LPGA majors in the years from 1955 to 1966, and from 1983 to the present. In those first twelve seasons, twenty-nine women recorded top tens in all four in a year—too many to consider it a significant accomplishment. Hats off, though, to Mickey Wright, who in 1961 won the U.S. Open, LPGA, and Western, and finished third in the Titleholders, for a "six-point" season that tops Tiger's best.)

NAME	U.S. OPEN	LPGA	NABISCO	DUMAURIER OR BRITISH	POINTS
Pat Bradley, 1986	T5	1	1	1	8
Annika Sorenstam, 2003	4	1	2	1	9
Juli Inkster, 1999	1	1	6	3	11
Ayako Okamoto, 1987	T2*	T3	T5	2	12
JoAnne Carner, 1983	T2	T4	T4	T2	12
Betsy King, 1987	T4	2	1	7	14
Betsy King, 1993	T7	T4	T2	2*	15
Betsy King, 1989	1	T8	T4	T2	15
Pat Bradley, 1989	T3	T4	T6	T2	15
Juli Inkster, 1992	2*	9	2*	3	16
Beth Daniel, 1990	T6	1	T6	3	16
Betsy King, 1990	1	T5	1	T10	17
Karrie Webb, 2000	1	T9	1	T7	18
Rosie Jones, 1987	T9	T3	4	3	19
Patty Sheehan, 1984	T5	1	T8	T8	22
Beth Daniel, 1984	T10	T2	4	T6	22
Jody Rosenthal, 1987	T4	T9	10	1	24
Tammie Green, 1995	T7	T8	T7	4	26

*tied for first, lost in a playoff

WHO WAS THE PERSON BEHIND . . .

The Stimpmeter: Edward Stimpson, a Massachusetts golfer and winner of the state's amateur championship in 1935, became interested in the subject of green speeds after the 1935 U.S. Open at Oakmont, whose fearsome greens ensured that no professional would break 75 in the final round. He invented a device to quantify the discussion: a wooden shaft, along which a ball would roll when it was raised at a sufficient angle. With the shaft's open end placed on the ground, the ball would continue onto the green; the distance it traveled over the grass would reflect the green's speed.

The device languished in obscurity until the 1970s, when Frank Thomas, the USGA's technical director, modified the design to ensure consistent operation, and with Stimpson's permission he christened it the Stimpmeter. Stimp readings provide a universal language for discussing the speed of putting surfaces—and have caused enormous problems for course superintendents who find themselves being pressed by club members to make the greens as fast as those they see on television.

Stimpmeter in use.

Stableford Scoring: Dr. Frank Barney Gordon Stableford lived from 1870 to 1959, and his name lives on in the scoring system that bears his name. A physician who served in England's Royal Army Medical Corps during the Somaliland uprising, the Boer War, and World War I, Stableford wrote that he developed the system after playing the second hole at the Wallasey Golf Club in Cheshire, England. Reflecting on the impossibility for most golfers of reaching the 458-yard par four in two, he decided to come up with a scoring method that would keep golfers from ruining their rounds at the very outset. His innovation reduced the negative effect of bad holes: A golfer receives one point for a bogey, two for par, three for birdie, and so forth; anything higher than a bogey is simply a zero. The first competition played under Stableford rules took place at Wallasey on May 16, 1932. A plaque at the second hole today commemorates the event.

Callaway Handicapping: The Official Callaway Handicap System was developed by Lionel F. Callaway, a Scottish golf professional who spent much of his life in Pinehurst, North Carolina. The system provides a way for players who do not have an established golf handicap to participate in a tournament on a net basis. Callaway also composed what he called "A Golfer's Pledge" in the mid-1950s, a simplified summary of golf etiquette for the uninitiated. His scoring system, described on page 286, has become the most prevalent method for "handicapping the unhandicapped."

Mulligans: There is considerable uncertainty about the origin of the free shot given (or taken) on the first tee—or at many other times, if your name is Bill Clinton. According to the most knowledgeable authority to have weighed in on the subject, the USGA (specifically, its museum curator, Dr. Rand Jerris), the most widely accepted progenitor is one David Mulligan, who played at the St. Lambert Club in Montreal during the 1920s. A variety of specific stories are told, each involving a day on which Mr. Mulligan, a hotelier who was part-owner and manager of the Biltmore Hotel in New York as well as several Canadian hotels, hit a terrible drive off the first tee and impulsively reteed and hit what he termed a "correction shot." His partners decided that the practice deserved a better name, and an illegal tradition was born. (A friend of ours invented the "provisional mulligan": Playing in an outing whose rules permitted one replay at any time, he drove his ball towards the edge of a blind fairway bordered by water. He reteed, declaring that his mulligan would take effect only if his first drive proved to be in the hazard; none of us could find grounds to disallow this imaginative effort. Yes, he is a lawyer.)

Baltusrol: Wealthy New Jersey farmer Baltus Roll was found murdered near his home in 1831. Two men were suspected of the crime; one committed suicide, and the other was tried and acquitted. The case remained a local legend, and when *Social Register* publisher Louis Keller decided in the 1890s to build a golf course on the land that been Roll's, he used the combined form of the name that had been applied to the "mountain" on which the land sat. Roll's tombstone is in the Revolutionary Cemetery in nearby Westfield, New Jersey.

The Haskell Ball: After the featherie, a leather pouch stuffed with feathers, there came the guttie, a ball shaped from the gum resin of the gutta percha tree. Sometime in the late 1890s, Coburn Haskell, a Cleveland industrialist, was visiting a friend named Bert Work at his place of employment, the B.F. Goodrich plant in Akron. Work was busy for the moment, so Haskell had a look around. He came upon some elastic thread in a waste container and took to rolling it in his hands. Haskell realized the elastic material was rubber and was soon bouncing the resulting mass on the floor. He had a brainstorm, perhaps inspired by his knowing that tennis balls were made from the material.

Haskell was a golfer who, like all golfers, was looking for a few extra yards. He suggested to Work that the material be used to make a golf ball. The company did just that. The ball consisted of rubber windings inside a cover rather than the solid piece of gutta-percha that had become the standard. Work, a Goodrich manager, developed a machine to do the winding. While the first efforts were difficult to control, the Goodrich team eventually hit upon a combination of resilient, stretched rubber windings around a noncompressible core that added stability while maintaining the advantages of increased liveliness.

The resulting product, patented in 1898, was the Pro V1 of its day. Haskell asked Joseph Mitchell, the pro at his club, to have a go at the ball when it was ready. Mitchell air-mailed a shot past a bunker that until then wasn't in play unless the ground was hard and the ball bounced in. The Haskell rubber-core ball went farther, bounced higher, and made many people fear that the golf courses of the day would soon be obsolete. The wound ball remained the standard for top players for nearly a hundred years, an extraordinary duration for any improvement in golf technology, until it was replaced by the current solid ball with multilayered covers. The original brass mold for that first rubber-core golf ball lives on; it has been made into the Mitchell Haskell Trophy, awarded to the winner of the Northern Ohio PGA Section's tour championship.

The Ryder Cup: Samuel Ryder was born in 1858, but didn't take up golf until he was fifty. He had become a wealthy man by selling seeds in penny packets, but his health was suffering, he was working too hard, and doctors advised him to get more fresh air and exercise. He enjoyed cricket, but he wasn't keen on golf; nonetheless, he decided to take up the game and hired English professional Abe Mitchell as his private tutor,

Ryder Cup team, 1927

engaging him for a year at a salary of £1,000. Ryder practiced every day but Sunday for a year, by which time he was playing to a six handicap.

Golf professionals in the 1920s were not held in high esteem; clubs frequently docked their pros' pay when they took time off to compete in a tournament. In 1923, Ryder created a tournament for professionals and named it after his Heath and Heather Seed Company. Three years later, he watched Mitchell and other British golfers defeat a team of American professionals in an informal match at Wentworth prior to the Open at St. Andrews. He thought this should become a regular affair, and he decided to put up a gold cup for competition between a team of American professionals and a team comprising British and Irish professionals. He ordered that the cup be made with a likeness of Abe Mitchell on top. The first official Ryder Cup was played in 1927 at Worcester Country Club in Worcester, Massachusetts. The U.S. team won, but more important, the British/Irish team traveled in style. As representatives of their countries, the pros were accorded respect that carried forward into their lives back home. A principle had been established, and the status of the golf pro was changed forever.

The Wanamaker Trophy: Rodman Wanamaker, who owned the department stores that bore his family name, was enamoured of the game of golf and its potential to engage new players. He believed that golf could play an important role in American sporting life, and in 1916 he hosted a luncheon for golf professionals and several prominent amateurs in the New York area; this gathering led to the creation of the Professional Golfers Association of America. Wanamaker donated the purse for the first PGA Championship, held later that year, as well as a trophy to serve as the champion's prize in perpetuity.

Wanamaker's Department Store.

Wanamaker was a man of many interests. He loved music, and at the time of his death in 1928 had amassed a collection of sixty rare musical instruments, among them works of Stradivari, Amati, and Guarneri. Fascinated with aviation, he built three huge planes in pre-Lindbergh days. In sports, he formed the Millrose Athletic Association as an outlet for employees of his department stores. (Millrose was the name of Wanamaker's country estate in Jenkintown, Pennsylvania.) The first Millrose Games were held in New York in 1908; the competition moved to Madison Square Garden in 1914. This prestigious track-and-field meet is the Garden's longest-running sporting event. The mile run, annually one of the highlights of the meet, is known as the Wanamaker Mile.

Walter Hagen won his fourth straight PGA Championship in 1927, and by tradition he took possession of the trophy until the following year, when Leo Diegel won. At that point, however, Hagen admitted that he had lost the trophy. It had disappeared after the 1927 event, when Hagen gave it to a taxi driver and asked him to take it to his hotel. The trophy was found by accident in 1930, while workers were looking through a warehouse in Detroit. They came across a leather trunk and found the trophy inside it. The warehouse was owned by the Walter Hagen Golf Company.

Colonel Bogey: In the late nineteenth century, golf clubs would occasionally hold competitions in which each player was pitted not against another golfer but against an assigned score for each hole. This score was the result that would be expected from a good amateur golfer. The winner of the competition would be the player who won the most holes at match play against this predetermined standard.

Playing in one such event at Great Yarmouth Golf Club in 1890, the *Oxford English Dictionary* tells us, a Major Charles Wellman referred to this mythical standard golfer as a "bogeyman," employing a term for a demon or ghost from a popular music-hall song of the day ("I'm the bogey man/Catch me if you can"). Golfers playing in such competitions came to think of themselves as playing against a Mister Bogey. Major Wellman subsequently decided that an opponent this tough would have to be a superior officer, and so he promoted his Bogey Man to Colonel. (Another explanation, offered by Robert Browning in his 1955 *History of Golf*, is that the promotion came from the United Services Club at Gosport, where the club secretary determined the standard for each hole. Since the club was for service personnel only, their Mister Bogey had to be granted a respectful rank.)

In the years before the Great War, Lieutenant F. J. Ricketts was stationed in the north of Scotland, where he liked to play golf in his off hours. At the local course he reportedly met an eccentric military officer who, for no apparent reason, didn't believe in shouting "Fore" like everyone else when his shots went awry. Instead, he would whistle out a descending minor third. This little phrase stuck in Ricketts's mind, and he used it as the beginning of a march that he published under his pseudonym, Kenneth Alford, in 1914. Whether or not that eccentric officer was actually a colonel and named "Bogey," or Ricketts had heard Wellman's term, which was by then in common usage, is lost to the mists of history. What is not lost is "The Colonel Bogey March" itself, used so effectively in the soundtrack of *The Bridge on the River Kwai.*

PLAYER NICKNAMES

Tommy Armour: Silver Scot. Born in Edinburgh. Had silver-white hair.

Miller Barber: X. Inscrutable behind his sunglasses.

Tommy Bolt: Terrible Tommy or Thunder Bolt. Known for his temper.

Julius Boros: Moose or Papa. Ambled along, genial, seemed like everybody's father.

Gay Brewer: Hound Dog. Looked like one.

Brad Bryant: Dirt, or Dr. Dirt. For his unscrubbed look

JoAnne Carner: Gundy or The Great Gundy. Maiden name Gunderson.

Billy Casper: Buffalo Billy or Mr. Cool. Ate buffalo meat while on a special diet. Didn't say much.

Bob Charles: Sphinx of the Links. Said very little.

Harry Cooper: Lighthorse. Writer Damon Runyon gave him the nickname at the 1926 Los Angeles Open, which he won. Runyon noticed that Cooper was light on his feet. He walked fast and he played fast.

Ben Crenshaw: Gentle Ben. Mild-mannered, courtly.

Bruce Crampton: Iron Man. Played and played and played, rarely taking time off.

John Daly: Wild Thing. No explanation required.

Glen Day: All Day. Slow PGA Tour player.

Roberto de Vicenzo: The Gay Gaucho. Friendly sort from Argentina.

Nick Dougherty: Georgie. After British soccer star Georgie Best, who liked to party, as does this young English tour pro.

Ernie Els: The Big Easy. Gangly and loping.

Al Geiberger: Skippy. Ate peanut-butter sandwiches on the course.

Paul Goydos: Happy or Chuckles. For the same reason a short man is called Stretch.

Walter Hagen: Sir Walter. Regal sort who lived high.

Ben Hogan: The Wee Ice Mon or The Hawk. Reputation as a cold-blooded competitor with no nerves.

Charles Howell III: Thurston. Reflects his name and initial, and refers to the millionaire character from *Gilligan's Island.*

Barry Jaeckel: Hollywood. Dressed the part. His father, Richard, was an Oscar-nominated actor.

Miguel Angel Jiménez: The Mechanic. His former job.

Bobby Jones: The Emperor.

Ky Laffoon: Chief. Native American ancestry.

Tony Lema: Champagne Tony. Ordered champagne for writers after winning 1964 British Open.

Gene Littler: Gene the Machine. Metronomic swing.

Davis Love III: DL 3.

Don Massengale: Bugs Bunny. Prominent front teeth.

Bill Mehlhorn: Wild Bill. His friend and fellow pro Leo Diegel wrote a piece for a New Orleans paper in which he said Mehlhorn went wild to start one round, making birdie after birdie. The name stuck.

Cary Middlecoff: Doc. He was a dentist.

Allen Miller: Best Monday Morning Qualifier. Had to qualify on Mondays for most tournaments and usually succeeded.

Johnny Miller: Desert Fox. For his domination of desert courses while winning in Arizona in the early 1970s.

Colin Montgomerie: Mrs. Doubtfire. Curly, high hairstyle and general lumpiness invited this nickname, after the character played by Robin Williams in the movie of the same name.

Orville Moody: Sarge. Served in U.S. Army.

Byron Nelson: Lord Byron.

Jack Nicklaus: The Golden Bear. Blond hair, and was as big as a bear when he was younger.

Greg Norman: Shark, or Great White Shark. A bold golfer who has gone deep-sea diving to encounter sharks.

Christy O'Connor: Wristy Christy. Very wristy swing.

Ed Oliver: Porky.

Masahi Ozaki: Jumbo.

Arnold Palmer: Arnie or The King or Harry Hitch. Hitched up his pants prior to every shot.

Henry Picard: Chocolate Soldier. Given the name because he was the pro at the Hershey Golf and Country Club. (Hershey, Pennsylvania, is the headquarters of the famous company that makes chocolate.)

Gary Player: Black Knight. Usually dresses in black.

Martin Roesink: Hercules. Muscular.

Bob Rosburg: Rossy or One Putt.

Gene Sarazen: The Squire. Lived on a farm in Brookfield, New York during his playing days.

Tom Shaw: Technicolor Tommy. Colorful wardrobe.

Charlie Sifford: Charlie Cigar. Always had a cigar in his mouth.

Horton Smith: The Joplin Ghost. From Joplin, MO.

Marilynn Smith: Mom.

Mike Souchak: Smokey the Bear. Big guy, resembled a bear.

Craig Stadler: Walrus. Hefty fellow with a mustache.

Peter Thomson: Thommo.

Bob Toski: Mouse. 5-foot-3, probably the best small player ever.

Lee Trevino: Super Mex.

Camilo Villegas: El Hombre Araña (Spiderman). Colombian-born pro assumes a low arachnidlike posture as he lines up a putt.

Tom Weiskopf: The Knife or Towering Inferno. The former for his ability to hit one-iron; the latter because he's tall and rages at the machine.

Joyce Wethered: Female Bobby Jones.

Tiger Woods: Urkel. Notah Begay called Woods Urkel when he first encountered him at Stanford University. He was then a skinny guy who wore glasses. Steve Urkel was the ultranerd played by Jaleel White on the sitcom *Family Matters.*

Lew Worsham: The Chin.

Kermit Zarley: The Pro from the Moon. For his somewhat extra-terrestrial name.

Best Player Nickname According to the Caddies

Miguel Angel Jiménez: Crime. He doesn't pay well, hence Crime, as in "crime doesn't pay."

Porky Oliver, getting a-round.

FAMOUS COLLAPSES IN MAJORS

Arnold Palmer, 1966 U.S. Open, Olympic Club, San Francisco

Palmer took a seven-shot lead over Billy Casper into the back nine at Olympic. How could he lose? Palmer was thinking about breaking the U.S. Open scoring record, which Ben Hogan had set in 1948 with 276 at the Riviera Country Club in Los Angeles. Casper told Palmer, with whom he was playing, that he wanted to finish second. He assumed he couldn't win.

The King stumbles.

Palmer bogeyed the 10th hole against Casper's par. His lead was six shots. It was still six as they headed for the 13th tee. Palmer bogeyed the par three after attacking the flag and finding a bunker, while Casper played away from the hole and made par. The lead was five, and it remained there after both Palmer and Casper parred the 14th hole. On 15, Palmer again attacked the flag and bogeyed the hole, while Casper birdied from twenty feet after playing to the safe side of the green. The lead was three shots.

"Hey, I can win this tournament." That's what Casper thought as he walked to the 16th tee. Palmer duck-hooked his drive into the rough and slashed at his ball with a three-iron, trying to move it well down the fairway. The ball stayed in the rough. Palmer in the end made a good bogey by getting up and down from a greenside bunker, while Casper birdied the hole. Palmer's lead was one shot.

Palmer bogeyed the 17th hole against Casper's par, and his lead was gone. Casper, feeling aggressive, chose to hit a driver off the 18th tee rather than the four-wood he'd used in earlier rounds. He hit the fairway, center cut. Palmer hit a one-iron, instead of the driver he'd used before, and found high rough to the left. He somehow ripped a nine-iron from there to the back of the green. Casper's wedge finished fifteen feet from the hole. They both two-putted, Palmer having to hole from four feet to make par. Casper had shot 32 on the back nine, and Palmer had shot 39.

Casper fulfilled a speaking engagement at a church that evening, and his eighteen-hole playoff with Palmer started at ten-thirty on Monday morning. Palmer took a two-shot lead into the back nine, but he bogeyed 11, 14, and 15, and double-bogeyed 16; Casper birdied the 11th hole and shot even par in from there to win, 69–73.

"As far as regret, or sorrow for not winning," Palmer said years later, "it's there, but it's more in the fact that I won only one Open and that would have made it two. The worst part was that I was very aware of Hogan's record [starting the back nine]. That was the part that ate at me. I wanted to break the record."

Casper said, "I was on the winning end. It brings better memories for me than for Arnold, I'm sure. I remember the shots I hit and some of the experiences I had with the gallery. As always when Arnold plays, there was a great army following him. But as I started catching him, many of the members of his army deserted ranks and they became Casper converts. I could really feel the momentum change. People root for underdogs in the U.S., and they all started yelling and screaming and hollering for me. It was a great feeling."

FAMOUS COLLAPSES IN MAJORS

Arnold Palmer, 1961 Masters

Palmer held a one-shot lead over Gary Player while playing the 72nd hole. After Palmer drove into the fairway, his good friend George Low called him over. Palmer walked up to Low, who congratulated him on having the tournament won. But he didn't have it won. He still had more golf to play. Palmer pushed his approach shot into a greenside bunker, went from there to another bunker, and double-bogeyed the hole.

"I let my mind wander when I still had golf to play," Palmer said. "But trying to win, that was my style. What the hell. So it was nothing new. I won lots of times doing that."

Not this time. Palmer's gaffe made Gary Player the first international golfer to win the Masters.

Palmer at the end. Never accept congratulations until the trophy's in hand.

LONGEST (MAYBE) AND WORST (LIKELY) SENTENCE IN A GOLF NOVEL

The pulses of the intent crowd throbbed with often baffled expectations, as the eye of the great golfer measured the ground between the ball and the hole again and again, and he grasped his instrument with fierce and felt energy in both hands, first one way, then another, now gently and deftly patting the turf immediately behind the ball, now, with glaring eye and bristling mustache, whirling the iron-shod club with an acrobatic twist of his whole body above his head and far behind him, with a force and determination so terrible as to strike cold fear into the hearts of the uninitiated bystanders, hitherto accustomed to hold such actions characteristic of cannibal islanders, ogres, and battle axe men in armor; then as if in face of duty beyond the power of mere humanity, sadly and slowly relaxing from this furious menace to a tamer and more peaceable attitude, till, from the rank of boomerang, battle-axe or two-handed sword, the driving-iron sank to the level of a mere pacific umbrella, spade, or walking stick, and the turf behind the ball was again gently, almost caressingly, patted by it.

If you can find a longer and worse sentence, please don't send it to us.

(from *The Great Refusal*, by Maxwell Gray, apparently a pseudonym for a woman who didn't want to be identified as such; London: John Long Publishing Co., 1906; 381 words)

THE YIPS—AND A FEW OTHER MOTOR DISTURBANCES

"Once you've had 'em, you've got 'em." That's what Henry Longhurst said of the yips, the scourge of all too many golfers who struggle to make a smooth putting stroke, usually from near the hole. Other names for the yips include the "staggers," "whiskey fingers," and "jitters."

Longhurst was a fine amateur golfer who won the 1936 German Amateur and was second in the 1938 French Amateur, but the yips got him in the end. He three-putted from three feet on the final green at the Old Course during a competition, and that was the end of golf for him. He was only in his late fifties, but he stopped playing.

"It does not come on all short putts," Longhurst wrote of the yips in his autobiography, "but you always know in advance when it is coming. You then become totally incapable of moving a piece of ironmongery to and fro without giving at the critical moment a convulsive twitch." Said Longhurst, "I am nothing more than a case for a mental hospital." The putting spasms can make a golfer feel this way.

YIPPERS

Tommy Armour

The Silver Scot is said to have coined the word *yips*. Armour won the 1927 U.S. Open and the 1930 PGA Championship, but he ran afoul of the yips over a two-foot putt on the 71st hole of the 1931 British Open at Carnoustie. He yipped the putt, and then on the final green faced a three-footer to win. Somehow he squeezed the ball into the hole, but he knew he'd gotten away with something.

"I took a new grip," Armour said of his experience, "holding the club as tightly as I could and with stiff wrists, and took a different stance. . . . From the instant the club left the ball on the backswing, I was blind and unconscious."

Harry Vardon

The six-time British Open champion suffered from what his fellow professional Henry Cotton called an "unbelievable jerking of the clubhead, in an effort to make contact with the ball from two feet or less from the hole." Vardon's affliction arrived in his mid-thirties, after he contracted tuberculosis. Here's how he described the results: "As I stood addressing the ball I would watch for my right hand to jump. At the end of two seconds I would not be looking at the ball at all. My gaze would have become riveted on my right hand. I simply could not resist the desire to see what it was going to do. Directly, as I felt that it was about to jump, I would snatch at the ball in a desperate effort to play the shot before the involuntary movement could take effect. Up would go my head and body with a start and off would go the ball, anywhere but on the proper line." In an effort to overcome the yips, Vardon tried weird diets, gave up drinking and smoking, and even resorted to using a foot-long putter when he got near the hole. Nothing worked.

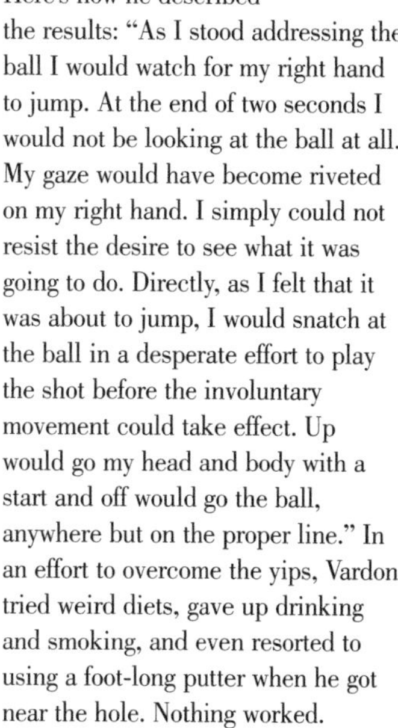

Harry Vardon, getting a grip.

Ben Hogan

Hogan suffered from the yips to the extent it sometimes seemed he could not bring the head of his putter back at all, and when he did, it was with a sudden shudder, like a fish jumping in the water.

Peter Alliss

Alliss, having played six Ryder Cups and won European Tour events, found himself in the 1967 Masters. Playing alongside Gene Littler, he was one under par and had chipped to within eight feet on the 11th hole.

"I settled over my putt in the normal way, and that was the last 'normal' thing I did for the rest of the round," Alliss said. "Somehow, I couldn't formulate a mental picture of letting the putter swing back and strike the ball. I just froze. I thought, 'Come on, Alliss, pull yourself together.' Then all I did was nudge the ball twenty feet past the hole. Gene Littler asked me if I was okay. I said I wasn't sure."

"A similar thing happened when I walked to the ball again. I think I hit the putt at least two or three times and I finished with an eight or nine. It could have been more or less. To be honest, my mind was that confused, I really didn't know for sure. I was thirty-six years of age. I had won twenty tournaments. . . . I carried on playing for a couple of years afterwards, but my own attack of the yips had a significant part to play in my calling it a day as a Tour player in 1969."

Alliss went on to a successful career as a broadcaster on British and American television.

Bernhard Langer

Langer, twice a winner of the Masters, has suffered from and overcome the yips a few times during his career; early on, while playing the European Tour, Langer, a slow player at the best of times, would slow his pace considerably as he neared the green, as if he didn't want to set foot there. Much later he five-putted during a final-round 80 in the 1988 British Open at Royal Lytham & St. Annes Golf Club.

"It's a weird situation," Langer says of the yips. "The yips can come back any time, and I haven't found anyone out there who understands them. And believe me, I have tried all sorts of remedies and talked to many people."

Johnny Miller

Miller was initiated into the yips in 1976, feeling the flinches coming on even while winning that summer's British Open. Miller neutralized the condition in an innovative manner. "I put a big red dot on the end of my grip," he said, "and all I did was watch it when I stroked a putt. I couldn't watch the clubhead." Miller played games with his mind and body while winning tournaments throughout his career. From time to time he would go so far as to pretend he was one of his sons: Johnny Miller wasn't putting, his kid was. He pretended he was his son John Jr., a teenager, when he unexpectedly won the 1994 AT&T National Pro-Am in Pebble Beach, California. Miller, with a one-foot putt to win, elected to look at the hole, not the ball. The ball fell, barely.

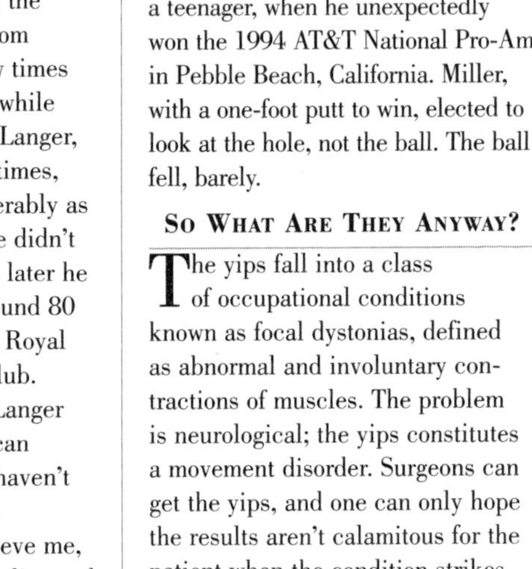

Johnny Miller in 1994.

So What Are They Anyway?

The yips fall into a class of occupational conditions known as focal dystonias, defined as abnormal and involuntary contractions of muscles. The problem is neurological; the yips constitutes a movement disorder. Surgeons can get the yips, and one can only hope the results aren't calamitous for the patient when the condition strikes. Musicians, dentists, pianists, calligraphers, baseball pitchers and catchers: They're all candidates to yip.

There's no sure cure for the yips, not hypnosis, meditation, yoga, visualization, nothing. Researchers at the Mayo Clinic in Rochester, Minnesota, have studied the yips and defined the problem as "a psychoneuromuscular problem that occurs in golf (especially during putting) when the golfer experiences freezing, jerking, or a tremor prior to initiating a putt. . . . [I]t is not clear whether this problem is purely physical or psychological."

Whatever the source, the result is an involuntary stab at the ball. Golfers afflicted with the yips are in pain. Byron Nelson, one of the greatest golfers ever, once put it this way: "Putting affects the nerves more than anything. I would actually get nauseated over three-footers, and there were tournaments when I couldn't keep a meal down for four days."

OTHER GOLFING TREMORS AND TRAUMAS

Full-swing yips: Hank Haney, Tiger Woods's coach, has written about the full-swing yips. He suffered from the yips with his driver and claims the full-swing yips is golf's untold affliction. The golfer afflicted with the full-swing yips makes an involuntary move, or two or three moves, during his swing. The problem usually doesn't manifest itself during a practice swing, or even with a real swing on the range, but only when the golfer is hitting the ball on the course. Haney maintains this is why practice doesn't help. Like classic putting yips, the full-swing yips represent an insoluble problem. So far anyway.

The shanks: Here's a nasty one. The ball shoots off the hosel of the clubface at nearly a right angle. Fear plays a part here as well. A member asked an old pro at the Royal Dornoch Golf Club to help him with the shanks. The pro invited the shanker to a corner of the course late in the day and offered every suggestion in his repertoire. The man kept shanking. Finally, the professional took the club and said, "Here, do it like this." He then shanked the shot himself. His next move was to leave. "I can't help you," he said, clearly shaken.

Atupsia: English writer Bernard Darwin identified this unusual condition. He wrote of a fellow who could get the club to the top of his swing well and smoothly enough, but then came to a halt. It was as if he were now thinking of where to go, what to do. Only with a fearsome lunge could he start down again. It was not a pretty sight.

For atupsiacs, this is a swing sequence.

An Englishman named John de Forest who suffered from atupsia still managed to play some excellent golf. He would come to a stop at the top of his swing and stand there as if frozen. But, somehow, as a writer in the mid-1930s put it, "suddenly down in de Forest something stirred." He came on down and through, and he managed to win the 1932 British Amateur at Muirfield in Scotland.

TOP TEN GOLFER/CADDIE EXCHANGES

GOLFER: I think I'm going to drown myself in the lake.

CADDIE: Do you think you can keep your head down that long?

GOLFER: I'd move heaven and earth to break 100 on this course.

CADDIE: Try heaven; you've already moved most of the earth.

GOLFER: Do you think my game is improving?

CADDIE: Yes sir, you miss the ball much closer now.

GOLFER: Do you think I can get there with a five-iron?

CADDIE: Eventually.

GOLFER: You've got to be the worst caddie in the world.

CADDIE: I don't think so, sir. That would be too much of a coincidence.

GOLFER: Please stop checking your watch all the time. It's too much of a distraction.

CADDIE: It's not a watch. It's a compass.

GOLFER: How do you like my game?

CADDIE: Very good, sir, but personally, I prefer golf.

GOLFER: Do you think it's a sin to play on Sunday?

CADDIE: The way you play, sir, it's a sin on any day.

GOLFER: This is the worst course I've ever played on.

CADDIE: This isn't the golf course. We left that an hour ago.

And the # 1 best golfer/caddie exchange:

GOLFER: That can't be my ball. It's too old.

CADDIE: It's been a long time since we teed off, sir.

THE GOLFER'S LIFE LIST

Take a Pure Golf Vacation with Buddies

Male bonding has surely never found a better friend than the golf trip. Jump into your van or cars, play according to an itinerary or play with no plan at all. Who knows where you'll land? It might be an up-and-down course called Killeen in Scotland, or a ten-hole links called Spanish Point, where you put your green fee in an honors box by the front door.

In the evening you meet in the designated hospitality room. You eat, drink, talk golf, tell lies, make up games for the next day, and then you have dinner and do more of the same. You have nothing to do but golf, golf, and golf some more. You're getting a Ph.D. in the buddy system of golf. It's pure golf because your only responsibility is to make your tee time, and because the purpose of the trip is golf and golf only. Best to leave your cell phones and BlackBerries in the room. On the course, and off as much as possible in these go-everywhere-with-the-office days, speak only golf. One language, all day and every day.

FAMOUS HAZARDS AND OBSTACLES

Rae's Creek: This body of water marks the low point of the property of Augusta National Golf Club; it runs behind the 11th green, in front of the 12th, in front of the 13th tee and along the left side of the fairway, and finally cuts across in front of the 13th green and to the right side below the putting surface. The creek is named for John Rae, who was responsible for building a Savannah River fortress that protected the town of Augusta from Indian attack. It was the site of a memorable ruling rendered by Bobby Jones's own father, Colonel Robert P. Jones, and recounted in David Owen's *The Making of the Masters.* A competitor had hit a poor shot that landed in a wet area near the creek. The player asked Colonel Jones, a rules official, if he was entitled to relief from casual water there. Jones asked the player how he was doing in the tournament; the player replied that he was 18 over par at that point. "Then what in the goddamn hell difference does it make?" the Colonel replied. "Tee the thing up on a peg for all I give a hoot."

Road Hole Bunker: The 17th hole at St. Andrews may be the hardest hole in the world. It begins with a blind tee shot aimed over a hotel sign, and then it requires a long approach to an unnervingly slender green guarded in back by a road and rock wall that are in play and in front by an unthinkably deep bunker. This sod-walled demon absorbed four blows from David Duval in the final round of the 2000 Open Championship, while the world watched thanks to a camera mounted in the bunker's face to record all the intimate and gory details. In the 1978 Open, Tommy Nakajima lay two on the right edge of the green, but his birdie putt caught the slopes near the hole and ran down into the bunker. He wound up taking a nine, and immortalizing "the Sands of Nakajima."

Barry Burn: A winding creek gives the final two holes at Carnoustie their sinister character. On the 17th, it meanders across the line of play twice, giving the golfer a choice between hitting to a virtual island fairway or trying to clear both of its cuts with his drive. On the final hole, a golfer must cross it three times, though the first viewing close in front of the tee is more of a psychological distraction than a strategic one. The Barry Burn is where Jean Van de Velde scratched his name off the Open Championship trophy in 1999. Not content with causing such end-of-round mischief, the Barry Burn runs in front of the 10th green as well.

THE DEVIL'S ASSHOLE AND HELL'S HALF ACRE: Pine Valley Golf Club boasts these two infernal obstacles, one famous for inducing claustrophobia, the other for requiring a caravan of camels to make one's way across it. The Devil's Asshole stands in front of the green on the 145-yard 10th hole, and draws its name from its depth and its conic shape. The small flat bottom, perhaps a third as wide as the opening at the top, is just broad enough to bury a ball, a golfer, and his hopes of a decent round. The wise and veteran player, upon plunking a ball into this aperture, declares an immediate unplayable lie and hits his third shot from the tee. Hell's Half Acre, in contrast, is a broad expanse of sand and scrub that divides the par-five seventh hole into two distinct sections. It begins at a distance of 280 yards from the tee, extends the full width of the playing area, and is over a hundred yards long. Thanks to this impressive interruption, no one has ever reached the green (itself ringed with sand and raised) in two shots.

KLONDYKE: On the 485-yard, par-five fifth hole at Lahinch, you hit your drive down into a valley bordered by long-grassed hills. As you look along the line of the fairway and contemplate your next shot, you see no green, no flag, just the fairway coming to an abrupt halt at a tall green hill. Welcome to the Klondyke. This thirty-foot-high mound must be cleared with your second shot to reach the fairway and green beyond it. If you have a caddie, send him on ahead, because you are responsible for making certain that no one is crossing behind this hill on the 18th fairway, which intersects the 5th at this point.

THE CHURCH PEWS: Between the third and fourth fairways of Oakmont Country Club lies the most famous bunker in American golf. The hundred-yard expanse of sand is legendary for its eight raised grassy interpositions that run perpendicular to the line of play. These three-foot-high hurdles turn an otherwise simple fairway bunker shot into a potential nightmare. The Pews are one of designer Henry Fownes's clever solutions to a problem posed by the land: Oakmont's heavy clay soil meant that deep bunkers would pose a drainage nightmare, while shallow ones would present little hazard. Another solution was to create a specially weighted rake with broad triangular teeth that carved furrows in the sand, making a playable lie all the more unlikely. The furrowing was abandoned in the 1960s, but the Church Pews remain, testament to the view expressed by Fownes's son William that "a shot poorly played should be a shot irrevocably lost."

THE HINKLE TREE: In the first round of the 1979 U.S. Open at the Inverness

Club in Toledo, Ohio, tour pro Lon Hinkle noticed that the approach to the sharp-angled dogleg-left 8th hole could be greatly simplified by playing his tee shot onto the 17th fairway instead. He took out a one-iron, aimed far left, put the ball in the adjoining fairway, hit a two-iron to the green, and two-putted for an easy birdie. Overnight, the USGA planted a twenty-five-foot-high black hill spruce to block the path that had cut about 60 yards off the hole's 528-yard length. (Hinkle played over it anyway in the second round as well.) The tree still stands, tribute to a golfer's imagination and an organization's single-mindedness.

DEVLIN'S BILLABONG: The pond that guards the 18th green of the South Course at Torrey Pines in La Jolla, California, earned its name during the 1975 Andy Williams San Diego Open. Aussie Bruce Devlin hit his second shot on the par five to the edge of the pond, and from a partially submerged lie he took six strokes to extricate the ball, winding up with a 10 on the hole that most other players considered a birdie chance. A plaque on the site commemorates his misadventure.

SPECTACLES: The upraised Spectacles bunkers lie side by side in the middle of the approach to the par-five 14th hole at Carnoustie, 50 yards short of the green. For the average player, the strategy of the 483-yard hole is dictated by whether or not he will try to carry the bunkers and reach the green in two. Despite the expansion of the hole to 513 yards for tournament play, most professionals don't even know these bunkers are there as they fly their approaches blithely by.

ELEANOR'S TEETH: There are fifteen greenside bunkers on the 326-yard fourth hole at the Apawamis Club in Rye, New York, but the nickname refers particularly to the two rows, five bunkers each, that are set into the hillside atop which the green sits. They were named for the prominent dentition of Eleanor Roosevelt.

YOUR NAME HERE?: The most photographed hazard of them all has no name. The lake that surrounds the island green on the 17th hole of the Stadium Course at the TPC Sawgrass is a manmade feature, suggested to architect Pete Dye by his wife, Alice, who knew the value of a good photo op. While several famous golfers have suffered at its hands, its most memorable victim may have been the worst ever to attempt it: Angelo Spagnolo of Fayette City, Pennsylvania, who played it in a "World's Worst Avid Golfer" competition in 1985. He put twenty-seven balls in the water, then played the hole along the ground by way of the pedestrian bridge, eventually reaching the green and putting out for a 66. Angelo's Aqua?

GREAT CAREER AMATEURS

Marlene Stewart Streit, b. Cereal, Alberta, 1934

When she was nineteen she won the 1953 British Ladies Amateur and when she was sixty-nine she won her third U.S. Women's Senior Amateur. In between Streit won eleven Canadian Ladies Amateurs, the 1956 U.S. Women's Amateur, and the 1963 Australian Ladies. She was inducted into the World Golf Hall of Fame in 2004, the first Canadian to be so honored.

Streit learned the game under the guidance of Gordon McInnis Sr. in Fonthill, Ontario, at the Lookout Point Golf Club. She thought only of smoothness, rhythm, and balance—her mantra. Barely five feet tall, she wore her opponents down with accuracy and her short game. Bob Toski said, "Marlene is the best small golfer I've ever seen. You don't get her longevity unless you have a good swing and a sound, orthodox method."

It helps to have plenty of fire in the belly. "Always aim for something on the horizon," Streit says. She still does.

Marlene Stewart (later Streit) in 1956, when she won her first USGA title. She was still winning them forty-seven years later.

THE EARLIEST WRITTEN GOLF INSTRUCTION

Thomas Kincaid was a young Edinburgh gentleman in the latter part of the seventeenth century. He took up golf and, obviously captivated by it, made some observations in his diary in January and February 1687 that, as it turns out, can be taken as the first words of instruction in the sport. Sir Guy Campbell, a golf course architect, historian, and accomplished player, in his seminal book *A History of Golf in Britain*, wrote, "These 'musings' of Kincaid make, I hold, the most important contemporary contribution to our knowledge of the game in its earlier days."

The Blackheath Golfer, *painted in 1778 by Lemuel Francis Abbott, shows a golfer in club dress, and a caddie in need of a bag.*

Kincaid summarized his views in verse:

Gripe fast, stand with your left leg first not farr;
Incline your back and shoulders, but beware
You raise them not when back the club you bring;
Make all the motion with your bodie's swinge
And shoulders, holding still the muscles bent;
Play slowly first till you the way have learnt.
At such lenth hold the club as fitts your strenth,
The lighter head requires the longer lenth.
That circle wherein moves your club and hands
At forty five degrees from the horizon stands
What at on stroak to effectuat your dispaire
Seek only 'gainst the nixt it to prepare.

In addition, Kincaid set down in verse what he believed to be "the generall rules of motion":

All motions with the strongest joynts performe
Lett the weaker second and perfect the same
The stronger joynt its motion first most end
Before the nixt to move in the least intend.
The muscles most with touie motion move
For which the gripping fast great helpe doth prove.

Kincaid refers again to golf in his diary, but offers no more advice. We don't know whether or not he mastered the game, or grew tired of it as he turned his attention to horse racing, wine, music, archery, making wax models, or, as he wrote, "the best way of studying any languadge."

THREE-HANKY GOLF

Davis and the Rainbow

Golf is not always a link between fathers and sons, but it certainly was for the Davis Loves. This was true from the very start: Davis Love Jr., a sometime touring pro who had played golf for Harvey Penick at the University of Texas, was the first-round leader in the 1964 Masters; the day after the tournament ended, Davis III was born.

Davis Jr. established himself as an outstanding teacher, first at Charlotte Country Club, then at Atlanta Country Club, and eventually at the *Golf Digest* teaching facility at the Cloister on Sea Island, Georgia. He taught his pupils in the simple, easily digestible style of his mentor, Penick, who was almost a second father to him. The one possible exception to this may have been his son, who became his most famous pupil.

Davis Love III stripes one down the fairway.

Davis Jr.'s expectations for his son were high, and the son absorbed those desires and made them his own. Ironically, the most significant thing lacking in the father's game—length off the tee—was one of the son's most conspicuous blessings. For Davis Jr., teaching his son golf was his clearest way of being a father; Davis III, called "Trip" for his numeral, came to recognize the lessons as expressions of his father's love. They weren't just father and son, teacher and pupil; they were also best friends and partners in the enterprise of young Davis's career.

In his first three years on Tour, Davis Love III established himself as an outstanding talent, with a win in Hilton Head and over half a million dollars in earnings. But the father felt his son was stagnating, and his third season had been particularly disappointing. Shortly before Davis III was to travel to Hawaii for the Kapalua Invitational in November 1988, his father asked him to go for a ride with him and delicately broached the subject of Davis's working with another teacher. "I'm wondering if I've taken you as far as you can go," he confided. "I just wonder if there isn't somebody else who could take you to the next level." Davis III was shocked, and he was adamant that he wanted only to continue working under his father's eye. He promised to increase his dedication to his practice regimen, and he flew off to Hawaii feeling invigorated.

While Davis III was in Hawaii, he ran into a pastor, an old friend of his parents'. He called home to check in and tell his folks about seeing their friend. His mother, Penta, told Davis that his father and one of his teaching associates, Jimmy Hodges, had taken a charter flight from Sea Island to Jacksonville en route to a seminar in Tampa, and that their plane had disappeared from the radar. Davis caught a flight from Hawaii to San Francisco, not knowing yet if his father was dead or alive. By the time Davis arrived in San Francisco and found a pay phone, the small plane had been found; there were no survivors.

Davis was devastated. He had lost the most important person in his life, along with one of his closest friends. For months after the crash, Davis would wake up sobbing uncontrollably. By his own admission, he went through the next year and a half in a daze. His talent assured him of a good living playing on Tour, but he wasn't getting better, and time was slipping away. In May 1990, while playing in a tournament in Japan, he had a bracing talk with the teaching pro Butch Harmon, who knows a thing or two about the influence of a strong father—his was also a legendary teacher, who won the 1948 Masters. The talk woke Davis out of his torpor; he finished third that weekend, and three months later he won his second Tour event.

In 1991, Davis won at Hilton Head again and finished eighth on the money list. Then, in 1992, in the tournament often referred to as the "fifth major"—the Players Championship—Davis won his biggest title yet, on the Sawgrass course that lies just a few miles from the site where his father's plane crashed. Starting the final day three strokes behind Nick Faldo, he shot the day's low round of 67 for a four-shot victory. The final round was played under gray skies, but as Davis putted on the final green for the victory, the sun peeked through the clouds, and in no time it was a bright and shining day. Robin Love, his wife, told him on that final green, "That's your dad, shining down at you in your moment of glory."

The years went by, and Davis continued to rank among the world's top players, but he increasingly found himself saddled with the title "Best Player Never to Have Won a Major." Some questioned his killer instinct; he was 1–5 in playoffs, and while his demeanor on the course was formal, perhaps even a little stiff, his fellow professionals knew him as someone who might be too nice to be a world-beater.

As 1996 wound down, Davis collaborated on a book describing the lessons he'd learned from his father. The title, *Every Shot I Take,* reflected how often Davis thought about his father's influence. He would later say that the process of putting his father's thoughts and teachings between hard covers—and of talking at length about his father's death, something that he, his mother, his brother, and his wife all did for the book—helped him view that tragedy from a different perspective, helped him recognize how time had passed and that he was ready for a kind of healing, a kind of acceptance that had eluded him so far.

In 1997, Davis's best finish in the year's first three majors was third place at the Masters, where he finished four strokes behind Tom Kite in the Merely Human Flight (Tiger Woods was an otherworldly twelve strokes ahead of Kite). But at Winged Foot for the PGA Championship, he tied for the first-round lead with a 66, adding another 66 on Saturday. He entered the final round tied for the lead with Justin Leonard; the two would play in the last Sunday pairing. After nine holes, Davis had opened up a five-stroke lead. On the par-five 12th, however, Leonard birdied while Love bogeyed, and on the 13th hole, Love hit his worst shot of the day, pulling the ball into long rough on the short side left of the green, while Leonard put his shot fifteen feet from the cup. But Davis hit a lob wedge that nearly went in, then made the two-foot putt to keep the lead at three.

Rains came throughout the last nine holes, but as Davis drove from the final tee with a four-shot lead, the skies began to lighten. As he walked up to the final green, the sun came through once again, just as it had at Sawgrass five years earlier. Only this time, there wasn't just sunshine; there was also a rainbow, framed by CBS's cameras in a view that ran it directly from the sky down to the hole as Davis approached his final putt. Rolling the twelve-foot birdie putt home, he then embraced first his friend Justin Leonard; then his brother and caddie, Mark; then his wife, Robin; and finally his mother, Penta. "Dad knows what you've done," she told him. "I know," he replied.

A Love story was requited at last.

FOOTNOTES TO HISTORY

Harry Bradshaw, 1949 British Open, Royal St. George's, Sandwich, England

The Brad, as his fellow Irishmen knew him, shot 68 in the opening round to take the lead, and started the second round with four consecutive fours—fine, controlled golf on the arduous Sandwich links. But he drove into the right rough on the 451-yard fifth hole and found his ball inside a broken beer bottle. "What villain dropped this relic on the links or how it ever came there, can never be known," Charles Mortimer wrote in his history of the first ninety years of the Open. However it got there, Bradshaw didn't want to wait for a ruling as to whether he could take a free drop—he could have—and chose to play it as it lay.

The Brad closed his eyes and took a whack at the bottle and his ball inside it. Glass flew, nobody was injured, and the ball finished some thirty yards down the course. Bradshaw later said it took him six more holes before he was able to settle down from his encounter with the bottled ball. He shot 77 and was tied for the halfway lead with the South African Bobby Locke. Bradshaw recovered with 68 and 70 in the last two rounds. Locke holed from three and a half feet on the final hole to tie Bradshaw.

The fellows played a thirty-six-hole playoff the next day. Locke's 67–68 won by twelve shots over the Brad's 74 and 73. The championship had turned sad for the Brad, but it never soured him on the game. He told the writer Peter Dobereiner that he hadn't lost a single second of sleep over the broken bottle incident and that "Locke was the better player. He deserved to win."

PGA Tour Money-Leaders at Ten-Year Intervals

1955 Julius Boros	$ 63,121.55
1965 Jack Nicklaus	$ 140,752.14
1975 Jack Nicklaus	$ 298,149.17
1985 Curtis Strange	$ 542.321.00
1995 Greg Norman	$ 1,654,959.00
2005 Tiger Woods	$10,628,024.00

Here's another way to put this in perspective: In 2005, Tiger Woods earned more official PGA Tour prize money than the career Tour earnings of Arnold Palmer, Gary Player, and Jack Nicklaus *combined.*

LPGA Tour Money-Leaders at Ten-Year Intervals

1955 Patty Berg	$ 16,492
1965 Kathy Whitworth	$ 28,658
1975 Sandra Palmer	$ 76,374
1985 Nancy Lopez	$ 416,472
1995 Annika Sorenstam	$ 666,533
2005 Annika Sorenstam	$2,588,240

European Tour Money-Leaders at Ten-Year Intervals (in British Pounds)

1965 Peter Thomson	£ 7,011
1975 Dale Hayes	£ 20,507
1985 Sandy Lyle	£ 254,711
1995 Colin Montgomerie	£1,038,718
2005 Colin Montgomerie	£1,885,884

RULES OF ETIQUETTE, 1899

The Rules of Golf begin not with Rule 1, but with a section on the etiquette of the game. Of course, those who most need to learn the etiquette of the game aren't likely to put their cell phones down long enough to read the rulebook, but it's nice that the USGA and the R&A give them the option. The first set of such principles was appended to the Rules in 1899, and while the current section is more extensive, the original list provides most of the guidance a player needs to get around the course without giving offense.

1. A single player has no standing, and must always give way to a properly constituted match.

2. No player, caddie, or onlooker should move or talk during a stroke.

3. No player should play from the tee until the party in front have played their second strokes and are out of range, nor play up to the putting-green till the party in front have holed out and moved away.

4. The player who has the honour should be allowed to play before his opponent tees his ball.

5. Players who have holed out should not try their putts over again when other players are following them.

6. Players looking for a lost ball must allow other matches coming up to pass them.

7. On request being made, a three-ball match must allow a single, threesome, or foursome to pass. Any match playing a whole round may claim the right to pass a match playing a shorter round.

8. If a match fail to keep its place on the green, and lose in distance more than one clear hole on those in front, it may be passed, on request being made.

9. Turf cut or displaced by a stroke should be at once replaced.

10. A player should carefully fill up all holes made by himself in a bunker.

FOOTNOTES TO HISTORY

Jenny Chuasiriporn, 1998 U.S. Women's Open, Blackwolf Run, Kohler, Wisconsin

For ninety-one holes, Chuasiriporn spelled "Cinderella."

As she approached her twentieth birthday, Chuasiriporn was playing in the U.S. Women's Open at the Pete Dye–designed Blackwolf Run. The Duke University junior had a putt of some forty-five feet on the final green of the championship. She needed the putt to have a chance of getting into a playoff with Se Ri Pak, who had won the LPGA Championship earlier in the year.

Chuasiriporn hit the putt exactly where she aimed and with what appeared to be the right speed. It looked good all the way, and it fell in. She covered her mouth in a gesture that asked, "What have I done?" NBC's Johnny Miller called the shot "one of the greatest putts ever in an Open championship."

"It was so overwhelming after it went in," Chuasiriporn said of the putt she made on the 72nd green. "I just kind of turned to my brother [her caddie] and he was just delighted, almost in tears, so I couldn't really think straight at that point."

Chuasiriporn could have won the 18-hole playoff with a par on 18, but she bogeyed, and Pak won the championship with a birdie on the second extra hole. Despite the promise she showed that week, Chuasiriporn never made it onto the LPGA Tour.

GOLF MYTHS EXPOSED

1. Gene Sarazen's double eagle on the 15th hole won him the 1935 Masters. His epic four-wood shot might still be the most famous swing of a club ever, but the leap from three to six under par only tied him for the four-round lead; he still needed to play thirty-six holes against Craig Wood the next day to determine a winner. Sarazen shot 71–73, Wood 75–74, and the legend of Mr. Double Eagle was complete.

Sarazen (right) putts out on the final green.

2. Bobby Jones embodied the golf ideal by remaining an amateur for life. With the Grand Slam safely in his pocket and his competitive career, as he saw it, at an end, Jones signed on with Warner Brothers to make a series of instructional films, and Spalding hired him to design and promote golf clubs. These commercial deals violated the USGA rules on amateur status; Jones wrote at the time of the Warner Brothers agreement, "I am so far convinced that [the contract] is contrary to the spirit of amateurism that I am prepared to accept and even endorse a ruling that it is an infringement." As noted in David Owen's book *The Making of the Masters,* written with access to the Augusta National archives, the Associated Press and other news organizations listed Jones as a professional during the first Masters, and Jones's own frequent collaborator O. B. Keeler hailed Charles Yates as low amateur though Jones finished three shots better.

3. Ben Hogan's famous one-iron on the 18th hole at Merion, photographed by Hy Peskin, capped his comeback from a near-fatal car crash with a U.S. Open triumph. As with the Sarazen double eagle, Hogan's great approach shot on Merion's final hole put him in position for a tie, which he earned with two putts. He then won the eighteen-hole playoff the next day, with a 69 to Lloyd Mangrum's 73 and George Fazio's 75.

4. Scheduling conflicts prevented Ben Hogan from trying to win the professional Grand Slam in 1953. While it's true that the finals of the PGA

Championship coincided with the qualifying rounds for the British Open in 1953, Hogan would not have entered the PGA even if they hadn't. After his auto accident in 1949, he recognized that the match-play grind that called for ten rounds in five days was too much for his legs. He didn't return to the PGA until 1960, its third year of stroke play.

5. In the 1960s and 1970s, Augusta National manipulated its rules to keep African American golfers out of the Masters. The most often cited evidence for this is that Charles Sifford won the Greater Hartford Open in 1967 but was not invited to play in the Masters. However, winning a tournament did not carry an automatic invitation to Augusta until 1972. Despite his victory, Sifford was not among the year's top money-winners nor automatically eligible under the other qualifying categories for the Masters; he was one of several tournament winners who didn't earn an invitation that year. Two years after the change in the Masters criteria, Lee Elder became the first African-American golfer to qualify when he won the 1974 Monsanto Open. Rather than manipulating its rules to keep Sifford out, it could be said that Augusta National changed its rules in a way that ultimately let Elder in. The automatic qualification for tournament winners was eliminated in 2000.

6. Payne Stewart's fifteen-footer on the 72nd hole at Pinehurst No. 2 in 1999 is the longest birdie putt ever made to win the U.S. Open on the final green. Stewart's putt was the longest ever made for an Open victory, but it wasn't for birdie; he had driven into the rough, laid up, and then pitched on, so the putt was for par.

Payne Stewart's moment in time.

7. The USGA makes its Open courses harder by converting short par fives to long par fours. This is one of the silliest arguments that we hear year after year. Golf was played for a couple hundred years before anyone thought of assigning perpetual par figures to every hole. A player's job is to get from point A to point B in as few strokes as possible; what difference does it make if the hole is called a par four or a par five? It doesn't make the hole any harder or easier if we call your four a par instead of a birdie. And if you think a green that's designed to receive a shot with a wedge is unfair when you're hitting a long iron or fairway wood to it, you can always lay up on your second and try to make four that way.

8. Jean Van de Velde's hideous course management on the final hole at Carnoustie cost him the 1999 Open Championship. When you have a three-shot lead on the 72nd hole, and that hole crosses a stream three times, it's hard to argue with those who say you should hit three seven-irons down the middle and then three-putt for a win. Van de Velde's choice of driver off the tee was consistent with how he'd played all week; the shot was lucky to stay out of trouble, but it did land safely in a clean lie. His second shot, a two-iron, had just 185 yards to cross the Barry Burn, no problem for a professional golfer. He hit a poor shot, but it may also have been the unluckiest shot in the history of golf: The ball, though pushed to the right, comfortably cleared the burn before hitting into the grandstand right of the green, from which, improbably, it bounced *backward,* toward him, back to his side of the creek into a nastily tangled lie. Had it behaved normally upon hitting the grandstand, Van de Velde would have been hitting from a drop zone clear of the water; instead, he faced a difficult pitch from an impossible spot and dumped the shot into the burn. After contemplating a shot from the water, he took his drop, pitched short into a bunker, then got up and down for a triple-bogey seven that put him in a four-hole playoff, which he lost.

In the 1996 movie *Tin Cup,* Rene Russo comforts Kevin Costner, who has just blown the U.S. Open, by telling him he just made the greatest 12 in the history of golf. Someone wins the Open every year, she tells him, but that 12 will live forever. Jean Van de Velde's name may not be on the Claret Jug, but will you ever forget him? And can you remember the name of the man who did win that playoff? (It's on page 51 if you can't.)

GREAT CAREER AMATEURS

Bill Campbell, b. Huntington, West Virginia, 1923

Campbell, a West Virginian, won four North and South Amateurs in Pinehurst, North Carolina. He played his first U.S. Amateur in 1938, was a semifinalist in the 1949 and 1973 U.S. Amateurs, and won it in 1964. Campbell's record in the Walker Cup was 7-0-1, which is at least as impressive as his fifteen West Virginia State Amateur championships.

Campbell started to play when he was three, joining his parents and brother on Sunday afternoons at the Guyan Golf and Country Club in Huntington, West Virginia. He learned the game early and maintained his form through thirty-three consecutive U.S. Amateurs.

Bill Campbell. Player. Always.

TOUR DE FARCE

Golfers come up with all sorts of ways to enjoy the game. Jim Fitchette, a Toronto teacher and writer, went to an exceptional length. He came up with an entire tour, which he dubbed the Tour de Farce.

Fitchette, who appointed himself the Tour's commissioner for life, started his series of tournaments in the mid-1970s. The schedule included twelve regular events, such as the Par Excellence, the Ricky Receptacle, the Grand Marnier, the Walker Percy Cup, Dante's Inferno Invitational, and the Pelican Guano Dip. The four majors—the Winter Rules, the Garbage Bag, the Golden Bear, and the Dog Day Afternoon—were the highlights of the year.

Every tournament on the Tour de Farce schedule was there for a reason. A sampling:

Winter Rules Open: This tournament started the season, so it was usually played in nasty weather. Fitchette's report on the 1988 Winter Rules, included in his annual media guide, mentions tees that were mud pies and greens that were "strangely quilted areas of short grass with rows and ridges of near rough, and dirt cups."

Garbage Bag: The Garbage Bag was modeled after the Masters. The winner received a green garbage bag that the previous year's champion placed on his shoulders. Each year's ceremony took place in a quiet corner of the host club's parking lot.

Bob Hope Dessert Classic: The golfers in this event participated in a most unusual ceremony at the close of play, when the winner teed up a cream-filled cupcake and aimed at his fellow competitors, who were lined up ten yards away.

Dog Day Afternoon: The commissioner felt strongly that this tournament, the third major, should be held in the most miserable conditions possible—hot, fetid, and nauseatingly humid, or bone-rattling cold, usually in late November. It was all the better if sleet was involved.

THE GOLF OF MEXICO: Each golfer wore a Band-Aid on his forearm, just as the Merry Mex Lee Trevino once did. The winner's trophy was a ceramic donkey and a peso mounted on a map of Mexico.

GOLDEN BEAR CLASSIC: Tour de Farce golfers played their final major at the Jack Nicklaus–designed Glen Abbey Golf Club. The winner received the clubhead from a Nicklaus Golden Bear driver. A Tour de Farce player had once smashed the driver that bore this clubhead against a tree after he'd hit a sickening drive. The head snapped off, making an ideal prize for the Golden Bear.

Commissioner Fitchette was diagnosed with brain cancer in 1990, and died in 1995. The Tour de Farce was his from its inception, so it hasn't been played again.

TEN MOST MEMORABLE LINES *from CADDYSHACK*

1. *Cinderella story. Out of nowhere. A former greenskeeper, and about to become the Masters champion. It looks like a mirac—it's in the hole!*

2. *I bet you've got a lot of nice ties . . . you want to tie me up with some of your ties, Ty?*

3. *"People say I'm an idiot or something because all I do is cut lawns for a living."*
"Oh, people don't say that about you, as far as you know."

4. *That's a peach, hon.*

5. *"You're crazy!" "That's what they said about Son of Sam."*

Judge Elihu Smails

6. *Oh, you're a funny kid. What time are you due back in Boys Town?*

7. *We're just about to tee off now, so call the hospital and move my appointment with Mrs. Bellows back thirty minutes. Oh. Well, just stick a tube down her nose and I'll be there in four hours.*

8. *This is the worst-looking hat I ever saw. You buy a hat like this, I bet you get a free bowl of soup with it.*

9. *If you ever want to rap or talk or just get weird with somebody . . . you know, buddies for life.*

10. *The last time I saw a mouth like that it had a hook in it.*

PALINDROMIC GOLF COURSES

Palindrome: from the Greek *palindrome,* meaning "running back again"—a phrase or sentence that reads the same way backward and forward. Some famous palindromes are "Madam, I'm Adam," "A man, a plan, a canal, Panama," and "A raga in Niagara."

But what does this have to do with golf? Consider the fact that the pars for the holes on each of Augusta National's nines form numeric palindromes: The front nine's pars are 4-5-4-3-4-3-4-5-4, and the back nine's sequence is 4-4-3-5-4-5-3-4-4. The course itself, however, is not a complete palindrome from start to finish.

The Old Course at St. Andrews, Scotland, is palindromic from the first through the last hole: 4-4-4-4-5-4-4-3-4; 4-3-4-4-5-4-4-4-4. It's worth noting that Bobby Jones loved the Old Course and tried to replicate its themes in Augusta National. Jones was instrumental in working out the architecture for Augusta National, along with principal designer Alister Mackenzie. Could this palindromic quality have anything to do with the drama that plays out every year on the back nine of the Masters?

Other nine-hole palindromes:

- Winged Foot (West), Mamaroneck, New York, front nine (as played in championships)
- Lagunita, Caracas, Venezuela, front nine
- Yomiuri, Tokyo, front nine

A hole can be a par three, four, or five, so the probability of it being any one of these, independent of design and thinking only of random events, is ⅓. The probability of the 1st hole having the same par as the 18th, then, is ⅓, and of the 2nd and 17th being the same is also ⅓, independent of the 1st and 18th.

The purely mathematical probability of the Old Course, or any course, being palindromic start to finish is therefore $(1/3)^9$ or 1/17,536. According to *Golf Digest,* there are approximately 32,000 courses in the world; thus, we should expect there to be two palindromic courses in the world. That makes it even more pleasing, and curious, that the Old Course—the oldest course—is one. There's magic, and mysticism, in its ancient links.

ONE-LINERS

1. *"Golf is like chasing a quinine pill around a cow pasture."*
—WINSTON CHURCHILL

2. *"Give me the fresh air, a beautiful partner, and a nice round of golf, and you can keep the fresh air and the round of golf."*
—JACK BENNY

3. *"You can make a lot of money in this game. Just ask my ex-wives. Both of them are so rich that neither of their husbands work."*
—LEE TREVINO

4. *"It took me seventeen years to get 3,000 hits in baseball. I did it in one afternoon on the golf course."*
—HANK AARON

5. *"Columbus went around the world in 1492. That isn't a lot of strokes when you consider the course."*
—LEE TREVINO

6. *"These greens are so fast I have to hold my putter over the ball and hit it with the shadow."*
—SAM SNEAD

7. *"Golf is a game in which you yell 'fore,' shoot six, and write down five."*
—PAUL HARVEY

8. *"They throw their clubs backwards, and that's wrong. You should always throw a club ahead of you so that you don't have to walk any extra distance to get it."*
—TOMMY BOLT, about modern players' bad tempers

9. *"Putting allows the touchy golfer two to four opportunities to blow a gasket in the short space of two to forty feet."* —TOMMY BOLT

10. *"Golf and sex are about the only things you can enjoy without being good at."*
—JIMMY DEMARET

THEIR WORST SHOTS

Jack Nicklaus: During the 1964 Masters I hit a shank on the 12th hole with Bobby Jones and Clifford Roberts out there watching. I shanked it over their heads, short of the water. Oh my gosh, I thought, with them standing right there. I pitched it on the green and made four. Where did that come from? I wasn't even nervous.

Kenny Perry: I was playing the 17th hole at Kingsmill [in Virginia]. That's the par three where all the people sit on the bank up there on the hillside. I hit it a little long and left and was chipping to my left with the people on my right on the hill. I had a sidehill lie, but it was pretty much a conventional shot. I cold-hosel shanked it with the gallery right there and hit some people sitting there. I cold shanked a chip. You don't ever imagine doing that.

Jeff Sluman: I topped my opening tee shot in my first World Series of Golf after winning the 1988 PGA. There was a fly on the ball and I stayed too long over it. The next thing I know I'm at the top of my swing and I'm hitting it. I don't even know how I made contact. It rolled forty yards. I hit the next one on the run, I was so embarrassed.

Steve Flesch: I was playing my state Amateur in Ohio. The first hole's a par five and I hit a three-iron for my second shot out of bounds four times. I felt like I kept making the same swing and the same setup. I was seventeen. There was nothing unusual about the shot, it was just a standard situation. I made 12 and shot 78.

Mark O'Meara: I was playing the 1985 PGA Championship at Cherry Hills [near Denver]. It was the 18th hole in the second round and I was playing with Seve [Ballesteros] and Tom Kite. I'd played all right the first day and okay the second for eight or nine holes and was on the leaderboard, in the top ten. But then I got on a downward trend and was off the board by the time I got to the 18th, a long, uphill par four where the fairway turns right to left and there's water on the left. I'm standing there and thinking, just don't snipe it left. I'd had a flat tire and the wheels were falling off. I'm saying just don't hit it in the water. I set up to it and took it back and I'm still thinking don't hit it in the water. I hit the ground ten inches behind the ball with my driver, coming from the inside, and I took a divot. I barely clipped the ball and it went forty yards into the water. Everybody was in shock. I looked at Kite and Seve but nobody said anything. I was going to re-tee but instead I walked up twenty yards and squeezed a three-wood down there and made triple. It looked like I'd miss the cut, I didn't know. I saw [Hank] Haney [his swing coach] and my wife there and they said, "Sorry about the triple, but you made the cut." I said I don't care, I'm quitting the game if I can hit a shot like that. Nobody can hit a shot like that. I go into the locker room and clean out my locker. The locker room guy says what are you doing, you made the cut Mr. O'Meara. I told him I'm quitting the game. He said huh? I gave him one hundred bucks and told him I'm quitting. I went to my car and backed it out almost through the chicken wire at the range. That night we went to an Italian place for dinner. I got a job application and started filling it out for a dishwasher. My wife is telling me I'm a psycho. I continued to play and finished in the top thirty.

ONE-LINERS

11. *"If you think it's hard to meet new people, try picking up the wrong golf ball."*

—Jack Lemmon

12. *"If you're caught on a golf course during a storm and are afraid of lightning, hold up a one-iron. Not even God can hit a one-iron."*

—Lee Trevino

Jack Lemmon, the cut-up who never made the cut.

13. *"He was the sort of player who does the first two holes in one under bogey and then takes an eleven at the third. The least thing upsets him on the links. He missed short putts because of the uproar of butterflies in the adjoining meadows."* —P. G. Wodehouse

14. *"If I'm on the course and lightning starts, I get inside fast. If God wants to play through, let him."*

—Bob Hope

15. *"The great thing to remember was to hold the breath on the backswing and not to release it before the moment of impact."*

—P. G. Wodehouse

16. *"In baseball you hit your home run over the right-field fence, the left-field fence, the center-field fence. Nobody cares. In golf everything has got to be right over second base."*

—Ken Harrelson

THE TALE OF THE TEE

The original Rules of Golf make three references to the tee: You must tee your ball within a club's length of the hole, your tee must be on the ground, and you may not change the ball which you strike off the tee. From this, we know that the word tee was used as both a noun and a verb, and that determining how to start the play of a hole was of great importance to the Rules makers.

Long before these rules were written down, golfers gave themselves a bit of an advantage on the opening stroke by creating a perch for the ball above the surrounding ground. They probably began by kicking at the turf to make a bump, much as some players do today. This caused an obvious problem of damage to the ground near the hole, even after later eighteenth-century codes increased the teeing distance to two-to-four club lengths. The answer, well into the twentieth century, was to take a small pile of dampened sand and form it into a cone shape, then set the ball on top.

The word *tee* is derived from the Gaelic word *tigh,* meaning "house." It appears to be related to the term *tee* in curling, which is the line through the center of the target circles, also called the *house.* If it seems odd to name golf's starting point after curling's target, remember that the golfing spot was defined by a club-length's circle around the previous hole. As a noun, *tee* probably referred at first to a place, and only later—much later—came to mean a device or technique for elevating the ball.

Towards the end of the nineteenth century, several people began to think of ways to make the tee a separate and reusable object. According to *The Singular History of the Golf Tee,* by Irwin R. Valenta, the earliest known portable golf tee was invented by two Scots, William Bloxsom and Arthur Douglas, in 1889; it consisted of a rubber slab that rested on the ground, with three vertical prongs or a hollow rubber tube extending upward to hold the ball in place. The first tee to anchor itself into the ground was the Perfectum tee, invented by Percy Ellis and patented in Britain in 1892; it consisted of a ring of rubber pins attached to a metal spike that was pushed into the ground.

The first two patents for teeing devices in America were registered to David Dalziel, a native of Glasgow, and Prosper L. Senat of Philadelphia, both granted in 1896. Dalziel's device is better described as a "golfing apparatus"; it was a large permanent structure to be buried in the teeing ground, containing a spring-loaded adjustable T on which to place the ball. The T would bounce back into position after the shot, ready for the next player, in the manner of an automated driving range. Senat's implement was more portable and practical. It consisted of a small piece of cardboard or paper, semicircular and ridged, with an interlocking notch creating a cone on which the golfer could place a ball.

The father of the modern tee in America was Dr. George F. Grant, who was awarded the U.S. patent for his 1898 invention consisting of a wooden peg, topped with rubber tubing, that could be pushed into the ground. Grant was one of the first two African Americans to graduate from Harvard Dental School; he eventually taught there as well, and invented an oblate palate for use as a prosthesis for patients with cleft palates.

Grant's patent application, specified as "an Improvement in Golf-Tees," describes its purpose in detail:

While the tee must firmly, yet lightly, support the ball until hit by the player's club, the tee must be so constructed that it will not in any manner interfere with the swing or "carry through" of the club in making the stroke. These requisites are possessed in full by my invention, and the annoyance and sometimes discomfort attendant upon the formation of a sand tee are obviated thereby.

Grant had the tees manufactured at a small shop near his suburban Boston home. He used them and he handed them out to friends, but he made no effort to market or capitalize on his invention. That task fell to another dentist, William Lowell, who invented the Reddy Tee in 1921. While Grant's two-piece device was similar to the Perfectum and Victor tees, the Reddy Tee was most like our modern tee in consisting of a single piece, shaped to hold a ball and be pressed into the ground. It had a distinctive red-painted top that made it easy to find and was manufactured in a variety of materials—first wood, then celluloid and assorted plastics. Lowell paid Walter Hagen and trick-shot artist Joe Kirkwood to promote the Reddy Tee, and the device took hold with the golfing public.

If it seems curious that two dentists were instrumental in developing the modern golf tee, take a look at the illustration that accompanied Grant's patent, number 638,920. The idea of a raised platform sitting above a surface line, anchored by a pointed extension below, would be a natural for someone who spent so much time contemplating teeth and their roots below the gumline.

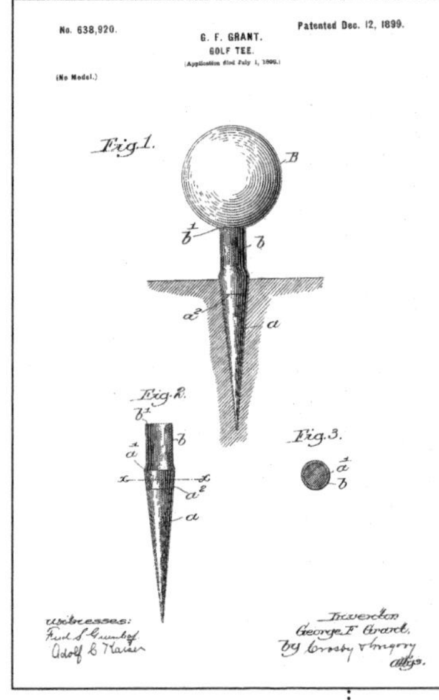

George Grant's drawing of his now-ubiquitous invention.

BEYOND THE GREEN JACKET

Every April, the Masters awards an item of haberdashery of which you may have heard to its winner, along with a rarely discussed amount of money and a replica of its permanent trophy. But that's not all that's awarded during the second week of April up the hill from Rae's Creek; here are some other items up for grabs:

- Gold Medal: Winner
- Silver Medal and Silver Salver: Runner-up
- Silver Cup: Low amateur*
- Silver Medal: Amateur runner-up*
- Crystal Vase: Each day's low score
- Large Crystal Bowl: Hole-in-one
- Pair of Crystal Goblets: Eagle
- Large Crystal Bowl: Double Eagle**

One additional gift is worth noting: From 1955 through 1992, the winner received a silver box (originally a cigarette case) engraved with the names of all the year's competitors. In 1968, the year that Roberto de Vicenzo signed an incorrect scorecard that kept him out of a playoff with Bob Goalby, Augusta National Chairman Clifford Roberts had an identical case made up for both players.

*Amateur awards are given only to players making the thirty-six-hole cut

**The bowl was first awarded after Bruce Devlin made a double eagle on the 8th hole in 1967, but Devlin did not receive his until one had been presented to Gene Sarazen in honor of his double eagle on the 15th in 1935. Jeff Maggert has the only other Masters double eagle, a two on the 13th hole in 1994.

THE GOLFER'S LIFE LIST

Take a Child Out for His or Her First Round

The family was in Wisconsin for a week, and Sis-in-Law was feeling a bit frazzled from the effort of entertaining her three kids, then ranging in age from nine to fifteen. "That's all right," the golfer said, "I'll get them out of your hair for the afternoon and take them over to the golf course."

The kids had been exposed to golf to some degree at an early age, because their grandfather was an avid player. They'd been to driving ranges and played pitch-and-putt and miniature golf; how big a stretch could this be? The golfer called a nearby executive course—nine holes, par 31, longest hole 300 yards—to find out when would be the best (i.e., emptiest) time to bring by a group of complete novices. They would be renting equipment, of course, adding those charges to the green fees as an extra inducement for the place to accommodate the group.

How, you might wonder, could nine holes played under such conditions take three hours?

The first thing to remember is just how difficult it is to hit a golf ball. The avid golfer takes for granted the a priori accomplishment of swinging a three-foot-long stick precisely enough to strike a 1.68-inch object. "Hit and go find it" is a wonderful summation of the game, but "take a few warmup swings and then swing and miss and giggle and start over" was a more accurate description that day.

Of course, once the ball is hit, it may well end up in places the course mowers had not anticipated. A surprising amount of time can be spent tiptoeing through flower beds and peering under bushes that were planted for purely decorative purposes—or so the planters thought.

The kids were relentlessly cheerful throughout these short-walks-spoiled. "Ooooh, good one!" would ring out, as the ball rose into the air (before falling to the ground fifteen yards away and at a seventy-degree angle to the target line). They bounced happily along, diligently totaled up their strokes (ignoring the misses, naturally and appropriately), were gleeful when the ball finally reached the green (this part of the game they *knew* they could handle), and high-fived each other when a putt finally rattled home (no gimmes allowed, at their insistence). They never got tired of it, never got discouraged—why should they? what expectations could they have?—and at the end they remembered the good shots they hit and didn't worry about the rest.

The golfer learned a lesson that day—but not from them. While the course had assured him that this was the least-busy time of day, an early cloudburst had shifted many morning golfers into the afternoon. Foursomes began to back up everywhere. On every hole, the family let at least one group, sometimes two, play through. Those golfers would arrive scowling at the slow play ahead of them—but then when they saw it was a single adult out with three youngsters, they all smiled and called out words of encouragement. They could see that something was being passed on, and they were willing to accept a little inconvenience to help it happen.

The group returned their rental clubs, got in the car, and headed for the nearest ice-cream stand. The golfer suspects they may remember the Rocky Road more than the par three over water, but he'll never forget their unfailing good humor in the face of golfing imperfection. He can't emulate it, but he sure does admire it.

JACK NICKLAUS'S EIGHTEEN PROFESSIONAL MAJOR CHAMPIONSHIPS

YEAR	MAJOR	COURSE	SCORE	RUNNER-UP
1962	U.S. Open	Oakmont	283 (–1)*	Arnold Palmer, 283
1963	Masters	Augusta National	286 (–2)	Tony Lema, 287
	PGA Championship	Dallas Athletic Club	279 (–5)	Dave Ragan, 281
1965	Masters	Augusta National	271 (–17)	Arnold Palmer and Gary Player, 280
1966	Masters	Augusta National	288 (E)*	Tommy Jacobs and Gay Brewer, 288
	British Open	Muirfield	282 (–2)	Doug Sanders and Dave Thomas, 283
1967	U.S. Open	Baltusrol	275 (–5)	Arnold Palmer, 279
1970	British Open	St. Andrews	283 (–5)*	Doug Sanders, 283
1971	PGA Championship	PGA National	281 (–7)	Billy Casper, 283
1972	Masters	Augusta National	286 (–2)	Bruce Crampton, Bobby Mitchell, Tom Weiskopf, 289
	U.S. Open	Pebble Beach	290 (+2)	Bruce Crampton, 293
1973	PGA Championship	Canterbury	277 (–7)	Bruce Crampton, 281
1975	Masters	Augusta National	276 (–12)	Johnny Miller and Tom Weiskopf, 277
	PGA Championship	Firestone	276 (–4)	Bruce Crampton, 278
1978	British Open	St. Andrews	281 (–7)	Ben Crenshaw, Simon Owen, Tom Kite, Ray Floyd, 283
1980	U.S. Open	Baltusrol	272 (–8)	Isao Aoki, 274
	PGA Championship	Oak Hill	274 (–6)	Andy Bean, 281
1986	Masters	Augusta National	279 (–9)	Tom Kite and Greg Norman, 280

*won in playoff as follows: 1962 U.S. Open—Nicklaus 71, Palmer 74; 1966 Masters—Nicklaus 70, Jacobs 72, Brewer 78; 1970 British Open—Nicklaus 72, Sanders 73

JACK NICKLAUS'S NINETEEN SECOND-PLACE FINISHES IN MAJOR CHAMPIONSHIPS

YEAR	MAJOR	COURSE	SCORE	WINNER
1960	U.S. Open	Cherry Hills	282 (–2)	Arnold Palmer, 280
1964	Masters	Augusta National	282t (–6)	Arnold Palmer, 276
	British Open	St. Andrews	284 (–4)	Tony Lema, 279
	PGA Championship	Columbus	274t (–6)	Bobby Nichols, 271
1965	PGA Championship	Laurel Valley	282t (–2)	Dave Marr, 280
1967	British Open	Hoylake	280 (–8)	Roberto de Vicenzo, 278
1968	U.S. Open	Oak Hill	279 (–1)	Lee Trevino, 275
	British Open	Carnoustie	291t (+3)	Gary Player, 289
1971	Masters	Augusta National	281t (–7)	Charles Coody, 279
	U.S. Open	Merion	280*(E)	Lee Trevino, 280
1972	British Open	Muirfield	279 (–5)	Lee Trevino, 278
1974	PGA Championship	Tanglewood	277 (–3)	Lee Trevino, 276
1976	British Open	Royal Birkdale	285t (–3)	Johnny Miller, 279
1977	Masters	Augusta National	278 (–10)	Tom Watson, 276
	British Open	Turnberry	269 (–11)	Tom Watson, 268
1979	British Open	Royal Lytham & St. Annes	286t (+2)	Seve Ballesteros, 283
1981	Masters	Augusta National	282t (–6)	Tom Watson, 280
1982	U.S. Open	Pebble Beach	284 (–4)	Tom Watson, 282
1983	PGA Championship	Riviera	275 (-9)	Hal Sutton, 274

*lost in playoff—Trevino 68, Nicklaus 71

SECOND-PLACE FINISHES IN MAJORS

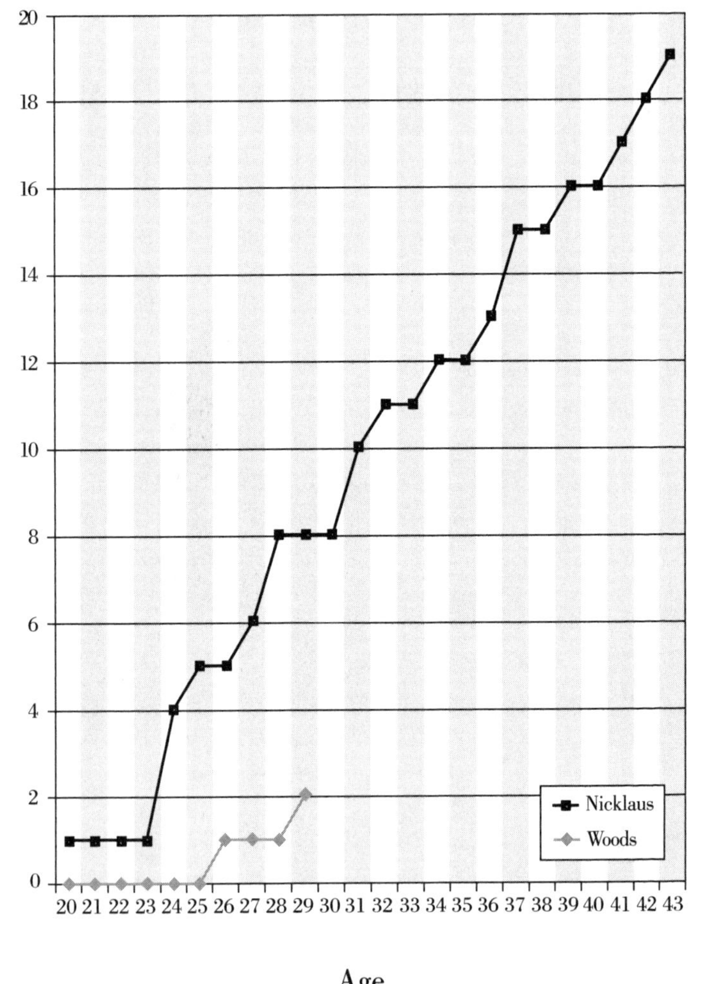

FOOTNOTES TO HISTORY

Ed Sneed, 1979 Masters, Augusta National Golf Club

With one round to go, Ed Sneed led Tom Watson by five shots and Fuzzy Zoeller by six. Things slipped away from him during the final round as Sneed tried to win his first major; still, he held a three-shot lead with three holes remaining.

But Sneed three-putted the 16th for bogey and missed a short putt for par on the next green. He hit the fairway on the 18th hole, but missed the green and then chipped within six feet of the hole. Sneed's putt to win the Masters was six feet, uphill. He left the putt hanging on the lip of the hole and hunched over it as he became aware it wasn't going to fall. It was the stance of a man who could not believe what had just happened, a man in shock.

Ed Sneed. Almost famous.

"It's extremely disappointing," Sneed said. "I'll just have to put it out of my mind, but it won't be easy. You don't get too many chances to win a big tournament."

Zoeller birdied the eleventh hole, the second in the sudden-death playoff against Sneed and Watson, to win.

GOLF MAGAZINE'S EIGHTEEN GREATEST HOLES IN THE WORLD

In 2000, *Golf Magazine*'s editors made their choices for the world's dream eighteen. They selected four par threes, four par fives, and ten par fours, from eight countries on four continents. Their selections:

Par Threes

Banff Springs Golf Course, Banff, Alberta, Canada. 4th hole (Rundle), 192 yards: From a point high above a glacial lake, the tee looks out at the granite cliffs of Mount Rundle, pines reaching spikily upwards. The green is ringed with bunkers, and slopes from back to front towards a steep bank in front of the putting surface.

Cypress Point Club, Pebble Beach, California. 15th hole, 139 yards: Traversing a small ocean inlet that is baby brother to the behemoth that follows it, Alister Mackenzie's little gem may be the most beautiful hole in the world. The green is surrounded by bunkers, with a tongue that projects between the two in front.

National Golf Links of America, Southampton, New York. 4th hole, 197 yards: C. B. MacDonald copied this Redan from his visits to North Berwick. It is one of several holes modeled after classic Scottish designs on this quintessential links on Long Island's eastern end.

TPC at Sawgrass (Stadium Course), Ponte Vedra Beach, Florida. 17th hole, 132 yards: Pete (or Alice) Dye's famous island green is surrounded at each Players Championship by throngs of fans who love to watch Tour pros sweat as much as they would. Tiger Woods, who had been six down, birdied it on the 35th hole of his final match to take his first lead against Trip Kuehne on the way to his first U.S. Amateur title.

Par Fours

Ballybunion Golf Club (Old), Ballybunion, County Kerry, Ireland. 11th hole, 453 yards: With sand dunes to the left and the Shannon estuary to the right, Ballybunion's most magnificent and challenging hole needs no bunkers to be fearsome. The fairway tumbles downward over shelves towards a green guarded by two sizable sandhills in front.

Bethpage State Park (Black Course), Farmingdale, New York. 5th hole, 451 yards: A. W. Tillinghast designed this beautiful monster that requires a fade off the tee and a draw into the green. The first shot must carry a vast natural bunker and hit a narrow angling fairway. The second, uphill to the green, must clear two bunkers and avoid the trees that guard the approach on the left. A new tee will make this hole longer for the 2009 U.S. Open.

Merion Golf Club (East), Ardmore, Pennsylvania. 16th hole, 428 yards: On the first of Hugh Wilson's famous three closing "quarry holes," the drive from an elevated tee lands in a fairway that ends abruptly 300 yards out. The second shot must cross the quarry to reach the green sitting below you; Merion's use of baskets instead of flags keeps you guessing about the wind at the green.

Mid Ocean Club, Tucker's Town, Bermuda. 5th hole, 433 yards: This emblematic Cape hole dares the golfer to select a line and carry as much water as he can. The hole doglegs around Mangrove Lake, sloping toward the water as it approaches the green.

Pine Valley Golf Club, Clementon, New Jersey. 13th hole, 448 yards: If Pine Valley is a multicourse French meal—too rich for everyday, but you wouldn't want a life without such occasional indulgences—the 13th is its cassoulet, a stout, hearty challenge. Tee off towards an unseen saddle of fairway, then play your second either straight over a wilderness of scrub and sand, or out toward the safety right of the green that leaves a tricky downhill chip.

Royal County Down Golf Club, Newcastle, County Down, Northern Ireland. 9th hole, 486 yards: From high above the natural-looking links—if you can tear your eyes away from the view of the crescent-shaped town of Newcastle, the waters of Dundrum Bay, and the steeple of the Slieve Donard Hotel—hit a firm drive over the marker at the crest of the hill to reach the lower fairway, then a second to a green protected front and left by bunkers.

Royal Melbourne Golf Club (West), Black Rock, Melbourne, Australia. 6th hole, 450 yards: A high tee presents a view of the nest of bunkers at the inner-right corner of the dogleg, 220 yards out. The fairway sweeps dramatically right, to a multitiered green sloped back to front.

St. Andrews (Old), St. Andrews, Fife, Scotland. 17th hole, 461 yards: The Road Hole. Hit your blind tee shot over the corner of a sign, then a long second to a shelf of green guarded in front by a bunker that's deeper than Kierkegaard and in back by a road and a stone wall that are both in play. No problem.

Shinnecock Hills Golf Club, Southampton, New York. 14th hole, 447 yards: The tee shot comes at a slight angle to a fairway that slopes away from its line. The uphill second shot is to a deep green along a rise that narrows as it elevates.

Southern Hills Country Club, Tulsa, Oklahoma. 12th hole, 445 yards: The hole plays downhill and doglegs right to left around a deep bunker, then over a blind water hazard to a green guarded on the left by bunkers and on the right by the continuation of the water. The raised green slopes back to front, and is flanked by trees that make the approach look equally picturesque and perilous.

PAR FIVES

Augusta National Golf Club, Augusta, Georgia. 13th hole, 510 yards: Many tough par fours are referred to as par-four-and-a-half holes; Augusta's 13th is a par five that deserves the designation. It doglegs at a near right-angle left from the tee line, and its fairway is steeply sloped from right to left. If you go for the green, you face a second shot over Rae's Creek to a heavily sloped green; if you don't, you have a tricky pitch to a hole that's usually tucked near the water. Pros expect a birdie here, which only increases the pressure.

Carnoustie Golf Links, Carnoustie, Angus, Scotland. 6th hole, 578 yards: Played at 490 yards by nonchampionship contestants, this flat yet strategic hole has a boundary fence left, two sod-walled bunkers straight ahead a bit more than two hundred yards from the tee, and Jockie's Burn entering from the right side to menace the second shot. In 1953, Ben Hogan played into the thirty-yard-wide strip left, between the bunkers and out-of-bounds, leaving the best angle into the green.

Durban Country Club, Durban, Natal, South Africa. 3rd hole, 513 yards: This long hole plays through a valley, over tumbling terrain guarded by trees on both sides and a deep bunker left. Two more bunkers forty yards from the green flank the landing area for the second shot and play havoc with the golfer's depth perception, and the green is small and elevated, with danger behind.

Pebble Beach Golf Links, Pebble Beach, California. 18th hole, 548 yards: The ultimate closing hole, with the Pacific Ocean on the left for its entire length. Two trees shrink the fairway landing area, and a cowardly drive hit too far right flirts with a bunker and out-of-bounds. This is a hole best played, as Dan Jenkins has written, with your left eye firmly shut.

THE WORD ON

Water

"As a Scotsman, I am naturally opposed to water in its undiluted state."

—Alister Mackenzie

"When your shot has to carry over water, you can either take one more club or two more balls."

—Henry Beard

"Splosh! One of the finest sights in the world: the other man's ball dropping in the water—preferably so that he can see it but cannot quite reach it and has therefore to leave it there, thus rendering himself so mad that he loses the next hole as well."

—Henry Longhurst

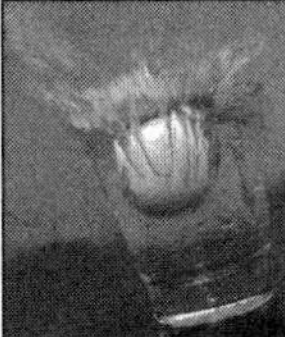

"The difference between a sand trap and water is the difference between a car crash and a plane crash."

—Bobby Jones

HOW TO TEND A FLAGSTICK

1. Stand beside the flag so that you are not in anyone's line and your shadow is not in the line of the person putting.

2. Hold the flag and flagstick together so that the flag does not hang or flap.

3. Lift the bottom of the flagstick out of the cup-liner to ensure that it does not stick in the liner and angle it away from the player.

4. Remove the flagstick once the putt is on its way and step away from the hole without stepping in anyone's line.

BUT I WANNA TELL YA, FOLKS . . .

Bob Hope played in the 1951 British Amateur, took lessons from Ben Hogan, told a few jokes along the way, and died in July 2004 at the age of one hundred. His jokes fill 85,000 pages in the Library of Congress's archives. Here are a few of his best golf jokes.

I hit a ball into the wind one day. I shouldn't have watched it with my mouth open. I'm the only guy around here with an Adam's apple marked "Spalding Pro-Flight."

On one hole, I hit an alligator so hard that he's now my golf bag.

Jimmy Stewart could have been a good golfer, but he speaks so slowly that by the time he yells "Fore!" the guy he's hit is already in an ambulance and on the way to the hospital.

Golf's a hard game to figure. One day you slice it, shank it, hit into all the traps, and miss every green. And then the next day, you go out and for no reason at all you really stink.

I've played all over the world, which means there isn't a country with a course where I haven't three-putted.

It's wonderful how you can start out with three strangers in the morning, play eighteen holes, and by the time the day is over, you have three solid enemies.

When I play golf I look like a polo player without a horse, or Grandma Moses trying to keep warm.

I played golf with [President Dwight Eisenhower] yesterday. It's hard to beat a guy who rattles his medals while you're putting. Ike uses a short Democrat for a tee.

Bob Hope and Gerald Ford, before surveying the damage.

In the first months after President Gerald Ford left office in 1977, he hit errant shots that conked spectators in several pro-am golf tournaments, including Hope's own Desert Classic. Hope said that Ford was "the man who made golf a contact sport," and in time he took more than a few shots at the man he called "the most dangerous 14-handicapper in the land."

You all know Jerry Ford, the most dangerous driver since Ben Hur.

Ford is easy to spot on the golf course. He drives the cart with the red cross painted on top.

Whenever I play with him, I usually try to make a foursome—the president, myself, a paramedic, and a faith healer. One of my most prized possessions is the Purple Heart I received for all the golf I played with him.

On the 18th tee Ford put a ball through the clubhouse window. It wasn't easy. It was behind him. That's when I remembered that the Russians used to say if we were really serious about disarmament, we'd dismantle his golf clubs.

It's not hard to find Jerry Ford on a golf course. You just follow the wounded.

THE LEGENDARY TITANIC THOMPSON

Who is the greatest golf hustler of all time? Probably someone we've never heard of, and never will. Golf hustling is a black art, best practiced in shadowy anonymity by men who are careful to keep their skin from tanning (lest you know how much they play) and who shake your hand with great feeling and care (to see if you have the calluses that would indicate long hours of practice).

One of the greatest, and certainly the most varied, was born Alvin Charles Thomas and became a renowned figure in golfing and gambling circles in the 1920s and for decades beyond. He was given the nickname "Titanic" at the pool table by observers who noticed he "was sinking everybody around here," he took the last name "Thompson" to go with it because he liked the sound. A contemporary and sometime partner of Nick "the Greek" Dandolos, he is thought to be the model for Sky Masterson in Damon Runyon's stories of the gamblers and the swells who made New York roar in the twenties.

Even as a child he had extraordinary hand-eye coordination. He spent hours throwing coins into a little box at the foot of his bed; years later, this skill paid off when he would bet he could throw silver dollars into a golf hole from ten feet away. He became a crack shot with rifle or pistol, an accomplished pool hustler, and a great poker player who knew all the ways that cards could be marked, spotted, or dealt from the middle.

His talents were remarkable, but he also knew how to avoid relying on them. Once, challenged to throw an orange to the top of a five-story building, he excused himself and substituted a lemon, which he knew was smaller and harder and easier to throw. He'd sit on a porch munching from a bag of walnuts, wait till someone got to chatting with him, and would bet he could throw one of them over a building across the street—which he could do, having planted in the bag a walnut shell he'd filled with lead shot.

It was inevitable that he'd turn his ingenuity to golf, which offered outstanding possibilities for fleecing the unwary. Here are some of his most famous exploits:

He would bet that he could make a forty-foot putt on his first try. The only condition was that the putt had to take place first thing in the morning. The night before, he would pay the greenkeeper to lay a forty-foot length of hose on the green and leave it there overnight. The hose would mat down the line, while the grass around it stood straight, creating a channel for the ball as true as the gutter in a bowling alley.

In a match against a young pro in Tulsa, Oklahoma, he offered his opponent three drives on every hole (except par threes) and the right to choose the best of the three. The pro got off to a strong start, but by the end of the round he was so arm-weary that Thompson swept the last several holes to win the bet.

He had a technique for heightening the pressure on an opponent, particularly if they were playing for the second time. The first round, Thompson would lose comfortably, and with great bonhomie he would pay off his wagers and offer congratulations. The second round, however, he would usually get a handicap, the stakes would be significantly increased, and if that wasn't unnerving enough, he would offer to bet thousands of dollars that the opponent would miss a putt; when the bet was invariably refused, he'd say contemptuously, "Okay, let's just make it for $100 then" (a figure that the mark could hardly turn down . . . and could not put out of his mind). He'd shower the player with extra bets on each hole—side bets on propositions and particular shots—until the comfortable game of the day before was replaced by so much money and math that his man's head would be spinning. The player who was used to such pressure—Thompson—would invariably rake in the winnings. He noted, "With business executives, this approach is a cinch. They won't admit they can't handle a complex mass of numbers simultaneously."

Thompson once found himself playing golf with a man who trained champion bird dogs and had brought one along. Seemingly out of nowhere, Thompson bet that he could get the dog to bark in under a minute. The trainer knew his dogs well and agreed quickly. What he didn't know was that Ti had seen a rabbit in a little ditch not far from the tee; he took out his driver and hit a screaming low liner at the ditch that just missed the rabbit and sent it running—with a loudly barking dog in fast pursuit.

GREAT CAREER AMATEURS

Carole Semple Thompson, b. Sewickley, Pennsylvania, 1950

The PGA of America awards its annual First Lady of Golf honor to a woman who has made a significant contribution to promoting the game. Thompson won it in 2005, a year before she would captain the U.S. Curtis Cup team during the matches at Bandon Dunes in Bandon, Oregon.

Thompson's accomplishments include winning both the U.S. Women's Amateur and the British Ladies Amateur in 1973. She won the U.S. Senior Women's Amateur four years running, from 1999 through 2002, and took the 1990 and 1997 U.S. Women's Mid-Amateurs. Thompson played on twelve Curtis Cup teams, holing a twenty-seven-foot putt from just off the 18th green to guarantee that the U.S. would retain the Cup in her last appearance in 2002. She is the only golfer to have played 100 USGA events.

Carole Semple Thompson at the 32nd Curtis Cup—her 12th—in 2002.

Her 1990 win was at her home course, the Allegheny Country Club in Sewickley. Her mother, Phyllis, a fine amateur in her own right, watched her. She was also at her daughter's side when Thompson won her first U.S. Senior Women's Amateur in 1999. Spectators couldn't take carts, but a player or her caddie could. Thompson's mother wasn't able to walk the course, so her daughter signed her up to be her caddie. Phyllis didn't offer a word of advice, and when asked the last time she had done so, she said, "When she was about twelve."

THREE-HANKY GOLF

The Hand on Weiskopf's Putter

Bert Yancey and Tom Weiskopf were ready to play the first round of the Franklin Quest Championship in Park City, Utah, on the Senior PGA Tour. The date was August 26, 1994, but everything suddenly changed. Yancey, who had been diagnosed with bipolar disorder years before, was going through his practice routine prior to teeing off in the first round when he suffered chest pains. Paramedics on site examined him and suggested he not play. But Yancey pressed on.

After hitting a few more balls, he was again in pain and needed oxygen. Yancey died on his way to the hospital. He was fifty-six years old.

Weiskopf, the winner of the 1973 British Open and fourteen PGA Tour events, was known for his elegant swing and sensitive temperament. He became close with Yancey and understood his friend's obsession with the golf swing. He'd designed some highly acclaimed courses and was playing the Senior PGA Tour only occasionally. Weiskopf had yet to win an official event there when he came to Park City.

Playing the 16th hole in the last round of the fifty-four-hole tournament, Weiskopf was three shots behind Dave Stockton. Yancey had for years coached his friend on the mechanics of putting, the weakest part of Weiskopf's game. In Park City, Weiskopf continued to hit the ball beautifully but wasn't making the putts to force the issue against Stockton.

But then Weiskopf holed an eighty-foot putt to birdie the 16th hole. He birdied the 17th hole, then made a fifteen-footer for birdie on the final hole. Weiskopf had closed with three consecutive birdies, and he found himself in a sudden-death playoff against Stockton.

Weiskopf felt something special was unfolding. How did he make those three consecutive birdie putts to get into a playoff? Yancey had told him time after time that he needed to keep his head still while putting, yet it came up no matter his intention. This time, however, Weiskopf was able to keep his head still during his run down the last holes. He didn't look up on his putt on the last hole of regulation play until it was halfway to the hole. "I knew it was going in," he said. "It was a miracle."

Weiskopf made a twenty-footer to birdie the first playoff hole and won the tournament. Later he said, "I didn't win this tournament. Bert Yancey made me win it. He was with me every step of the way. My mind was not on golf, but I just had a feeling I was going to make every putt. It sounds crazy, but I told [my caddie] I was going to birdie the last three holes."

Weiskopf was in tears at the presentation following his win. He asked that the Senior PGA Tour and the Franklin Quest Championship put both his and Yancey's name on the trophy. "It would mean a lot to me to recognize his contribution to this victory."

Visitors to Park Meadows today might notice a plaque on a boulder near the practice area where Yancey collapsed. The plaque reads, "Bert Yancey was a tenacious champion with unusual courage, determination and wisdom." It goes on to say, "His quest for excellence remained remarkably intense and focused as he executed his final shot from this area."

Weiskopf's final shot came two days later, and it was a winning putt. "If there is such a thing as destiny, I was certainly feeling it out there today," he said.

TIME GOLF COVERS

Editors of major non-golf publications rarely put golfers on their covers. *Time* magazine has had ten golf covers since it began publication in 1923, and only Bobby Jones has been on the cover twice. Here is the list.

August 25, 1924

Edith Cummings

Edith Cummings won the 1923 U.S. Women's Amateur at the Westchester Country Club in Rye, New York. Cummings was a glamorous young woman who traveled in elite social company, so much so that F. Scott Fitzgerald based his character Jordan Baker in *The Great Gatsby* on her. She was the first woman to make the cover of *Time*.

August 31, 1925

Bobby Jones

Jones was about to defend his title in the U.S. Amateur, which would be played at the Oakmont Country Club near Pittsburgh. Jones defeated Watts Gunn 8 & 7 to win his second straight national amateur championship.

September 22, 1930

Bobby Jones

Jones had won the British Open and the British Amateur, and also the U.S. Open, and was headed back to the Merion Cricket Club to try to win golf's Grand Slam. Jones beat Eugene Homans 8 & 7 in the final match of his competitive career.

June 6, 1938

Johnny Goodman

Goodman, a twenty-eight-year-old amateur from Omaha, Nebraska, had won the 1933 U.S. Open and the 1937 British Amateur. Having not lost a match in two previous Walker Cups, he had traveled to Scotland to represent the United States at St. Andrews in another Walker Cup the week he was on *Time*'s cover. The U.S. team lost the Cup and Goodman lost both of his matches.

January 10, 1949

Ben Hogan

Hogan is depicted in an illustration with clubheads coming out of his own head, in a stroboscopic pattern. There's more than a hint of the application of science to the golf swing in the cover illustration, which is appropriate given the precise technique that Hogan was famous for.

JUNE 21, 1954

Sam Snead

By the time the 1954 U.S. Open came around, Sam Snead had won just about everything in golf—except for this championship. He prepared hard for it, hitting drives into an area marked off thirty-five yards wide—the width of Baltusrol's fairways. He putted into small golf holes so that they would look bigger to him at Baltusrol. But Snead tied for 11th, six shots back of winner Ed Furgol. Snead played seventeen more U.S. Opens and never did win one.

MAY 2, 1960

Arnold Palmer

Powerman Palmer: That's how the cover story referred to the man with the bulging forearms who tore at the ball. He'd won the Masters the month before and was looking forward to the U.S. Open at Cherry Hills in Denver. He won that too, driving the green on the par-four first hole and shooting 65 in the last round.

JUNE 29, 1962

Jack Nicklaus

Having turned professional after winning the 1959 and 1961 U.S. Amateurs, Nicklaus won the U.S. Open in his first year of playing the game for a living. The *Time* story following his win suggested, "With at least a dozen good playing years ahead of him, there seems to be no limit to the heights he may reach."

JULY 19, 1971

Lee Trevino

Trevino had won the U.S. Open, and then the Canadian Open, and now he'd taken the British Open the previous week. "Trevino: Golf's New Superstar" was the way *Time* put it on this cover. Trevino attributed his popularity to being the pro from the driving range who appealed to, as he said, "the municipal player, the truck driver, the union man, the guy who grinds it out."

AUGUST 14, 2000

Tiger Woods

The longest period in the magazine's history between golf covers ended when Woods got the call. Woods had won the U.S. Open at the Pebble Beach Golf Links by fifteen shots in June and the British Open at the Old Course at St. Andrews by eight shots. Woods was pictured on a black background, face on his fingertips, as if he were a Buddha of the links, with the words, "Tiger's Tale: How the greatest golfer in the world risked it all in his quest to become the greatest golfer in history."

BYRON NELSON'S ANNUS MIRABILIS

For pure domination of the golfing scene, there has never been a year anything like Byron Nelson's 1945: nineteen victories, including eleven in a row, and the only "major championship" contested that year, the PGA. For the year, his stroke average was 68.4; his average margin of victory in stroke-play tournaments during his streak was 6.67. His earnings were an unprecedented $63,335; today, he could earn more by finishing 16th at the PGA Tour's Disney World stop.

In examining such a commanding season, it is natural to wonder whether the competition was diluted by World War II. To address this, we have listed some of the prominent golfers who competed in each tournament. Sam Snead played in twenty-five of the thirty-one tournaments Nelson entered; Nelson won fourteen of those events, Snead won six. Lieutenant Ben Hogan's name appears frequently towards the end of the year. Other major winners who competed during the year include Gene Sarazen, Jimmy Demaret, Craig Wood (referred to in newspaper accounts as the "duration national champion" for his victory in the 1941 U.S. Open), Lloyd Mangrum, Claude Harmon, Denny Shute, Henry Picard, and Jim Ferrier. If the average field was weaker than it would be in the pre- and postwar periods, his accomplishment is epic nonetheless.

TOURNAMENT	PLACE	NELSON'S SCORE	WON/ LOST BY	OTHER COMPETITORS (winner in CAPS)
Los Angeles Open	T2	284 (E)	–1	SNEAD, McSpaden, Shute
Phoenix Open	1	274 (–10)	+2	Snead, McSpaden, Shute, Harmon
Tucson Open	2	269 (–11)	–1	R. MANGRUM, Snead, McSpaden, Wood
Texas Open	2	269 (–15)	–1	BYRD, McSpaden, Harmon, Demaret
Corpus Christi Open	1	264 (–16)	+4	McSpaden, Demaret, Wood
New Orleans Open	1	284 (–4)	0	McSpaden (lost playoff), Snead, Harmon, Shute
Gulfport Open	2	275 (–13)	0	SNEAD (beat Nelson in playoff), Shute, Harmon
Pensacola Open	2	274 (–14)	–7	SNEAD, Harmon, McSpaden, Harrison
Jacksonville Open	T6	275 (–13)	–9	SNEAD, McSpaden, Harmon
Miami Four-Ball	1	Match play	8 & 6	(with McSPADEN), Snead, Hogan, Wood
Charlotte Open	1	272 (–16)	0	Snead (lost playoff), McSpaden, Harmon
Greensboro Open	1	271 (–13)	+8	Snead, Wood, Byrd
Durham Open	1	276 (–4)	+5	Snead, McSpaden, Wood
Atlanta Open	1	263 (–13)	+9	Snead, Demaret, McSpaden
Montreal Open	1	268 (–20)	+10	McSpaden, Furgol
Philadelphia Inquirer Open	1	269 (–11)	+2	Snead, McSpaden, Wood
Chicago Victory National	1	275 (–13)	+7	McSpaden, Harmon, Wood
PGA Championship	1	Match play	4 & 3	Byrd, Harrison, Shute, Sarazen

Lord Byron, in 2003.

TOURNAMENT	PLACE	NELSON'S SCORE	WON/ LOST BY	OTHER COMPETITORS (winner in CAPS)
All-American Open	1	269 (–19)	+11	Hogan, Sarazen, McSpaden
Canadian Open	1	280 (E)	+4	Snead, McSpaden, Wood, Harmon
Spring Lake Pro-Member*	1	140 (–4)	+1	Snead, Sarazen, McSpaden, Wood
Memphis Invitational	T4	276 (–12)	–6	FRED HAAS JR., Snead, McSpaden
Knoxville Invitational	1	276 (–12)	+10	Hogan, Snead, McSpaden
Nashville Invitational	T2	269 (–15)	-4	HOGAN, Snead, Johnny Bulla
Dallas Open	3	281 (–7)	–5	SNEAD, Hogan, McSpaden
Tulsa Open	4	288 (+4)	–11	SNEAD, Hogan, Demaret, McSpaden
Esmeralda Open	1	266 (–22)	+7	Hogan, Snead, McSpaden
Portland Open Invitational	2	275 (–13)	–14	HOGAN, Snead, McSpaden
Tacoma Open	T9	283 (+3)	–8	HINES, Hogan, Snead, Ferrier, McSpaden
Seattle Open	1	259 (–21)	+13	Hogan, Snead, McSpaden
Fort Worth Open	1	273 (–11)	+8	Hogan, Snead, Demaret, McSpaden

*Not a Tour event, so not considered part of the streak.

THE GOLFER'S LIFE LIST

Spend a Full Day in a Practice Bunker

Most golfers would prefer to mow the lawn, paint the house, or do just about anything other than spend a day in a bunker. But if tour pros, who know how to play the many varieties of sand shots, do this from time to time, why shouldn't other golfers? Practice your sand game and you'll be much more confident when you find a bunker.

The interesting aspect of spending time in the sand is that you'll soon recognize how to play the basic shot, and then you can go on to the fried egg lie, the buried lie, and half-buried lie, the uphill lie, the downhill lie, the uphill sidehill, the downhill sidehill, the ball under the lip, the shot from firm sand, from fluffy sand, from wet sand. Take a lesson on bunker play from a professional, or go in there with just about any instructional guide, and practice the shots. You'll get into it, and you'll be amazed at how soon you'll enjoy the process. Best of all, you'll lose any fear of the sand you might have. Tour pros always say the basic bunker shot is easy because the idea is to let the ball ride out on a cushion of sand. You don't hit even the ball, so the shot is a cinch. Supposedly. You'll discover this only if you spend those hours in the sand. But discover it you will.

Gary Player, one of the game's best bunker players, has written that most amateurs worry about embarrassing themselves by leaving shots in bunkers. Most amateurs don't like bunkers, Player observes. Well, familiarity will help. Get into a bunker and make it your home for a day. The discipline and training will be good for your game, increasing your satisfaction and lowering your scores.

HERBERT WARREN WIND, WRITER

Herbert Warren Wind joined *The New Yorker* in 1947, where he wrote on a variety of subjects for departments such as Talk of the Town and Television. (He actually wrote his first Talk piece in 1940, and he contributed a poem in 1941.) Wind also wrote profiles. His first golf piece, on Robert Trent Jones Sr., was published nearly two months after the U.S. Open was held on the South course of the Oakland Hills Country Club in Birmingham, Michigan. The United States Golf Association had brought Jones in to bring the course up to a standard that would adequately test the players. Ben Hogan won with descending scores of 76–73–71–67, one under par for the championship. Wind's essay was much more about Jones than it was about the course, yet the reader learned everything there was to know about its challenges by getting to know the architect. Wind's piece ran into the usual 10,000–15,000 words, and it was a pleasure to read. Where Wind wrote about the Open and the course, he did so with a casual eloquence. "After getting over their first sense of humiliation at their inability to pick up their usual strings of birdies, most of the pros admitted, with decreasing reluctance, that the revised Oakland Hills rewarded them when they played good shots."

Wind left *The New Yorker* in 1954 for *Sports Illustrated,* and remained there until 1960, when he returned to the magazine where he started the Sporting Scene department. While at *Sports Illustrated,* Wind helped Ben Hogan write a series of instructional pieces in 1957 that became *Five Lessons: The Modern*

Fundamentals of Golf. It's still one of golf's bestselling instructional books, and has never been out of print.

Back at *The New Yorker,* Wind became well known for his golf writing, but he also dug into many other sports and athletes. He wrote about the Montreal Canadiens, a team he loved to watch. He wrote about the Boston Bruins' superstar defenseman Bobby Orr. He wrote about Larry Bird and Bjorn Borg and Chris Evert and Roger Bannister and Wimbledon and pelote and place-kicking and squash and about the Holmenkollen Festival of skiing near Oslo, Norway. He wrote on subjects beyond sports, including a three-part series on Wallace K. Harrison, the architect and director of planning for the United Nations headquarters in New York City, and a story about the House of Baedeker, the publisher of travel books.

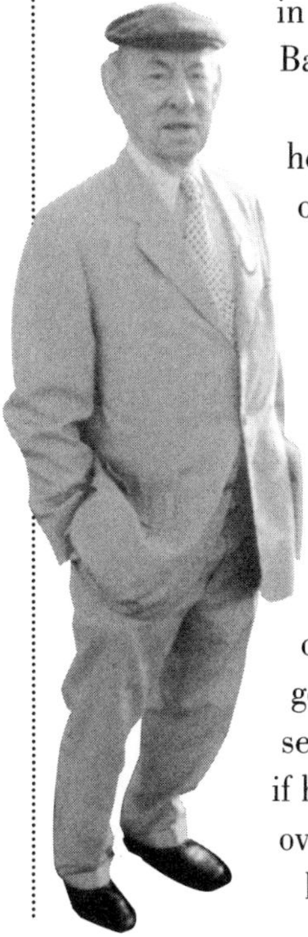

Wind captured golfers; the reader knew that he had walked the course as they played and observed the shots they hit. He watched Tom Watson on his way to winning the 1977 British Open at Turnberry, and wrote, "What impresses you most is the quickness and decisiveness with which he plays his shots, the freedom of his hitting action, and the sharpness with which he strikes the ball." Of Jack Nicklaus, Wind wrote, "Out on the fairway, surrounded by thousands of exuberant fans, he wears the tournament golfer's invariable frown of concentration, but he seems completely relaxed—as much at home as if he were talking a solitary walk in the country over a pleasant stretch of land he has known all his life."

Beyond his magazine work, Wind wrote books that are staples in any self-respecting golfer's library, beginning with *The Story of American Golf*, published in 1948; he brought it up to date in 1956 and 1975. He helped Jack Nicklaus with his early autobiography, *The Greatest Game of All*, and Gene Sarazen with his memoir, *Thirty Years of Championship Golf*.

Wind died on May 30, 2005, at the age of eighty-eight. He cared about every word he wrote. He collected many of his essays in *Following Through* (New York: Ticknor & Fields, 1985). His entire body of work for *The New Yorker* can be found in *The Complete New Yorker*, a DVD-ROM collection of every issue of the magazine from its first issue in 1925.

Bob Charles, the first left-handed golfer to win a major.

Left-Handed Golfers Who Have Won Majors

1. Bob Charles, British Open, 1963
2. Mike Weir, Masters, 2003
3. Phil Mickelson, Masters, 2004; PGA, 2005; Masters, 2006

Left-Handed Golfers Who Have Won Majors but were Actually Right-Handed

1. Bob Charles
2. Mike Weir
3. Phil Mickelson

ON THE VALUE OF GOLF FOR HEALTH: REPORT FROM THE *JOURNAL OF THE AMERICAN MEDICAL ASSOCIATION*, AUGUST 6, 1898

Long before the Columbian rediscovery of America, our hardy Caledonian ancestry amused themselves by playing the royal and ancient game which has been defined as the putting of little balls into little holes with instruments very ill-adapted to the purpose. Today we find a game with a long pedigree taken up and assimilated from Scotland, and so fascinating as to have spread around the English-speaking world. There is no danger to the game and consequently no accidents ensue.

To be more explicit, I may say that in all affections marked by slowing of exudation, or in those consequent upon intoxication by the products of organic disassimilation, the game of golf is to be recommended as the best adjuvant method of bringing about a cure.

The obesity and degeneration of middle age, when the biceps has diminished and one's energy is wanting, may be helped by devotion to golf. The further tendency of exercise is to eliminate the so-called diatheses and thus do away with gout, lithemia, headache and dyspepsia; while its hygienic and therapeutic consequences are admissible in cardiac and pulmonary affections.

Although moderation is advisable in such circumstances, there can be no doubt of the benefit derived in some cases of cough, nervous asthma, and in affectations of the bladder and prostate.

But it is pre-eminently in functional nervous disease that our great Anglo-Saxon game is to be recommended, both as prophylactic and curative. No exercise or recreation is better for the mentally overworked, the hysterical, the melancholic; none helps to preserve the concerted action of eye, brain, and muscle known as the psychological moment; none, perhaps, with the exception of swimming, gives one so good an appetite; there is not a more sovereign remedy for dyspepsia, and as to insomnia, such a thing scarcely exists among the devotees of golf.

FOOTNOTES TO HISTORY

Mike Reid, 1989 PGA Championship, Kemper Lakes Golf Club, Hawthorn Woods, Illinois

Mike Reid, one of the quietest players in professional golf and one of its straightest drivers, took a three-shot lead into the final round. Radar, as he was called for his accuracy and his resemblance to the character Radar O'Reilly on the popular television show *M*A*S*H,* appeared ready to win his first major championship. At the same time, he admitted to feeling nervous. Asked if he would have butterflies in his stomach during the last round, he said, "There's always butterflies. Sometimes they're in there playing hockey."

Reid maintained his three-shot lead until the 16th hole, where he drove into the water and made bogey. He now held a two-shot lead over Payne Stewart, Curtis Strange, and Andy Bean. Stewart, playing ahead, birdied the 18th hole with a twelve-foot putt to draw a shot closer.

Reid missed the green on the 17th hole, and came up fifteen feet short of the hole with his chipped sand wedge. He ran his par putt over the left edge of the hole, thirty inches by, and missed the bogey putt. Stewart, watching on television in the scorer's tent, was shocked by what had transpired. Bean, watching in the press room, was equally stunned. Reid needed to birdie the last hole to force a playoff with Stewart.

After a drive more typical of a golfer nicknamed Radar, Reid hit a five-iron within seven feet of the hole. But he missed the putt to the left. Stewart, thirty-two, had won his first major championship. He'd shot five-under-par 31 on the back nine and 67 for the round. But Reid's unexpected collapse was the story of the day. In the end, he tied for second with Bean and Strange. He shed a few tears after his round, saying, "I cry at supermarket grand openings." Reid, ranked 184th on the PGA Tour in driving distance out of 185 players, had come painfully close to winning the championship. He became a "nearly" man.

THE LAST TIME A U.S. OPEN CHAMPION . . .

- Birdied the last hole to win by a stroke: Bobby Jones, 1926
- Birdied the last hole to get into a playoff: Hale Irwin, 1990
- Had no rounds in the 60s: Geoff Ogilvy, 2006
- Had four rounds in the 60s: Lee Janzen, 1993
- Had a round in the 80s: John McDermott, 1911, playoff (also first round)
- Had a round of 77: Sam Parks Jr., 1935, first round
- Had a round of 76: Johnny Miller, 1973, third round
- Had a round of 75: Payne Stewart, 1991, playoff
- Had a round of 74: Steve Jones, 1996, first round
- Got into the Open through sectional qualifying: Steve Jones, 1996
- Got into the Open through local and sectional qualifying: Orville Moody, 1969
- Was an amateur: Johnny Goodman, 1933
- Missed the cut the next year: Michael Campbell, 2005–6

CADDIE–PLAYER RELATIONS

How to Be Good to Your Caddie

1. Tip well. Nothing speaks like cash. Assuming the caddie fee is in the normal $50–80 range, a tip of $20–40 puts you in the "good-to-excellent" category. If the fee is higher, tip about a third of the fee, and remember that at many places the caddie fee does not go 100 percent into the caddie's pocket.

2. He's a person—include him in your conversation. If you're talking sports, ask him what he thinks. Treat him like a valued employee—because that's what he is for you, this day. You want him to want to do his best for you.

3. He's a person—understand if he makes a small mistake. If he tells you to aim two balls left, and it should be two cups left, don't make a big deal of it—it might be a matter of how hard you hit it. If he tells you to aim two cups left and the putt *breaks* to the left, don't make a big deal of it—but don't ask him to read any more putts.

4. Believe him on distances. "One guy, when I told him the shot was 147, walked up to the sprinkler head and paced it back, and told me, 'It's 149,'" one caddie says. "So I told him, 'Okay, then use your 149 club.'"

5. Know your game. If you like to make the choice between three-wood and driver once you're on the tee, tell him at the start of the round; otherwise, he might walk ahead into forecaddying position with the club you want to hit. Most players hit driver on most par fours and fives, even if they shouldn't; let him know you're one of those who knows how to think.

6. Be sensible. If he's caddying a double and your partner's on the other side of the green, it won't kill you to rake a trap. Do *not* grumble that "he oughta be paying me," unless you know you'll be hitting every shot thereafter into a *very* visible position.

CADDIE–PLAYER RELATIONS

How to Be Good to Your Player

1. One read per putt. Look it over, tell him your best judgment with confidence, and stick to it. There's nothing worse for a player than to be standing over the ball and hear, "On second thought, maybe it's a cup outside." Could you make a putt under those circumstances?

2. Find a common language, and be consistent. If you told him on the second green that the putt "breaks two feet to the left," don't tell him on the fourth green to "aim two cups to the left"—the resulting confusion will spread doubt into every read. If the shot is 150 yards, but playing uphill and into the wind, does he want to hear all of that, or does he simply want you to say, "Play it like 175"? Or would he rather just know the distance and then make his own adjustments? Figure this out early, and stick to it.

3. Don't give too much information. The funniest thing we've ever heard from a caddie was on an approach shot at Whistling Straits: "You've got 179 yards to the pin, and the wind is from the left, but will only affect the first two-thirds of the shot." Maybe "Bones" Mackay can get away with saying that to Phil Mickelson, but what's a handicap player supposed to do with the information?

4. Be observant. Know when your player's getting annoyed, and give him some room. And be aware of the rest of the group; if your player starts talking when someone else is about to swing, a raised finger should be enough to keep the peace in the foursome. (Choose the finger wisely.)

5. Be kind. Don't tell the player who's just come up short with his four-iron second shot that you hit driver/eight-iron on Monday.

6. When he hits the green from a good distance, give him his putter. There's nothing more satisfying to a golfer than a long walk down the fairway with a putter in his hand.

7. Accept blame. If a slight push causes a lipout, say that you should have warned him about the subtle break on that three-footer. You want your man in a positive frame of mind, even if it means shouldering some fault that wasn't really yours. He'll know what you're doing, and he'll reward you for it in the end.

TIGER VS. ANNIKA

It is very possible that the greatest male golfer and greatest female golfer in history are both in the primes of their careers right now. As if that's not unusual enough, the two also are friendly with each other, exchanging text messages about their accomplishments in a tournament-based version of "Anything You Can Do, I Can Do Better."

Measures of historical greatness are difficult in golf because we require accomplishment over such a long time before we are willing to pass judgment. Comparing a man and a woman is at least as difficult. No one would expect Annika to have a chance head-to-head with Tiger, but that's irrelevant; the question ultimately is, which of them is more dominant in his or her own sphere?

Here's a look at how they match up in their PGA and LPGA careers, through 2005 (for statistical purposes on facing page, except for "Events Played Before First Win," Tiger's career is deemed to have begun with the Greater Milwaukee Open in 1996, his first tournament as a professional; Annika's begins with the 1994 season, her first year qualifying for the LPGA Tour):

TIGER		ANNIKA
December 30, 1975	Date of Birth	October 9, 1970
18	Events Played Before First Win *Advantage: Tiger*	35
46	Official Wins *Advantage: Annika*	66
10	Professional Majors *Advantage: Tiger*	9
85	Books About *Advantage: Tiger*	3
$55,770,760	Official Career Earnings *Advantage: Y Chromosome*	$18,332,821
A jillion	Career Endorsement Earnings *Advantage: Tiger*	A lot less
10, twice (1997 US–1999 British; 2002 British–2004 PGA)	Most Consecutive Majors Without a Victory *Advantage: Tiger*	17 (1996 DuMaurier– 2000 DuMaurier)
3 (2000)	Most Majors in a Season *Advantage: Tiger*	2 (2003, 2005)
9 (2000)	Most Wins in a Season *Advantage: Annika*	11 (2002)
6 (1999–2003, 2005)	Vardon or Vare Trophies (Lowest Scoring Average) *Advantage: None*	6* (1995–96, 1998, 2001–02, 2005)
7 (1997, 1999–2003, 2005)	Player of the Year Awards *Advantage: Annika*	8 (1995, 1997–98, 2001–05)
.246	Career Winning Percentage *Advantage: Annika*	.266
.450 (2000: 9/20)	Best Winning Percentage, Season *Advantage: Annika*	.500 (2005: 10/20)
.433	Career Top-3 Percentage *Advantage: Annika*	.492
.700 (2000: 14/20)	Best Top-3 Percentage, Season *Advantage: Tiger*	.667 (2004: 12/18)
.647	Career Top-10 Percentage *Advantage: Annika*	.706

*Annika had the lowest scoring average on the LPGA Tour in 2004, but played two rounds too few to qualify for the Vare Trophy.

"Now, Tiger, maybe when you've won as many tournaments as I have, then I'll let you read the putt."

TIGER		ANNIKA
.850 (2000: 17/20)	Best Top-10 Percentage, Season *Advantage: Annika, and she has two other seasons higher than Tiger's best*	.889 (2004: 16/18)
.408	Money-Winning Percentage** *Advantage: Annika*	.454
.630 (2000)	Best Money-Winning Percentage** in a Season *Advantage: Annika, but to be fair, both figures are sensational*	.645 (2002)
2 (1999, 2000)	Most Years with Money-Winning Percentage** above .500 *Advantage: Annika*	4 (2002–05)
61	Lowest Round *Advantage: Annika*	59
8–1	Career Playoff Record *Advantage: Tiger*	13–5
17–20–3	Ryder/Presidents/ Solheim Cup Record *Advantage: Annika*	16–7–2
No	Last Name Necessary? *Advantage: None*	No

**Money-Winning Percentage compares a player's official earnings to the first-place money paid in the tournaments that player entered. For any golfer to have a year in which he wins half the money available to him is extraordinary; for comparison purposes, in 2004 Vijay Singh had a sensational year in which he won nine tournaments including a major, had over $11 million in official earnings, yet his money-winning percentage for the year was just .384.

THE BIGGEST WINNER

The record for most official professional wins is held not by Sam Snead, nor Jack Nicklaus, nor Arnold Palmer, nor any other man. It belongs to Kathrynne Ann Whitworth, who didn't take up the game until she was fifteen years old. Within three years she was winning state amateur championships in New Mexico; two years later she joined the LPGA Tour, and by the time she stopped winning she had set a standard that seemed unapproachable until the twin supernovae of Tiger Woods and Annika Sorenstam came on the scene.

The graph below shows the career win trajectories for Whitworth, Snead, Woods, and Sorenstam, through the 2005 season. (The age assigned to the player for a year's wins is his or her age on July 1 of that year.) Annika is charging hard at Whitworth, while Tiger maintains a solid edge over Snead at comparable ages, and has only just fallen behind Whitworth's pace as he's exited his twenties.

TOUR WINS BY AGE

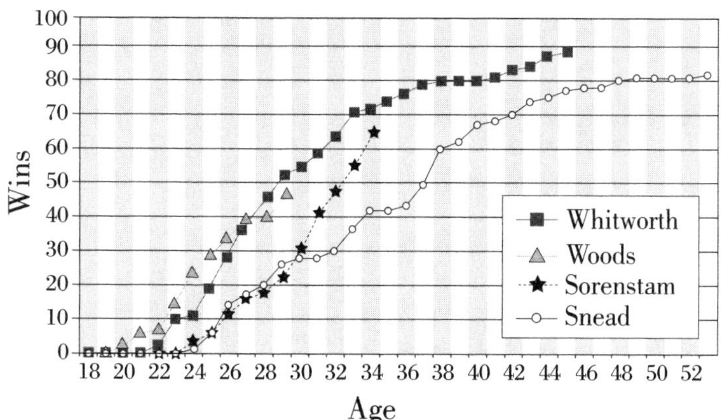

CONTRASTING SWING ADVICE

Newton's Third Law of Motion states that for every action, there's an equal and opposite reaction. The equivalent in golf is that for every swing thought, there's an equal and opposite swing thought. Some examples follow.

Reaching for the Ball

TOM WATSON: You should never feel you're reaching for the ball.

JOHNNY MILLER: Reach for the ball but not so much that your weight is back on your heels.

Pinching the Knees

PETER KOSTIS: Forget all you've heard about pinching your knees together. That's nonsense.

BEN HOGAN: During the golf swing, the knees work toward each other. Since they do, let's start them that way to begin with, each knee pointing in. In my opinion, this is a very valuable shortcut.

The Force that Controls the Swing

DAVID LEADBETTER: Both the direction and the speed of the clubhead are controlled by your torso. Your hands and arms remain passive—think "active body, passive hands."

ERNEST JONES: The body and all its parts should be treated as disastrous leaders but as wholly admirable followers of the action of the hands and fingers. The basic action of the swing is the proper action of the hands and fingers.

Attitude of the Body at Address

BOBBY JONES: The keynote of the address position should be ease, comfort, and relaxation.

BEN HOGAN: Right off the reel, it will help [the golfer] if he realizes that pure relaxation is something he can't attain and shouldn't want to.

Head Games

JACK NICKLAUS: All kinds of golfing evils stem from head movement.

JIMMY BALLARD: The head must move with the spine during the swing if you are to generate any real power.

Grip Strength

HARRY VARDON: The club should be gripped firmly with the thumb and forefinger of the right hand.

BEN HOGAN: Gripping firmly with these two fingers is a swing-wrecker.

The Left Arm

J. H. Taylor (five-time British Open champion): I go so far as to say that if the left arm be kept straight on the way back, it is impossible to get the left wrist into position under the shaft at the top of the swing, and so obtain the necessary freedom of movement.

Gene Sarazen: Without the straight left arm it is well nigh impossible to ever become a consistently good golfer, for there is too much leeway for error.

Weight Shift

Jim McLean: As the backswing starts, there is first a feeling of slight weight shift off the inside of the left instep, with a constant increase of weight shift to the inside of the right foot (toward the right heel) and right leg. I like to see the weight shift occur early as the club head travels away from the target.

Ernest Jones: When I found myself on one leg [Jones's right leg was amputated below the knee after he was wounded in 1915 while serving in the British Army] I didn't have any difficulty playing golf. You swing the club and trust the swing. You hear all this talk about, "Should your weight be on the right leg or the left leg?" When you come to play on one leg you don't worry about transferring your weight from one leg to the other. You swing the club and that maintains you in a state of balance. Balance is simply a state or condition governed by force. If you want to balance a top, you spin it.

Starting the Swing

John Jacobs: Swing your left arm directly back from the ball, allowing it to move progressively upward and backward—i.e., to the inside of the target line—as a natural response to the rotation of your shoulders around the axis of your spine.

Gary Player: I distinctly favor the method of Ben Hogan, who starts back moving hips, arms and shoulders together. This is commonly called the "one-piece swing," and results in a nice wide arc, with the club-head being taken back close to the ground.

Starting the Downswing

Sam Snead: The last two fingers of the left hand pull down on the club handle to start the downswing:

Nick Faldo: My left knee and left shoulder make the first move towards the target, while the right side of my body holds momentarily.

Faldo makes his move.

MOON SHOT

Alan B. Shepard was the first American in space and the fifth to walk on the moon. He commanded the Apollo 14 mission that started on January 31, 1971, and returned to earth on February 9. Lunar module pilot Edgar Mitchell and command module pilot Stuart Roosa accompanied Shepard.

Shepard, then forty-seven, announced en route that he had with him a couple of golf balls and a clubhead from a six-iron. He also had a handle into which was fitted a slot for the clubhead. The handle has been said, variously, to be a converted soil sampler, an implement to collect rocks on the lunar surface, or, according to Mitchell, a tool related to the capsule's thermonuclear generator.

The crew worked for some four hours on February 6, with each minute accounted for according to a set of assigned tasks. When they were finished, Shepard removed a couple of golf balls and the "club" from the cumbersome spacesuit he was wearing. Because his uniform was so heavy, Shepard was able to swing with his right hand only.

Following is an excerpt from Apollo 14's Lunar Surface Journal that records the conversation around the shots:

Shepard (facing the TV camera): Houston, while you're looking that up, you might recognize what I have in my hand as the handle for the contingency sample return; it just so happens to have a genuine six-iron on the bottom of it. In my left hand, I have a little white pellet that's familiar to millions of Americans. I'll drop it down. Unfortunately, the suit is so stiff, I can't do this with two hands, but I'm going to try a little sand-trap shot here. (pause)

Jones (on the ground in Houston): He topped and buried it on the first swing. I assume that the six-iron was snuck on board.

Mitchell (to Jones): In his suit pocket. (to Shepard) You got more dirt than ball that time.

Shepard: Got more dirt than ball. Here we go again.

[Al's second swing pushes the ball about two or three feet, mostly along the line toward the TV camera, rather than along the line of the swing.]

Fred Haise (on the ground in Houston): That looked like a slice to me, Al.

Shepard: Here we go. Straight as a die; one more. (long pause)

[Al's third swing finally connects and sends the ball off-camera to the right, apparently on a fairly low trajectory. He drops a second ball, which rolls left and toward the TV camera. Al gets himself in position and connects again. The trajectory of this shot appears to be similar to the previous one.]

Shepard: Miles and miles and miles.

Haise: Very good, Al.

The ball didn't go miles and miles, however. Shepard later amended his estimate to between two hundred and four hundred yards. Michell, meanwhile, picked up a rod that resembled a window shade after Shepard was finishing hitting golf shots and threw it some fifty feet. Claiming Shepard's longest ball went about the same distance, he referred to their sporting escapades as the "lunar Olympics."

Shepard died in 1998, in Pebble Beach, California. President Bill Clinton said that Shepard "lived every golfer's dream" by hitting a golf ball on the moon and that he'd hit the ball for those "miles and miles," thereby preserving the fiction that Shepard himself had recanted.

RULES YOU OUGHT TO KNOW BETTER

WATER HAZARD VS. LATERAL WATER HAZARD

When you hit your ball into a *water hazard,* which is marked by *yellow* stakes, you have three options:

(1) play the ball as it lies;

(2) play the ball as near as possible to the spot where you hit the shot that went into the water; or

(3) drop a ball behind the water hazard, keeping the spot where the ball last crossed the margin of the hazard directly in line between your drop and the hole.

Options (2) and (3) carry a one-stroke penalty.

When you hit into a *lateral water hazard,* marked by *red* stakes, you have two additional options:

(4) drop a ball within two club-lengths of where it last crossed the margin of the hazard but no closer to the hole; or

(5) drop a ball within two club-lengths (but no closer to the hole) of the opposite margin of the hazard, equidistant from the hole.

These two additional options also cost you a stroke.

Let's say you hit a shot to a green guarded in front by water. The ball hits on the slope past the hazard line but short of the green, and bounces back into the water. Are you allowed to take your drop on the green's side of the hazard or not? The answer depends on the color of the line or stakes. If they're red, it's a lateral hazard, and you may drop within two club-lengths of the point near the green where the ball last crossed the margin. If they're yellow, you must keep the point of entry between you and the hole, and drop on the side of the hazard nearer to the tee.

A PROVISIONAL BALL

If you hit a ball that you think might be out-of-bounds or lost (but *not* in a water hazard), you can—and should—play a provisional ball from where you just played before going to look. Simply declare a provisional to the rest of the group, and then hit the ball in turn (after everyone else if you're on the tee). If you're unable to find the first ball, or if it's out-of-bounds, then you take your provisional as your ball in play, under the appropriate stroke- and-distance penalty.

Why can't you hit a provisional for a ball in a water hazard? Because stroke-and-distance is only one of the possible options, and you're not entitled to know how the shot will work out before deciding whether to hit another or take a drop.

What if your provisional ball winds up well short of where you have to look for your first? Keep playing it, provisionally, until you reach the area of the first ball. If the first one is playable, you are not charged for any strokes taken with the provisional.

What if your provisional might be out of bounds or lost? Play another provisional—and hope that you've used a ball with a different number or markings than your first one. (If the first ball and the provisional might be lost in the same area, and you only find one, it's presumed to be your provisional unless you can prove otherwise.)

Taking a Ball Out of Play

A ball is unfit for play if it's visibly cut, cracked, or out of shape. If you think your ball became damaged in this way during the play of a hole, you're allowed to lift the ball to examine it, so long as you announce your intentions to your fellow golfers. Any of them can check the ball as well, and they must agree that the ball is unfit for play. If it is, you can place another ball on the spot where the original ball lay (you did remember to mark it, didn't you?) and play on without penalty.

A ball is *not* unfit for play because it has mud or any other material stuck to it, or its surface is scratched or scraped for any reason (such as hitting a cart path), or its paint is damaged or discolored.

Grounding a Club in a Hazard

You may not ground your club in a hazard, which includes sand traps as well as water hazards; the penalty is two strokes in stroke play, loss of hole in match play. Scraping the sand in your backswing is considered grounding your club. If you're losing your balance, you may steady yourself with your club without penalty (but if that becomes a habit, your friends might think you're testing the sand). Taking multiple clubs into the hazard and laying the ones you're not going to use on the ground is fine; so is bringing a rake into a bunker with you so you don't waste time walking though the sand to get to it.

Knocking the Ball Off the Tee

Moving a ball in play when you address it violates Rule 18-2(b); you're supposed to replace the ball at a penalty of one stroke. Why is it okay to put a ball back on the tee if you knock it off? Should you charge yourself a stroke? No. A ball on the tee is *not yet* a ball in play. Put it back on the tee, and tell your friends who called out, "That's one!" to read the Rules *and* get a life.

THE BIRTH OF AMEN CORNER

During the final round of the 1958 Masters, Arnold Palmer hit his tee shot on the par-three 12th hole over the green and into an area that had been softened by persistent rain earlier in the week. The ball plugged in the turf, so Palmer felt he could lift and clean the ball and drop it out of its plug mark. However, Arthur Lacey, the official at hand, disagreed and insisted that Palmer play the ball from its original position. Palmer was not pleased and said he would then play two balls, one from the plugged lie and another that he would drop. Lacey said he couldn't do this, either.

Palmer played his first ball and double-bogeyed the hole. He then returned to the spot where his ball had embedded and played another, parring the hole with that ball. He next eagled the par-five 13th after hitting the green with a three-wood from a sidehill lie and holing a downhill putt from eighteen feet. While playing the par-five 15th, Palmer learned from Jonathon Winters, the chairman of the rules committee, that the par with his second ball on 12 would stand. Palmer went on to win the Masters, his first of four victories in the tournament and the first of his seven major championships.

Herbert Warren Wind, then writing on golf for *Sports Illustrated,* realized that the events on the 12th hole had effectively won the tournament for Palmer—his victory was by only a single shot, after all. Wind wanted to come up with a name for what he described as "that far corner of the course where the critical action had taken place—some colorful tag like those that Grantland Rice and his contemporaries loved

Mezz Mezzrow inspired a memorable monicker.

to devise: the Four Horsemen, the Manassa Mauler, the House that Ruth Built, the Georgia Peach, and so on."

Wind was a man of wide-ranging interests, one of which was jazz. He remembered from his college days hearing a song that Chicago clarinetist Milton "Mezz" Mezzrow had recorded, called "Shoutin' in that Amen Corner," the reverse side of a more popular number called "35th and Calumet." Mezzrow doesn't even mention the song in his autobiography, *Really the Blues,* but the title had stuck with Wind. The more he thought about those two words—Amen Corner—the more he believed they suited what had transpired at the Augusta National Golf Club while Palmer was on his way to winning his first Masters.

The piece that Wind wrote for *Sports Illustrated,* "The Fateful Corner," appeared in the issue of April 21, 1958. Wind's opening lines were: "On the afternoon before the start of the recent Masters golf tournament, a wonderfully evocative ceremony took place at the farthest reach of the Augusta National course—down in the Amen Corner where Rae's Creek intersects the 13th fairway near the tee, then parallels the front edge of the green on the short 12th and finally swirls alongside the 11th green." It's interesting that the picture Wind drew was of the holes in reverse order.

The name "Amen Corner" caught on, although most people believe it means the entire 11th, 12th, and 13th holes. Strictly speaking, it's the second half of the 11th hole, the 12th, and the first half of the 13th hole. Said Wind of the 12th, the heart of the corner and the heart of that 1958 Masters, "You hit a good shot, you're fine. But if you hit it in the water, say 'Amen.'"

HOW TO GET ON THE OLD COURSE

Unlike most major championship venues in the United States, the Old Course in St. Andrews, Scotland, is a public golf course. This doesn't mean you can just show up with your clubs and spikes and walk on, but you also don't have to pay through the nose to an exclusive tour operator for the chance to play it. Here are a few ways to get your shot at Hell Bunker, the Road Hole, and the Valley of Sin:

1. Book the year before.
Reservations for the following calendar year are accepted beginning on the first Wednesday in September. You can email reservations@standrews.org.uk, or send a fax to +44 (0) 1334 477036. Prime summer times go quickly, but if you're reasonably flexible you stand an excellent chance of getting your foursome on when you want. (You will be required to book a time on one of the other St. Andrews courses for every Old Course reservation requested, but that's no hardship—some people prefer the New Course to the Old, and the Jubilee is another excellent course that should not be missed.) Keep in mind that advance reservations are not accepted for Saturdays, and the course is closed on Sundays.

2. Book the day before.
A ballot for available tee times is held daily; according to the St. Andrews Links Trust, half of all Old Course times are allotted by this lottery. You and your group (two to four golfers) have to

sign up in person or by phone—call +44 (0) 1334 466666—before 2 P.M. for the next day's times. Results of the lottery are announced by 4 P.M., posted at various sites in St. Andrews and on the Internet at www.linksnet.co.uk/barononline/ballot.aspx.

3. Pay through the nose to an exclusive tour company. The Old Course Experience is a tour company that has an arrangement with the Links Trust; it can offer prime tee times that you may not be able to get otherwise. A two-night package includes prime tee times on the Old and New or Jubilee Courses, local transportation, hotel accommodations, full Scottish breakfast, lunch in the Links Clubhouse (which lies beside the first tee of the New and Jubilee Courses, and is not to be confused with the famous clubhouse of the R&A), a three-course dinner on your first evening, and a souvenir photo and merchandise—all this for £1,205 to £1,325 per person in April, May, and October. (Prime summer months require a three-night package at £1,705 to £1,890, and add a round at Kingsbarns or Carnoustie.) Details are available at www.oldcourse-experience.com.

4. Show up with your clubs and spikes. Singles without reservations can go to the starter's hut and will be entered onto a list to be matched up with a group that has an opening.

A few words of warning: The green fees for high season in 2006 have gone up to £120 ($210 at this writing), no longer the bargain it once was. A round on the New or Jubilee will add £57 ($100) in high season, April 17 to October 15. You can effect a substantial savings—about 50 percent—by playing in low season, November 1 to February 28, but you'll have to play your shots on the Old Course off a mat that you carry with you. (March through mid-April and the second half of October are designated "shoulder season"—the charges are somewhere between high and low, but you won't have to use the mat.) Up-to-date information is available at www.standrews.org.uk/golf/book_golf/green_fees.html. The reservation form asks for the home club and handicap of each golfer in the group, and you may have to show a handicap card to play. Green fees must be paid at the time the reservation is accepted and are nonrefundable.

THE GOLFER'S LIFE LIST

Organize a Tournament

Golf is a solitary pursuit undertaken in good company. Corporate life is a collective undertaking pursued by many bad companies. What could be better than mixing the two?

Whether you're putting together a company outing, or just getting all your golfing friends together, there's nothing like the pleasures and pressures of running a one-day tournament. Every golf course worth playing (and many that aren't) will be happy to help you with the arrangements, providing tee times and carts and food and beverages, setting out "Closest to the Pin" and "Long Drive" signs, and painting the center line for "Straightest Drive." So there's no reason for you to get stressed out, is there?

Except that a week before the outing, five people will drop out, then three will come back in, then two more will bail, and one person will be nowhere to be found on the day of the event. An entire foursome will call the day before and tell you that they were *sure* they had clubs but can't seem to find them—and two of them will be lefties. The CEO will decide to play at the last minute, and he'll want to play with the one person who made you promise he wouldn't have to play with the CEO. The weather will be threatening all day, with occasional rumbles of thunder that drive one foursome (and one foursome only) to head for the clubhouse in the middle of the round. As a result, there will be a forty-minute gap between the next-to-last group and the last. During this interminable wait, the eventual runner-up will have too many beers, and the winner will be long gone by the time you calculate the handicaps, using the methods described on pages 286–287. (If you're using the Callaway system, you'll lose the adjustment sheet; if you're playing a Peoria, your calculator batteries will die.)

Still, it's a day of golf, and you'll have a great time as host, though of course you'll play terribly thanks to all the distractions—and it would be bad form to win your own tournament anyway, right? But as with labor pains, you'll forget about what you went through once the results are in. And the best moment of all will take place the day after: No, not when everybody thanks you for all your efforts, but when the balls you'd ordered with the tournament logo finally arrive.

ONE-LINERS

17. *"After all these years, it's still embarrassing for me to play on the American golf tour. Like the time I asked my caddie for a sand wedge and he came back ten minutes later with a ham on rye."*

—CHI CHI RODRIGUEZ

18. *Tommy Bolt, toward the end of one of his infamous temperamental, high-volume, club-throwing rounds, asked his caddie for a club recommendation for a shot of about 155 yards. His caddie said, "I'd say either a three-iron or a wedge, sir." "A three-iron or a wedge?" asked Bolt. "What kind of stupid choice is that?" "Those are the only two clubs you have left, sir," said the caddie.*

19. *"Listen, mate. I want you to know that I have a horse at home that is better bred and has more brains than you. If you remember that, we will get along fine."*

—EAMON DARCY to Frank McBride, his new caddie

20. *"Mr. Vardon, did you ever see a worse shot?" "No," Vardon answered.*

—BOBBY JONES to Harry Vardon after he fluffed an easy shot

GOLF SCENES IN NON-GOLF MOVIES

In this selective guide, we have excluded movies specifically about golf and golfers (*Tin Cup, Follow the Sun, Pat and Mike*). The list is not exhaustive.

SIDEWAYS (2004): Paul Giamatti takes out some of his rage on a casual round of golf with Thomas Haden-Church.

LOST IN TRANSLATION (2003): Bill Murray hits a drive towards Mt. Fuji in a rare moment of familiarity in the disconcerting world of modern Tokyo.

GOLDFINGER (1964): James Bond defeats Auric Goldfinger in a match filmed at Stoke Park Club at Stoke Poges, north of London in Buckinghamshire. (More memorable than the match is Goldfinger's caddie and henchman, Oddjob, crushing a golf ball in his bare hand.)

M*A*S*H (1970): Donald Sutherland and Elliott Gould hit balls off the helicopter pad, practice putting while being detained by MPs, rampage through a golf club, and perform surgery while wearing plus-fours and spikes.

*M*A*S*H surgeons at work.*

ANIMAL HOUSE (1978): Delta brothers Otter and Boone (Tim Matheson and Peter Riegert) work on their games on a hillside while Niedermeyer (Mark Metcalf) abuses their pledges during ROTC drills; Otter then takes dead aim and drills Niedermeyer's horse in the rear, causing it to bolt and drag its imperious rider.

DIRTY DANCING (1987): Jerry Orbach is practicing six-footers on the putting green and advising his wife ("You're overcorrecting, Marge") when daughter Jennifer Grey comes up to ask him for $250 that she'll use to pay for a friend's abortion. Orbach makes both putts he attempts in the scene, the second one doing a 360 around the lip before dropping.

SPACE JAM (1996): Was there going to be a Michael Jordan movie *without* a golf scene? That would be Looney. Jordan gets pulled down into a hole by the cartoon gang to play some hoops and save Bugs and friends.

THE CONSTANT GARDENER (2005): Ralph Fiennes barges onto a golf course in Kenya to confront an official of the drug company that has been conducting improper testing.

Welcome to Mooseport (2004): Gene Hackman plays a former U.S. president who is used to having unlimited mulligans, frequent gimmes, and Secret Service agents throwing his ball into the fairway from the woods. He and Ray Romano play a golf match in the midst of their race for mayor of a small town.

Swingers (1996): Jon Favreau and Ron Livingston demonstrate dreadful golf etiquette (talking during each other's swings, counting up their strokes while standing at the hole) on the first hole of L.A.'s Los Feliz par-three golf course in Harding Park.

Days of Heaven (1978): Sam Shepard hits a few balls on a rudimentary course with his stepdaughter in Terrence Malick's beautifully filmed drama.

Three-Iron (2004): Kim Ki-Duk directed this Korean film in which a mysterious intruder enters the homes of several people, and the life of one. Golf shots are struck with the title club—occasionally as a means of assault, but mostly into nets and with a ball tethered to a tree, exercises that serve as a metaphor for the purposelessness of human endeavor.

Fahrenheit 9/11 (2004): George W. Bush declares America's resolve to track down and stop international terrorists, then adds, "Now watch this drive," and laces one, presumably down the fairway (and if not, see *Welcome to Mooseport,* above).

Ordinary People (1980): The tensions in the marriage between Mary Tyler Moore and Donald Sutherland simmer away through a mixed foursome afternoon at the golf club.

Sunset Boulevard (1950): Struggling screenwriter Joe Gillis (William Holden) can't get his agent to return his calls, so he confronts the agent in the place where all unfeeling characters spend their time: on a golf course in Bel-Air.

The Best Years of Our Lives (1946): As Dana Andrews, Fredric March, and Harold Russell are returning home from the war, their transport plane flies over a golf course, and they comment about how they can't imagine being able to do anything so normal.

The Philadelphia Story (1940): In the opening scene, Katharine Hepburn throws her husband Cary Grant and his belongings out of the house. The last item she tosses is his golf bag, from which she picks out a club and breaks it over her knee.

Carefree (1938): Fred Astaire does a solo to "Since They Turned 'Loch Lomond' Into Swing" and demonstrates a pretty good swing of his own by hitting a series of drives while he dances and twirls.

MAESTRO GEORGE SPEAKS

Golfers who knew George Knudson well called him the "maestro" because of his ability to control the ball. Knudson, who was born in Winnipeg and moved to Toronto as a young man, won eight PGA Tour events and finished second in the 1969 Masters—without making a putt longer than a few feet until the 16th hole of the last round. He fashioned his game after Ben Hogan's, and it was said of Knudson that in the way he walked and talked and swung the golf club he looked more like Hogan than Hogan himself. He wasn't interested in putting, didn't study it, and, like Hogan, felt the game was about shot making more than about putting. "When I walk around the green waiting my turn to putt," Knudson said, "I feel lost. And then when I stand over the ball, I have to decide what the hell kind of stroke I'll make. I look down at the ball and sometimes I don't even see it. I can't get into it. I'll see cigarette butts, or the shades of green on the grass, but not the ball."

Knudson and Hogan liked to play "call-shot" golf when they were in the same group together during a tournament; each would call his shot before playing it. They were concerned with the quality of the shot as much or more than the result.

Some Knudsonian maxims:

You don't play golf to relax. You relax to play golf.

It's not what you do that matters. It's what you attempt to do.

Never do anything at the expense of balance.

Knudson knew.

Golf is a stationary ball game in which we make a motion towards a target. The ball simply gets in the way of the motion.

You give up control to gain control.

If you start in a good position and you finish in a good position, not much can go wrong in between.

FAMOUS GOLFERS WHO DIED ON GOLF COURSES

Julius Boros

Interestingly, none of them died during a round of golf.

Tony Lema: The thirty-two-year-old pro, winner of the British Open in 1964, died on July 24, 1966, when the small plane in which he was flying crashed onto a golf course, the Lansing (Ill.) Sportsman's Club. He was en route from the PGA Championship in Akron, Ohio, to an exhibition match in the Chicago area—though not, as is occasionally reported, at the same course where the plane crashed.

Julius Boros: Boros, who won three majors (the 1952 and 1963 U.S. Opens and 1968 PGA), died of a heart attack on May 28, 1994, near the 16th hole of Coral Ridge Country Club in Ft. Lauderdale, Florida. He had driven a cart out to the bridge near the 16th hole and was found sitting in the cart under a willow tree. He had been in poor health and was no longer able to play golf, but the spot where he was found was known to be one of his favorite places.

Bing Crosby: Crosby was in Spain to film a television special when he died of a heart attack at La Moraleja club outside Madrid on October 15, 1977. The crooner was on his way to the clubhouse from the 18th green after a round of golf when he suddenly dropped to the ground. His wife, Kathryn, told reporters, "I can't think of a better way for a golfer who sings for a living to finish the round."

THE WORD ON: THE 17TH AT SAWGRASS

By the numbers:

4: Depth in feet of the water that surrounds the island green

6: Number of holes-in-one made during the 24 years of the Players Championship.

12: Score that Bob Tway made in the third round of the 2005 Players, moving him from 10th to 72nd place. He hit four balls in the water.

55: Square footage of the front bunker.

75: Yardage from the drop area to the center of the green.

121: Yardage from championship tee to the front of the green.

138: Number of holes-in-one made by amateurs and professionals since the course opened in 1980.

146: Yardage from middle of back tee to back edge of green.

1,200: Number of boards, each 6 inches by 10 feet, placed around the green for support.

3,912: Square footage of green.

50,000: Amount of dirt in cubic yards removed to make the island green.

150,000: Number of balls hit in the water each year.

"*Standing there, it's all different. The green just shrinks in the tournament. It's got a lot to do with the mind.*"

—VIJAY SINGH

"*You're playing great in the tournament and all of a sudden, in one hole, you might as well be finishing last.*"

—BOB TWAY

"*It's just a hole that scares you. It creates a lot of anxiety when you're on the tee. I actually can feel my heart through my shirt on the hole.*"

—FRED FUNK

"*It's such an easy shot, a nine-iron, eight-iron, big green. It's easy to walk on a one-foot plank one foot above the ground, but 100 feet above the ground it's tough to do."*

—Robert Damron

"In practice it's fine, it's no problem. You pull a club and you hit it, it doesn't seem such a difficult hole. Then you get in the tournament and there are all sorts of things happening before and after. You can cut the tension in the air down there, especially if you're going well. It's a strange hole."

—Padraig Harrington

"It builds all the way and finishes you off with the hardest part of the course. I once stood on the 17th tee with a six-shot lead and I was still worried about getting it across the water. I know if I put one in the drink, I might put 10 in. It's one of those feelings."

—Steve Elkington

"It's like having a three o'clock appointment for a root canal. You're thinking about it all morning and you feel [bad] all day. You kind of know, sooner or later, you've got to get to it."

—Mark Calcavecchia

ONE-LINERS

21. *"Who's going to be second?"*

—Walter Hagen, on many a first tee

22. *"I'm not saying my golf game went bad, but if I grew tomatoes, they'd come up sliced."*

—Lee Trevino

23. *"Golf is not a funeral, though both can be very sad affairs."*

—Bernard Darwin while watching a British Amateur match between Frank Stranahan and R. J. White—both were playing poorly and very slowly

24. *"He hits the ball 130 and his jewelry goes 150."*

—Bob Hope on Sammy Davis Jr.'s golf game

25. *"It does look like a very good exercise. But what is the little white ball for?"*

—Ulysses S. Grant, after watching a beginner swing and miss repeatedly

26. *"The only time he opens his mouth is to change feet."*

—David Feherty on Nick Faldo

LONG, LONGER, LONGEST, LONGESTER

Every year, it seems, a new record is broken for length on the pro tours. Par fours stretch to five hundred yards; par threes creep up toward the three-hundred-yard mark. Augusta National gets longer every year; the courses for the U.S. Open and Open Championship constantly top their previous marks by one or two yards (despite the impossibility of such four-round precision when you consider the placement of tee markers and hole locations). As a result, it is fruitless to try to list the longest championship-level holes or courses; a longer one will crop up as soon as the ink is dry.

The lengthiest nontournament golf course has for many years been the Pines at the International in Bolton, Massachusetts, which plays to an unearthly 8,325 yards from its back, Tiger tees. It was originally designed in 1957 by Geoffrey Cornish, with help from Francis Ouimet among others, but was reworked in 1972 by Robert Trent Jones Sr., who added the length that gives the course its notoriety. The scorecard alone is breathtaking, and the authors fervently hope that if the day arrives when such distances are standard, we will be playing the game with titanium limbs and jet-powered balls.

HOLE	1	2	3	4	5	6	7	8	9	OUT	
Yardage	*405*	*460*	*674*	*180*	*715*	*530*	*277*	*412*	*535*	***4,188***	
Par	4	4	5	3	6	4	3	4	4	**37**	
HOLE	**10**	**11**	**12**	**13**	**14**	**15**	**16**	**17**	**18**	**IN**	**TOTAL**
Yardage	*440*	*590*	*567*	*250*	*437*	*487*	*270*	*440*	*656*	***4,137***	***8,325***
Par	4	5	4	3	4	4	3	4	5	**36**	**73**

At Jade Dragon Snow Mountain, the holes are long but the scenery is spectacular.

A recent contender for the crown is the Jade Dragon Snow Mountain Golf Club in the Chinese province of Yunnan. The course totals 8,548 yards from its Record tees, has four par fours in excess of 500 yards each, no par three shorter than 236 yards, and unlike the International, it calls its 700-yarder a mere par five. However, this length must come with an asterisk, because the site is near the Himalayas, at an elevation of over 10,000 feet, and shots travel nearly 20 percent farther through the thinner air.

In November 2005, the Asian Tour played its Double A International Open at St. Andrews Hill Golf Club in Rayong, Thailand. The course, designed by Desmond Muirhead, has two par sixes, but one of them was converted to a par five for the pros. The remaining par six, the first to be played on any major pro tour, clocked in at an imposing 878 yards. It features a choice of fairways divided by a lake, with the green protruding into the water; pros reported playing it as driver, four-iron, three-wood, wedge.

COMBAT ON THE COURSE

The media in 1991 took to referring to the Ryder Cup held on the Ocean Course in Kiawah Island as the "War by the Shore." *Golf World*'s Gary Van Sickle began his account of the U.S. victory by writing, "We thumped Iraq. We whipped Communism. And now, at last, we put Europe in its place. We're a lean, mean, fighting machine. We're the United States of America. . . . The War by the Shore is over, and we won." But that war was figurative, not literal. Golf courses or sites very near them have in fact been the sites of various battles, duels, and other war-related events. Here are a few.

BATTLEFIELD COURSE, LEGENDS ON THE NIAGARA, ONTARIO

Battle of Chippawa, July 5, 1814

The War of 1812 between American and British troops led to some protracted engagements, but none took longer to resolve than the Battle of Chippawa. The battle, the first of the Niagara campaign, was fought on farmland near the banks of the Niagara River. The fierce battle on open ground lasted into the evening, ultimately costing the lives of two hundred men. The Americans prevailed, but lost a decisive battle on July 25 that marked the end of the war. A memorial cairn on the Battlefield course reminds golfers that a genuine war was waged there, not just a golf war.

WAWASHKAMO GOLF CLUB, MICHIGAN

Battle on Mackinac Island, August 5, 1814

During the War of 1812, American forces tried unsuccessfully to regain Mackinac Island from the British. In 1898, Chicago cottagers built a nine-hole course on the battlefield. Chippawa Chief Eagle Eye observed a group of golfers out on the course and remarked that they "wa-wash-kamo," or "walk a crooked path." *Golf Digest* in 1996 designated Wawashkamo an American Historic Landmark of Golf.

SAN FRANCISCO GOLF CLUB

Duel in the Dell, Sept. 13, 1859

Senator David Broderick and Chief Justice of the Supreme Court of California David Terry were opponents in an election contest for Terry's seat in the summer of 1859. Terry, a pro-slavery Democrat, did not appreciate Broderick's campaign tactics, although his own were not exactly gentle. Terry—a member of the Democratic Party's "Chivalry" wing that wanted to maintain slavery—had portrayed Broderick as being in the pocket of abolitionists.

Broderick was elected chief justice and soon took to calling Terry a "dishonest, miserable wretch of a judge." Terry challenged Broderick to a duel. It took place early in the morning of September 13, 1859, on property that much later became the site of the par-three, 190-yard seventh hole at the ultraexclusive A. W. Tillinghast–designed San Francisco Golf Club. The duelists started back-to-back, then paced ten steps before turning to shoot. Broderick's gun discharged into the ground. Terry shot his opponent in the right shoulder, felling him. He died three days later.

The site is a California Registered Landmark, so noted by two granite markers in a grove of cypress trees on the spot where Broderick and Terry stood to commence their duel. Before dying, Broderick said, "They killed me because I was opposed to the extension of slavery and the corruption of justice." In the face of widespread contempt, Terry left San Francisco. He retired to Stockton and came to a violent end himself: On a train near Stockton on August 14, 1889, he pulled a knife on U.S. Supreme Court Justice Stephen Field, who was having breakfast. The two had served together on the California Supreme Court, and Terry, unhappy with some of Field's decisions, sought to kill him. U.S. Marshal David Neagle, assigned to protect Field, shot Terry to death.

On November 25, 1998, an unidentified private collector purchased at auction in San Francisco the two Belgian .58-caliber pistols with which Broderick and Terry dueled. The set sold for $34,500.

PRINCE'S GOLF CLUB, SANDWICH, ENGLAND

A Princely Landing

Laddie Lucas, a pilot in the Royal Air Force and one of Britain's best amateur golfers, returning to his base during World War II was forced to ditch his plane. The Prince's golf course on England's southwest coast loomed ahead, but Lucas missed his target by a mile, and later said, "I could never hit that first fairway with a driver, I don't know why I thought I could hit it with an airplane."

TURNBERRY, SCOTLAND

Runway Tees

During World Wars I and II, Turnberry's courses on the southwest coast of Scotland were used as military training bases. The fairways became concrete runways, portions of which are still evident today.

Are Kabul Stones Loose Impediments?

The nine-hole Kabul Golf Club was built in 1967, when life was relatively relaxed in this now troubled part of the world. The mood changed after the Soviet Union invaded Afghanistan during the 1980s. The army took up positions near the seventh hole and assumed control of the course, which became a battleground. Local pro Mohammad Afzal Abdul was arrested, allegedly because he was a U.S. spy, and the course was used to store tanks and artillery.

Abdul was freed after the Soviets left. He went to Pakistan and returned just before the Taliban took control of the country in the mid-1990s. The fundamentalist Taliban wanted nothing to do with the game, perceiving it as an egregious example of capitalism. When it was learned that Abdul used to work with foreigners, he was thrown in jail again, where he spent three months.

Golf—as opposed to combat—wasn't seen on the property until after U.S. and Afghan troops defeated the Taliban in 2001. Paul McNeill, an aid worker from North Carolina, who had already helped reclaim golf courses in Rwanda and the Soviet republic of Georgia following wars there, worked with Abdul to do the same at the Kabul Golf Club. McNeill wanted to leave some missile launchers and rusted tanks on the course, "as a testament to history," he told *Time* correspondent Tim McGirk. But Abdul wanted a fresh start and cleared the course of these reminders of war. The course had also been studded with land mines; Abdul bought some sheep from a local nomad and sent them out on the course as a means of clearing the mines. The property for a while became a training ground for demining.

A tournament with some forty golfers was held on November 24, 2004, at the course. The U.S. Central Command, hearing of the tournament, sent Col. James Waurishuk as a goodwill ambassador. Waurishuk, the deputy director of the Central Command, was a USGA member and a twenty-five-year veteran of the military. He didn't play and in fact had to wear his military uniform, including a Kevlar vest. Waurishuk walked the course with the players and participated in the awards presentation following play. "It was just a moving experience," he said. He asked Abdul what would be the one thing he could do to help out. "Grow grass," the pro told him.

By the fall of 2005 the course was still dry but had about sixty members who paid the annual membership fee of $60. They putted on greens that were mixtures of oil and dirt, and more black than green. But at least the Kabul Golf Club was a home for the game again, occupied by golfers, not soldiers.

FOOTNOTES TO HISTORY

Billy Joe Patton, 1954 Masters

"Look, Ma—no bogeys!"

After eleven holes of the final round, Patton, an amateur from Morgantown, North Carolina, led the Masters by a shot. He'd made a hole-in-one on the sixth hole, then birdied the eighth and ninth holes to shoot four-under-par 32 on the front side. Patton, a twenty-eight-year-old lumber salesman, was a big hitter. Writer Charles Price said that his homemade swing "made him look like a drunk at a driving range." The swing was good enough for Patton to win the long-drive contest at the Masters, held on the preceding Wednesday, with a boomer of 338 yards.

Patton had shot 70-74 to lead after two rounds. Smooth-swinging Cary Middlecoff, an analytical sort who was both a dentist and a professional golfer, sniffed, "If this guy wins the Masters, he'll set golf back fifty years." Patton made Middlecoff happy the next day when he shot 75 against Ben Hogan's 69, while Sam Snead shot 70. Hogan was five ahead of Patton while Snead was two shots in front of him.

Following the 32 that Patton shot on the front nine the last round, he was tied with Hogan. And then he was leading the Masters by a shot after eleven holes. He parred the 12th and hit a big drive down the par-five 13th hole. From there he went for the green, but found the creek in front and made a double bogey. He birdied the 14th hole and bogeyed the par-five 15th hole. He shot 39 on the back nine, and his 71 for the round put him a shot out of a playoff with Hogan and Snead. Snead won the playoff with a 70 to Hogan's 71.

Patton went on to play twelve more Masters, finishing eighth in 1958 and 1959. He was invited to become a member at Augusta National and accepted. His hole-in-one the last day remained a vivid memory. "I remember that like it was yesterday," he said fifty years later. "I used a five-iron and it hit the hole on the fly and wedged between the flagstick and the edge of the cup." He added, "Even though I didn't win the tournament, the 1954 Masters changed my life."

INGREDIENTS *of the* MOST POPULAR SANDWICH SOLD *at the* MASTERS

- Pimento cheese—pasteurized processed American Swiss cheese consisting of: American cheese, Swiss cheese (milk, salt, cheese culture, enzymes), water, cream, sodium citrate, salt, sodium phosphate, sorbic acid (as a preservative), lactic acid, pimento
- White bread consisting of: wheat flour, water, high fructose corn syrup; contains 2 percent or less of each of the following: soybean oil, yeast, salt, mono-calcium phosphate, mono- and diglycerides, sodium stearol lactylate, calcium stearoyl-2-lactylate, corn flour, calcium sulphate, calcium propionate (a preservative), enzyme, active soy flour, wheat flour, ammonium sulphate, whey, potassium bromate, azodicarbonate, ferrous sulphate
- Mayonnaise consisting of: soybean oil, water, whole eggs, vinegar, egg yolks, salt, sugar, lemon juice concentrate, natural flavor, calcium disodium EDTA (to protect flavor), paprika

Bread, cheese, mayo. That's what I like about the South!

THE GOLFER'S LIFE LIST

Play Cross-Country

When man first put club to ball, the path to the hole was not lined with bunkers, or trees, or borders of intermediate and secondary rough. Point A was here, point B was there; how you traveled between the two was up to your talent and ingenuity.

That open spirit lives when you put scorecard and architectural intention aside and, late in the day if the course is empty enough, play with your friends from the first tee to, say, the seventh green. You think the best route is dead right off the tee, down the ninth fairway, and the length of the eighth hole. Harry thinks it's better to go down 1, over the culvert toward 6, and up from there. There are as many possible paths as there are imaginative golfers; take your best guess, and count 'em up on the distant green. Low score picks the next target. If you're not laughing out loud by the time you hole out, you're doing something wrong.

The mother of all cross-country games was described by Dan Jenkins in his classic story "The Glory Game at Goat Hills." It ran from the first tee at Worth Hills in Fort Worth ("Goat Hills" was its nickname) to the third green at Colonial Country Club, roughly fifteen blocks away. The authors of this volume wish to state clearly that they do not sanction the use of public roads as golfing thoroughfares, regardless of how light the traffic might be at the time of teeing off.

MOST FAMOUS SHOTS, BY CLUB

DRIVER: Arnold Palmer, 1960 U.S. Open, Cherry Hills. Trailing by seven shots at the start of the fourth round, Palmer drove the green on the 346-yard first hole and two-putted for a birdie. This bold start set him on his way to a 65 that gave him his only U.S. Open title and cemented his reputation for final-round charges.

HONORABLE MENTION: Annika Sorenstam, 2003 Colonial Invitational. Just by hitting the fairway (and mock-quaking afterwards with relief), Sorenstam got one of the most scrutinized rounds in PGA Tour history off to a good start.

THREE-WOOD: Bob Gilder, 1982 Westchester Classic, Westchester CC. Playing the par-five 18th hole during the third round, Gilder holed his three-wood second shot from 251 yards for one of the few double eagles ever shown on live TV. The shot gave him a six-stroke lead, and he cruised to victory on Sunday. His 261 total is still the tournament record.

When David Toms made his ace at the PGA, did he have to buy drinks for the field?

FOUR-WOOD: Gene Sarazen, 1935 Masters. By holing out his second shot on the par-five 15th, Sarazen made up three strokes on the leader Craig Wood. In only the second Masters, Augusta National was already becoming known as a place where exciting things could happen down the stretch.

HONORABLE MENTION: Corey Pavin, 1995 U.S. Open, Shinnecock Hills. Pavin held a one-stroke lead over Greg Norman as he played the 18th. A famously short hitter, Pavin had 228 yards to the green on the 450-yard hole. His four-wood shot bounced up and finished five feet above the hole, as he sprinted thirty yards up the fairway to get a better look. His two putts, combined with Norman's subsequent bogey on 17, gave Pavin a two-stroke winning margin.

FIVE-WOOD: David Toms, 2001 PGA, Atlanta Athletic Club. Toms aced the 243-yard 15th hole in the third round of the PGA, an eagle that gave him the lead on the way to his first major championship.

Hybrid: Todd Hamilton, 2004 British Open, Royal Troon. Most golfers use their hybrid clubs to replace harder-to-hit long irons, but the shot that won the British Open for Hamilton was a running chip from thirty yards short of the green. Hamilton put the ball three feet from the hole and made the putt to seal his playoff win over Ernie Els.

One-Iron: Jack Nicklaus, 1972 U.S. Open, Pebble Beach. On the 17th hole of the final round, hitting into the wind, Nicklaus laced a one-iron that struck the flagstick and wound up just inches from the hole. The birdie clinched his victory and kept his Grand Slam hopes alive.

Honorable mention: Ben Hogan, 1950 U.S. Open, Merion Golf Club. The approach shot to the 18th green, captured by Hy Peskin's famous photograph, led to a final par and put Hogan in the Open playoff just a year after his near-fatal auto accident.

Two-Iron: Mark Calcavecchia, 1991 Ryder Cup, Ocean Course at Kiawah Island. One of the worst pressure shots ever hit. Needing only a half on the hole to win the match—and with Colin Montgomerie already having put his shot in the water—Calcavecchia's cold top-smother on the par-three 17th went into the hazard a good hundred yards short of the green. Unable to get up-and-down (or up-and-up-and-down) from the drop zone, he wound up earning just half a point for a match he led by four with four to play.

Honorable mention: Christy O'Connor, 1989 Ryder Cup, the Belfry. Deadlocked with Fred Couples on the 18th hole, O'Connor's drive left him with 240 yards to the flag, while Couples was just a nine-iron away. His two-iron wound up four feet from the hole, and the birdie gave him a 1-up victory, crucial in the 14–14 tie that let Europe retain the Cup.

Three-iron: Jack Nicholson, 1994, Los Angeles. The Academy Award–winning actor allegedly used a three-iron to retaliate against a driver who had allegedly cut him off on the road. Nicholson allegedly smashed the car's windshield and battered its roof. The parties reached a civil settlement, and charges were dismissed. There was no testimony as to why he allegedly selected a whippy club like a three-iron, rather than a heavy-headed club like a sand wedge.

Honorable Mention: Bob Goalby, 1968 Masters. In the final round Goalby played the 13th, 14th, and 15th holes in four under par, an electrifying stretch capped by his three-iron second shot to eight feet on the par-five 15th. The eagle gave Goalby a one-shot lead, until Roberto de Vicenzo birdied the 17th—the birdie that was recorded as a par on his ill-fated scorecard.

OTHER MENTION: Phil Mickelson, 2006 U.S. Open, Winged Foot. From a trampled lie in the rough, Mickelson tried to carve a three-iron around a tree and reach the 72nd green. The shot hit the tree instead and rebounded towards him, the key blow in his double-bogey collapse.

FOUR-IRON: Seve Ballesteros, 1986 Masters. Seve would prefer not to be known for hitting the most famous shot with this club, but he's the pick. Ballesteros had a one-stroke lead over Jack Nicklaus, who was charging in the group ahead, as he played the par-five 15th. Ballesteros was two hundred yards from the green in the middle of the fairway, and he took out a four-iron and eased up on his swing; the shot found the water in front of the green. He said later he should have hit a hard five-iron rather than smoothing the four-iron. Nicklaus went on to win the Masters; Ballesteros says he didn't put this bad shot behind him until he won the 1988 British Open.

FIVE-IRON: Jerry Pate, 1976 U.S. Open, Atlanta Athletic Club. Leading by one shot on the final hole, Pate drove into the right rough, but with his ball sitting up atop the grass he played a 190-yard five-iron over the water to two feet. A plaque marks the spot from which Pate hit his shot.

SIX-IRON: Alan Shepard, 1971, Fra Mauro GC. Imperfect contact may have prevented a true test of the carry characteristics of lunar gravity, but Shepard's clandestine effort remains, as far as we know, the only golf shot in which there was no risk of hitting the Earth first.

HONORABLE MENTION: Craig Parry, 2004 Ford Championship at Doral. Parry holed a 176-yard approach shot in sudden death for an eagle, defeating Scott Verplank on the first playoff hole.

SEVEN-IRON: Shaun Micheel, 2003 PGA, Oak Hill CC. On the 72nd hole, with a one-shot lead, Micheel drove into the short left rough, leaving him 174 yards to the pin. His seven-iron second shot bounced twice on the green and then rolled to a stop two inches from the hole. The birdie gave him a two-shot win over Chad Campbell.

HONORABLE MENTION: Robert Gamez, 1990 Nestle Invitational, Bay Hill. Not all of Greg Norman's disappointments came in majors; he was in the clubhouse with a one-shot lead when Tour rookie Gamez holed out from the 18th fairway for an eagle and the win.

EIGHT-IRON: Sam Snead, 1939 U.S. Open, Philadelphia CC (Spring Mill): Snead's disastrous play on the final hole of the Open began with a drive into the rough and an ill-considered three-wood from a trampled lie. But the shot that undid him was his third, played from a buried lie in a bunker a good hundred yards from the green. Sammy slammed this effort into the collar, from which he could only hit out into another bunker before pitching onto the green and three-putting. Had he known he only needed bogey to make the playoff, he'd have pitched out from that first bunker, needing only to pitch on and two-putt for his six.

NINE-IRON: Gary Player, 1972 PGA, Oakland Hills CC. Player had just bogeyed the 14th and 15th holes in the final round, falling back into a tie with Jim Jamieson, when he sliced his tee shot wildly right on the dogleg-right 16th into grass trampled down by the gallery. He had to stand on a chair to see the flagstick, then lofted a nine-iron over trees and past the pond that guards the green, to within four feet. The birdie putt, followed by two pars, gave him the win.

PITCHING WEDGE: Nick Faldo, 1995 Ryder Cup, Oak Hill CC. Faldo was one-down to Curtis Strange after sixteen holes of their singles match, but a combination of his solid shots and some Strange mistakes found them even as they played the 18th hole. Faldo drove deep into the rough and had to lay up to ninety-three yards from the hole. Strange, from the fairway, left his approach shot in the rough just short of the green. Faldo hit his pitching wedge to three and a half feet, and made his par putt after Strange missed his from ten feet. The one-up victory was vital as Europe went on to win 14½–13½.

SAND WEDGE: Tom Watson, 1982 U.S. Open, Pebble Beach. Watson and Nicklaus were tied for the lead when Watson hit his two-iron into the rough left of the green, just eighteen feet from the hole. His caddie, Bruce Edwards, told him to hit it close. Watson replied, "Get it close, hell—I'm going to make it." He popped it into the air, and it ran to the flagstick and down into the hole. Watson then birdied 18 for a two-shot victory.

HONORABLE MENTION: Larry Mize, 1987 Masters. On the second hole of sudden death, Greg Norman lay comfortably on the green, while Mize pushed his second shot wide right of the green. He took a sand wedge from 140 feet, bounced the ball up the bank to the green, and watched it run and run directly into the hole.

HONORABLE MENTION: Birdie Kim, 2005 U.S. Women's Open, Cherry Hills. With coleader Morgan Pressel watching from the fairway below, Kim blasted out of the right greenside bunker and saw her ball steam across the green until it found the center of the cup. Kim noted later that she's generally not a good bunker player, and that her club was a relatively new one that was "not yet used to me."

Lob wedge: Phil Mickelson, 2005 PGA, Baltusrol. Tied for the lead on the par-five 72nd hole, Mickelson put his second shot beside the green in ankle-deep rough. His lob-wedge shot landed ten feet from the hole and rolled to about three feet as Mickelson thrust his arms into the air in triumph. The putt gave him his second major win.

Putter: Bernhard Langer, 1991 Ryder Cup, Kiawah. Possibly the most pressure-packed golf shot in history. Final match, final green, opponent's putt conceded for bogey, two teams watching tensely, six feet for a par that would mean a second consecutive 14–14 tie and keep the Cup in European hands. Langer's putt slid by the hole, and he threw his head back in anguish. (This miss might have devastated a lesser man; a week later, Langer rolled in a fifteen-foot putt to win the German Masters in a playoff.)

Honorable mention: Bobby Jones, 1929 U.S. Open, Winged Foot. Jones faced a twelve-foot putt for par (with at least a foot of break) on the final hole to tie Al Espinosa for the Open lead. He made it, and crushed Espinosa by twenty-three strokes in the thirty-six-hole playoff the next day. (In 1954, to celebrate the 25th anniversary of this putt, four golfers who had played in the 1929 Open—Tommy Armour, Craig Wood, Gene Sarazen, and Johnny Farrell—attempted a putt from the same location; nobody came close.)

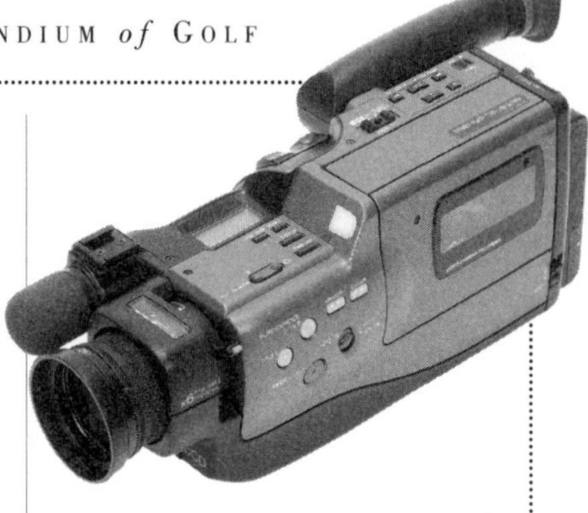

Television camera: Tiger Woods's ball, 2005 Masters. Tiger's remarkable birdie chip-in on the par-three 16th of the final round—up the slope, then slowly down and curling to the cup—was made all the more memorable by the televised close-up that lingered on the ball and its logo as it shuddered on the edge of the hole before finally dropping.

Honorable mention: Lew Worsham's wedge shot, 1953 Tam O'Shanter World Championship, Tam O'Shanter CC. The first nationally televised golf tournament in the United States utilized just one camera, mounted on the grandstand behind the 18th green, to capture one hour of action. That camera was rolling when Lew Worsham hit the winning shot, a 121-yard wedge that landed on the front of the green, ran fifty or sixty feet, and fell in the hole for an eagle. (Jimmy Demaret, on the radio broadcast, exclaimed, "The sonofabitch went in!") This experiment in TV coverage was deemed a success, and the next year saw the first telecast of the U.S. Open.

ROYAL, AND ANCIENT

The first written reference to golf is in a royal proclamation by James II of Scotland, in 1457: "Ye fut bawe and ye golf be uterly cryt done and not usyt." He was concerned that his soldiers were playing football and golf instead of sharpening their archery skills. This condemnation of the game did not stamp it out, however, and his grandson, James IV, felt compelled to issue his own order in 1491: "In na place of the realme be usit fut bawis, gouff or uthir sic unproffitable sports."

James IV (aka James I of England), First Gouffer.

A dozen years later, however, this same James IV ordered a set of clubs from a bowmaker in Perth, and a year after that he engaged in the first golf match of which there is a record, against the Earl of Bothwell. What changed his mind?

In 1502, James IV became engaged to Princess Margaret Tudor of England, whose brother would become Henry VIII. In this period of relative peace between the armies of Scotland and England, it may no longer have seemed essential that soldiers practice more martial arts, or that craftsmen apply themselves solely to weapons. Or maybe James just needed a way to get out of the castle once in a while.

FLYING BLIND

Blind holes, charming though they often are, tend to produce a special kind of tension. Driving over the white rock in the sandhills at Royal County Down in Newcastle, Northern Ireland, and then scampering to the other side; hitting over a marker in the hill to the green that's squeezed between dunes on the par-three fifth hole, the famous Dell, at the Lahinch Golf Club near Limerick; playing one blind hole after another at the twelve-hole Shiskine Golf Club on the Isle of Arran Golf Club in Scotland; lofting one's approach high over the hill that intervenes between fairway and green on the fifth hole at the Devil's Paintbrush course in Caledon, Ontario; hitting across the ridge sixty yards short of the sixth green at Sand Hills Golf Club in Mullen, Nebraska, toward the hole cut in the left front half of the green: On these holes the golfer feels a mixture of anxiety and anticipation and hope as his ball flies into the unknown and unseen. Then, walking forward, and reaching the other side of the intervening hill, dune, or other obstacle, the golfer, pent up, spots the ball. It's on the fairway, or in the rough, or it's close to the hole, or just through, or it caught a slope and rolled into a bunker.

Among modern architects, Pete Dye and Tom Doak in particular have not been afraid to build blind holes. The short par-four 12th hole at Dye's Tournament Players Club in Ponte Vedra Beach, Florida, is a useful illustration. The approach shot to a back left hole location becomes blind to the golfer who has hit his tee shot too far to the left side of the fairway or into the rough there. The penalty is that he won't be able to see the hole. The more Dye can induce confusion in a player's mind, the more he feels he's built holes that offer a substantial test.

Doak, who worked closely with Dye when he was learning his craft, is aware of the safety issues a blind hole can create; still, he's written, "I think the rare blind shot adds interest to the course, because it adds variety and because so many players are uncomfortable with it."

Doak included what he called his All-Blind Eighteen in his book *The Confidential Guide to Golf Courses.* Here is the list.

HOLE	PAR	COURSE
1	4	Elie, Scotland
2	4	National Golf Links of America, Southampton, New York
3	4	Yale Golf Club, New Haven, Connecticut
4	4	Royal Melbourne (West), Victoria, Australia
5	4	Long Cove, Hilton Head Island, South Carolina
6	3	Lahinch, Ireland
7	5	Ekwanok, Manchester, Vermont
8	4	Pebble Beach Golf Links, Pebble Beach, California
9	4	Royal County Down, Newcastle, Northern Ireland
10	4	Shinnecock Hills, Southampton, New York
11	4	Sunningdale (Old), London, England
12	4	Old Course, St. Andrews, Scotland
13	4	Rye, England
14	5	Carnoustie, Scotland
15	4	Prestwick, Scotland
16	5	Roaring Gap CC, Roaring Gap, North Carolina
17	4	Prestwick, Scotland
18	4	Riviera CC, Pacific Palisades, CA

Notes on some of Doak's choices:

1. Elie. The starting hole is unusual, to say the least: A thirty-foot hill stands just fifty yards from the tee. It appears to be a wall in the golfer's face. The starter has to look from his shed through a periscope taken from a World War II submarine to be sure the way is clear.

7. Ekwanok. The Australian Walter Travis won the 1900 and 1901 U.S. Amateurs, and started *American Golfer* magazine, a first-rate publication. He also designed courses. Ekwanok was his first course in the United States, and later he did the Garden City Golf Club on Long Island, New York. Here, the golfer finds a hill that's 60 yards across, and directly in line on the 595-yard hole. There's no getting around it. The only way is over.

9. Royal County Down. Old Tom Morris was partial to blind shots, or, to put it another way, he didn't mind them when the terrain suggested them. This is one of five blind tee shots on the famous course in Northern Ireland.

10. Shinnecock Hills. This par four troubled the competitors during the 2004 U.S. Open. The tee shot and the second shot, if it's from the valley, are blind. Very few players chose to lay up to the upper part of the fairway, from where they would have a clear view of the green. Most players drove into the valley. The greens were absurdly firm during the championship, and many players couldn't hold this green even with a short iron.

12. Old Course. Doak chooses this short par four because the bunkers aren't visible from the tee. The flag on the green is visible, but as on the entire Old Course, the mission statement is to stay out of the bunkers.

13. Rye Golf Club. Here the second shot on the par four must carry over a craggy dunescape. There's a white fencepost as an aiming point, and nothing but sky beyond. Anybody but a long hitter will be using a mid to long iron on this Alps hole, which only makes the shot that much more onerous.

18. Riviera Golf Club. The tee shot here must carry the hill to a blind fairway. The famed clubhouse high on another elevation behind the green is visible, but not the fairway. The tee shot is made even more daunting by the fact that, following the first hole that plunges from the tee in front of the clubhouse, the rest of the course until the 18th is all but flat. Suddenly the golfer has to hit a mighty, uphill, blind shot. Architect George Thomas confounded the player in many ways, this being one of the most drastic.

THE MOST AMAZING SWING

Purists can debate whether Steve Elkington, Sam Snead, or Mickey Wright had the prettiest swing ever seen, and golf magazines and cable channels can search for the world's ugliest, but the most incredible swing ever seen was reported by Greg Miles of the magazine *Golf Chicago!* Playing with a stranger at Countryside Golf Club in Mundelein, Illinois, Miles noticed that his playing partner appeared to be recovering from some kind of injury. The man explained that he had damaged both of his shoulders and that he could not pull his left arm back past his right side, nor could he swing through with his right arm past his left side. Generating a full swing required him to address the ball with both hands on the club, take the club back with his right arm to the top of his backswing, bring the club down, and at some point evidently transfer the club, because the follow-through was accomplished *with his left arm only.*

Miles is careful to wait until a round is over before describing this swing to his subsequent playing partners; it will ruin someone's game faster than "Do you inhale or exhale on your backswing?" And for anyone interested in trying this remarkable technique, he offers this final observation: "I have absolutely no idea whether, at impact, he had one or two hands on the club—*or none.*"

Mickey Wright, whose swing we understand.

EIGHTEEN FACTS ABOUT THE FIRST MASTERS, IN 1934

1. A Calcutta (a type of gambling auction in which players are sold, with the proceeds going to the tournament's top finishers—not unlike today's fantasy leagues, except the players often participated) was held in the ballroom at the Bon Air Vanderbilt Hotel the night before the first round. Prohibition was repealed at the end of 1933, which helped make for an enjoyable evening for the guests. (Masters Calcuttas were held at Augusta National until 1952.)

2. The first round of the first Masters was held not in April, but on March 22. The thinking was that sportswriters who had been to spring training with the baseball teams would be heading north and that they would happily stop in to cover the tournament.

3. The first starting time was scheduled for 10 A.M., but the leadoff twosome of Ralph Stonehouse and Jim Foulis Jr. started fifteen minutes ahead of time. Stonehouse hit the first ball off the first tee in this first Masters, down the fairway. He hit the green with a five-iron and made par.

4. Stonehouse had won the Miami Open to start the tour that year. He was twenty-nine years old, the pro at the Coffin Golf Club in Indianapolis, and he had a first-class short game. The sportswriter Grantland Rice put it this way: "This Ralph Stonehouse fellow thinks about getting down in two any time he's within 150 yards."

5. The 1st hole then is the 10th hole now. The nines were switched after this Masters, because the club had noticed that today's front nine warmed up first on frosty mornings.

6. The 1st (now 10th) green was located just past and to the right of the amoebalike bunker that still sits in the middle of the fairway. The green was moved to its present place in 1937.

7. This first Masters was one of the first seventy-two-hole tournaments to schedule single rounds over four days. Most every other tournament had a thirty-six-hole final day.

8. The official program for the tournament ran forty-four pages, including a hole-by-hole description by course co-designer Alister Mackenzie. It cost twenty-five cents and contained much advertising, since space was provided to the club's creditors in lieu of payment.

9. Alister Mackenzie was not on hand to watch the tournament. He had died two and a half months earlier.

10. After opening with a two-over-par 74, Stonehouse shot 70 to lie two shots out of the lead after thirty-six holes. But he shot 75 on a cold, wet Saturday, and 76 in worse weather in the last round. He finished sixteenth, a shot behind Bobby Jones and Walter Hagen.

11. C. Ross (Sandy) Somerville, the six-time Canadian Amateur champion who had won the 1932 U.S. Amateur, made the first hole-in-one in the Masters, on the 7th hole (now the 16th, but a completely different hole before Robert Trent Jones redesigned it in 1947).

12. Bobby Jones and Walter Hagen were paired together in the third round, not because of their scores. (Players were not routinely grouped by their standing until decades later.) Tournament officials knew that ticket holders would want to follow this twosome, so they left an open tee time ahead of and behind the players, allowing ample room for the crowd.

13. Ticket sales for the week added up to $8,011, which didn't cover the expenses of conducting the tournament. A full week's ticket cost $5.50.

14. The official name of what would become the Masters in its sixth year was the Augusta National Invitation Tournament. Most players called it "Bobby Jones's tournament," but some writers were already calling it the "Masters' tournament."

15. There were only three rounds in the 60s, none of them by the winner, Horton Smith. Scores of 69 were recorded by Ed Dudley in the second round, runner-up Craig Wood in the third round, and Harold (Jug) McSpaden in the fourth.

16. The tournament paid the top twelve finishers, with prize money running from $1,500 to $100, and had to pass the hat among the membership to cover the expense.

17. Not all invitees made the trip to Augusta. Olin Dutra, the 1932 PGA champion who went on to win the 1934 U.S. Open, felt he could not take the time away from his duties at Brentwood Country Club in Los Angeles. Gene Sarazen couldn't play because of a prior commitment to play an exhibition in South America with Joe Kirkwood; they had to leave a week before the tournament. Sarazen was disappointed that he couldn't play, but promised he would the next year. He did play and, of course, he won.

18. The most important measure to the club of the tournament's success is that it induced eighteen to twenty attendees to join Augusta National, increasing the membership's size by approximately 25 percent. Patrons today are not generally afforded the same opportunity.

FAMOUS COLLAPSES IN MAJORS

Patty Sheehan, 1990 U.S. Women's Open, Atlanta Athletic Club, Riverside Course

Patty Sheehan, as things got away from her.

Poor weather meant that players had to contend with a thirty-six-hole Sunday. Sheehan, who had finished second in the 1988 Open and tied for seventeenth in 1989 after being coleader going into the last round, had shot a record 66–68 to reach 10 under par after two rounds. She held a nine-shot lead halfway through the third round.

But Sheehan started making mistakes, perhaps because she was tired and perhaps because she was in the lead at the Women's Open. She'd won two LPGA Championships, but this was the tournament she most wanted. Sheehan hit a fat four-iron into the lake in front of the 18th green in her morning round and finished with a double bogey and a 75, the first time in twenty-seven rounds she hadn't shot par or better.

Still, Sheehan held a four-shot lead over Mary Murphy and five over Betsy King, the defending champion. She had only thirty-five minutes between her third and fourth rounds, hit just fifteen practice shots, and was on the tee. A bogey on the second against King's birdies on the third and fourth holes meant that Sheehan's lead was down to two shots. Her game was unraveling and so was her once-commanding lead. Tied for the lead, she missed the 17th green by thirty yards and bogeyed the hole. King was in at four-under-par 284, and Sheehan needed to birdie the last hole to tie. She didn't, and King had successfully defended her championship. Sheehan's 76 hurt, so much so that she broke down in tears during a post-round interview.

"It hurts to know that all I had to do was play my game and I would have won," Sheehan said. She added, "I know I'm going to win the U.S. Open some day." Two years later, she did.

THE WORD ON

Golf Architecture

"*The trick for the developer, as devised through his architect, is to build something that is photogenically stunning, however impractical, extravagant, or absurd. Never mind the golfer, that most gullible of all citizens.*"

—PETER THOMSON

"*I want to build a course my mom can enjoy.*"

—DAVIS LOVE III

"*A good golf course is like good music. It does not necessarily appeal the first time one plays it.*"

—ALISTER MACKENZIE

"*Courses built for 300-yard tee-shot artists are not great courses.*"

—PETER THOMSON

"*The chief object of every golf architect or greenkeeper worth his salt is to imitate the beauties of nature so closely as to make his work indistinguishable from nature itself.*"

—ALISTER MACKENZIE

"*The best architects feel it to be their duty to make the path to the hole as free as possible from annoying difficulties for the less skillful golfers, while at the same time presenting to the scratch players a route calling for the best shots at their command.*"

—ROBERT HUNTER

"*The course [Crooked Stick] is so long I had to take the curvature of the Earth into consideration.*"

—DAVID FEHERTY

MEN'S MAJOR CHAMPIONSHIP COURSES *in* *the* UNITED STATES THAT ARE OPEN TO THE PUBLIC

Pete Dye created Ireland-on-Lake-Michigan, Whistling Straits (12th hole shown here), from a flat piece of property and a lot of imagination. And money.

Bethpage State Park (Black)
Farmingdale, NY
(2002 U.S. Open)

French Lick Springs Resort
(Hill), French Lick, IN
(1924 PGA)

Hershey Golf Club (West)
Hershey, PA
(1940 PGA)

Keller Golf Course
St. Paul, MN
(1932 and 1954 PGAs)

Kemper Lakes Golf Club
Hawthorn Woods, IL
(1989 PGA)

Pebble Beach Golf Links
Pebble Beach, CA
(1972, 1982, 1992, 2000
U.S. Opens; 1977 PGA)

Pecan Valley Golf Club
San Antonio, TX
(1968 PGA)

PGA National (Champion)
Palm Beach Gardens, FL
(1987 PGA)

Pinehurst No. 2
Pinehurst, NC
(1936 PGA; 1999 and
2005 U.S. Opens)

Seaview Marriott Resort & Spa
Absecon, NJ
(1942 PGA)

Tanglewood Park
(Championship)
Clemmons, NC
(1974 PGA)

Whistling Straits (Straits)
Kohler, WI
(2004 PGA)

GREAT CAREER AMATEURS

Michael Bonallack, b. Chigwell, England, 1931

Bonallack won the 1961, 1965, 1969, and 1970 British Amateurs. He was six-down to Clive Clark after twelve holes of their morning round during the 1965 championship and three-down when they went to lunch. Bonallack whiled away a few moments by donating some coins to a betting machine, and suddenly he pulled the jackpot. He figured things were turning his way and overcame Clark in the afternoon. Bonallack's most dominating victory was in 1970 at Royal County Down in Northern Ireland, when he was one-down to American Bill Hyndman after the morning round in their final match, but won 8 & 7.

Bonallack played on nine Walker Cup teams. He won five English Amateur championships at match-play and four at stroke-play. He became an R&A member in 1960 and was working for a property developer when somebody suggested he apply for the job of secretary. Keith Mackenzie had just retired. Bonallack applied, got the job in 1983, and was secretary for sixteen years. Upon his retirement he was made R&A captain. Queen Elizabeth II later knighted him.

NUMBER OF ENTRIES INTO THE U.S. OPEN, AT TEN-YEAR INTERVALS

To enter U.S. Open qualifying today, you must have a USGA handicap index of 1.4 or lower, and pay a $150 entry fee. Five hundred and fifty players advance from local to sectional qualifying. There are 156 spots in the U.S. Open field, of which more than half go to players exempt from qualifying by virtue of various accomplishments on the pro Tour. The last player to win the Open after playing in local and sectional qualifying was Orville Moody in 1969.

Orville Moody, a fully qualified U.S. Open champion.

1895...... 11

1905...... 83

1915...... 141

1925...... 445

1935...... 1,125

1945...... no tournament, World War II

1955...... 1,522

1965...... 2,271

1975...... 4,214

1985...... 5,274

1995...... 6,001

2005...... 9,048, including 535 on the last day, April 27, and 75 in the last hour

NUMBER OF ENTRIES INTO THE U.S. WOMEN'S OPEN, AT TEN-YEAR INTERVALS

Entrants must have a USGA handicap index of 4.4 or lower and pay a $150 fee. Four hundred golfers advance to sectional qualifying, and as with the men's championship, the final field is 156, with at least half of it exempt from qualifying by virtue of their achievements on the pro Tour.

1955. 49
1965. 84
1975. 175
1985. 626
1995. 826
2005. . . . . . 1,158, including ten-year-old Alexis Thompson of Coral Springs, Florida

Young Tom Morris

HOLES-IN-ONE WHILE WINNING A MAJOR

CENTURY	PLAYER	TOURNAMENT	HOLE
19th	Young Tom Morris	1869 Open Championship	Prestwick, 8th
19th	Jamie Anderson	1878 Open Championship	Prestwick, 17th
20th	Jock Hutchison	1921 Open Championship	St. Andrews, 8th
21st	David Toms	2001 PGA Championship	Atlanta AC, 15th

THE GOLFER'S LIFE LIST

Play Pasture Golf

Who needs Augusta National Golf Club and Seminole Golf Club and Oakmont Country Club and the golf cart–ridden, overwatered, overmanicured, over-fertilized, absurdly expensive courses that get all the ink? Rough-and-tumble golf can be the real adventure. Check it out at www.pasturegolf.com.

You'll find the old way of playing. You'll find golf in a field, just whacking a ball around from here to there, hither and yon. Be a golfing rebel. Grab your clubs and a few balls and find a meadow. Bang the ball around during a quiet time in your local park, even for five minutes. Hit toward a tree, a garbage can. The idea is so simple, just to swing, swing, swing. It's golf the way it was hundreds of years ago when some folks got the idea that it's fun to hit a ball toward a target. The rougher the ground, the better.

For a serious look at pasture golf, read Scotsman David Ewen's book *Par 10,000: A Golfing Odyssey Across Mountains, Moors and Fields*. Ewen was ten years old when he played front-garden golf. (By the way, three-time major champion Nick Price learned the rudiments of the game by playing what he called "golf in the garden" at his home in Harare, Zimbabwe.) Ewen enjoyed his garden golf, and much later, as he writes, "I found myself on the edge of the North Sea with my driver drawn and nothing to aim at but Scotland. The plan: to skelp a ball across the birthplace of the game, this time negotiating roads, towns, fields, rivers and mountains."

He did it, too. He skelped. He golfed. He played pasture golf all across Scotland. Why don't you try it, wherever you are?

TEN MOST MEMORABLE LINES *from CADDYSHACK*

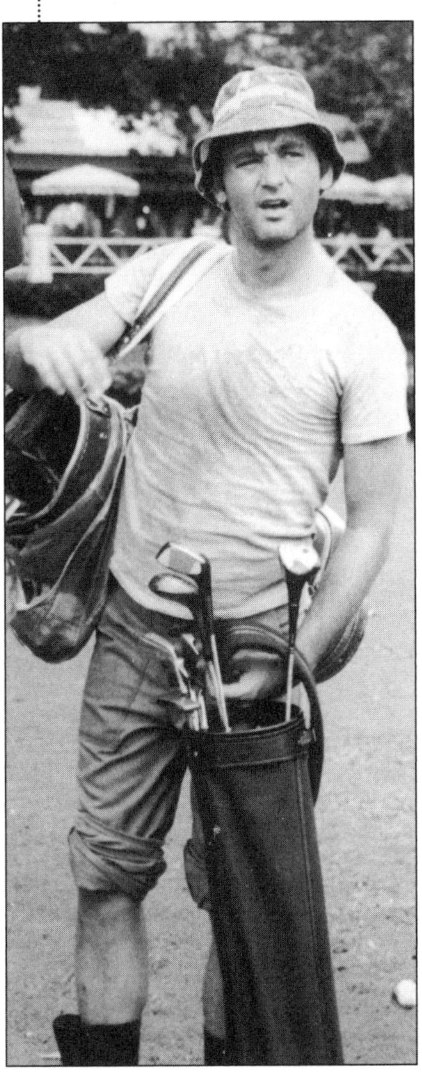

1. *I tell you, this steak still has marks from where the jockey was hittin' it.*

2. *Hey, Moose! Rocco! Help the judge find his checkbook, will ya?*

3. *So what brings you to this nape of the woods . . . neck of the wape . . . How come you're here?*

4. *Noonan!*

5. *Fifty bucks the Smails kid picks his nose.*

6. *Nobody likes a tattletale, Danny—except, of course, me.*

7. *"What do you do for excitement?"*
"Oh, I play a lot of golf."
"Golf???? Nixon plays golf."

8. *She's been plucked more times than the Rose of Tralee.*

9. *In one physical model of the universe, the shortest distance between two points is a straight line . . . in the opposite direction.*

10. *Fifty bucks more says he eats it.*

Carl Spackler

NAME THAT CLUB (IF POSSIBLE)

It's tricky to compare the golf clubs that Andra Kirkcaldy, Old and Young Tom Morris, and Willie Auchterlonie used more than one hundred years ago to those Ben Hogan, Jack Nicklaus, and Tiger Woods used or are using in the modern era. But golfers, whenever they come across an old wooden-shafted club, enjoy trying to understand to which modern clubs they can compare the cleeks or niblicks or mashies of old-time golf. Is a cleek by any other name still a cleek, or a two-iron? Is a spade mashie used for shaping potatoes or the golf ball, and what was its loft anyway? Old Tom Morris, an esteemed clubmaker as well as a British Open champion, spoke of the "music" that a heavy head could extract from a seriously stiff shaft. Tiger Woods speaks of the way a golf ball reacts off the face of a wedge. Today's clubs look about as close to clubs of many years ago as does a jet to the contraption that the Wright Brothers flew that December day in 1903 at Kitty Hawk, North Carolina. Before we can make comparisons, it helps to look at how clubs evolved, and why.

COURSE CONDITIONS

Consider the condition of the courses golfers played on during the early days of the game. They were playing on ground that wasn't much more than a field, barely cleared. Courses weren't so much maintained as they were accepted. Then there was the first golf ball, the featherie. Not exactly durable, it was prone to splitting. The result was that the golfer needed to hit a ball that could fall apart and could become heavy when it got wet. He had to get it out of holes, ruts, and cuppy lies. He had to chop it low along the ground in a seaside breeze (sometimes, a gale), or loft it over unkempt, deep sand pits. Greens were barely distinguishable from fairways—indeed, the word *fairway* wasn't used in golf until the turn of the twentieth century.

So the golfer was whacking a sewn bag full of feathers, or a rounded piece of tree resin (the gutta percha, introduced in 1848), over rough ground until he reached the putting area, and even then he hardly found himself facing anything smooth.

THE CLUBS

Our golfing ancestors were using clubs based on equipment derived from tools used in other field sports. Ball-and-club games such as the Dutch *kolven* or the Flemish *chole* used clubs shaped more like hockey sticks. The shafts were long and the heads were skinny and bowed. The general shape was concave, to make it easier to lift the ball from the ruts and higher grass.

The clubs that lasted into the gutta-percha age had shafts and heads made of wood, formed by master craftsmen. Hugh Philp, a St. Andrean and one of the most esteemed clubmakers, worked from 1812 until his death in 1856. A carpenter and cabinetmaker before he turned to clubmaking, Philp used thorn, apple, and pear in his clubheads and ash in the shafts before moving to hickory when it became widely available.

A player's set began with the "play-club," which the golfer often used to start a hole, as if somebody were saying "Play away." Today we would call such a club a "driver," but as historian Robert Browning observed, a golfer didn't "drive" toward a target, he "played upon it." They also used "spoons," so called because they were shaped like a spoon, with their concave heads. There was a long spoon, a mid-spoon, and a short spoon. The player who needed to hit yesteryear's equivalent of a lob shot—over a bunker, for instance, and meant to stop quickly on the green—used a "baffing" spoon. (To "baff" was to contact the ground just before the ball, which would then ride up the concave face of the spoon and soar quickly.)

INFLUENCE OF THE GUTTA-PERCHA BALL

The advent of gutta-percha led to several changes. Harder than the featherie, it could damage the skinny wooden-headed clubs. Many golfers found their clubs breaking where the neck joined the head. Clubmakers designed smaller, deeper heads to better absorb the blow against the harder guttie. The clubhead began to assume its squat appearance. A club called the "bulger" for the shape of the face—it bulged forward—was used. A "brassie" found its way into the game, so called because of a piece of brass put on the sole of the club to prevent possible damage when it hit hard ground, such as the roads or footpaths that were found on courses. The brassie was close in loft to the driver, and later the word was used for a two-wood.

The Influence of the Rubber-Core Ball

The rubber-core ball came along in 1902, and clubs changed again as golfers flocked to it. The ball was softer, it bounced and ran, and it could take the blow from a piece of hardwood. Persimmon—wood from the namesake fruit tree—came into vogue for club heads, and remained popular until golfers switched to metal "woods" in the 1980s and 1990s.

The rubber-core ball also meant that clubheads made of iron became popular. They existed much earlier—the first Rules of Golf written in 1744 make reference to an iron club—but they were hard on the featheries, particularly as their faces became scored and pocked. The best irons were forged in blacksmiths' shops, and with the resilient rubber-core ball coming into fashion, golfers discovered the advantages of backspin available from grooved metal clubfaces.

Niblicks

The niblick in its original form was a wood-faced club with a short, small snout, more like a baffing spoon than what it would become in its iron days. Browning isn't sure of the derivation of the word, but believes it hails from *neb laigh,* which means "broken nose," a reference to the club's short head, the better to dig into a small rut and extricate the ball.

The niblick eventually developed into a club like today's eight- or nine-iron. The mashie niblick, approximating today's seven-iron, soon came along, and the march to the matched iron set known only by their numbers was on and not to be stopped.

Composition of a Set of Clubs

"Nearly every golfer has in his pack one good iron," John Low wrote in 1903, "one that stands out among the mediocrity of its

fellows and is the admiration of the player's friends. Suppose this is a driving mashie, I should recommend the following plan: If the owner has a good local club-maker take it to him; if not, send it to one of the St. Andrews makers, and request the three clubs be made of exactly the same shape and lie, but with three greater grades of loft. The player should then have: (1) his ordinary driving mashie, (2) the same club with rather less loft than the ordinary medium iron, (3) ditto with rather less loft than the ordinary mashie, and (4) ditto with rather more loft than the ordinary mashie. He will have what few golfers have, viz.—a set of irons of the same weight and lie, the same balance, the same class of shaft, and the same thickness of grip."

Low was a thoroughly modern golfer. He knew to blame the club for a poor shot, not himself; he wrote that "when a new shaft is put in an iron, and what was a true club becomes an untrue club, the blame must lie in the stick." Golfers around the world know this. Never mind the fact that when steel shafts were made legal in 1929, standardization and uniformity became the order of the day, and the excuse provided by handmade implements of variable woods became as antiquated as a play club.

A Champion's Clubs: Willie Park's Clubs When He Won the 1887 and 1889 British Opens

Bulger-driver, straight-faced driver, spoon, brassie, cleek, iron, mashie, iron-niblick, wooden putter, and Parks Patent putter. (Golfers sometimes carried one nearly straight-faced putter for use near the hole, and another, slightly more lofted one, to run the ball from near the green onto it and then have it roll.)

Then and Now

Lofts have changed over the years, so it's impossible to conclude that a club of an earlier generation equates to a modern club. After all, the loft of a nine-iron in 1975 was forty-six degrees, and it's now down to forty-one degrees, which was a seven-iron then. A mashie niblick's loft was approximately forty-one degrees, so one might say, well, that would be a seven-iron. But it played more like a nine-iron because of the stubby, short head. It's important to take these comparisons with a grain of salt, or perhaps even understanding. Consider the cleek. Well, which cleek? The driving cleek, the lofting cleek, the putting cleek, the plaid-backed putting cleek?

With these caveats, then, we present our effort to equate clubs of vastly different golfing times. Lofts are the means of comparison, rather than shape or size of heads.

- Play club: driver
- Brassie: two-wood
- Spoon: three-wood
- Baffy: four-wood
- Cleek (one type of cleek, anyway): one-iron
- Mid-iron: two-iron
- Mid-mashie: three-iron
- Mashie iron: four-iron
- Mashie: five-iron
- Spade mashie: six-iron
- Mashie niblick: seven-iron
- Pitching niblick: eight-iron
- Niblick: nine-iron
- Jigger: wedge
- Baffing spoon: lob wedge
- Putter: putter. Always.

ONE-LINERS

27. *"That gives me the Greater Slam."*
—MARK BROOKS on winning the Greater Hartford, Greater Greensboro, and Greater Milwaukee Opens

28. *"I always said you have to be really smart or really dumb to play this game well. I just don't know where I fit in."*
—BETH DANIEL

29. *"Watch out for buses."*
—BEN HOGAN, asked in 1990 if he had any advice for young players

30. *"All four days I didn't think. I just hit. Squeeky [Jeff Medlen, his caddie] said kill and I killed it."*
—JOHN DALY, on winning the 1991 PGA Championship after getting into the field as the ninth alternate

John Daly in 1991, when it all began.

FAMOUS COLLAPSES IN MAJORS

Tom Kite, 1989 U.S. Open, Oak Hill Country Club, Rochester, New York

By this U.S. Open, many observers felt that Kite, one of the game's most consistent players, might never win the national championship—or, for that matter, any major. He'd won twelve PGA Tour events, including the Players Championship nearly three months prior to the U.S. Open. But he was on the cusp of winning the U.S. Open now. Kite had taken a one-shot lead over Scott Simpson into the final round and was three ahead after a birdie on the third hole against Simpson's bogey.

But things changed quickly. Kite drove into the creek to the right of the fifth fairway. Even after a penalty drop, his only play was to pitch back out to the fairway, which he did. He reached the green and had a twelve-foot putt for a bogey, ran that eighteen inches by, and missed the return putt. Kite's triple bogey reversed his forward direction and now he and Simpson were tied. A double bogey at the par-five 13th hole, where Kite missed a three-foot putt after driving in the rough and failing to get out with his four-wood second, effectively put him out of contention. Curtis Strange won, thereby defending the title he'd won the year before at The Country Club in Brookline, Massachusetts. Kite shot 78 and said, "My play stunk." He also said he'd cope well with the experience and that he would win a major one day.

"You bet I damn will," a defiant Kite said. Kite won the 1992 U.S. Open at Pebble Beach.

GAMBLING GAMES

NASSAU: The most basic of all golf variations was invented by John B. Coles Tappan, club captain at the Nassau Country Club on Long Island around 1900. It turns a round into three separate bets, usually of equal size: front nine, back nine, and full eighteen. It is most often played at match play, with full handicaps, though stroke play is also an option for individuals.

The most common format in a foursome is to play a better-ball, two-on-two match for a designated amount in each of the three segments ($2 is the usual minimum, though in Texas bets under $10,000 are considered insulting to all participants). The trailing side on any nine may "press," or create a new bet for the remainder of the nine for the same amount, while the original bet continues. (Some groups that like a lot of action play automatic presses as soon as one side falls two-down, or even one-down. In such a game, think of the stakes as at least double or triple the amount agreed to at the start.)

Since a Nassau prevents a complete blowout by starting a new bet after nine holes, it's a good game for players at any level. As with all betting games, know what the rules and stakes are before the start of the round, and only bet with people whose handicaps (and ethics) you can trust.

STABLEFORD: Popular throughout the world—though familiar to most Americans only via the modified system used at the International, the PGA Tour event held each year at Castle Pines—Stableford scoring keeps the game moving across a large field of players. Stableford games are generally held at full handicap; players receive one point for a net bogey, two for a net par, three for a net birdie, and four for a net eagle. When net bogey is no longer possible, you pick up and go to the next hole. Pairs can compete at total points; foursomes can play as best-three-of-four scores.

SKINS: A simple game, particularly good for threesomes, played for a set amount per hole; the winner of a hole collects from the others. If there is no outright winner—the game can be played at full handicap, though half is fairer—the money is added to the stake for the next hole, and the hole after that, and so on until someone wins one. Variations might include giving a double payoff for winning a hole with a natural birdie, or by getting up and down from sand.

BINGO, BANGO, BONGO: On each hole, there are three points available. One point goes to the player who hits the green first. Another goes to the player who is closest to the hole once all players are on the green.

The third goes to the person who holes out first, playing strictly by who is away. Bets are paid off on a set amount per point.

While this seems to be an innocuous variation on regular golf, it's actually a very different game. There can be a definite advantage to conceding the first point and missing the green with your approach shot if you're a good chipper and putter. Your chip will most likely wind up closer than your opponent's longer shot, and you'll have a better chance of holing out first.

VEGAS: A team game, pair against pair. Each team's scores on every hole are combined to create a two-digit number, the lower score first: A four and a six becomes a 46, and would be worth eleven points against a team scoring a five and a seven for 57. Stakes are set in a unit per point; if you're playing for a dollar a point, the team scoring 46 would be up $11 against the team with a 57. This is a good game for the solid player teamed with an erratic one; the consistent scores will ensure that the tens digit never gets too high, and the effect of the up-and-down player's bad scores will be restricted to the ones digit, while his occasional brilliances pay off in tens.

NINE POINTS: A game for threesomes. On each hole, nine points are at stake: five for the winner, three for finishing second, one for finishing

BET YOUR WAY TO BETTER PUTTING

Twenty-one is a game you should play whenever you have some time with another player on a practice green. Each player alternates selecting a target hole, of any length or difficulty. If a player sinks his first putt, he gets five points. The player closer to the hole after each has hit his first putt gets one point. If you three-putt, your *opponent* gets three points. First player to reach twenty-one points wins.

This game emphasizes accurate lag putting and simulates the pressure on short putts that you feel out on the course in a match. It's also a great way to rehearse and strengthen your powers of concentration.

last. If all three tie, they get three points each. If two tie for first, they get four each (with one for the third player); if two tie for last, they get two each while the winner still gets five.

LOW TOTAL: A game for foursomes that keeps a weak player from being wholly carried by a strong one in a better-ball match. There are two points at stake on each hole: one for the low individual score, another for the low team total. One variation is to play "high-low," or one point for the lowest score and one for the lower of the two highest scores.

WOLF: At the start of a round, choose a rotation so that each player in the foursome will take four turns being the "wolf" over the first sixteen holes. The wolf tees off first; then, as each player tees off in turn, the wolf declares whether he will take that player as his partner for the hole or pass and select from the remaining players. The wolf can also decide to pass on all three players and go it alone against everybody; if so, the bet for the hole is doubled. Whoever is behind in the betting gets to be wolf for the last two holes.

SNAKE: This can be played in conjunction with any other kind of betting game. Whoever three-putts first in a round has to carry the "snake" (this needn't be literal, but it's more fun when someone has a big rubber snake dangling from his bag) until someone else three-putts, when the snake is transferred to the new victim. Whoever has the snake at the end of the round pays a set amount to the other players, or buys the drinks—a traditional folk remedy for snakebite.

INSTANT REPLAY: In a one-on-one game, instead of getting strokes from a stronger player, the higher-handicap player gets the right to demand that his opponent replay a set number of shots, usually corresponding to the difference in their handicaps. Strategy comes into play in the selection of when to invoke the replays; the best times include trouble shots played successfully and long putts holed, but there is a definite psychological advantage to holding the threat of a replay over someone's head for as long as possible. (Of course, you might finish the round with one fewer friend than when you started.)

STICKS: Aimed at keeping a match close, this game can be combined with any other bet. When one player falls one (or perhaps two) holes behind, he can remove one club from his opponent's bag. (Some people play that the putter is off-limits.) Knowledge of the course and your opponent's strengths are key to picking the clubs to remove; go first for the short-yardage "scoring" clubs, then tailor the selection to the par threes ahead.

THE GOLFER'S LIFE LIST

Be the First Golfer Out on a Course, and the Last In

Out first, in last. Any golfer can do this at any course. Walking onto the first tee at your favorite course at dawn during the long light of summer, play your morning round, and then return in the evening for a second round. Your first round shouldn't take more than two and a half hours, and your evening round the same.

One satisfying way to be first out, last in, is by playing on your own. Sling your clubs over your shoulder and walk onto the tee as soon as the course opens, or, if you can get permission, a few minutes prior to the first official starting time. You'll have a clear course ahead, and you'll feel as if you're out for a hike while hitting golf balls along the way. The round will flow, and you'll probably move more quickly as the round progresses. You'll gather momentum, due to the excitement at being out alone on the quiet course. Players will soon come along, but you'll feel they're on another course. The walk will invigorate you, while the fairways and greens will appear inviting from start to finish.

Perhaps your pace will slow as you walk up the last fairway as the light fades. The course will again be empty. Finish the hole, and then turn around and look down the course. First out, last in. It's golf to savor.

PLAYOFFS

There are few crucibles of pressure in sports that compare to the final round of a major golf championship. In the history of men's professional majors that dates back to 1860, there have been seventy-nine occasions when those who survived that ordeal found that they still had more golf to play because they were tied for the lead. (This total includes match-play finals in the PGA Championship that went to extra holes.) The methods used to decide a winner have varied from thirty-six-hole playoffs—even when the tournament itself was only thirty-six holes, as in the nineteenth-century British Opens—to sudden death. Currently, the four majors differ on how to resolve seventy-two-hole ties: the Masters uses sudden death, the U.S. Open holds to the eighteen-hole medal format (followed now by sudden death), the British Open pioneered the four-hole aggregate-score playoff, and the PGA uses a three-hole aggregate. Regardless of the method used, these playoffs form an unusual hothouse environment in which to examine a player's abilities. (Or perhaps just his luck.)

Special mention for stick-to-itiveness must go to Craig Wood, who lost playoffs in each of the four majors before winning both the Masters and the U.S. Open in 1941. Had the concept of professional majors existed in the 1930s, Wood would have been a serious contender for the mantle of "Best Player Never to Have Won a Major" that has haunted so many players to this day.

Players Who Lost Multiple Majors in Playoffs

NAME	PLAYOFFS
Michael Brady	1911 U.S. Open, 1919 U.S. Open
Bobby Jones	1925 U.S. Open, 1928 U.S. Open

NAME	PLAYOFFS
Craig Wood	1933 British Open, 1934 PGA, 1935 Masters, 1939 U.S. Open
Byron Nelson	1939 PGA, 1941 PGA, 1946 U.S. Open
Ben Hogan	1942 Masters, 1954 Masters, 1955 U.S. Open
Arnold Palmer	1962 U.S. Open, 1963 U.S. Open, 1966 U.S. Open
Gene Littler	1970 Masters, 1977 PGA
Greg Norman	1984 U.S. Open, 1987 Masters, 1989 British Open, 1993 PGA
Colin Montgomerie	1994 U.S. Open, 1995 PGA
Justin Leonard	1999 British Open, 2004 PGA
Chris DiMarco	2004 PGA, 2005 Masters

Players Who Lost a Playoff in a Major and Never Won a Major (through 2005)

NAME	PLAYOFFS
Andra Kirkaldy	1889 British Open
MacDonald Smith	1910 U.S. Open
Michael Brady	1911 U.S. Open, 1919 U.S. Open
George Simpson	1911 U.S. Open
*Roger Wethered	1921 British Open
Bobby Cruikshank	1923 U.S. Open
Harry Cooper	1927 U.S. Open
Al Espinosa	1929 U.S. Open
*George Von Elm	1931 U.S. Open
Harold "Jug" McSpaden	1937 PGA
Harry Bradshaw	1949 British Open
George Fazio	1950 U.S. Open
Dave Thomas	1958 British Open
Jackie Cupit	1963 U.S. Open
Phil Rodgers	1963 British Open
Tommy Jacobs	1966 Masters

NAME	PLAYOFFS
Don Massengale	1967 PGA
Doug Sanders	1970 British Open
Jack Newton	1975 British Open
Ed Sneed	1979 Masters
Dan Pohl	1982 Masters
Scott Hoch	1989 Masters
Mike Donald	1990 U.S. Open
Colin Montgomerie	1994 U.S. Open, 1995 PGA
Loren Roberts	1994 U.S. Open
Costantino Rocca	1995 British Open
Kenny Perry	1996 PGA
Brian Watts	1998 British Open
Jean Van de Velde	1999 British Open
Bob May	2000 PGA
Stuart Appleby	2002 British Open
Thomas Levet	2002 British Open
Len Mattiace	2003 Masters
Chris DiMarco	2004 PGA, 2005 Masters

*Neither Wethered nor Von Elm ever won a professional major, but Wethered took the 1923 British Amateur and Von Elm won the 1926 U.S. Amateur, which were at least as important at the time.

Players Who Won Their First Professional Major in a Playoff

NAME	PLAYOFF	WON OTHERS?
**Bob Martin	1876 British Open	Yes, 1
Willie Fernie	1883 British Open	No
Harry Vardon	1896 British Open	Yes, 6
Willie Anderson	1901 U.S. Open	Yes, 3
Fred MacLeod	1908 U.S. Open	No
John McDermott	1911 U.S. Open	Yes, 1

NAME	PLAYOFF	WON OTHERS?
Francis Ouimet	1913 U.S. Open	No (but 2 "major" Amateurs)
Bobby Jones	1923 U.S. Open	Yes, 6 (plus 6 "major" Amateurs)
William Macfarlane	1925 U.S. Open	No
Tommy Armour	1927 U.S. Open	Yes, 2
Johnny Farrell	1928 U.S. Open	No
Billy Burke	1931 U.S. Open	No
Denny Shute	1933 British Open	Yes, 2
Paul Runyan	1934 PGA	Yes, 1
Lawson Little	1940 U.S. Open	No (but 2 previous "major" Amateurs)
Vic Ghezzi	1941 PGA	No
Lloyd Mangrum	1946 U.S. Open	No
Lew Worsham	1947 U.S. Open	No
Bobby Locke	1949 British Open	Yes, 3
Jack Fleck	1955 U.S. Open	No
Dick Mayer	1957 U.S. Open	No
Jerry Barber	1961 PGA	No
Jack Nicklaus	1962 U.S. Open	Duh
Bob Charles	1963 British Open	No
Don January	1967 PGA	No
Lou Graham	1975 U.S. Open	No
Tom Watson	1975 British Open	Yes, 7
Lanny Wadkins	1977 PGA	No
John Mahaffey	1978 PGA	No
David Graham	1979 PGA	Yes, 1
Fuzzy Zoeller	1979 Masters	Yes, 1
Craig Stadler	1982 Masters	No
Larry Mize	1987 Masters	No
Curtis Strange	1988 U.S. Open	Yes, 1

Ernie Els needed 20 extra holes for his first major win.

Mike Weir defeated Len Mattiace on the first extra hole, five to X.

NAME	PLAYOFF	WON OTHERS?
Mark Calcavecchia	1989 British Open	No
Paul Azinger	1993 PGA	No
Ernie Els	1994 U.S. Open	Yes, 2
Steve Elkington	1995 PGA	No
Mark Brooks	1996 PGA	No
Paul Lawrie	1999 British Open	No
Retief Goosen	2001 U.S. Open	Yes, 1
Mike Weir	2003 Masters	No
Todd Hamilton	2004 British Open	No

**Martin won the 1876 Open Championship in a walkover; see The Playoff That Never Was on page 48.

STEPPING OUT WITH IRON BYRON: SEVENTEEN THINGS ABOUT THE SWING MACHINE

1. The True Temper company was looking in 1963 for a way to test new shafts. Gordon Leslie, a vice president of the company, decided the best strategy would be to develop a mechanical golfer. Repetition, he concluded, would lead to reliability.

2. Leslie engaged the Battelle Memorial Institute, a research and development facility in Columbus, Ohio, that George Battelle founded in 1929 and which already had more than 3,000 employees. The Xerox copier was invented by Chester Carlson, a Battelle researcher. George Manning, a twenty-eight-year-old mechanical engineer, guided the research that tried to answer the question: How do we build a machine that will produce an efficient swing time after time after time?

3. Manning and his associates took film of golfers to study their swings. The scientists were particularly interested in the efficient transfer of energy.

4. Byron Nelson hadn't played competitive golf since 1947, but he still had his swing. Manning determined that Nelson's was the model swing and set to work to design a machine based on it. The mechanical golf club swinger cost $250,000. By 1966, when the machine was developed, Manning had left Battelle to work with True Temper. There he met Bob Bush, who would go on to become perhaps golf's most knowledgeable person about shaft technology.

5. The mechanical golfer was first called the Golf Club Swing Device.

6. The United States Golf Association took delivery of its first Golf Club Swing Device in 1972.

7. Joe Schwendeman—a USGA employee working on the association's magazine, *Golf Journal*—took to calling the machine Iron Mike after the automated baseball pitching device of the same name. He mentioned Iron Mike to the magazine's editor, Bob Sommers, one day. Sommers didn't like the name and said, "Stop calling it

Iron Mike. If you want to call it anything, call it Iron Byron. The machine's swing was patterned after him." Iron Byron was born.

8. The USGA used Iron Byron on an outdoor range at its headquarters in Far Hills, New Jersey, to test golf balls for conformance to its Overall Distance Standard (ODS). The requirement was that ODS, combining carry and roll, could not exceed 296.8 yards (280 yards plus a tolerance of 6 percent) when tested under specified conditions.

9. Specified weather conditions: wind no higher than four miles an hour, temperature between 55 and 95 degrees Fahrenheit, ideal test temperature considered 75 degrees.

10. Specified swing conditions: Iron Byron swung at 109 mph, considered representative of the average PGA Tour professional. The machine was set so that the ball would take off at a ten-degree launch angle and speed of 250 feet per second, which translated to the 109 mph figure.

11. Iron Byron swung a Spalding laminated wood with an extra-stiff steel shaft. It was set to hit a ball every thirty seconds. It hit between 1,000 and 2,000 balls a day during the summer. The shaft snapped about once every 9,000 swings.

12. Iron Byron was so reliable that the balls it hit wore out a strip of turf where they landed. The USGA had to replace the turf every two years.

13. As reliable as Iron Byron was, its limitations became evident in time. Golfers such as Tiger Woods and John Daly could swing at speeds 20 mph faster than Iron Byron. The machine wasn't replicating the swing speeds of these longer hitters. Golf balls that met the USGA's test under Iron Byron were going too far.

14. Because of weather restrictions, the USGA could test balls only thirty to fifty days a year, when conditions were as mandated. The outdoor test also couldn't isolate factors such as aerodynamic lift and drag on a ball that influenced distance.

15. It had become evident by the mid- to late 1990s that Iron Byron was no longer useful as a testing mechanism. The USGA began to develop a protocol to be used indoors. Its Indoor Test Range (ITR) was designed and built. Iron Byron was retired. Frank Thomas, a scientist with a heart, said, "He's a great, great guy, but he's old technology. Iron

Iron Byron and caddie

Byron has done an absolutely, positively wonderful job for us, because he was the only consistent, untiring ball-launching device we could use to develop the ODS. But now he's past his sell-by date."

16. Iron Byron has gone to a happy retirement. He took up residence in the World Golf Hall of Fame as part of its Byron Nelson exhibit. Meanwhile, golf teacher Paul Wilson bases his instruction on Iron Byron, writing in his book *Swing Machine Golf: The Fastest Way to a Consistent Swing* that he wants his students to "understand the true simplicity of the swing," as Iron Byron demonstrated it, and that the golfer can expect consistency from working with the principles on which it is based.

17. The last word goes to Bob Bush: "To this day, even the best golfers in the world can't provide [Iron Byron's] level of consistency."

THE GOLFER'S LIFE LIST

Go to St. Andrews

St. Andrews has been welcoming pilgrims for more than a thousand years. The relics of St. Andrew were what first drew visitors to the area, along with its designation as the seat of the Bishop of Alba in 906. Construction on St. Andrews Cathedral began around 1160, though it was not finally consecrated until 1318. It stands today in ruins, its stone walls open to all who wish to walk among its echoes. The University of St. Andrews, established by Papal Bull in 1413, is the oldest in Scotland, with the attractive campuses of St. Salvator's and St. Mary's Colleges lying within the town confines.

There are also a few golf courses.

Walk along The Links over to Golf Place, noting the low rail fence that is the only boundary between fairway and town. Stand beside the 18th green of the Old Course for a while, and imagine the space thronged with spectators roaring as the new Open champion approaches. Lean on the fence along the last fairway and watch golfers play up to the green; note their confusion as they try to decide between flying the ball in the American way, or running it up through the Valley of Sin, the preferred Scottish shot. Stop in the Tom Morris Golf Shop. Have a drink in the bar at Rusacks Hotel, overlooking the 1st and 18th fairways. Hang out in the pub at the Dunvegan Hotel, 112 yards from the Old Course. Walk directly across the street to the Quarto Bookshop and browse among more golf books—old and new—than you could read in a lifetime. (The shelves also bulge with superb volumes on Scottish history and landscape, of the non-golf variety.) Take Granny Clark's Wynd

Scottish troops were said to have crossed the Swilcan Bridge en route to the Crusades.

through the middle of the double fairway on your way to the beach where they filmed *Chariots of Fire,* and realize you're on a road that every great golfer has crossed several times in his life. (All except Ben Hogan, that is.)

If it's Sunday, there won't be any golf to watch, but you can walk the course as it reclaims its role as the town green. Linger at the Swilcan Bridge. Stare down into the Road Hole Bunker. Walk to Hell and back. Or walk farther, all the way out to the loop, comprising the 7th through 11th holes at the far reaches of the links. Time your walk so that you return to town as the sun is setting.

Go, whether you'll be able to play golf there or not. Just go.

ARE ATHLETES GOLFERS?

It can be debated endlessly whether or not golfers are athletes, and whether or not golf is a sport. A casual observer coming across Tiger Woods in the sauna would most likely believe he was seeing an athlete; someone observing Tim Herron in similar circumstances would feel otherwise. The authors do not consider any aspect of this discussion to be of vital importance, though we do note the power of the Larry Laoretti Argument: Nothing should be considered a sport if you can compete in it while smoking.

Golf is certainly the second-favorite sport of most professional athletes—and it's not clear that it isn't actually their favorite, no matter what other sport pays the bills. Through the years, a number of athletes have attempted to bring their skills onto the pro tours. Here are some who have been the most successful:

SAMMY BYRD: The only man to play in the World Series and the Masters, Byrd spent eight seasons in the major leagues, with the New York Yankees and Cincinnati Reds. He earned the nickname "Babe Ruth's Legs" for his frequent role as a late-inning replacement for Ruth. (In 1933, he appeared in eighty-five games, but had only 107 at-bats.) He played on the PGA Tour in the 1940s, winning six titles; he reached the finals of the 1945 PGA Championship, losing 4 & 3 to Byron Nelson. He also played in five Masters, finishing third in 1941, and nine U.S. Opens.

JOE LOUIS: The boxing champion wasn't the most successful golfer, but he was certainly a passionate one. He took up the game shortly after winning the heavyweight title, and his managers soon demanded that he play no more than every other day while in training.

In the 1940s, Louis received the equivalent of sponsor's exemptions to play in some PGA events, even though PGA bylaws explicitly restricted membership to "Professional Golfers of the Caucasian race." At the San Diego Invitational in 1952, Louis was permitted to compete as an invitee, but Bill Spiller—an African-American professional who had qualified for the tournament—was not; Louis reacted angrily, declaring, "I want people to know what the PGA is. We've got another Hitler to get by." A compromise was worked out, and at the next tour stop in Phoenix, four black professionals (Spiller, Ted Rhodes, Eval Clark, and Charlie Sifford) qualified for the event, while Louis shot an 81 and did not. A week later, in Tucson, Louis was in the field and started out 69–72; he had a third round 78, and did not complete his fourth round, but he nonetheless was among the earliest African Americans to make the cut in a PGA tournament.

ELLSWORTH VINES: After a tennis career that included Grand Slam singles wins at Forest Hills in 1931 and 1932 and Wimbledon in 1932, Vines competed on the PGA tour in the years after World War II, finishing as high as 12th on the money list in 1947. He played in four U.S. Opens and three Masters, his best finishes being ties for 14th in the 1948 and 1949 Opens, and 24th in the 1947 Masters.

Ty Cobb

TY COBB: After his retirement from baseball, the crotchety Hall of Famer belonged to as many as eight country clubs, one of which was the Olympic Club in San Francisco. One year he reached the finals of the club championship, only to lose to a twelve-year-old boy. Cobb hated the teasing that followed this defeat so much that he left Olympic and didn't return for many years. The boy, Bob Rosburg, would win the PGA Championship in 1959.

KEN HARRELSON: In 1971, the twenty-nine-year-old outfielder, three seasons removed from leading the American League in RBIs, announced that he was quitting baseball to become a pro golfer. Maybe he thought there was room on the Tour for someone else nicknamed Hawk, because Ben Hogan had just competed in his final PGA event. Harrelson soon learned about the gap between country club play and tournament golf; he traveled the circuit, trying to get into fields through Monday qualifying, but played only seven events between 1971 and 1973. One was the 1972 British Open at Muirfield, where he missed the cut by a single stroke. The only cut he made on the PGA Tour came in 1981, at the Pleasant Valley Jimmy Fund Classic in Sutton, Massachusetts; he finished 75th.

RALPH TERRY: Terry won two of his three starts for the Yankees in the 1962 World Series, including a game-seven 1–0 shutout. This was redemption for the right-hander, who had two years earlier given up one of the most famous home runs in baseball history, Bill Mazeroski's blast that won the Series for the Pirates. Terry won 107 games in twelve seasons, then became a golf pro upon retiring from baseball. He appeared in five PGA Tour events between 1974 and 1982, missing all five cuts, then tried the Senior Tour when he turned fifty in 1986. In ninety-six Senior events he had one top-ten finish, in the Showdown Classic in 1989, where he tied for 10th. He earned a little over $162,000 in his years on the tour, and is one of only two pro athletes to have earned fully exempt status there.

JOHN BRODIE: "My wife said to me the other day, 'My God, you may get to sixty-five without ever working a day in your life,'" said Brodie, reflecting on his career as a football player, announcer, and member of golf's Senior Tour. Brodie was always an outstanding all-around athlete; in high school in Oakland, he jumped center against Bill Russell and played baseball against Frank Robinson. He attended Stanford, where he led the nation in passing and total offense in his senior year, 1956. He was the San Francisco 49ers quarterback for seventeen years, and won the NFL MVP Award in 1970. Always an outstanding golfer, he played in the 1959 U.S. Open during the NFL offseason and qualified again in 1981—possibly the longest gap between appearances in Open history. He won more than $735,000 in a thirteen-year Senior Tour career that began in 1985, capped off by a victory in the 1991 Security Pacific Senior Classic, in which he defeated Chi Chi Rodriguez and George Archer in a playoff.

FRANK CONNER: After winning the U.S. Juniors singles title in tennis at age seventeen, Conner became an All-American in the sport at Trinity University and played in two U.S. Championships at Forest Hills, in 1966 and 1967. He made it to the PGA Tour in 1975, and over the next eighteen years won just under $750,000, with eighteen top tens and one victory, the 1988 Deposit Guaranty Classic. He earned an additional $2.5 million on the Senior circuit from 1995 through 2002.

PETE BOSTWICK: Son of a legendary polo player, Bostwick joins Vines and Conner as the three men to have played in the U.S. Open (or Amateur equivalent in pre-Open tennis days) in tennis and golf. He appeared at Forest Hills in 1952 and Winged

Foot in 1959. His greatest fame, however, has come in other racquet sports: he won U.S. championships in court tennis and hard racquets, and national age-group titles in squash.

Rick Rhoden: Rhoden pitched in parts of sixteen seasons in the majors, compiling a record of 151–125 for the Dodgers, Pirates, Yankees, and Astros. Since turning fifty, he has tried to qualify for the Senior Tour three times; in 2003 he missed out by one stroke. He was in contention in the final round of the Allianz Championship in 2003 before finishing tied for fifth; his only other Champions Tour top ten is a tie for eighth in the 2005 Constellation Energy Classic. He finished in a tenth-place tie in the 2005 Q School and has conditional exempt status for the 2006 Champions Tour.

Grant Fuhr: The Hall of Fame goalie for the Edmonton Oilers and five other teams was on the verge of qualifying for the Canadian Tour with a 13th-place finish at Q School when he signed an incorrect scorecard and was disqualified.

Mark McGwire: While only time will tell if the slugger of 583 home runs will take a run at professional golf, he has demonstrated considerable talent already. In the made-for-TV ADT Golf Skills Challenge in 2003, McGwire finished first in a field that included Greg Norman, Nick Faldo, Padraig Harrington, Paul Azinger, Colin Montgomerie, Rich Beem, Peter Jacobsen, and Dudley Hart. McGwire won the long-drive portion with a 319-yard clout, finished second in the bunker, trouble shot, putting, and chipping competitions, and put a short-iron shot inside two feet to clinch the win.

Scott Draper: On the same day in January 2005, Draper played the opening round of the Victoria Open, his first tournament as a member of the Australasian golf tour, and won the semifinals of the mixed doubles at tennis's Australian Open with Samantha Stosur. He missed the cut in the golf, but went on to win the mixed doubles title the next day. Draper's highest singles ranking in tennis was 42 in 1998; he's played in thirty-three Grand Slam singles tournaments, reaching the fourth round of the French Open in 1995 and 1996 and the U.S. Open in 1997.

Mark McGwire has shown unquestionable skills in golf.

IN A CLASS BY HERSELF

Mildred "Babe" Didrikson Zaharias was quite possibly the greatest athlete ever to put a tee in the ground. Before taking up golf, she was an All-America selection in basketball, toured the country with a barnstorming baseball team, and won three medals in track and field at the 1932 Olympics. She carved out her legend at the 1932 Amateur Athletic Union Track Championships, which served as the women's Olympic trials. She competed in eight events and won six of them, leading her team to the overall title—though "leading" is rather a misstatement, since she was the only person on the team. (She had thirty points for the meet, eight points ahead of the twenty-two-member second-place University of Illinois team.) At the Olympic Games in Los Angeles, she was restricted to three individual events by the rules of the time; she won the 80-meter hurdles in world-record time, won the javelin throw, and was awarded the silver medal in the high jump despite clearing the same height as the gold medalist. The judges ruled her jump style was illegal, since her head preceded her body over the bar.

Encouraged to try golf by sportswriter Grantland Rice, Didrikson Zaharias won the Texas State Amateur title two years after she began. The USGA soon declared her a professional because she had competed in other sports for pay. She regained her amateur status in the 1940s, and in 1946–47 won seventeen consecutive amateur tournaments. She won the U.S. Amateur in 1946, and she became the first American to win the British Ladies Amateur in 1947. Turning pro again, she earned approximately $100,000 through exhibitions and promotions. A founding member of the LPGA, she won forty-one professional tournaments including ten majors, four of which she won as an amateur. She was voted Associated Press Woman Athlete of the Year six times: in 1932 for her track-and-field accomplishments, and in 1945, 1946, 1947, 1950, and 1954 for her golf exploits. She was stricken with cancer in 1953, underwent surgery, and played in a tournament just fourteen weeks after the operation. The cancer returned to stay in 1955, and she died in September 1956, at forty-five years of age.

In 1950, the Associated Press voted her the greatest woman athlete of the first half of the twentieth century. In 1999, ESPN ranked her tenth on its list of the greatest athletes of the century, the highest ranking given to any woman.

HOW TO GET ONTO AUGUSTA NATIONAL

You probably have a better chance of becoming a Supreme Court justice than you do of becoming a member at Augusta National, and if you know a member who can get you on you've undoubtedly used that connection already and aren't reading this. All things considered, your best chance of getting onto Augusta National is . . . by qualifying for the Masters. Masters participants may come to Augusta National for practice rounds once they have qualified. Here's the complete list of ways to get into the Masters, as of 2006:

1. Masters winners (eligible for life)

2. U.S. Open champions (previous five years)

3. British Open champions (previous five years)

4. PGA champions (previous five years)

5. Winners of the Players Championship (previous three years)

6. Current U.S. Amateur champion and runner-up, if they remain amateurs

7. Current British Amateur champion

8. Current U.S. Amateur Public Links champion

9. Current U.S. Mid-Amateur champion

10. Top sixteen, including ties, in previous year's Masters

11. Top eight, including ties, in previous year's U.S. Open

12. Top four, including ties, in previous year's British Open

13. Top four, including ties, in previous year's PGA Championship

14. The forty leaders on the PGA Tour money list for the previous year

15. The ten leaders on the PGA Tour money list as of the week before the Masters

16. Top fifty in the World Golf Ranking at the end of the previous year

17. Top fifty in the World Golf Ranking as of the week before the Masters

FOOTNOTES TO HISTORY

Bob May, 2000 PGA Championship, Valhalla Golf Club, Louisville, Kentucky

May began the final round one shot behind Tiger Woods, the third-round leader. Woods and May had grown up only twenty minutes from one another in southern California, but had never played together in a tournament; now they would be paired in the last twosome of a major championship.

Bob May, a few steps short of Valhalla.

May, a three-time All-American at Oklahoma State University and a member of the U.S. team in the 1991 Walker Cup, was a thirty-one-year-old golfer who had played five years on the European Tour, finishing fifth on the 1999 money list. He was even with Woods after the first nine, then went four under par over the next eight holes—but so did Woods, whose birdie on 17 brought him back into a tie for the lead as they played the 72nd hole. They both hit the green of the par five in two, but each was left with a difficult putt for birdie after long approach putts. May holed his, from fifteen feet, after which Woods rolled in his six-footer to force a playoff.

The PGA of America was using a three-hole aggregate score playoff for the first time. The playoff began on the par-four 16th hole, where May's 70-foot chip for birdie stopped just inches from the hole. Woods then made a birdie putt from twenty feet, following it in while pointing his right index finger at the hole. Both players saved par on the 17th. Woods drove well left on 18, his shot hitting a sycamore tree, bouncing off a cart path, and hitting the tree again before coming to rest. May, with a chance to capitalize on a rare Tiger mistake, drove into the left rough as well, hit his second into the rough on the other side of the fairway, and left himself a 40-footer for birdie on the big 18th green. Tiger, meanwhile, put his third shot into a bunker, then blasted out to two feet. May's birdie putt just missed, and Woods tapped in for his third PGA Championship. May had played brilliantly, shooting a 66 in the final round with a back-nine 31, then made three pars in the playoff, but in the end he was just another golfer who almost won a major but didn't.

LED OR SHARED THE U.S. OPEN LEAD AFTER FIRST, SECOND, AND THIRD ROUNDS BUT DIDN'T WIN

YEAR	PLAYER	HIS FINAL ROUND	WINNER	HIS FINAL ROUND
1908	Willie Smith	78	Fred McLeod	77*
1912	Mike Brady	79	John McDermott	71
1960	Mike Souchak	75	Arnold Palmer	65
1968	Bert Yancey	76	Lee Trevino	69
1984	Hale Irwin	79	Fuzzy Zoeller	70
1985	T. C. Chen	77	Andy North	74
1992	Gil Morgan	81	Tom Kite	72
1998	Payne Stewart	74	Lee Janzen	68

*McLeod defeated Smith in a playoff, 77–83

NAMES OF THE HOLES ON SPYGLASS HILL GOLF COURSE

All of the hole names at Spyglass Hill, on California's Monterey Peninsula, are based on *Treasure Island,* by Robert Louis Stevenson, who supposedly wandered through the area looking for inspiration for his novels. These descriptions and associations are provided by the course guide.

1. Treasure Island. The first green is actually an island in the sand. To hit the green in par figures is to be rewarded.

2. Billy Bones. Like the character in the book, he appears early, doesn't stay long, but is long remembered.

3. The Black Spot. There is no alternative. Either the player hits the green or is in the sand and on the spot.

4. Blind Pew. Unless the tee shot is perfectly placed, the second shot to the green is absolutely blind.

5. Bird Rock. A one-shotter directly toward Bird Rock.

6. Israel Hands. Now we meet the pirates in the woods, and number six is a real rogue.

7. Indian Village. In keeping with the local lore, a difficult five par and many a player may be captured in the Indian Village.

8. Signal Hill. Again, a local name. Number eight is all uphill and could be a signal to a good or bad round.

9. Captain Smollett. Captain of the whole front nine and a tough taskmaster.

10. Captain Flint. Silver's parrot may well be echoing "pieces of eight" in the ears of the money players.

11. Admiral Benbow. Eleven green will provide a safe harbor for those who negotiate the lake.

12. Skeleton Island. The shape of the green and the lake guarding it lead the way to the treasure.

13. Tom Morgan. A pirate if there ever was one. One of the most deceiving holes on the course; longer than it looks.

14. Long John Silver. This double dogleg five par will dominate the whole card.

15. Jim Hawkins. The only kindly hole on the course. Just a little bit of a shot, but . . .

16. Black Dog. The most scurrilous of them all; a name well deserved. Not many will be able to cope with the length of this infamous four par.

17. Ben Gunn. Liked by all, a friendly character, not too long but full of suspicion.

18. Spyglass. The home hole toward the sign of the Spyglass.

FAMOUS COLLAPSES IN MAJORS

Phil Mickelson, 2006 U.S. Open, Winged Foot

With three holes to play, Mickelson was three over par and had a two-stroke lead in pursuit of his first U.S. Open title. When he bogeyed 16 and Colin Montgomerie birdied 17, the lead was gone—but Montgomerie double-bogeyed 18, leaving Mickelson one shot ahead of Geoff Ogilvy, who had finished at five over.

Mickelson had found just two of thirteen fairways to this point, but chose to hit driver and went far left, bouncing off a hospitality tent and into the rough. Rather than play safely back into the fairway he tried a big slice around a tree, hit the tree, and wound up just twenty-five yards closer. Shot number three flew over the trees and into a greenside bunker, but in a fried-egg lie. Mickelson blasted out across the green and into the long grass ringing the putting surface. His last-ditch chip for bogey ran by the hole, handing the trophy to Ogilvy. Only Sam Snead's catastrophic triple in 1939 can compare in U.S. Open history with Mickelson's last-hole double-bogey.

"I still am in shock that I did that," he said after the round. "I am such an idiot."

GOLF'S MOST UNDERRATED PLAYER?

Billy Casper won the 1959 and 1966 U.S. Opens, and the 1970 Masters. Only five players have more than his fifty-one PGA Tour victories. He won five Vardon Trophies for the low stroke average on the PGA Tour and represented the United States in eight Ryder Cups. Casper had his best years while Arnold Palmer, Jack Nicklaus, and Gary Player were in top form. They were called the Big Three. Casper was left out of a group that could easily have been called the Big Four.

Billy Casper drives for show at the 1973 Ryder Cup.

After winning the 1959 U.S. Open at Winged Foot Golf Club in Mamaroneck, New York, Casper noticed Ben Hogan near him. Hogan was all too aware that Casper had had a tremendous week on Winged Foot's crusty, fast greens, taking only 114 putts and three-putting only once. He said, "Son, if you couldn't putt, you'd be selling hot dogs out on the tenth tee." Perhaps this is one reason Casper didn't get the respect he deserved: Too many people saw him as a superb putter and not a complete golfer. However, Arnold Palmer told writer Jim Dodson that he feared Casper more than any other player.

Casper long ago resigned himself to how others see him. He has always handled himself gracefully in public, even when he shot 106 in the first round of the 2005 Masters. During the round he told his caddie, Brian Taylor, "I shouldn't be here." Taylor told his seventy-three-year-old friend, "Yes, you should. You're a Masters champion."

The media surrounded Casper after his round. He hadn't turned in his scorecard; speaking softly, as he always did during good times and bad, "I've got the card right here and I'm going to frame it. The score doesn't mean anything. My kids wanted me to play and I'm proud to finish."

Casper spoke at length and didn't leave until the last person had asked the last question. At that moment, one wanted to remember his stellar career and all the wins, but this somehow seemed an apt coda: A golfer who had done so much and been recognized so little, and now, having shot 106 in the Masters, standing and talking and being graceful and grateful. Casper distinguished himself there behind the 18th green where he met the media, just as he had distinguished himself during his career.

It's a shame so few people noticed.

THE WORD ON

The Game

"Golf is a day spent in a round of strenuous idleness."

—WILLIAM WORDSWORTH

"If profanity had an influence on the flight of the ball, the game of golf would be played far better than it is."

—HORACE HUTCHINSON

"Golf appeals to the idiot in us and the child. Just how childlike golf players become is proven by their frequent inability to count past five."

—JOHN UPDIKE

"It's good sportsmanship not to pick up lost balls while they are still rolling."

—MARK TWAIN

"Don't play too much golf. Two rounds a day are plenty."

—HARRY VARDON

MASTERS TIMELINE

1931

Purchase of Fruitland Nurseries as site for Augusta National Golf Club. Bobby Jones figured the land was made for a golf course, something everybody who has ever seen a property for a course seems to have felt. Dr. Alister Mackenzie retained as course architect. Construction begins.

1932

Augusta National opens in December.

1933

Club formal opening January 12–16. Even in its first years, the club closed every summer, as it still does today.

1934

First Augusta National Invitation Tournament. Horton Smith champion. Club and tournament cofounder Bobby Jones makes first tournament appearance since winning the Grand Slam in 1930; he finishes thirteenth.

1935

Golf course nines reversed because frost on the first hole, which was then number 10, delayed play.

1935

Gene Sarazen makes double eagle on number 15 to force playoff with Craig Wood. Sarazen wins thirty-six-hole playoff by five strokes. Maybe thirty people watched Sarazen hit the shot. In the years since, about 30,000 people have claimed they were there.

1936

Horton Smith becomes first player to win two Masters.

1937

Members begin to wear the green jackets that would become emblematic of the club and the Masters. (Members and winners aren't supposed to wear the jacket off the property, which is a good thing. They're that gaudy.) Byron Nelson scores 2–3 on numbers 12 and 13 to pick up six strokes on Ralph Guldahl and win his first Masters.

1939

Tournament officially renamed the Masters.

1940

Lloyd Mangrum shoots a course-record 64.

1941

Underground network of telephone cable installed for scoring system. First radio tower put in use.

1942

Byron Nelson defeats Ben Hogan 69–70 in playoff.

1943–44

Club closes during World War II.

1945

Club reopens for members.

1946

First postwar Masters is played. First photographers' tower installed, beside the 18th green.

1947

Magnolia Lane, the entrance to the club, is paved. First scoreboards are built and used on the course. Jimmy Demaret wins and becomes the first player to break par each day.

1948

General Dwight D. Eisenhower joins Augusta National.

1949

Ike's Pond is built. Sam Snead wins the Masters and is the first champion to receive a green jacket. A spectator's guide is published. The 11th fairway becomes the first to be roped off for gallery control.

1950

Jimmy Demaret becomes the tournament's first three-time champion.

1952

Defending champion Ben Hogan begins the tradition of the Masters Club, a pretournament dinner for past champions. General Eisenhower is elected U.S. president.

1953

Ben Hogan breaks seventy-two-hole scoring record by five shots with 274.

1953

Press building for the Masters is erected. It's a Quonset hut, like those used by the U.S. Navy in World War II, a prefabricated structure of corrugated iron known for its durability.

1954

Amateur Billy Joe Patton misses out on playoff after finding water on numbers 13 and 15 in final round. Patton made ace on the par-three sixth hole earlier in final round.

1954

Sam Snead edges Ben Hogan in eighteen-hole playoff for third Masters win.

1955

All holes serviced by phone for scoring system. Sarazen Bridge dedicated at 15th hole in celebration of twentieth anniversary of his double eagle. Cary Middlecoff sinks a seventy-five-foot putt for eagle on the 13th hole en route to victory.

1956

First television broadcast of tournament, with holes 15–18 shown.

1956

Amateur Ken Venturi's collapse on the final day paves the way for Jack Burke Jr.'s victory.

1958

Hogan Bridge at number 12 green and Nelson Bridge at number 13 tee dedicated on April 2.

1958

Par-three course built. Arnold Palmer, after getting favorable ruling on number 12, wins his first Masters. Herbert Warren Wind comes up with the name Amen Corner to describe holes 11–13 in *Sports Illustrated* article.

1959

Record Fountain, located left of number 17 green, dedicated on twenty-fifth anniversary of tournament. Art Wall Jr. birdies five of final six holes to win tournament.

1960

Par-three contest is held for first time, and Sam Snead is inaugural winner. Over-par and under-par scoring method for leaderboards introduced. Arnold Palmer birdies 17 and 18 in final round to win by a shot. The tradition of interviewing the Masters winner begins with tournament chairman Clifford Roberts. Another tradition begins in that nobody who has won the par-three contest has won the tournament.

1961

Gary Player becomes first international champion.

1962

First observation stand (never called "bleachers") erected to improve sightlines for patrons (never called "fans"). Arnold Palmer wins first three-man playoff, defeating Gary Player and Dow Finsterwald.

1963

Jock Hutchinson and Fred McLeod serve as honorary starters. Attendance limitations instituted. Jack Nicklaus becomes youngest champion and wins first of six Masters.

1964

Butler Cabin built. Arnold Palmer becomes the first four-time Masters champion.

1965

Television studio in Butler Cabin for the first time. Jack Nicklaus defeats Arnold Palmer and Gary Player by nine strokes for then-largest victory margin. Nicklaus's 17-under-par 271 sets a tournament record. Bobby Jones makes the now-famous comment that Nicklaus was playing a game with which he wasn't familiar.

1966

Jack Nicklaus becomes first back-to-back champion, winning three-way playoff against Gay Brewer Jr. and Tommy Jacobs. First golf broadcast in color. Players within ten strokes of the lead are included in the final two rounds. Resolution makes Bobby Jones president in perpetuity at Augusta National. He is still listed as such, thirty-five years after his death.

1967

First overseas broadcast as BBC televises the tournament via satellite. Bruce Devlin makes a double eagle on the par-five eighth hole, the first player to make a double eagle since Gene Sarazen in 1935. Ben Hogan shoots 66 in third round and is so exhausted at the end that he hardly has enough energy to make it up the hill to the 18th green.

1968

Roberto de Vicenzo signs an incorrect scorecard, denying himself a chance at a playoff with Bob Goalby.

1970

Rear-operated scoreboard used on course for first time. Television coverage extended to the 13th hole for the first time. Billy Casper defeats Gene Littler in an eighteen-hole playoff.

1971

Bobby Jones dies at age sixty-nine on December 18.

1972

Patron badge list closed and waiting list established.

1973

Television coverage extended to the 12th hole. First delayed television coverage to Japan.

1975

Jack Nicklaus sinks forty-foot putt on 16th hole en route to fifth win, a Masters record. Lee Elder becomes first African American golfer to compete in Masters.

1976

Sudden-death playoff format announced. Ray Floyd matches seventy-two-hole scoring record with total of 271. First live broadcast to Japan.

1977

Clifford Roberts dies at age eighty-three on September 29 and is named chairman in memoriam after his death. Tom Watson birdies the 17th hole in the final round to win his first Masters.

1978

Tommy Nakajima has the highest score on an individual hole in tournament history, taking a 13 on the par-five 13th. Gary Player wins for third time thanks to final-round

64 while making birdies on seven of the last ten holes.

1979

Masters rookie Fuzzy Zoeller wins the first sudden-death playoff in tournament history, defeating Ed Sneed and Tom Watson on second playoff hole (number 11).

1980

Tom Weiskopf scores a 13 on the par-three 12th, matching the highest score on an individual hole. Seve Ballesteros becomes youngest champion and second foreign winner. Greens changed in the fall from Bermuda to bentgrass.

1981

First Masters played on bentgrass greens. Heating and cooling system installed under 12th green. Gene Sarazen, Byron Nelson, and Sam Snead become honorary starters.

1982

First and second rounds televised for first time. Craig Stadler defeats Dan Pohl in tournament's only one-hole playoff.

1983

Seve Ballesteros starts final round birdie, eagle, par, birdie, and goes on to win for second time. Players given the option of using their own caddies rather than those who work at the club.

1984

Ben Crenshaw holes a sixty-foot putt on the 10th hole in the final round en route to his first Masters victory.

1986

Nick Price establishes a new course record with a 63 in the third round. Jack Nicklaus becomes oldest champion with sixth victory, shooting a final-round 65 after going seven under par the last ten holes.

1987

Augusta native Larry Mize holes 140-foot pitch and run on the 11th hole to win in sudden-death playoff. He defeats Greg Norman and Seve Ballesteros.

1988

Sandy Lyle hits a seven-iron from the fairway bunker and makes birdie on the final hole to win.

1989

Scott Hoch misses short putt on first sudden-death hole, allowing Nick Faldo the chance to win. Faldo holes from twenty-five feet for birdie on the next hole, number 11, to win.

1990

Flood causes heavy damage at Amen Corner. The 11th green and the 13th tee are destroyed, and the 12th green is damaged. Nick Faldo becomes second player to successfully defend title as he defeats Raymond Floyd in sudden-death playoff.

1992

Fred Couples gets a lucky break when his ball stays on the bank at the 12th hole as he wins first major. Masters lore has it that the area wasn't mown that morning, as it should have been.

1993

Trailing eventual winner Bernhard Langer, Chip Beck decides to lay up on the 15th hole. Beck loses by four strokes. Armchair quarter-backs have argued since that he should have gone for the green. Easy for them to say.

1994

Jeff Maggert scores a double eagle on the 13th hole. It's the third double eagle in tournament history.

1995

Practice-round tickets are limited and sold in advance for first time. Plaque commemorating Arnold Palmer's career placed on fountain at number 16. Jack Nicklaus makes eagles on the par-four fifth hole in the first and third rounds. Ben Crenshaw, saddened by the death earlier in the week of his mentor Harvey Penick, wins for second time.

1996

Greg Norman matches the course record of 63 in the first round. Nick Faldo shoots 67 in the final round to overcome a six-shot deficit and win his third Masters. Greg Norman's 78 represents the worst collapse in tournament history. Norman faces the music, though, and speaks with the media at length. This can't be said of all golfers who have been in similar situations.

1997

Tiger Woods shoots 40 on his first nine yet goes on to establish a new seventy-two-hole scoring record of 270 and win the Masters in his first appearance as a professional.

1998

Jack Nicklaus's achievements are honored with new fountain between the 16th and 17th holes. Mark O'Meara birdies the last two holes to win. Hootie Johnson elected chairman.

1999

Second cut of fairway increased. Qualifications for invitation to Masters changed. World rankings are part of new qualifications; victories in PGA Tour events are no longer a criterion for an invitation. José Maria Olazabal overcomes mysterious foot condition that put his career on hold to win for second time.

2000

Jack Nicklaus, Arnold Palmer, and Gary Player are in the same group for the first time in tournament history.

2001

Tiger Woods wins the Masters for his fourth consecutive major victory. Tournament chairman Hootie Johnson announces significant changes to Augusta National that will lengthen the course by almost three hundred yards. Nine holes are altered in an effort to combat the distances players are hitting the ball.

2002

Tiger Woods becomes the third player to win the tournament in consecutive years. Nine holes are changed on the course. Television coverage extended to eighteen holes for the first time. Sam Snead serves as honorary starter; he dies a month later.

2003

Mike Weir becomes the first Canadian male to win a professional major and the first left-hander to win the Masters, defeating Len Mattiace in a playoff on the first extra hole. Martha Burk tries to get the world to notice that Augusta National doesn't have any female members. Lots of commentary leading up to the Masters and through the week amounts to Augusta National doing . . . nothing. The club is private, doesn't have to do anything, and makes that clear. The Masters is televised without commercials, to reduce potential pressure on its sponsors.

2004

Phil Mickelson holes a birdie putt on the last hole to win, making him the fourth player to win with a birdie on the final hole. Whaddya know? Mickelson is no longer the "Best Player Never to Have Won a Major." Arnold Palmer plays in his fiftieth consecutive, and his final, Masters.

2005

Tiger Woods chips in for birdie on the 16th hole in the last round. His ball hangs on the lip of the hole for an instant, with the Nike logo there for all the world to see. He thereby creates an instant commercial. Woods goes on to win in a playoff over Chris DiMarco. It's his fourth Masters win. Jack Nicklaus famously predicted Woods will win more Masters than he and Arnold Palmer combined, which would mean he needs to win eleven. The prediction might yet come true.

2006

Phil Mickelson wins his second Masters using two drivers, one to draw the ball for distance and the other to fade it for control. Billy Payne replaces Hootie Johnson as chairman of Augusta National.

THE HIMALAYAS

The Himalayas—neither caddies nor Sherpas needed.

The first-time visitor to the Old Course at St. Andrews is likely to wonder just what that huge area of humpty-dumpty ground is, short of and to the right of the first green, and to the right of the second tee. Children, often along with older men and women, perhaps their grandparents, are seen scampering along the ground, which appears to be some sort of golf area. As it happens, they're putting, on a course that was founded in 1867 and that is the home of the Ladies Golf Club. It's the oldest such club in the world, it started as a putting club, and it remains a putting club. The Himalayas (pronounced *hih-mol-yas*), named for the mountain range in Asia, is open to the public, and it's usually a busy spot.

Putting round the Himalayas is a popular recreation for St. Andreans and visitors alike. The course is full most fine days and summer evenings when the light is long. The competition is also keen and takes many forms. The members of the St. Rule Club, a ladies' club at St. Andrews, play an annual match against R&A members. It's one of the oldest interclub matches in the game.

The Himalayas have always been a thing apart from the Old Course. But in 2005, a new tee for the second hole was placed at the edge of an unused portion of the Himalayas, forty yards behind the original tee. The hole was longer than in any previous British Open, but a few days later this back tee became only a curiosity. People were back on the Himalayas, putting the day and evening away.

THE GOLFER'S LIFE LIST

Read at Least One Book by Bernard Darwin

Herbert Warren Wind wrote that we think of Darwin "as the man who invented golf writing." Darwin wrote on golf for *The Times* of London from 1907 through 1953 and for the British weekly *Country Life* from 1907 through 1961, where his column was titled "A Golf Commentary." His name didn't appear under the column; he was called the magazine's "golf correspondent," which was appropriate. It was as if he were sending letters to his readers from courses and tournaments. Darwin didn't interview players, as he believed his readers were interested in what he had to say and not what the golfers had to say. He wrote based on what he saw on the course, and he didn't write about what he didn't see. Or, if he did, he'd likely inform his readers, "A kind friend told me that."

Grandson of the naturalist Charles, Bernard Darwin evolved into one of the world's finest golf writers.

Darwin also wrote books. His columns were collected into volumes from time to time, and he also wrote a biography of the British golfer and architect James Braid. His book *The Golf Courses of the British Isles,* with paintings by Harry Rowntree, is a classic. Darwin was inducted into the World Golf Hall of Fame in November 2005, where John Hopkins, the current *Times* golf correspondent, spoke about him.

"Darwin's writing," Hopkins said, "was that of a master craftsman. He chipped away paragraphs until they were as clear as a pane of glass. He chiseled at sentences with the care of the craftsmen who built Chartres Cathedral. At all times he wrote with gusto."

Darwin could play as well as write. He reached the semi-finals of the 1909 and 1921 British Amateurs, and he always knew when a golfer had played a sound shot as opposed to when he might have gotten a good result; there's often a difference, as he understood.

Many subjects inspired Darwin. He read Charles Dickens avidly and often quoted from his novels. Once, having learned that Mozart enjoyed billiards, and that he was sometimes moved by the way the ball rolled to stop to jot down a theme that later made its way into his music, Darwin decided to take this as a departure point for one of his golf pieces. He imagined that Mozart would have enjoyed golf:

"Set him alone on a wide stretch of the links, where there is no rough to make him hunt for lost balls and no other tiresome players to shout an angry 'Fore' at him, and he tastes some of the intensest joys of living. Let the time be that of evening drawing in, when the rest of the world is at tea and a light or two begin to shine out in the clubhouse windows, and he may enjoy mute ecstasies in which he feels capable of composing almost anything."

Yes, read Darwin.

HOW TO GET KIDS INTERESTED IN GOLF

The Manawatu Way

Manawatu Golf Club, in North Palmerston, New Zealand, has a thriving junior golf program. One aspect of it, an excellent and simple idea for any course, is to have special "junior tees" set considerably down the fairway from even the regular forward or red tees. For kids just learning, even a 300-yard hole can seem impossibly long, and a scorecard full of 9s and 10s grows discouraging quickly when you know "par" is four. A tee box that creates a junior par four of 180 yards caters to youngsters for whom getting the ball in the air is still an accomplishment. It doesn't require special dedicated land, and it's no inconvenience for the regular players to have a small patch of fairway groomed like a tee box. This beginners' course-within-a-course can provide a great way in for the novice golfer.

Johnny Miller's Way

In his book *I Call the Shots,* Johnny Miller provides a step-by-step blueprint for how to get a child between the ages of three and eight interested in the game:

1. Take the child to a course that has a pond or stream. Bring along a bag of old balls and a child-sized club or two.

2. Rent a golf cart, seat the child on your lap or let him or her stand in front of you, and drive out onto the course while he/she does the steering. This alone will be a big kick for a child. Head for a spot next to the water hazard where you won't be in anybody's way.

3. Take out a few balls and let the child make some practice swings, brushing the grass, maybe whacking the top of a weed or dandelion. Then let the child hit balls into the water. ("There's something about watching the ball splash that makes a little kid ecstatic," Miller notes.)

4. Praise every shot. If it goes into the water, it's a great shot. If they miss or just dribble it a few feet, it's a great swing.

5. After five or ten balls, *stop.* Go down to the water, let the kid chase butterflies, catch a frog, talk with your child about nature or the sky or anything under the sun.

Johnny Miller, out of the basement and into the winner's circle.

6. Go back to hitting balls. Spread six balls on the ground and let them go at it again. This time, *stop the game after four shots.* Pocket the two balls, no matter how much he or she wants to hit those last two. Say that you'll do this again soon, but that it's time to go home. Let the child steer the cart on the way back to the clubhouse.

7. You've now whetted the appetite. The next time, give two days' notice, so that the child can look forward to the trip to the golf course with a specific memory in mind. Add something next time—but not something related to golf. Maybe bring a fishing pole, or a favorite book you'll read together. The goal is to create a sense of anticipation and pleasure that the child will always associate with going to the golf course; the love of the game will almost inevitably follow.

Johnny Miller's Father's Way

When Johnny was five, his father Larry nailed a big green canvas tarp to the basement ceiling, gave his son three instruction books and told him to copy the swing positions from them while looking in a mirror, and had him hit balls in the basement into that tarp for three years. Johnny learned the feeling of striking the ball solidly without worrying about where it was going and could only dream of the day when he might get to take his swing out to a real course. Larry Miller's method created a great golfer with a deep love of the game, but isn't it interesting that Johnny's own recommended method is so different?

SO YOU WANNA JOIN THE R&A

Okay, Mr. Club Collector, you know who you are. Between your limitless income and your limitless ego, you've managed to get your name onto the rolls of an agglomeration of the world's great golfing venues. Winged Foot, Pine Valley, and Seminole fell readily into your lap. Overseas membership at Royal Dornoch—why not? Ballybunion likewise. Maybe you'll get there once every couple of years, but it's good to know you'll be welcomed like a brother. But if you really want to brighten up a *vitae* and dazzle your friends, there's nothing like placing the words "Royal" and "Ancient" into close conjunction.

Needless to say, joining the R&A isn't a matter of collecting enough Weetabix box tops and sending in an application. No, when a club's bylaws declare one of its objects to be "[t]o maintain the position of St Andrews as the Home of Golf," it's unlikely to base this on an open-door policy. (Likewise its stated desire "[t]o be a members' golf club having a club house with high quality facilities and reasonable access to first class golfing facilities. . . ." You might say they've overachieved on that score.)

The procedures for considering membership are not that different from those of the country club down the street, provided that your street is a part of Seventeen-Mile Drive. You must be proposed and seconded by members of the club (three if you live in the United Kingdom, two if you live overseas), there's a nomination form that has to be filed, you must be available for an interview, and those proposing you must attest to your character, your history, and your likelihood to partake in the activities of the club. Seems pretty standard, although your local club probably does not have a Rules of Golf Committee and an Implements and Ball Committee that are empowered to nominate one candidate per year separate from anyone nominated by individuals on those committees. Your club also probably doesn't have a category of honorary members intended for "Princes of the Blood-Royal," "distinguished Members of the Club," and "distinguished professional golfers," who are exempt from paying an entrance fee or annual subscription.

There is a General Committee that conducts elections for members; a candidate must normally be listed in the Candidates' Book for a year before the election will take place, though it can be accelerated if the committee considers it "advisable in the general interest of the Club." (That's a loophole large enough to drive a lorry-leasing magnate through.) The good news for those of you who have, ahem, strong personalities is that the vote of the General Committee need not be unanimous; you must receive more than 80 percent approval, however, to be accepted.

Looking for a way to increase your chances of acceptance? If acquiring some of that blood-royal is out of the question, and it's too late for you to win multiple Open Championships (calling it the British Open will not make you any friends), we do have a few practical suggestions:

1. Become the RAF's commanding officer at Leuchars. This Royal Air Force base is familiar to anyone who's heard the incongruous sound of military aircraft flying overhead while trying to extricate himself from Hell Bunker. (There is no St. Andrews BritRail station; the nearest stop to the Old Course is the one at Leuchars, pronounced *loo-cars.*) The officer in command there may be invited to become an Extraordinary Member, which is a nice phrase to drop when you're chatting up the lasses. Regular officers of the United Kingdom or Allied Forces, while on duty in the counties of Fife, Perthshire, or Angus, may also be nominated for such membership.

2. Learn to put "Sheriff" and "Fife" in the same sentence without thinking of Don Knotts. If you can put aside your memories of the ineffectual Barney Fife in Andy Griffiths's town of Mayberry, you will discover that others who share similar status with the officer in command at Leuchars are the lord lieutenant and sheriff principal of Tayside, Central, and Fife; the sheriff at Cupar; and the principal of the University of St. Andrews. Extraordinary Members pay no initiation or annual fees, but the membership can be terminated at any time without citing a reason—like, say, forgetting to pronounce "lord lieutenant" with a *leff.*

3. Move to Trinidad and Tobago.

Membership is strictly allocated by geography. The United States is restricted to a maximum of 275 "Ordinary Members"—though there is probably little less ordinary than an ordinary member of the R&A. With a population of 295.7 million (according to the 2000 *World Almanac*), this permits only one member for every 1,075,273 persons. Three other major countries are allowed 110 members each; their rates of membership are one in 181,818 (Australia), one in 298,182 (Canada), and one in 402,727 (South Africa). It might seem your best bet is to move to part of what is considered the Home Territory—the U.K., Ireland, Channel Islands, and Isle of Man—but even with a whopping 1,150 slots reserved for the home team, that's still a rate of one in 55,652. Far better is to go for a Rest of the World country, whose only restriction is that there may be no more than 50 members from any such country (among the 750 permissible Overseas Members). However, there are two ways of looking at the numbers: (1) Divide the population of, say, Trinidad and Tobago by fifty to reach a figure of one in 22,000, your best odds yet. (2) Assuming the other countries are fully subscribed, the overall limit of 1,900 members means that there are only 145 spots available for the entire remaining population of the world. This puts your chances at one in 41,297,241 and getting worse every day. (The best way to understand such fractions is to listen to the mathematician who said of any individual's odds in a national lottery, "Your chances of winning are roughly the same whether or not you buy a ticket.")

On second thought, maybe you should aim for something easy like Augusta National instead.

NAMES OF HOLES AT HIGHLANDS LINKS, INGONISH, NOVA SCOTIA

Canadian golf's finest meeting of mountain, forest, and (unseen) sea.

1. Ben Franey—Franey Mountain visible

2. Tam O'Shanter—for the shape of the green

3. Lochan—plays over a small loch, or lake

4. Heich O'Fash—Heap O'Trouble

5. Canny Slap—a small opening in a hedge or fence

6. Mucklemouth Meg—for a young Scottish lady whose mouth was wide enough to swallow a turkey's egg

7. Killiecrankie—this 570-yard par five moves along a fairway named for a long and narrow pass

8. Caber's Toss—have to play up and over a hill

9. Corbie's Nest—for a corbie, or crow, whose nest is on high ground

10. Cuddy's Lugs—donkey's ears, named after the shape of the bunkers

11. Bonnie Burn—a pretty stream

12. Cleugh—a deep gully or ravine with steep sides

13. Laird—a Scottish landowner

14. Haugh—a small hollow or, sometimes, a valley

15. Tattie Bogle—potato pits

16. Sair Fecht—hard work

17. Dowie Den—after a ballad of the same name

18. Hame Noo—home now

IF T. S. ELIOT WERE IN THE BROADCAST BOOTH . . .

As Greg Norman shoots 76 in the last round of the 1996 Masters and loses the six-shot lead he had over Nick Faldo, who wins:

"*April is the cruellest month.*"
—"The Waste Land"

His version of "grip it and rip it":

"*Cling, swing.*"
—"Landscapes: I. New Hampshire"

As a player stands over an important shot:

"*The time is now propitious, as he guesses.*"
—"The Waste Land"

While a phalanx of R&A members and officials from other clubs line up with players at a ceremony:

"*Those are the golf club captains, these are the scouts.*"
—"Coriolan: I. Triumphal March"

"I have seen the moment of my greatness flicker."

As a player tries to decide whether to gamble on a shot, and finally chooses to lay up:

"*The right time and the right place are not here.*"
—"Ash Wednesday"

About slow play:

"*All that time, what did he do?*"
—"Sweeney Agonistes, Fragment of an Agon"

When players hate a course:

"*This is the dead land.*"
—"The Hollow Men"

As Tiger Woods was winning the 2005 British Open at the Old Course in beautiful weather:

"*Pleasure in the wind, the sunlight and the sea.*"
—"Animula"

While a player prepares to hit a bunker shot:

"*Sweat is dry and feet are in the sand.*"

—"The Waste Land"

While the wind howls on the par-three 17th hole at the Tournament Players Club in Ponte Vedra Beach, Florida, its island green appearing such a small target:

"*The menace and caress of waves that breaks on water.*"

—"The Dry Salvages"

During a storm, while players try to compose themselves and study yardage books with their caddies:

"*Men and bits of paper, whirled by the cold wind.*"

—"Burnt Norton"

Watching a player fight the yips:

"*As the mind deserts the body it has used.*"

—"La Figlia che Piange"

Studying a player working with his swing coach:

"*Where is the knowledge we have lost in information?*"

—Choruses from *THE ROCK*, III

Observing a golfer, perhaps Colin Montgomerie, hearing sounds everywhere:

"*What is that noise now? What is the wind doing?*"

—"The Waste Land"

T. S. Eliot, would-be author of The Waste Area.

Tiger heading to the interview tent:

"*There will be time, there will be time*
To prepare a face to meet the faces that you meet . . .
And time for all the works and days of hands
That lift and drop a question on your plate"

—"The Love Song of J. Alfred Prufrock"

Players missing the Q-school cut by one shot:

"*We are the hollow men.*"

—"The Hollow Men"

LUCY'S RULES

On the episode of *I Love Lucy* aired on May 17, 1954, Fred and Ricky want to keep Lucy and Ethel from taking up golf—and intruding on their game—so they take the wives out onto the course and invent a series of complicated rules designed to make the game seem impossible. (In addition, they provide wrong terms for nearly everything, like "stymie" for a driver.) Those rules:

1. All players grip the driver fist-over-fist like baseball teams "choosing up"; the person who is fourth from the top hits first.

2. Before swinging, you must say, "May I?" If you fail to do so, you are penalized ten points and must take one giant step forward (perpendicular to the line of play) with your right leg only.

3. If you swing and miss three times (which is likely because Lucy is instructed to look only down the fairway, never at the ball), that's a "dormie," after which you are entitled to pick up the ball and throw it forward under your left leg.

4. You are not permitted to do a normal "stymie" (this is the term for a drive and a driver) if your partner has "dormied." Your opponent, upon saluting, may ask his partner for permission to shoot out of turn. If permission is granted, the opponent may take his stance, flap his arms and whistle, and then hit a drive. This is what's known as "a birdie."

5. If you swing and miss on a "birdie," your opponent may start counting; you must kick the ball before he gets to ten, or you're out. If you do kick the ball in time, the opponent does not get to drive on the hole.

6. If the person who hit first got the ball farther down the fairway than the third person's ball, the first person gets to carry all the bags.

7. The green must be approached by playing leapfrog over each other.

8. If you touch your ball when it isn't a dormie (see rule 3), you get a "mashie" for a penalty. This is accomplished by your opponent mashing your ball into the ground with his foot.

9. Everybody putts at once. The object of putting is both to get your ball into the cup and to keep your opponents' balls from getting in.

10. The person who gets the ball into the hole first gets to carry all the bags to the next hole.

11. If you hit the ball farther than your husband, you have to hop to the next hole while rubbing your stomach and patting your head. (This might not be an actual rule, though it is enforced by Fred against Ethel.)

12. If your ball misses the sand trap completely and lands on the green, you are penalized ten points. (This penalty is enforced by Lucy and Ethel against the golfer who joins up with them—Jimmy Demaret.)

TEN MOST MEMORABLE LINES *from* *CADDYSHACK*

1. *But the man worthwhile/Is the man who can smile/When his shorts are too tight in the seat.*

2. *Will you come and loofah my stretchmarks?*

3. *Hey, baby, you're all right. You must have been something before electricity.*

4. *"My uncle says you have a screw loose." "Your uncle molests collies."*

5. *He was night putting. Just putting at night. With the fifteen-year-old daughter of the Dean.*

6. *So we finish eighteen, and he was going to stiff me. And I said, "Hey! Lama! How about a little something, you know, for the effort." And he said, "Oh, there won't be any money, but when you die, on your deathbed you will receive total consciousness." So I got that goin' for me. Which is nice.*

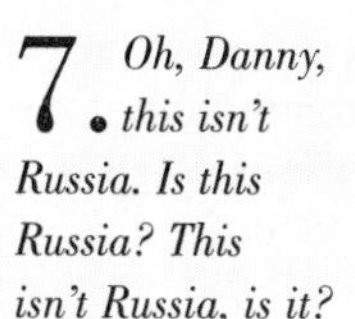

7. *Oh, Danny, this isn't Russia. Is this Russia? This isn't Russia, is it?*

8. *I was born to love you/I was born to lick your face/I was born to rub you/But you were born to rub me first.*

9. *I tell you, I never saw dead people smoke before.*

10. *Find your center. See nothing. Hear nothing. Be the ball.*

GOLF CART ETIQUETTE

Purists hate them (and rightly so, say the authors, both purists), but golf carts are a necessary evil on some of the far-flung landscapes that pass for courses in the Age of the Developer. Some people don't, or can't, or won't play golf without them. Without passing judgment on them, let's agree that the cart creates a need for certain new principles of etiquette. Our suggestions:

1. Wait at the tee box until everyone's hit. Your club won't get lonely if it has to wait a minute before rejoining its mates. Leaving the tee to go sit in your cart while others hit is unsociable, and deprives the other players of a set of eyes that could help spot a wayward drive. This will also keep you from rattling your club into your bag during someone else's swing.

2. Have an extra ball in your pocket at all times. A good general principle, this one is especially important when your golf bag might be more than a few steps away. In fact, carry two extras, and replenish your pockets if you lose one. It's not impossible that your second drive will go in the same godforsaken direction as the first.

3. Take extra clubs with you. If the course has mandated "cart paths only"—the three most loathsome words in golf—bring at least three clubs with you: the club you think you'll need, and one club longer and shorter. You might want to bring a "safe" club, too, one that you'd use to lay up to a comfortable distance. There's nothing worse than getting to your ball and then deciding you need a club you don't have with you—nothing worse for you, your partners, or the group in back of you.

4. Anticipate needs. If you're in a greenside bunker, bring your putter along with your sand wedge. And, because the occasional bunker shot has gone through the green in the past, bring a club you like to use for chipping, too.

5. Remember that there are two of you. Keep the cart in a reasonable state of cleanliness, and make sure there's always at least one empty cup-holder for your fellow rider. Dump your trash periodically; your friend was kind enough not to object to your cigar at 9 A.M., but this doesn't mean he wants to ride around all day with the butt floating in your leftover coffee.

6. Don't be stupid. Surprising how often this advice is ignored. When you're getting out of a car, you wait until it comes to a full stop, right? Do the same with a golf cart; soft spikes are good for traction in grass but can be slippery on a floor mat. Same for getting in; save your complex boarding maneuvers for cable cars and trolleys.

7. Carts should be neither seen nor heard. As much as possible, keep the cart out of other golfers' lines of sight. If you're sharing the cart with a right-handed golfer, park to the left of where he'll stand for his next shot. Don't hit the brake when someone else is swinging; this includes players on the next tee if you're approaching a green that's close to it.

8. Carry your clubs with you into the cart. If players are waiting behind you, hit your shot, get into the cart, and sort your clubs into their appropriate compartments after you get to your ball for the next shot.

9. Notice if the cart is carrying a rake. If it is, assume that you're expected to bring it with you to the bunker, and keep the rake with your clubs so that you won't forget to bring it back to the cart.

10. Park in the direction of the next tee. Assuming you know the course or can tell where you're going, leave the cart around the green so that you're on your way to the next hole, and so you won't have to circle several bunkers to get to the cart. In general, you always want to leave the cart somewhere that won't require walking back to it.

11. Carts are not soundproof. Other players can still hear you talking on your cellphone even if you're sitting in the cart. Don't do it. (Cellphones are a whole category of transgressions unto themselves; taking or making a call during the play of a hole should carry a two-stroke penalty at all times. Let your voice-mail take a message, and call back at the turn.)

THE GOLFER'S LIFE LIST

Play a Three-Club Round

Rule 4-4 allows a player to start a round "with not more than fourteen clubs." But nothing compels the golfer to use the fourteen clubs allowed. One of the pleasures of golf is to use fewer than the maximum number allowed, even far fewer. Many clubs have an event each season in which they stipulate that players must restrict themselves to five or six clubs. Some even insist that competitors use but one club.

Three clubs seems just about right. Take a club to use from the tees on longer holes, perhaps a five- or seven-wood or a hybrid club. Knock the ball down to get more distance. Open it up to turn it into a more lofted club. Use it for long chip and run shots, as Todd Hamilton did to seal his win in the 2004 British Open. Tiger Woods used a fairway wood up a sharp greenside slope at the Congressional Country Club during the 1997 U.S. Open, and holed the shot. Anybody can play this shot; you don't need to be Tiger Woods to improvise.

For shots into the green, and others around the green, and even in sand, a seven-iron works well. You can close it down and turn it into a longer iron, open the blade to hit a hard slice, or close it to hit a low hook. Open it up wide, very wide, and you'll have a sand wedge or even a lob wedge in your hands. You'll feel like Seve Ballesteros, master of the short game. (Well, *maybe* you'll feel like him.)

Your third club is your putter, but it doesn't have to be a conventional putter. If you feel you need a sand wedge, you could convert this into a putter by using the leading edge on the greens. Sometimes tour pros resort to this when they're putting poorly and have given up or broken their putters. Focusing on contacting the ball with the thin leading edge concentrates the mind. You might even putt better.

Using only a few clubs frees you from playing golf by rote, by yardage. You'll play by feel and instinct. You'll lose your mind and come to your senses, as Fritz Perls, the founder of Gestalt therapy, said; he wasn't a golfer, but the maxim applies. Play three-club golf and find more shots than you knew you had. You'll invent shots, and you'll have nothing but fun.

PRICES OF CONCESSIONS DURING 2006 MASTERS, INCLUDING 7 PERCENT SALES TAX

SANDWICH (CHOICE OF BAR-B-Q, EGG, PIMENTO CHEESE, TURKEY, OR HAM AND CHEESE): $1.50

MASTERS CLUB SANDWICH: $2.50

SOFT DRINKS: $1.00

PINK LEMONADE: $1.00

BEER: $2.00 (NO BEER SOLD AFTER 4 PM)

IMPORTED BEER: $3.00

BOTTLED WATER: $1.25

CANDY: $.75 (SNICKERS, MILKY WAY, CRUNCH)

ASPIRIN OR TYLENOL: $.50

CRACKERS: $.75

HEADACHE POWDER: $.50

FOOTNOTES TO HISTORY

Marty Fleckman, 1967 U.S. Open, Baltusrol Golf Club, Springfield, New Jersey

Fleckman, the son of a lumber dealer in Port Arthur, Texas, was a well-known amateur who had been on the University of Houston team that won three NCAA Championships, and was also on the U.S. Walker Cup team that defeated Great Britain and Ireland a few weeks before in England. Fleckman, then twenty-three, shot 67–73–69 to take a one-shot lead over Jack Nicklaus, Arnold Palmer, and Billy Casper heading into the final round at Baltusrol.

Fleckman didn't have a restful night sleeping on the lead. "I couldn't stop thinking about it," he said. "I was always an early riser, but in this case I was up at 2 A.M. and my tee time wasn't until 2 P.M."

Baltusrol's spectators welcomed him warmly. "I felt like a Hollywood star," he said of walking to the first tee of the final round. "I saw a sea of people and I don't remember whether I pushed my way through or they parted for me, but I shook so many hands and signed so many autographs I almost wore my arm out."

Fleckman was playing with Casper in the last twosome, with Nicklaus and Palmer just ahead. Fleckman's round got off to a bad start when he drove into trees to the right and bogeyed the hole. He shot 80, while Casper also faltered and fell out of contention. Palmer shot 69 but Nicklaus's 65 gave him a new U.S. Open record of 275, one better than the record score that Ben Hogan had posted nineteen years earlier.

Fleckman turned pro that fall and immediately won the Cajun Classic in Lafayette, Louisiana, becoming the first player to win his first tournament as a professional. He stayed on the PGA Tour for thirteen years but never won again, and turned to a career as a teaching professional.

HOW TO CALCULATE A HANDICAP

1. List your twenty most recent rounds.

2. Apply Equitable Stroke Control* to your hole-by-hole results in those rounds to determine an Adjusted Score.

3. Subtract the Course Rating for each course from your Adjusted Score to determine a Differential for each round.

4. To factor in the difficulty of each course, calculate a Slope Rating Adjustment by dividing 113 by the designated Slope.**

5. Multiply the Differential by the Slope Rating Adjustment.

6. Multiply that figure by 0.96.

7. Rank your twenty results from lowest to highest.

8. Calculate the average of your ten lowest results from those twenty most recent rounds. This figure is your handicap index—a measure of what your handicap would be at a course of average difficulty.

9. At any actual course, use the handicap index conversion chart to see what your handicap is at that particular course for your particular index.

*Equitable Stroke Control is intended to keep a few bad holes from excessively raising a player's handicap index. It sets maximums for the score you can have on any single hole when you're preparing your rounds to be included in your handicap. The maximums, which depend on your handicap at the particular course, are as follows:

COURSE HANDICAP	MAXIMUM
1–9	double bogey
10–19	7
20–29	8
30–39	9
40 and up	10

**113 is the Slope Rating assigned to a course of exactly average difficulty.

WHEN IS A BOGEY PAR?

The term *bogey* came into golf in the late nineteenth century, in British competitions that consisted of match play against a designated standard for each hole. The score represented the expectation for a good player. It was an era when Open Championships were won by players scoring in the 80s, and bogey scores were generally set at that level by the individual clubs.

In the United States, the game was still quite young when national organizations became involved in the process. In the 1890s, the United States Golf Association began efforts to standardize the handicap system, which led in 1911 to a yardage-based definition of par for each hole. (The term *par* was taken from finance, where the par value of a stock represents its normal or market price.) A hole of up to 225 yards was a par three; from 225 to 425 yards was a par four; 426 to 600 yards was a par five; anything longer was a par six.

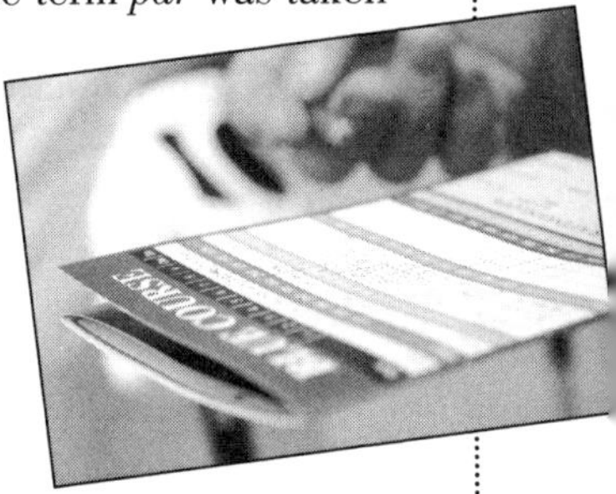

The British courses were slow to change their bogey figures to reflect the way scores were dropping—much as courses today cling to 70–72 as a par when a more realistic figure for flawless play by professionals would be 66–68. So while "bogey" and "par" were intended to mean the same thing, in reality the bogey figures were significantly higher. Americans began to use "bogey" derisively for a hole score of one over par. That meaning eventually took hold on both sides of the Atlantic, and bogey became an evil to be avoided instead of a tough spectral opponent.

THE GOLFER'S LIFE LIST

Play Pebble Beach

Walk the fairways where Dean Martin staggered.

It sits on one of the most beautiful and expensive pieces of real estate in America. We've watched Jack and Tom and Tiger win there, seen Jack Lemmon struggle and Dean Martin stagger and Bill Murray mug for the cameras. You don't have to love the game to appreciate the salt air and the conjunction of land and sea. Pebble Beach is the one course on earth that you simply must play if you want to call yourself a golfer.

True, there are a number of ordinary holes. Yes, the price for a round is exorbitant, even more so when you factor in the cost of the night's stay that's a near necessity to make your tee-time reservation. (While we have nothing against the Lodge, our preference is for the Inn at Spanish Bay, which offers a level of comfort and customer service most of the world's other resorts can only aspire to.) But when you stand on the 7th tee and choose your club for that tantalizing little tee shot, or launch a ball across Stillwater Cove hoping to see it land on the 8th green, or walk up the 18th fairway with the sea lions barking and the sea spray tickling your nose, you'll be in the midst of the most spectacular environment the game has ever known, and you'll be soaking up the moments and wishing they could last forever.

DEBUNKING THE MYTHS ABOUT GOLF EQUIPMENT

Frank Thomas was technical director of the United States Golf Association for more than a quarter of a century. In that time he directed the development of the testing procedures that govern all aspects of equipment and literally wrote the rulebook on what's permitted and what isn't. Prior to joining the USGA, he worked at Shakespeare Sporting Goods, where he invented the graphite shaft. Today he is a consultant to the golf industry, chief technical advisor to *Golf Digest* and the Golf Channel, answers questions on his Web site (www.franklygolf.com), and has designed putters that translate his theoretical knowledge into practical form. The following, adapted from his upcoming book, *Just Hit It,* describes what he considers the biggest myths about golf equipment, with his commentaries on each:

The lower the loft, the farther you'll hit your driver.

When the USGA began testing equipment with a mechanical model, it was exactly that—a mechanical model of what was considered to be the ideal swing. Today, computer models of flight trajectories can determine the optimum launch conditions for hitting a golf ball as far as possible. Those conditions, using the average clubhead speed for a touring pro, are a launch angle of about 12 to 12.5 degrees and a spin rate of about 2,000–2,300 rpm.

The crucial variable is *swing speed.* The pros average 116 mph; fewer than 10 percent of all amateur golfers swing as fast as 95 mph. The slower the swing speed, the higher the launch angle should be to get maximum distance. Your macho playing partners might brag about using a nine-degree, eight-degree, even a six-degree driver. Let them. Your higher-lofted driver will give you the most efficient way to get the ball out there as far as you can with your actual swing.

The shaft plays a vital role in keeping the clubface from twisting at impact.

A lot of golf equipment marketing is based on maintaining belief in this fiction. The duration of impact is so incredibly short—in the neighborhood of 450 *microseconds,* or .00045 seconds—that the shaft has no time to have an effect. (For comparison, the blink of an eye takes .10 seconds.) By the time the shaft comes into play at all, the ball is long gone.

The clubface does rotate during impact on mishits, but it does so around its own center of gravity, at or behind the sweet spot on the face. This is why, when you hit the ball on the toe of the club, it generates draw spin, while a hit on the heel will fade. This "gear effect" is the result of the clubface rotating around its center on imperfect contact. If the clubface rotated around the shaft at impact, those two mishits would fly the same way.

Club fitting is an essential expenditure for the serious golfer.

Golf is a very mature sport. People have been playing it for hundreds of years now, and through a long process of trial and error we've come up with a set of approximate standards for equipment that have held up very well through the ages.

Most club fitting these days is done to sell new clubs to the average golfer. The club fitter examines your stance, your setup, and your swing, and determines the very slight tweaking that will give you the theoretically perfect result every time. The problem is, you and I don't swing perfectly every time, we don't set up exactly the same way every time, and try as we might we just aren't as consistent as we would like to be. (Given what some of our swings look like, that inconsistency might be a blessing.) With the exception of lie angle, which does affect ball flight and depends on your posture and swing plane and shaft flex, fitting for all the rest of the bells and whistles is just window dressing that makes the customer feel special because he is getting a "customized set." For most of us, comprehensive club fitting will at best provide a placebo effect—and a pretty expensive one at that.

The better the player, the stiffer the shaft he should use.

In general, the higher your swing speed, the stiffer your shaft should be, because you're applying more force in the swing, "loading" the shaft with more energy, and a more flexible shaft will bend too much for you to be able to control the clubhead. It's important to have a feel for where the clubhead is as you swing; "swing the clubhead" is the mantra of many a good teacher. If the shaft is too whippy, you'll get a big kick as the clubhead catches up with your hands, or it will lag behind so that timing and controlling the head at impact will be almost impossible. On the other hand, if the shaft is too stiff, you won't get any significant bend at all, you'll lose feel for where the head is, and you won't transfer the most possible energy to the clubhead for impact.

Golfers know that the pros use X (for extra-stiff) or Double-X shafts, and their macho instincts tell them that that's what "real golfers"—that is, "real men"—ought to use. So they buy their equipment by trying the stiffest possible shafts first, then move towards more flexible shafts until they find one they can begin to control. That's a backward way of thinking about the problem; you'll be better off starting with the most flexible shaft, and moving toward the stiffer shafts for as long as you can still feel the clubhead throughout the swing.

Something must be done to rein in the new equipment, or pros will soon be hitting drives four hundred yards, and all classic courses will be rendered obsolete.

There has been a revolution in golf at the professional level over the past ten years; if the gains in distance over that time are extrapolated forward, the prospects are truly alarming. In 1980, the average driving distance on the PGA Tour was 256.9 yards. From 1980 to 1995, the average increased a total of 8.1 yards, or just about 1.6 feet per year. Since 1995, this figure has jumped by a startling 23.6 yards, a rate of seven feet per year.

Will innovation continue at the same phenomenal rate? I don't see how it possibly can.

When we consider the distance figures from twenty-five years ago, we're comparing titanium drivers and solid, multilayer balls launched under computer-analyzed optimum conditions to wooden-headed drivers and softer, wound balls hit using methods honed using the naked eye. What kind of material will be as much of an advance over titanium as that ultralight metal was over persimmon woods?

Even just taking the increases since 1995—which coincide with the springlike effect from thin-faced titanium drivers as opposed to steel or other metal clubheads—there has been a definite leveling off in the last two years:

YEARS	GAIN IN AVG. DRIVING DISTANCE (yards)	YEARLY RATE OF INCREASE (in feet)
1999–2001	from 272.6 to 279.4	10.2
2001–2003	from 279.4 to 286.6	10.8
2003–2005	from 286.6 to 288.6	3.0

I would estimate that about ten yards of the difference is attributable to the club, about five to the ball, and the rest to an effect of synergy between the two that results from an increased awareness of how to optimize launch conditions.

Right now, the ball is about as resilient as it can get—it has a little way to go, but not much—and the spring in the club is as efficient as it's going to get, especially with the recent rules putting a limit on the degree of bounceback, the oft-cited "coefficient of restitution," or COR. It is possible to gain a little bit from improved aerodynamics in ball design, but even there we're probably as close to ideal as we can get, with only a few yards additional benefit yet to come.

The only way we're going to see further quantum leaps in distance is if golfers somehow learn to swing faster, more powerfully, without a simultaneous loss of control. We've been trying to do that since Angus first swung his shepherd's crook at a rock, and we haven't managed it yet. The rules that will keep that from happening were observed by Newton, not written by the USGA.

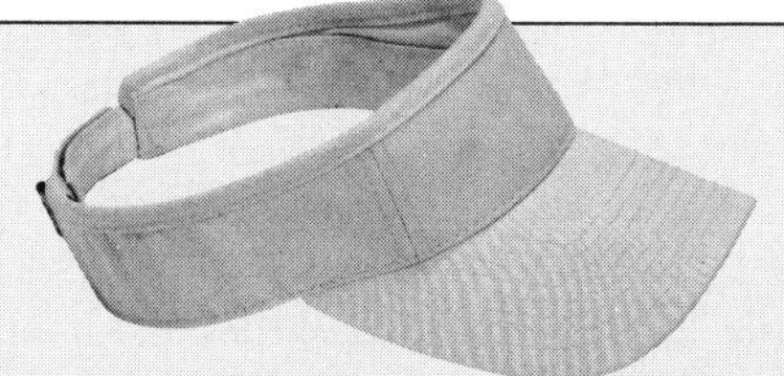

MASTERS MERCHANDISE AND PRICES (2006)

- 13th hole throw: $55
- Cap: $20
- Visor: $15
- Valuables pouch: $24
- Flag: $22
- Shoe bag: $29
- Two ball markers and ball repair tool: $22
- Screen saver: $12
- Golden Bell Candle: $18
- Masters pillow: $30
- Yardage book: $7
- Fleece blanket: $30
- Driver headcover: $15
- Calendar: April 2006 through April 2007: $16

NICKNAMES OF SOME TOUR CADDIES

Asbestos: Steve Duplantis. Thought to be fireproof because no matter what he did, Jim Furyk wouldn't fire him. However, Furyk did finally let him go after he was late one too many times. Also known as Spring Break because he believed every day was spring break. Caddied for Rich Beem when Beem won the 1999 Kemper Open, his first PGA Tour victory. Beem credited Duplantis with calming him down and helping him believe he could win.

Bambi: Ron Levin. Works for Todd Hamilton, the 2004 British Open champion. Started when he was twenty.

Big Country: Scott Tway, PGA Tour player Bob Tway's brother. Works for Scott Verplank. A big guy from Oklahoma, he shares the nickname with former Oklahoma State basketball player Bryant Reeves.

Big E: Eric Bagas. Caddies for Neal Lancaster. He's big and wide.

Boats: Greg Rita. Has worked for Mike Donald and Gil Morgan. Feet the size of boats.

Bones: Jim Mackay. Phil Mickelson's caddie. Tall and lanky.

Crispy: Chris P. Jones. Caddies for Paul Claxton. Chris P. Crispy. Get it?

Fluff: Mike Cowan. Caddied for Peter Jacobsen and then Tiger Woods until March 1999. Was with Tiger when he won his first Masters, in 1997. When he started caddying, he had little or no money and drove a beat-up old green Chevrolet van. Caddies who rode with him paid for his gas and his hamburger breakfasts. He now works for Jim Furyk.

Killer: Sammy Foy. Worked for Hale Irwin and Phil Blackmar. Ladies' man, hence the nickname.

Lucky: Peter Coleman. Caddied for Bernhard Langer.

Overkill: Don Thom. Worked for Craig Barlow, spends more time on the course studying it than any other caddie.

Professor: Brad Klein. Caddied for Lon Hinkle, Bernhard Langer, and Don Pooley. Holds doctorate in political science and has taught at various universities.

Road Runner: Mark Cairns. Caddies for James Driscoll. Runs to the ball.

Squeeky: Jeff Medlen. Nick Price's long-time caddy. Had John Daly's bag when Daly came out of nowhere to win the 1991 PGA. Known for his high-pitched voice. Died of leukemia in 1997.

Stump: Mike Harmon. Works for Hunter Mahan. Short and stocky.

Tobacco Lou: Ralph Coffee. Always had a cigarette in his mouth.

THE GOLFER'S LIFE LIST

Play a Round Without Using Yardages

Trust your eyes and your judgment; your golfing brain is smarter than you think.

This probably sounds like heresy. How can you play without knowing the exact distance to a hazard, the front of the green, the middle of the green, the pin? But really, how can you not? Very few people do anymore—a generation of golfers has grown up who rely on yardage books, and many are also using GPS systems now.

Try it and you'll be surprised. You'll find that you can rely on your own senses far more than you thought you could. You don't have an exact distance to the car ahead of you when you brake. You don't know the distance in yards or even feet to the wall when you're playing squash, or to the net when you play tennis. You trust what you see and feel. You trust your mind's eye. You rely on your experience, not someone else's tape measure. You rely on yourself.

Let your eye and your senses guide you around the course. The wager here is that you'll hit a greater variety of shots, that you'll be more involved in your round, and that you'll enjoy it in new ways. You'll probably also score better.

GOOD WORDS *for* BAD SHOTS

Steven Pinker wrote in *The Language Instinct* that it's just an urban legend that Eskimos have forty different words for snow. It is not a legend that there are nearly that many words in golf for bad shots: chili-dip, chunk, flub, foozle, shank, skank, stub—to cite a few.

It must say something about the game that golfers have such a colorful vocabulary for poor shots but almost nothing for a good shot. ("Ace" for a hole-in-one doesn't count; the occurrence is all too rare, and nothing about the word tickles the tongue.) What do we say when somebody happens to hit a good one? We say "nice shot" or "great shot" or—the highest accolade, and dullest term—"golf shot." But you don't need adjectives for a poor shot, not when the language offers so many delicious words. Here's a catalogue, in alphabetical order:

Banana Ball

Blade

Block

Blue Darter

Chili-dip

Chunk

Cold-top

Dub

Duck Hook

Duff

E.A. (Elephant's Ass—it's high and it stinks)

El Hosel

Fat

Flub

Fluff

Foozle (rarely used anymore, unfortunately; means any type of bad shot)

Hack

Heel Job

Lateral

Quacker

Sclaff (when the golfer hits the ground before the ball; rarely used today)

Scuff

Shank

Skank

Skull

Sky

Smother

Snap-hook (or Snapper)

Socket

Thin

Top

Whiff

Yip

GREAT CAREER AMATEURS

C. Ross (Sandy) Somerville, b. London, Ontario, 1902, d. London, Ontario, 1991

Bobby Jones wrote the following for the front page of *The Mail and Empire* of Toronto on September 18, 1932, the day after Somerville became the first Canadian to win the U.S. Amateur:

"I believe that for the championship to be won by some other than an American is a good thing. Particularly, this is true when the winner is a fine golfer and a sportsman like Sandy Somerville."

Somerville was a man of few words, so few that he was called Silent Sandy. His friends liked to tell the story of when he was at a cocktail party, and a lady said to somebody standing nearby that she bet she could get Somerville to say three words. Overhearing her, he turned and said, "You lose."

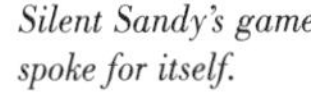

Silent Sandy's game spoke for itself.

FAMOUS COLLAPSES IN MAJORS

MacDonald Smith, 1925 British Open, Prestwick

Born in Carnoustie, and owner of a graceful swing, Smith moved to the United States before he was twenty years old. He tied for the U.S. Open in 1910 at the Philadelphia Cricket Club when he shot 71 in the final round. Alex Smith, one of the men he tied, was his brother and shot 71 to beat him in the playoff. Smith shot 77. Johnny McDermott, the third golfer in the playoff, shot 75.

Mac Smith wasn't seen much in championship golf for some time following his loss, when he worked in a shipyard. But he returned to golf in 1923 and took the lead into the final round of the 1925 British Open. Smith was at 221, which staked him to a five-shot advantage going into the last round. The Englishman Long Jim Barnes shot 74 in that round to finish at 300. Nobody was closer as Smith was out on the course, followed by a huge crowd. He needed to shoot 78 or better to win.

Crowds walked with the players then and got very near to them. They certainly got very near Smith, unsettling him. Many of Prestwick's holes converged on one another, which made the crowding only worse, and people watching one player commingled with those watching another. Smith lost shot after shot in "a tragedy of frittering," to use Bernard Darwin's felicitous phrase, and came in with 82 to finish in fourth place, three shots behind Barnes. He was understandably bitter and disappointed. Smith won three Western Opens and the 1926 Canadian Open, but he never did win a major championship. Darwin wrote that he "deserves serious consideration for the depressing honor of being the best player who never won a championship."

THE WORD ON

Augusta National

"We wanted to make bogeys easy if frankly sought, pars readily obtainable by standard good play, and birdies, except on par fives, dearly bought."

—BOBBY JONES

"The first time I played the Masters, I was so nervous I drank a bottle of rum before I teed off. I shot the happiest 83 of my life."

—CHI CHI RODRIGUEZ (His first Masters round was actually a 77, but it's still a nice line.)

"The Masters is the only tournament I ever knew where you choke when you drive through the front gate."

—GARY PLAYER

"If you ever see me on the 11th green in two, you'll know I missed my shot."

—BEN HOGAN

"They built eighteen great holes, every one of which is perfectly fair and provides a problem. It seems to me that each one demands that a player shall firstly and foremostly use his brains and not merely his physical and, in these days, his almost mechanical ability to hit a target from a particular range. It restores the ideas of some of the old original golf links which furnished the world with those great players upon whose methods and tremendous skill the modern game is now based."

—LEONARD CRAWLEY

"There's no other golf course like this, anywhere. Never has been. Its greens and its challenges on and around the greens are just super, super tough. So they are fun to play, in sort of a morbid way."

—BEN CRENSHAW

THREE-HANKY GOLF

Tom Watson and Bruce Edwards

"Yes," caddie Bruce Edwards said with a punch in his voice when Tom Watson, his employer and friend, holed a six-iron from 171 yards on their third hole of the first round of the 2003 U.S. Open. Watson was playing the 12th hole, and this was the first sign that the day might become something special. "That completely changed my round," Watson, who was fifty-three, said later. "It opened up the airwaves and everything was free-wheeling from there."

Edwards helped make Watson a champion; then Watson championed Edwards's cause.

But Edwards, freewheeling in spirit and still at his man's side after some thirty years of caddying for him, couldn't freewheel in other, important ways. He'd learned in January 2003 that he had ALS—amyotrophic lateral sclerosis, also known as Lou Gehrig's Disease. Gehrig, the baseball Hall of Fame first baseman, died of the disease in 1941. Now Watson and Edwards were at the Olympia Fields Country Club just outside Chicago. It was twenty-one years since Edwards had caddied for Watson at Pebble Beach during his first and only U.S. Open win. Watson was on his way to a 65 in the opening round.

Watson said that it wouldn't matter if he shot 90 in the second round. Maybe. Maybe not.

Watson shot 72 in the second round, 75 in the third, and a final 72 to tie for twenty-eighth in the championship. He spoke about ALS throughout the week, using what he called his "bully pulpit" to discuss the condition and to emphasize the importance of raising money for research. He had read widely about ALS and become an advocate for research into the disease. With Edwards and his wife Marsha, Watson had started a website called Driving4Life.org. Marsha spoke at Olympia Fields of her husband and Watson having relived the magic there that they had felt so often in the past. But she was thinking about the future and what it might hold, what it seemed sure to hold. ALS was usually fatal within three years of diagnosis.

Watson along with Bruce and Marsha continued to try to raise awareness of ALS in the months following the U.S. Open. Edwards remained mostly at home, as his condition worsened. He hoped to be able to attend the Golf Writers Association of America's annual awards dinner the night before the first round of the 2004 Masters, but he couldn't make it. His father, Jay, was there to accept the Ben Hogan Award on his behalf. The award is given to someone who remains active in golf despite a physical handicap or serious illness. Watson received the USGA's William Richardson Award that evening for his work in raising awareness of and money for ALS.

Watson's wife, Hilary, received a phone call from Marsha Edwards at six-thirty the next morning, not long before the first round of the 2004 Masters would start. Marsha was calling to say that her husband had just died. Watson was already at the Augusta National Golf Club, where Hilary had dropped him off. She returned to inform her husband of the news. Edwards had last caddied for Watson the previous fall. They had last seen each other during the PGA Tour's event at the Bay Hill Club in Orlando, in March. They talked about death, Edwards telling Watson he wasn't afraid to die. Over the following weeks they had e-mailed each other frequently.

Only fifteen months had passed since Edwards had been diagnosed with ALS. Watson would continue, in the name of his friend and all people diagnosed with ALS, to work to eradicate the disease. He would also remember a Thursday at the U.S. Open when he shot 65, another day when he listened to his caddie Bruce Edwards, a day not unlike so many during the years they had together.

A TRIVIA QUESTION THAT IS GUARANTEED TO STUMP YOUR FRIENDS

Looking to win free drinks at the bar after your round? Here's a simple question with a famous golfer as the answer, yet even the most golf-obsessed history buffs won't get it right:

Who was the first golfer to have four rounds under par in a U.S. Open? See page 275 for the answer.

THE WORD ON

The Mental Game

"*The correlation between thinking well and making successful shots is not 100 percent. But the correlation between bad thinking and unsuccessful shots is much higher.*"

—DR. BOB ROTELLA

"*Let your attitude determine your golf game. Don't let your golf game determine your attitude.*"

—DAVIS LOVE JR

"*A leading difficulty with the average player is that he totally misunderstands what is meant by concentration. He may think that he is concentrating hard when he is merely worrying.*"

—ROBERT TRENT JONES

"*Of all games, golf exposes fraud and self-delusion most efficiently.*" —*Jim McLean*

FORECAST: PAIN

The Ko'olau Golf Club in Kaneohe, Hawaii declares itself to be the "World's Most Challenging Golf Course." Its slope rating, from the tournament tees, is a 152, with a course rating of 75.7. From the championship tees, the figures are merely 145 and 73.5, respectively. (The less-masochistic blue tees, at 6,406 yards, have a slope of 135 and rating of 71.7.)

The course is in a beautiful setting, carved out of a rain forest not far from Oahu's famed Pali Lookout and providing views of the 2,000-foot Ko'olau Ridge Mountains. Whether its notion of "challenge" is one you wish to take on is up to you. Before setting your sights on Ko'olau, however, you might want to consider the following local rule as posted on Ko'olau's scorecard:

A ball lost in a ravine crossing a fairway is a one stroke penalty and the next shot will be played from the marked DROP AREA on the opposite side. Holes 1, 5, 6, 7, 8, 10, 11, 12, 14, 16 and 18.

A local rule that provides a drop area beyond a difficult hazard is a valid option and can be necessary and helpful in keeping play on a course moving. A course that not only provides but *requires* this option on eleven of its eighteen holes (ten of its fourteen par fours and fives) qualifies for the category that *Golf Digest*'s Ron Whitten has dubbed "Architorture."

U.S. OPEN PHILOSOPHY, AS STATED BY THE UNITED STATES GOLF ASSOCIATION IN 2005

The USGA selects venues for the U.S. Open that rank among the most challenging courses in the United States. We intend that the U.S. Open prove the most rigorous examination of golfers. A U.S. Open course should test all forms of shot making, mental tenacity, and physical endurance under conditions of extreme pressure found only at the highest levels of championship golf.

At the same time, we try to ensure that a well-played stroke produces a positive result for an Open competitor. We formulate a detailed, careful plan for conducting the Open over four-to-five days, but unanticipated variations in weather and other conditions may force consideration of daily adjustments to maintain appropriate playing conditions.

The following list of 14 factors impact overall U.S. Open course set up. The mix of these factors varies from course to course, year to year. Evaluation of course set up should not focus on any single element but consider the composite result.

1. Length, variation, and playing characteristics of individual holes

2. Length of overall golf course relative to total par

3. Teeing ground locations (i.e., angles of play, variation of distance day to day)

4. Fairway width and contours

5. Fairway firmness and speed

6. Green speed relative to percentage slopes and contours of the putting greens

7. Putting green firmness

8. Rough height, density, and stages of severity

9. Bunker preparation (i.e., create challenge of recovery)

10. Green surrounds (e.g., closely mown areas vs. primary rough)

11. Hole locations (relative difficulty, balance in location of left vs. right, front vs. back, anticipated wind, anticipated length of approach shot)

12. Risk and reward options

13. Anticipated weather conditions

14. Pace of play

There is no USGA target score for a U.S. Open. While the final score at some U.S. Open sites will be at or near par, the USGA does not try to formulate a course set up that will only produce a winning score of at or near even par.

The Association typically begins preparing for a U.S. Open five to seven years in advance of the actual championship. This preparation process continues regularly throughout that extended period. The complexities of course set up, gallery management, traffic, transportation and parking, lodging, security, volunteers, media, corporate hospitality, and player needs continue to increase annually. Our goal is to provide everyone attending a U.S. Open with the finest experience possible, whether they are located inside or outside the ropes.

U.S. OPEN PHILOSOPHY, AS STATED BY PLAYERS

"*I'm glad I brought this course, this monster, to its knees.*"

—BEN HOGAN, after shooting 76-73-71-67 to win the 1951 U.S. Open at Oakland Hills Country Club, Birmingham, Michigan

"*I don't know whether to practice or cut my wrists.*"

—JOHN SCHLEE, 1974 U.S. Open, Winged Foot Golf Club, Mamaroneck, New York

John Schlee

"*The USGA can rest easy. Par has been preserved.*"

—HALE IRWIN at presentation ceremony after winning in 1979 at Inverness Club in Toledo, Ohio, having finished double bogey, bogey

"*I will never, ever play an Open [again] at Oakmont, even if I'm lucky enough to be defending champion. The rough is ridiculous.*"

—DAVID GRAHAM, 1983 U.S. Open, Oakmont Country Club, Oakmont, Pennsylvania

"*The pin at 18 was a joke. I had a three-footer [downhill for a double bogey] and I didn't have a chance.*"

—TOM PERNICE after final round, 1989 U.S. Open, Oak Hill Country Club, Pittsford, New York

"*If we played a course like this every week, there wouldn't be anybody left at the end of the season. We'd all quit the game.*"

—MARK CALCAVECCHIA, 1990 U.S. Open, Medinah Country Club, Medinah, Illinois

"*If they want greens like this, I'm going to take up topless darts, I think. It would be easier to catch them in your teeth today.*"

—Nick Faldo, following the final round of the 1992 U.S. Open, Pebble Beach Golf Links

"*Trying to find a ball in this rough is like trying to find a crouton in the bottom of a salad.*"

—David Ogrin, 1994 U.S. Open, Oakmont Country Club, Oakmont, Pennsylvania

"*You can't tame this course, you can only survive it.*"

—Tom Lehman, 1995 U.S. Open, Shinnecock Hills Golf Club, Southampton, New York

"*I don't think even Mickey Mouse knows how to play this hole.*"

—Jeff Maggert, after triple-bogeying the par-four 18th hole in the second round of the 1996 U.S. Open, Oakland Hills Golf Club, Bloomfield, Michigan

"*It's a U.S. Open. I can't smile.*"

—Brad Faxon, after a fan asked him to smile for a photo, 1997 U.S. Open, Congressional Country Club, Bethesda, Maryland

"*I think the U.S. Open historically has always been very difficult. They say they're trying to identify the best player. I felt they're always trying to identify the person who drives the ball the best.*"

—Tiger Woods, two days before the start of the 2000 U.S. Open at Pebble Beach, which he won by fifteen shots

"*You're hitting a three-iron off a downhill lie to an uphill green that can't be held with a nine-iron. My caddie [Jimmy Johnson] had the best line. He said to me, 'The green is thirty-four yards deep, but it has a twenty-two-yard false front.' If you did this at any other club, they'd kill the superintendent.*"

—Nick Price on the 18th hole, 2001 U.S. Open, Southern Hills Country Club, Tulsa, Oklahoma

"*This is a great golf course, one of the best ever to host a U.S. Open, but what they did to it is horrible.*"

—Ernie Els, 2002 U.S. Open, Black Course, Bethpage State Park, Farmingdale, New York

"*[The USGA] has caved in to the whole technology scare, the idea that you have to hit the ball straight and forever to play the game.*"

—Scott Verplank, 2002 U.S. Open, Black Course, Bethpage State Park

"*I'm looking at holes wondering how in the world I'm going to get it anywhere near the pin, and . . . but it's fun. It's fun. It's a fun challenge. We only see this probably once or twice a year. And it's a fun challenge. What I really like, though, is that your short game is back into play, all around the greens you can chip and putt."*

—PHIL MICKELSON, 2004 U.S. Open, Shinnecock Hills Golf Club, Southampton, New York

"Some of those greens, they're really hard. It's really hard. With the wind blowing today as it was, it's just hard to control your putts, to control your speed. Some putts are really, really quick, some putts are fairly slow, so it's just—it just feels exactly like a U.S. Open."

—SERGIO GARCIA, 2004 U.S. Open, Shinnecock Hills Golf Club

Fun-loving Sergio Garcia had no fun at Shinnecock Hills.

ANSWER TO THE TRIVIA QUESTION GUARANTEED TO STUMP YOUR FRIENDS [PAGE 270]

In 1947, Sam Snead, who never won the U.S. Open, became the first player to have four subpar rounds in an Open, carding 72-70-70-70 to tie for the lead at the par-71 St. Louis CC, then adding another 70 in the playoff that he lost to Lew Worsham's 69.

Only five other golfers have managed four subpar rounds in a U.S. Open:

- Billy Casper, Olympic, 1966 (69-68-73-68-69, including playoff round), won
- Lee Trevino, Oak Hill, 1968 (69-68-69-69), won
- Tony Jacklin, Hazeltine, 1970 (71-70-70-70), won
- Lee Janzen, Baltusrol, 1993 (67-67-69-69), won
- Curtis Strange, Oakmont, 1994 (70-70-70-70), finished 4th

Sam Snead: an Open first, but no Open title.

FAMOUS GOLF FOODS

Pimento cheese sandwiches: A staple at the Masters from the beginning. For a complete list of the ingredients in the examples sold in Augusta, see page 176.

Snapper soup: Served at Pine Valley Golf Club at least since 1936; both the British/Irish and American sides in the Walker Cup that year commented favorably on this item on the lunch menu. No record was made of whether they added to the soup from the traditional decanter of sherry.

Olympic's hamburgers: Available at the stand located behind the sixth green of the Lake Course at the Olympic Club in San Francisco. Shaped like a sausage, slathered with condiments, and served on a hot-dog bun. A necessary early-round pick-me-up after the course's tough opening stretch.

Ginger snaps: Cookies on the bar counter at the halfway house at Seminole Golf Club, Juno Beach, Florida.

Whisky Mac: Ginger wine and whisky, popular at Littlestone Golf Club in Rye, England.

Pretzels: Not an ordinary bag, but made-to-order big pretzels baked after your round at Whisper Rock in Scottsdale, Arizona. The course also offers "sliders"—miniburgers of chicken, beef, and tuna (separately) that are the choice of about four-fifths of the people who eat there.

Peanut-butter sandwich: Al Geiberger carried the sandwiches in his bag and ate them to keep his blood sugar up while winning the 1966 PGA Championship; the habit won him an endorsement deal with Skippy.

Pepto-Bismol: Rich Beem, en route to the 2002 PGA Championship, swigged the pink upset-stomach remedy before each round to quiet his nerves.

Volcanic sand: Jesper Parnevik claimed he ate this to cleanse his system. Your mileage may vary.

Arnold Palmer: He drinks it, he gave it its name—half iced tea and half lemonade. Ahhhhhh.

Champagne: Tony Lema celebrated his first win by drinking it with the sportswriters instead of beer. "Champagne Tony" was born.

Fried chicken: In one of the most expensive jokes in the history of ethnic humor, Fuzzy

Zoeller commented on Tiger Woods's first Masters win by saying he hoped that at next year's annual champions dinner Woods wouldn't serve "fried chicken . . . or collard greens or whatever the hell they serve." The joke cost Zoeller considerable endorsement money and some of his popularity.

Wine: Beginning with the highly regarded Greg Norman Estates wineries in southeastern Australia and California, wineries have become nearly as much a part of PGA Tour life as courtesy cars. Ernie Els, Arnold Palmer, David Frost, Mike Weir, Nick Faldo, and Johnny Miller have developed wines or purchased wineries; the Tour itself has a line of wines under the Players Cellars label.

HOW TO SOUND AND ACT LIKE A GOLFER

Golfer: You've just made a five on a par five. Your playing companion asks what you scored on the hole. You answer, "I made par."

Non-golfer: "I shot par," or, "I shot a par."

Golfer: "Who's away?"

Non-golfer: "Who's closer?" Or, "Who's farther away?"

Golfer: "What do you lie?"

Non-golfer: "How many do you lie?"

Golfer: Marks the scorecard on the way to the next tee, or every few holes.

Non-golfer: Stands on the green, looking back at the hole and pointing to where he hit his shots from, while counting.

Golfer: Stands to side of fellow player, facing him, while he's hitting a shot.

Non-golfer: Stands behind fellow player.

Golfer: Walks off rear of green.

Non-golfer: Walks off front of green.

SOME TRICKS YOU CAN DO

With just a little practice, you can learn how to amaze your friends with these feats. The authors take no responsibility for bodily harm visited upon anyone who thought he could use them as the basis for a wager.

Two balls, three putts: From a distance of thirty feet or so, offer the observation that you are confident you can sink two balls in three strokes. When onlookers express skepticism, you place the two balls on the green, side by side. With one stroke, hit both balls toward the hole—which is really no more difficult than putting with one ball. Make both of your remaining putts. (The trick requires little more than adequate lag putting and a steady hand on the short ones.)

Tour juice made easy: Who isn't impressed by a shot that backs up on the greens? That's why your friends who've seen you play will be surprised to hear that you can hit a ball out of a bunker and make it fly way up high in the air, then come zipping back upon landing. Yet this shot is as foolproof as it is illegal. Go to a bunker with a sandy face. Embed a ball completely in the face just on the upslope, and place another ball on top of and behind it. With a pitching wedge or a nine-iron, hit an easy shot, trying to catch the visible ball cleanly. The effect of driving the ball into the embedded ball will cause the one you struck to go flying in the air with a huge amount of backspin, and it will come racing back toward you when it hits the ground.

The wrong-way wedge: One of Phil Mickelson's signature shots is a wedge shot hit back over his own head. He explained to *Golf Digest*'s Bob Verdi how to hit it (or, at least, how he hits it): Place the ball on a steep incline, like the lip of a bunker. Brace yourself with your "front" foot behind the ball and your weight on your back (lower) foot. Open a sand or lob wedge as far as you can, and keep it open through impact by cupping your left wrist and keeping it that way. Your right hand should stay under the club and feel as though you're pitching a softball. *Don't* roll your wrists, and *don't* shift your weight. Swing *up* on the ball and it should go flying back over your head in the direction your shoulders are pointing. *Do* practice this before showing it to anybody, and practice it in an area with nothing breakable nearby.

THE GOLFER'S LIFE LIST

Reread Harvey Penick

"Take dead aim." "Go to dinner with good putters." "If you have a bad grip, you don't want to have a good swing." These and other maxims exemplified the genial, story-telling nature of the wisdom of *Harvey Penick's Little Red Book.* His main point, it seemed, was to draw more pleasure from the game of golf, and through that, you will play better.

But this determinedly nontechnical book also contained the following, and much more:

"Hold a clubshaft along the front of your thighs to see where you're aimed."

"To start your downswing, let your weight shift to your left foot while bringing your right elbow back down to your body."

"The first and foremost fundamental [of chipping and putting is]: keep your hands ahead of or even with the clubhead on the follow-through. All the way through."

"Never practice your full swing when the wind is at your back."

In addition to the stories and the wisdom, there's some pretty clear and specific information being conveyed there. Reread *Little Red* and your game will improve, but not just because of your feelings.

WHO GETS INTO A TOURNAMENT?

Every PGA Tour event selects its field according to a priority ranking of entry qualifications. The system below was in effect for the 2005 season; here is how the field for the BellSouth Classic, played in Atlanta the week before the Masters, was filled.

1. Winners of the PGA Championship or the U.S. Open prior to 1970 or in the last ten calendar years. (Beginning in 1998, this became a five-year exemption.) Rich Beem, Mark Brooks, Steve Elkington, Retief Goosen, Steve Jones.

2. Winners of the Players Championship in the last ten calendar years. (Beginning in 1998, this became a five-year exemption.) Lee Janzen.

3. Winners of the Masters in the last ten calendar years. (Beginning in 1998, this became a five-year exemption.) Phil Mickelson.

4. Winners of the British Open in the last ten calendar years. (Beginning in 1998, this became a five-year exemption.) None.

5. Winners of the World Series of Golf from 1995 to 1997. (Ten-year exemption.) None.

6. The Tour Championship winners in the last three years. (Beginning in 2002.) None.

7. Winners of official money World Golf Championships events in the last three years. Stewart Cink, Kevin Sutherland.

8. The leader in PGA Tour official earnings in each of the last five calendar years. None.

9. Winners of PGA Tour cosponsored or approved events (except team events) within the last two calendar years, or during the current year; winners receive an additional year of exemption for each additional win, up to five years. Jonathan Byrd, John Huston, Zach Johnson, J. L. Lewis, Frank Lickliter II, Len Mattiace, Kenny Perry, Rory Sabbatini, Joey Sindelar, Heath Slocum, Bob Tway.

10. A. Members of the last-named U.S. Presidents Cup team. None.

B. Members of the last-named International Presidents Cup team provided they were PGA Tour members at the time they were named to the team. Robert Allenby, Stephen Leaney, Peter Lonard.

C. Members of the last-named U.S. Ryder Cup team provided they were PGA Tour members at the time they were named to the team. Chris Riley.

D. Members of the last-named European Ryder Cup team. Thomas Levet.

11. Leaders in official PGA Tour career earnings, as follows:

A. Players among the top fifty in career earnings as of the end of the preceding calendar year may elect to use a one-time, one-year exemption for the next year. Rocco Mediate, Tom Kite, Billy Mayfair.

B. Players among the top twenty-five in career earnings as of the end of the preceding calendar year may elect to use this special exemption for a second year, provided that the player remains among the top twenty-five on the career money list. None.

12. Sponsor exemptions (a maximum of eight, which may include amateurs with scratch handicaps or less), on the following basis:

A. Not less than two sponsor invitees can be PGA Tour members not otherwise exempt for the tournament. Larry Mize, José Maria Olazabal.

B. Not less than two of the top thirty finishers and ties from the last qualifying tournament, as well as players ranked 2 through 20 from the previous year's Nationwide Tour money list, if not all of them can otherwise be accommodated. (PGA Tour members may receive an unlimited number of sponsor invitations. Non-Tour members may receive a maximum of seven per year.) Bill Glasson and Will McKenzie (qualifying), Craig Bowden, Angel Cabrera, Joakim Haeggman, Miguel Angel Jiménez, Matt Kuchar, Tim O'Neal, Casey Wittenberg (unrestricted).

13. Two international players designated by the commissioner. Shingo Katayama.

14. The current PGA Club Professional champion for a maximum of six open events (three must be from open tournaments held opposite the British Open and the World Golf Championships), in addition to any sponsor selections. None.

15. PGA Section champion or Player of the Year of the Section in which the tournament is played. Tim Weinhart.

16. Two members of the PGA Section in which the tournament is played, who qualify through sectional qualifying competitions. Scott Curiel, Billy Jack.

17. Four low scorers at open qualifying, normally held on Monday of tournament week. Eric Axley, Camilo Benedetti, Scott Dunlap, Nick Gilliam.

18. Past champions of the particular event being played that week, if cosponsored by the PGA Tour and the same tournament sponsor (except for team events), as follows:

A. Winners prior to July 28, 1970; unlimited exemptions for such events. None

B. Winners after July 28, 1970, and prior to January 1, 2000; ten years of exemptions for such events. Scott McCarron.

C. Winners after January 1, 2000: five years of exemptions for such events. None.

19. Life members (who have been active members of the PGA Tour for fifteen years and have won at least twenty cosponsored events). None.

20. If not exempt under special [above] exemptions, the top 125 PGA Tour members on the previous year's official money list, in order of their position. Ted Purdy, Bo Van Pelt, Duffy Waldorf, Tom Pernice, Harrison Frazar, Carl Pettersson, Arron Oberholser, Alex Cejka, Skip Kendall, Tim Petrovic, Joe Durant, Brian Bateman, Michael Allen, J. J. Henry, Brett Quigley, Hank Kuehne, Hunter Mahan, Hidemichi Tanaka, Cameron Beckman, Daniel Chopra, John Rollins, Neal Lancaster, Chris Smith, Dennis Paulson, Kent Jones, Jay Williamson, Steve Allan, Brian Gay, Aaron Baddeley, Billy Andrade, Tag Ridings.

21. Players who earned more than the 125th-place finisher on the previous year's official money list as nonmembers. None.

22. Major Medical Extension: If granted by the commissioner, if not otherwise eligible, and if needed to fill the field. Craig Barlow, Tom Gillis, Andrew Magee, Brandt Jobe, Paul Goydos, Glen Hnatiuk.

23. Leading money winner from the 2004 Nationwide Tour. Jimmy Walker.

24. Top ten and ties among professionals from the previous open tournament whose victory has official status are exempt into the next open tournament whose victory has official status. Brett Wetterich, Lucas Glover.

25. Top thirty and ties from the previous year's PGA Tour qualifying tournament, in order of their finish, and players who finished ranked 2 through 20 on the previous year's Nationwide Tour money list. Brian Davis, Charles Warren, Jason Bohn, Ryuji Imada, Doug Barron, Joey Snyder III, Franklin Langham, Jason Allred, Danny Bridges, D. A. Points, D. J. Trahan, Darron Stiles, Kevin Stadler, Nick Watney, Scott Gutschewski, Scott Hend, James Driscoll, Sean O'Hair, Brendan Jones, Gavin Coles, Mark Wilson, Omar Uresti, Dean Wilson, Phillip Price, Mario Tiziani, Paul Gow, Jeff Hart, Roland Thatcher, John Elliott, Jim Carter, D. J. Brigman, Charlie Wi, Rob Rashell, Carl Paulson, Hunter Haas, Hideto Tanihara, Justin Bolli, Chris Anderson, Paul Claxton, J. P. Hayes, Michael Long,

Bradley Hughes, Matt Davidson, Jeff Brehaut, Bob Heintz, David Hearn, Tjaart van der Walt.

26. Players winning three Nationwide Tour events in the current year, in priority determined by the date they win their third event. None.

27. Minor Medical Extension. None.

28. Next 25 PGA Tour members after the top 125 PGA Tour members from the previous year's official money list if needed to fill the field, in order of their positions on the list. Olin Browne, Mathias Gronberg, Brenden Pappas, Glen Day, Danny Ellis, Arjun Atwal.

29. Nonexempt, Major Medical Extension. None.

30. Past champions, team tournament winners, and veteran members beyond 150th on the money list: if not otherwise eligible and as needed to fill the field, past champion members, team tournament winners, and veteran members beyond 150th place on the previous year's money list, in order of their combined official PGA Tour and Nationwide Tour earnings in the previous year. Steve Stricker, Spike McRoy, Dan Forsman.

31. Past champion members: if not otherwise eligible and if needed to fill the field, past champion members, in order of the total number of cosponsored or approved events won, excluding team events. If two or more players are tied, the player who is higher on the PGA Tour career money list will be eligible. Alternates: Grant Waite, Scott Simpson, Jay Delsing, Robin Freeman, Mike Heinen, Garrett Willis, Blaine McCallister, Guy Boros, Tom Scherrer, David Edwards.

32. Special temporary: If during the course of a PGA Tour season, a nonmember of the PGA Tour wins an amount of official money (for instance, by playing in PGA Tour events through sponsor exemptions, open qualifying, etc.) equal to the amount won in the preceding year by the 150th finisher on the official money list, he will be eligible for the remainder of the year. None.

33. Team tournament winners: If not otherwise eligible and if needed to fill the field, winners of cosponsored team championships, in order of the total number of team championship tournaments won. If two or more players are tied based on the number of such tournaments won, the player who is higher on the official PGA Tour career money list will be eligible. None.

34. Veteran members: If not otherwise eligible and needed to fill the field, veteran members (players who have made a minimum of 150 cuts during their careers), in order of their standing on the PGA Tour career money list. None.

FAMOUS COLLAPSES IN MAJORS

Greg Norman, 1996 Masters, Augusta National Golf Club

Norman had everything that Central Casting could ask for in a Masters champion: good looks, a swashbuckling style, and a Great White Nickname. By 1996, the Shark had been so snakebit in major championships that he had become a sentimental favorite as well as a crowd-pleaser.

Norman and Faldo after their final-round eleven-stroke swing.

Augusta National should have been the perfect venue for him, a course that rewards bold play. But Fate had other plans for him. In 1986, his bogey on the 72nd hole clinched Jack Nicklaus's final major victory. In 1987, Larry Mize's stunning chip shot in sudden death again snatched the green jacket from Norman's grasp.

Everything seemed different in 1996. He opened with a 63 that tied the course record and entered the final round with a six-shot lead over Nick Faldo. But as a worldwide audience watched, what should have been a victory lap turned into a death march. Norman pulled his second shot on the 8th hole into the trees, backed his second on the 9th off the green and down the hill in front, bogeyed the 10th with a poor pitch shot, three-putted the 11th, and dumped his tee shot on 12 into Rae's Creek—a five-hole stretch that turned a four-shot advantage into a two-stroke deficit. Norman finished with a 78 while Faldo, with whom he was playing in the last group, shot 67 to win his third Masters.

"Yeah, I know I screwed up," Norman said. "But it's not the end of the world for me. I'm disappointed. I'm sad about it. I'm going to regret it. But I'm not going to fall off the face of the earth because of what's happened. It's not going to affect my life. Please believe me."

Perhaps not, but we can only wonder how much of his fortune he would happily trade for the one green jacket that must be won and not bought.

LONGEST GAP BETWEEN MAJOR VICTORIES

MEN

- Ben Crenshaw, 11 years (1984 Masters–1995 Masters)
- Henry Cotton, 11 years (1937 British Open–1948 British Open)
- Julius Boros, 11 years (1952 U.S. Open–1963 U.S. Open)
- Hale Irwin, 11 years (1979 U.S. Open–1990 U.S. Open)
- Lee Trevino, 10 years (1974 PGA–1984 PGA)

WOMEN

- Juli Inkster, 10 years (1989 Kraft Nabisco–1999 LPGA and U.S. Open)
- Mary Mills, 9 years (1964 LPGA–1973 LPGA)
- Meg Mallon, 9 years (1991 LPGA and U.S. Open–2000 du Maurier)
- Sandra Haynie, 9 years (1965 LPGA–1974 LPGA and U.S. Open)
- Donna Caponi, 9 years (1970 U.S. Open–1979 LPGA)
- Betsy Rawls, 9 years (1960 U.S. Open–1969 LPGA)

HOW TO RUN A ONE-DAY TOURNAMENT/OUTING

The two most popular ways of running a one-day event in which many of the participants do not have handicaps are the Callaway Scoring System and the Peoria System.

CALLAWAY

A player's Callaway score (net score) is his gross score minus his highest scores on a designated number of holes. The higher the player's score, the more holes he deducts.

The following is the procedure for converting a gross score to a Callaway net score:

1. Start with the player's gross score—with the understanding that the highest possible score on any one hole is double par (six on a par three, eight on a par four, ten on a par five).

2. Use the chart below to determine the number of holes that are to be subtracted from the gross score.

3. Subtract the scores (or half-scores) for the player's highest results on holes 1 through 16. (Holes 17 and 18 may *not* be subtracted.)

—	—	70	71	72	NO HOLES, NO ADJUSTMENT
73	74	75	—	—	½ worst hole
76	77	78	79	80	1 worst hole
81	82	83	84	85	1½ worst holes
86	87	88	89	90	2 worst holes
91	92	93	94	95	2½ worst holes
96	97	98	99	100	3 worst holes
101	102	103	104	105	3½ worst holes
106	107	108	109	110	4 worst holes
111	112	113	114	115	4½ worst holes
116	117	118	119	120	5 worst holes
121	122	123	124	125	5½ worst holes
126	127	128	129	130	6 worst holes
–2	**–1**	**0**	**+1**	**+2**	**Adjustment to deduction**

4. Add or subtract the adjustment value listed on the bottom of the chart for the player's original gross score.

Example: Say a player shoots a 104 as follows:

5	8	4	6	4	5	6	7	9	54	
8	5	4	5	8	6	4	5	5	50	TOTAL: 104

Looking up 104 on the chart, this player should deduct the three-and-a-half worst scores—a nine, two eights, and half of another eight, for a total of 29. Then add one more stroke to the adjustment as shown on the bottom line, and the player's final net score is 74.

PEORIA

Under the Peoria System, the tournament organizer selects six holes in secret—either two par threes, two par fours, and two par fives, or one par three, one par five, and four par fours—and uses those holes to determine a handicap for each player. The number of strokes that player shot over par for those six holes is multiplied by three to determine his handicap for the entire round; there is usually a limit on the score for each hole that can be used for this purpose (double par, for example; or perhaps three strokes on par threes and fours but four strokes on par fives). In some modifications, the six-hole score is multiplied by 2.8 instead, or only 80 percent of the handicap adjustment is used. It is essential that the participants not know which holes have been selected prior to the end of the event.

Example: Let's take that same 104 as above, assigning pars to each hole:

Hole	1	2	3	4	5	6	7	8	9		10	11	12	13	14	15	16	17	18		
Par	4	5	4	3	4	3	4	5	4	Out	4	4	3	5	4	5	3	4	4	In	Total
Score	5	8	4	6	4	5	6	7	9	54	8	5	4	5	8	6	4	5	5	50	104

Suppose the selected holes were the 2nd, 6th, 9th, 12th, 15th, and 18th (it is generally a good idea to use three holes from each nine, to prevent a hot or cold streak from overly influencing a player's handicap). The golfer played those six holes in 13 over par, with the total reduced to 12 to bring the adjustment for the 9th hole down to the double-par maximum. The golfer's handicap for the round would thus be 36, for a net score of 68. The luck factor is large, since a different selection of holes (3rd, 6th, 8th, 13th, 16th, and 17th) could have resulted in a total handicap for the round of just 18, and a net score of 86 instead.

THE MORE THINGS CHANGE . . .

The people involved in playing, managing, and writing about the highest levels of golf have been bemoaning the ill effects of new equipment for as long as there has been equipment. Does this mean it has always been a problem? Or that the problem is always blown out of proportion by those who feel the game they know—or knew—was the only game that should be? Consider the following pairs of quotations:

"*Our longest holes are little more than a drive and a putt. My feeling is that if the game continues to improve in the matter of its length and we get just a little more resiliency in the ball and a little better clubs than we have now, the game in [the] future will be relegated to the only place where it can be played, and that is on the great prairies of our Western country.*"

—R. H. ROBERTSON, USGA president, 1902

"*We don't have a championship golf course in the world today [by] any standards, including this golf course here [Augusta National]. All of the golf courses . . . the golf ball has gotten beyond them.*"

—JACK NICKLAUS, 2005

"*The game has been waging a battle against the inventor. The one aim of the inventor is to minimize the skill required for the game.*"

—JOHN LOW, 1905

"*It's all about keeping the skill factor. At the moment, equipment has brought everyone closer together. It's harder to separate from the field.*"

—TIGER WOODS, 2005

"*If the carrying power of golf balls is to be still further increased, all our golf courses will be irretrievably ruined as a test of the game.*"

—*GOLF ILLUSTRATED*, 1910

"*If all these 'classic' courses are becoming obsolete due to the distance the golf ball flies, why have only two venues designed post-1960 been selected to host a U.S. Open Championship within the past forty-five years?*"

—WALLY UIHLEIN, chairman and CEO of Acushnet Company, October 2005

"The longer you make the courses, the more you make it a power game. Of the top five money winners last year, none of them were in the top twenty-five in driving accuracy. All five of those guys have won major championships, so they've driven the ball in the fairway when they needed to, but they choose not to. They would much rather play a sand wedge out of the rough than a six-iron out of the fairway because they can still spin the ball out of the rough with the grooves they've got. It's a different game. It's a totally different game than I played."

—JACK NICKLAUS, 2005

"I'd rather play a wedge second shot out of the rough than a five-iron from the fairway if I gain forty or fifty yards by doing it."

—SAM SNEAD, 1937

"The principal topic of conversation . . . last week was the standardisation [sic] of the golf ball. When one sees the first hole . . . driven with a drive and an iron shot, and 11 years ago . . . when I made the course, it took two full shots and a pitch to get on the green, it is surely time that something was done to prevent golf courses from being entirely spoilt."

—WILLIE PARK JR., 1910

"A hole of about 600 yards will occasionally be reached by two of [Abe] Mitchell's best shots, and these days there are other hitters of almost equal power. Of course the ball has made such distances possible, and unless some regulation is devised, the ball will force us on and on in this mad race for yardage."

—ROBERT HUNTER, 1926

"The issue I have is not how far [the ball] goes. You can always change the golf courses. The issue I have is that if you aren't a power player, you can't play. You take the Gary Players, the Jackie Burkes, the Ben Hogans, Gardner Dickinsons, there's hundreds of guys who are small of stature who didn't have the clubhead speed that they have today. But they could compete when they played well on certain golf courses they could play on. That's not the case today, because of all the length and because of all the power and because of the emphasis on how far the golf ball goes."

—JACK NICKLAUS, 2005

"He plays a game with which I am not familiar."

—BOBBY JONES, 1965, describing Jack Nicklaus

PLAYERS WHO QUALIFY DIRECTLY INTO THE U.S. OPEN

Players who meet any of these criteria are exempt from local and sectional qualifying.

- U.S. Open champions of the last ten years
- 2005 U.S. Amateur champion and runner-up (if still an amateur)
- Winners of the Masters in the last five years
- British Open champions of the last five years
- PGA Championship winners of the last five years
- Winner of the 2006 Players Championship
- 2005 U.S. Senior Open champion
- The fifteen lowest finishers and ties from the 2005 U.S. Open
- Top thirty on the 2005 PGA Tour official money list
- Top fifteen from the 2005 PGA European Tour money list
- Top ten on the 2006 PGA Tour official money list through May 28
- Any multiple winner of PGA Tour cosponsored events whose victories are considered official from April 27, 2005, through June 4, 2006
- Top two through May 29 from the official 2006 European PGA Tour money list
- Top two from the official 2005 Japan Golf Tour money list, provided they are within the top seventy-five point leaders of the world rankings at that time
- Top two from the 2005 final official PGA Tour of Australasia money list, provided they are within the top seventy-five point leaders in the world rankings at that time
- Top fifty point leaders in the current world ranking, as of May 29, 2006
- The USGA Executive Committee awards special exemptions as it sees fit.

PLAYERS WHO QUALIFY DIRECTLY INTO THE U.S. WOMEN'S OPEN

Michelle Wie finished 3rd in the 2006 U.S. Women's Open, after the USGA saw fit to give her a special exemption.

- U.S. Women's Open champions from the last ten years
- U.S. Women's Amateur champions from the last two years and runner-up for the most recent year (if still amateurs)
- Winners of the LPGA Championship for the last five years
- Winners of the Women's British Open Championship for the last five years
- Winners of the Kraft Nabisco Championship for the last five years
- The forty leading money-winners on the 2005 final official LPGA Tour money list
- The thirty-five leading money-winners on the 2006 official LPGA Tour money list through May 29
- The twenty lowest scorers and anyone tied for twentieth place from the 2005 U.S. Women's Open
- Winners of LPGA Tour cosponsored events, from the conclusion of the 2005 U.S. Women's Open to the beginning of the 2006 U.S. Women's Open
- Top three point leaders from the 2005 Ladies European Tour Order of Merit
- The two leading money-winners form the 2005 Japan LPGA Tour
- The USGA awards special exemptions as it sees fit.

EXEMPTIONS FROM ALL QUALIFYING FOR THE BRITISH OPEN (2006)

1. First ten and anyone tying for tenth place in the 2005 Open Championship.

2. Past Open champions aged sixty-five or under on July 23, 2006.

3. The first fifty players on the Official World Golf Ranking for week 22, 2006.

4. First twenty in the PGA European Tour Final Order of Merit for 2005.

5. The BMW Championship winners for 2004–06.

6. First three and anyone tying for third place, not exempt, in the top twenty of the PGA European Tour Order of Merit for 2006 on completion of the 2006 BMW Championship.

7. First two European Tour members and any European Tour members tying for second place, not exempt, in a cumulative money list taken from all official PGA European Tour events from the British Masters up to and including the French Open and including the U.S. Open.

8. The leading player, not exempt, in the first ten and ties of each of the 2006 French Open, 2006 Smurfit European Open, and 2006 Barclays Scottish Open. Ties will be decided by the better final-round score and, if still tied, by the better third-round score and then by the better second-round score. If still tied, a hole-by-hole card playoff will take place starting at the 18th hole of the final round.

9. The U.S. Open champions for 2002–06.

10. The U.S. Masters champions for 2002–06.

11. The U.S. PGA champions for 2001–05.

12. The U.S. Tournament Players Championship winner for 2003–05.

13. First twenty on the official money list of the U.S. PGA Tour for 2005.

14. First three and anyone tying for third place, not exempt, in the top twenty of the official money list of the U.S. PGA Tour for 2006 on completion of the FedEx St. Jude Classic.

15. First two U.S. PGA Tour members and any U.S. PGA

Tour members tying for second place, not exempt, in a cumulative money list taken from the U.S. PGA Tour Tournament Players Championship and the five U.S. PGA Tour events leading up to and including the 2006 Western Open.

16. The leading player, not otherwise exempt, having applied (15) above, in each of the 2006 Buick Open, the 2006 Western Open, and the 2006 John Deere Classic. Ties will be decided by the better final-round score and, if still tied, by the better third-round score and then by the better second-round score. If still tied, a hole-by-hole card playoff will take place starting at the 18th hole of the final round.

17. Playing members of the 2005 Presidents Cup teams.

18. First and anyone tying for first place on the Order of Merit of the Asian PGA Tour for 2005.

19. First two and anyone tying for second place on the Order of Merit of the Tour of Australasia for 2005.

20. First and anyone tying for first place on the Order of Merit of the Southern Africa PGA Sunshine Tour for 2005/2006.

21. The Canadian Open champion for 2005.

22. The Japan Open champion for 2005.

23. First two and anyone tying for second place, not exempt, on the official money list of the Japan Golf Tour for 2005.

24. The leading four players, not exempt, in the 2006 Mizuno Open. If still tied, a hole-by-hole card playoff will take place starting at the 18th hole of the final round.

25. First two and anyone tying for second place, not otherwise exempt, having applied (24) above, in a cumulative money list taken from all official Japan Golf Tour events from the 2006 Japan PGA Championship up to and including the 2006 Mizuno Open.

26. The Senior British Open champion for 2005.

27. The [British] Amateur champion for 2006.

28. The U.S. Amateur champion for 2005.

29. The European Individual Amateur champion for 2005.

27 to 29 are applicable only if the entrant concerned is still an amateur on July 20, 2006.

FOOTNOTES TO HISTORY

T. C. Chen, 1985 U.S. Open, Oakland Hills Country Club, Birmingham, Michigan

The little-known Taiwanese golfer T. C. Chen got off to a rousing start at his first U.S. Open, recording a double-eagle on the second hole of his first round. He shot 65-69-69 to take a two-shot lead over Andy North into the final round. He had moved four shots ahead after four holes of the final round and hit a good drive down the fairway on the 457-yard, par-four fifth hole.

Chen, wearing a white cap with the Taiwanese flag on the side, came out of his four-iron second shot and pushed the ball well short of the green into heavy rough. Trees intervened on his line to the hole, but it appeared he could get his ball on the green from his position if he kept the ball underneath the branches.

Chen tried to get cute with his shot, hoping to cut sharply beneath the ball so that it would pop out and land softly on the green. But he didn't reach the green with his third shot and was still in the high rough.

Chen took a hard cut at the ball for his fourth shot. The ball came up almost straight in the air in front of him; he could have reached out and caught it.

His clubface was caught for an instant in the thick grass, then continued forward and contacted the ball, which was hanging almost lifelessly in the air. The extra hit altered the ball's flight path and sent it to the left beside the green. Chen's double hit meant a penalty stroke. Everybody in the vicinity was shocked, nobody more than Chen. Jim Engh and Tim Nugent, then a couple of teenaged golf fans, watched Chen's misfortune. They picked up, and kept, the blob of turf he'd dislodged. Engh and Nugent went on to become course architects.

Lying five beside the green, Chen chipped past the hole and two-putted from there for a quadruple-bogey eight. He and North were tied for the lead. North went on to win his second U.S. Open. Chen tied for second with Dave Barr and Denis Watson, one shot behind North.

From double eagle to double hit. Some people began to refer to T. C. Chen as "Two-chip." But never to his face. Never.

THE WORD ON

Putting

"*It's so bad I could putt off a tabletop and still leave the ball halfway down the leg.*"
—J. C. SNEAD

"*When I putt, my emotions collide like tectonic plates. It's left my memory circuits full of scars that won't heal.*"
—MAC O'GRADY

"*Half of golf is fun; the other half is putting.*"
—PETER DOBEREINER

"*It is not necessary to go back and through the same length [when putting]. That's hogwash, unless it happens to work for you.*"
—JIM MCLEAN

"*The key to pressure putting is wanting it. Looking at it as an opportunity. And understanding that something is not really fun unless it's also a little scary.*"
—RAYMOND FLOYD

WINNER'S PRIZE MONEY THROUGH THE YEARS AT THE MAJORS

	MASTERS (US$)	US OPEN (US$)	BRITISH (GB£)	PGA (US$)
1860			0	
1864			6	
1876			10	
1889			8	
1893			30	
1905		200	50	
1910		300	50	
1920		500	75	500
1931		1,000	100	1,000
1939	1,500	1,000	100	1,100
1946	2,500	1,500	150	3,500
1954	5,000	6,000	750	5,000
1960	17,500	14,400	1,250	11,000
1965	20,000	26,000	1,750	25,000
1970	25,000	30,000	5,250	40,000
1975	40,000	40,000	7,500	45,000
1977	40,000	45,000	10,000	45,000
1978	45,000	45,000	12,500	50,000
1983	90,000	72,000	40,000	100,000
1985	126,000	105,000	65,000	125,000
1990	225,000	220,000	85,000	225,000
1993	306,000	290,000	100,000	300,000
1997	486,000	465,000	250,000	470,000
2000	828,000	800,000	500,000	900,000
2002	1,008,000	1,000,000	700,000	990,000
2005	1,260,000	1,170,000	720,000	1,125,000

TAKE THESE JOKES . . . PLEASE

There are jokes, there are bad jokes, and then there are golf jokes. Or, to put it another way, there are jokes, there are knock-knock jokes, there are chicken jokes, there are mother-in-law jokes, there is the entire career of Pauly Shore, and then, down on the bottom of the pile, are golf jokes.

If you're on a golf course, and you're about to tell a joke that ends with any of the punchlines listed below, do yourself a favor and stop. No one ever needs to hear it again.

"Are You gonna screw around, or are You gonna play golf?"

"Hit the ball, pick up my clubs, drag Charlie . . ."

"They brought Rabbi Nicklaus."

"Oh—that was my mulligan."

*"Don't tell me—you missed the *&#^%&! putt!"*

"I'll bet that makes his putter stand up."

"If that happens, I get here at ten minutes to seven."

"I don't mind about the operation—but how dare you play from the red tees?"

"It's the least I could do; we were married twenty-five years."

"I hit him six, maybe seven times . . . oh, just put me down for a five."

"And God said, 'Yeah, but who can you tell?'"

THEMES AND VARIATIONS

Rule 1-1, right there at the start, declares, "The Game of Golf consists of playing a ball with a club from the teeing ground into the hole by a stroke or successive strokes in accordance with the Rules." This clarity has not kept clever tinkerers from developing their own versions of the game, tweaking one element here, eliminating another there, or keeping all the basics in place but radically changing the goal. Some of the more popular games have developed their own professional circuits; others are currently available only in certain corners of the globe. But all of them are tribute to the ingenuity of a human mind with too much time on its hands.

Disc golf: The most successful variation on golf takes its essential purpose and eliminates all of its traditional equipment. There is no ball, no club, no hole in the ground—yet the game is unmistakably golf, albeit a version played with aerodynamic discs.

Disc golf (or Frisbee golf) came into existence not long after the Frisbee itself. Much as bored shepherds had whacked stones towards bushes with their upturned crooks, Frisbee enthusiasts enjoyed testing their prowess by selecting a distant object—generally a tree—and seeing how many tosses it took to hit the target. The game took formal life with the invention in 1975, by the same Ed Headrick who had patented the original Frisbee, of the Disc Pole Hole, a catching device consisting of an upturned basket set upon a pole, with a set of ten loosely hanging parabolic chains extending upward to help direct a toss down into the basket. The first course was set up in Oak Grove Park in Pasadena, California, and was an immediate success.

The beauty of the game lies in its obviousness and simplicity. Each "hole" begins with a throw from a tee area; wherever your disc lands, you go to it, pick it up, stand behind the spot where it lay, and take your next throw. You are permitted to change discs in the course of play, and most disc golfers use a "driver" for distance, a "midrange" for approach tosses, and a "putter" for those final throws from close in. Courses can be laid out in open grassy public parks or, for an additional challenge, they can be routed through wooded areas. Because the rules of disc golf prohibit damaging local flora in the play of a round, the game is extremely eco-friendly, and many courses laid out on public land can be played for free. Most courses mirror the conditions of the game they call "ball golf," with nine or eighteen (or, in some cases, twenty-seven) holes, divided among par threes, fours, and fives.

There is a Professional Disc Golfers Association, which sanctions events at various levels of competition for professionals and amateurs. The 2005 U.S. National Tour champion, Dave Feldberg, earned $29,408 in prize money in twenty-five events. The PDGA website www.pdga.com lists courses in twenty-five countries, and provides an easy-to-use interface for finding courses anywhere in the world.

SPEED GOLF: For those who don't think swinging a club and chasing a beer cart are enough exercise, there's Speed Golf. Invented in 1979 by Steve Scott, American record holder in the mile, the game requires players to run from shot to shot and hole to hole while carrying their clubs and playing golf by conventional rules. The score for a round consists of your number of strokes added to your time for completing eighteen holes; a round of 80 that took fifty-seven minutes would give you a 137.

Most golfers find that their scores are not much different from their scores in "slow golf," and some even improve, since the nature of the game keeps them from spending too much time thinking. Step up, hit, and move on—just like the Scots, though with a bit more sweating.

A different kind of speed golf consists of a team of golfers spread across a course, trying to propel a ball as quickly as possible from the first tee to the 18th hole. The listed record for this endeavor is under ten minutes, but in terms of accomplishment this is akin to baking the world's largest chocolate chip cookie—fun for all, but not exactly nourishing.

EXTREME GOLF: Upon first viewing the site of the former Fruitland

Nurseries in Augusta, Georgia, Bobby Jones just knew this landscape was crying out to have a golf course on it. Doug Keister felt the same way about the alkali flats of Nevada's Black Rock Desert.

Lucifer's Anvil Golf Course is just one of many corrective reactions to the manicured and pampered face of so much modern golf. Intrepid individuals have been inspired to plant golf's flag on ungroomed mountain slopes, glacial fields, the desert floor—the more unlikely the terrain, the more tempting the target. These adaptations of the game can be grouped under the rubric of "extreme golf."

The golfer at Lucifer's Anvil faces the bleakest landscape in North America. The sun-baked surface will add two hundred yards of roll to an ordinary two-hundred-yard drive. The land is virtually but not completely flat, and small deflections from the ground will send a ball wildly off line. The "greens" are marked with biodegradable spray paint in imaginative colors, with no effort to bring an unnatural greenness to the area. (The longest hole on the course, a 702-yarder dubbed "Hell," features a motif of curling flames and demons.) The nine-hole course hosts the annual Black Rock Desert Self-Invitational, open to all comers. The game is played like regular golf (although you can tee your ball on every shot, in deference to the hard-packed ground); it fulfills all the demands of Rule 1-1, which says nothing about requiring bushes, trees, or even grass.

A very different prospect greets participants in the U.X. Open, played on mountain terrain usually visited by skiers in winter. Players hit from a designated teeing area, but they'll find no smooth fairways awaiting them; instead, they play over ravines and moraines, around rugged boulders and escarpments, toward a designated twenty-foot circle that serves as the "hole." Golfing skills are helpful, but stamina and a good pair of boots are essential as you make your way up and down the ten-hole course.

Lost balls are a common occurrence in the natural landscape, so the penalty is reduced to one stroke only. The other major modification to the rules permits improving your lie within a one-club area, though you may not improve your stance. Range finders are helpful, as are Sherpas.

The U.X. Open has no dress code. Neither does the World Ice Golf Championship, though layers are recommended. Held every March in Uummannaq, in northern Greenland, the tournament is played on a course that must be laid out anew each year. To quote from the tournament's Web site, "The real architect of the course every year is the ocean, which interacts with the weather and the formation of icebergs in January and February to create an external framework for the course. The course itself is laid out in March on the fjord ice. . . . [I]ts shape is determined largely by the positions of icebergs in the fjord. . . . Be prepared for the fact that the foundation is variable and can be very different from hole to hole. On one side of an iceberg there can be a lot more snow than on the other, and the ice is very different to that on a European ice rink. Over the very hard ice surface lies a layer of approx. 1–2 cm frozen 'powder,' which makes the surface itself rough and uneven." Putting surfaces on the three-foot ice pack are cleared of snow, and you are permitted to scrape powder from the line of your putt; holes are twice the normal size.

The tournament is conducted under the R&A-approved Rules of Golf, with local rules that permit a ball to be lifted, cleaned, and placed within a club length if it lies "through the white." The organizers also note, drolly, that carry bags are recommended, "as trolleys cannot be used on the course." Steel-shafted clubs are also preferred, as graphite shatters under the frigid conditions. The winner is saluted by being held aloft on a dogsled, while his fellow competitors cheer.

And then, like golfers everywhere, extreme or otherwise, they all repair to the bar and tell lies about their round.

GOLFCROSS: Pasture golf with a Kiwi twist, GolfCross was invented by New Zealand's Burton Silver. It uses regular golf clubs to hit a ball not into a hole, but into a goal raised above the ground and resembling the goalposts of American football.

Silver's major innovation was to create an oval ball that is hit from a rubber "tee cup." The ball is hard and dimpled like a regulation golf ball, but because of its shape it is almost impossible to hook or slice by accident. It flies end over end through the air, and makes an unusual thwong! sound when you hit it. (To make the ball curve on purpose, simply tilt the ball in the direction you want its flight to bend.) GolfCross holes are of similar length to golf holes, and the ball will go about 130–150 yards, with roll.

The GolfCross goal has a net behind its posts and is set in a fixed position. If your ball lies in an area designated as "the yard"—about the same size as a green, surrounding the goal—you are allowed to turn the goal so that the opening faces toward you. An important strategic aspect of the game is deciding whether to go for the goal or to lay up from a distance; if you miss the goal, the shot will almost certainly carry past the yard, and you'll have no shot at the goal from behind.

There are a handful of GolfCross courses springing up around the world. They require only minimal maintenance, since the ball is never played directly off the ground and there's no need for an even putting surface. If you do wind up at a GolfCross course, having an extra ball in your pocket will be helpful, but having a second tee cup is vital—you're more likely to lose the tee cup than the ball.

SWIN GOLF: This smaller-course offshoot was developed in France, where there are approximately fifty sites dedicated to the game. Its rules are essentially the same as regular golf, and the courses look similar to those of "executive" courses, with holes about half the length of regulation golf holes. The variation lies entirely in the equipment.

Swin golf is played with a rubber ball that's slightly larger and softer than a regulation ball. It's the club that makes the real difference, however: Each swin golfer carries just one club, which has a triangular head to provide three different striking faces. The three are cut to different lofts, for pitching, chipping, and putting. The swing is the same as a regulation golf swing, but because no great distance is required, the game is beginner friendly. With only one club to carry, the round is an easy walk for kids, and a great way to introduce them to golflike games.

CROSSE-GOLF: A game played cross-country, crosse-golf is also known by the name *chole* and is native to the Maubeuge region in the north of France and Mons in Belgium. The game is believed to date back to the thirteenth century, and it is likely an ancestor of golf rather than an offshoot.

The game is played in fields outside those towns that have crosse societies; courses generally consist of nine holes, ranging in length from five hundred yards to a mile. An egg-shaped ball made of wood is hit with a wood-shafted club (also called a crosse) that has an iron head. The head of the club has two hitting surfaces: one flat-faced for distance, the other with a curved shovellike face for digging the ball out of holes, muck, and the occasional cowpie. (This multifaced head may have inspired the three faces of the swin golf club.)

Rather than playing into a hole, the ball is played toward a plank, seven feet high and eight inches wide, called a *planche.* An unusual aspect of the game is that you hit your ball three times towards the target, and then your opponent gets to hit your ball in some other direction or toward an obstruction.

The ranks of crosse players are dwindling with age, but the continued existence of the game is a reminder that golf began as a game of local conditions and myriad variations.

THE GOLFER'S LIFE LIST

Sneak onto a Course at Night

Rule #1 of Night Golf: No penalty for lost balls.

Full moon and empty tees? You're driving by your favorite local course on a bright summer night. You've got your clubs in the trunk and a bag of balls. Seems a shame to let a perfectly good golf opportunity go by just because it's after dark, doesn't it?

Don't let it go. Take a lofted club or two, and some balls you won't mind losing. Pick out a place where you're hitting in the direction of the moon. The target's not the point; the illicit pleasure is. Notice how smooth your swing is when you can't exactly see where the ball is going. Remember what it was like when you were younger, and you wouldn't leave the course until the last hint of light disappeared in the west. Rediscover the joy of purposeless play. Stolen pleasures are the sweetest kind.

Stomp down the edges of your divot holes. Pick up the balls you can find; don't worry about the rest. Go home, sleep well, and draw on that unhurried rhythm the next time you play.

THE MYSTERIOUS MAN WHO WROTE *THE MYSTERY OF GOLF*

Arnold Haultain opened his 1908 book *The Mystery of Golf* by declaring, "Three things there are as unfathomable as they are fascinating to the masculine mind: metaphysics; golf; and the feminine heart." He believed that the German people "pretend to have solved some of the riddles of the first," while the French had "unravelled some of the intricacies of the last." But, he asked, "Will some one tell us wherein lies the extraordinary fascination of golf?"

Haultain from that question launched a far-reaching and far-out inquiry into what he called the "infection" that is golf. His investigation had staying power, even if it didn't entirely resolve his questions. The last time the authors investigated the matter, a first edition of Haultain's tome was available for just under \$3,500, up from \$750 in the early 1990s. Originally published in an edition of 440 copies, the book examines golf from a variety of angles, including the philosophical, psychological, neurological, and even metaphysical, with chapters such as "Necessarianism," "Mind and Matter," and "Anatomical Analysis."

But who was Arnold Haultain?

He was born in Cannanore, India, in 1857 to English parents—his father was a major general in the British army. The family eventually immigrated to Canada, settling in Peterborough, about one hundred miles northeast of Toronto. Haultain studied at the University of Toronto, and eventually worked as private secretary to Goldwin Smith, a political writer and historian whose book *The United States: An Outline of Political History* was highly regarded. Haultain's job in the main was to look after whatever Smith wanted.

Haultain enjoyed golf, perhaps having been made aware of it as a British export to India. An interest in the sport certainly ran in his family: His brother Charles went out west to Fort Macleod, a small town in southwest Alberta, and introduced the game there in 1885, while Frederick W. G. Haultain, a cousin, was president of the Regina Golf Club in the western Canadian province of Saskatchewan.

In 1900, Haultain wrote about Harry Vardon's visit to Canada, during which the golfing legend played matches in Toronto and Montreal. Haultain had a distinctively romantic perspective on golf. He liked the flight of a well-struck ball and wrote that "Vardon's play was a pure aesthetic pleasure." Haultain enjoyed the outdoors, which is one reason he liked to be out on a golf course. Among the books he wrote are *Two Country Walks in Canada* (1903) and *Hints for Lovers* (1908), which suggests he also enjoyed indoor activities.

The Mystery of Golf came out of an essay of the same name that Haultain wrote for the July 1904 issue of *The Atlantic* magazine. It's been reprinted a number of times, including in a 1986 *Classics of Golf* edition for which Herbert Warren Wind wrote a foreword and John Updike an afterword. Wind claimed that Haultain had managed to delve into the puzzle that is golf more deeply than any subsequent writer. While some find Haultain ponderous, many regard the book as a classic that asks the hard questions, the primary one being, Why can't we hit the ball better, since it sits still? As Haultain describes it, that stillness is the very source of the problem. Golf is not a reaction or reflex game—the golfer, in short, has too much time to think about what to do.

As Haultain wrote about the mystery of golf, he became a mystery in turn. Leaving Canada after Smith's death in 1910, he settled in London's Whitechapel Court. Haultain died in 1941, but little is known of how he lived out his last three decades. Perhaps there are papers somewhere in which Haultain further expounded on the mysteries of golf. *The New York Times* review of Haultain's book had said, "The author ambles pleasantly in discussion of the perversities of golf, its humors, its insoluble problems, its perpetual charm." Maybe Haultain spent his years in England still ambling pleasantly in the game. Many writers have come and gone since Haultain wrote his treatise nearly a hundred years ago, but perhaps none has written anything like, for example, the following from his chapter on mind and matter:

"If the physical mysteries of golf are so recondite," Haultain writes, having tried to analyze brain function as it pertains to generating the swing, "what of the psychic? These, I fear, be beyond us. How analyse the complexities of the human soul? How tread the labyrinthine mazes of temperament and of character? How unravel the mesh-work of feelings and emotions . . . or how explain the disturbances these bring about in the higher layers, and the resulting delinquencies of the motor muscles? In golf we see in its profoundest aspects that profound problem of the relation of mind to matter."

How's that for golf writing? One hundred years on, the mystery of golf remains.

Three of Haultain's observations

A false stroke in golf is more keenly felt than a rejected proposal.

Until a man has learned to keep his eye on the ball, he will not play golf. He may be an excellent fellow; he may be the most jovial of companions, the sagest of counsellors, the truest of friends; but unless he can keep his eye on the ball never will he be a golfer.

What exasperates the ordinary man about golf is that it seems to be a game utterly and absolutely unamenable to reason. You may speculate in stocks; you may lay odds on a horse race; but the money-market and the turf are child's play compared with the uncertainties of golf.

IF YOUR GRANDFATHER HAD ONLY KNOWN . . .

- Cost of joining Augusta National in 1932: $350.00 (plus tax and $60 annual fee)
- Number of invitations sent out: tens of thousands
- Number of members anticipated: 1,800
- Actual number of members at the time of the first Masters: 76

GREAT CAREER AMATEURS

Joe Carr, b. Dublin, 1922

There's never been a finer Irish amateur, and there have been few finer Irish professionals. The Dubliner dominated Irish and British golf for many years. He won four Irish Amateur Close championships, the 1953, 1958, and 1960 British Amateurs, and he was low amateur in the 1956 and 1958 British Opens.

Carr wasn't above a bit of gamesmanship. He was twice the age of Ivan Morris, whom he played in a match during the 1967 Irish Amateur Close championship at Lahinch Golf Club. Morris was two-up on the much more experienced Carr after fourteen holes but lost the fifteenth and then the sixteenth when he three-putted from forty-five feet. Carr, now even with Morris, said, "I have been in this position thousands of times, you know." Morris said that the remark "unhinged him." Carr went on to win the match and the championship.

He was on the receiving end of a needling remark one day when he was struggling with his game at Rosses Point in County Sligo. His caddie asked him, "Have you ever played Rosses Point before, Sor?" He answered, "Oh, yes, many times," to which his caddie said, "You know they play the West of Ireland championship here, Sor." Carr came back with, "I know. I won it twelve times." The caddie, not a bit disconcerted, replied, "It must have been fierce easy to win in those days, Sor."

Carr lives near the Portmarnock Golf Club, where his father was the manager. His house shares a wall with the home where the poet W. B. Yeats lived. He knows his records will endure, for, as he told writer Lewine Mair, "Today nobody has the chance to put together a record like mine or Michael Bonallack's. They aren't around for long enough before they turn professional." They might not have his, or Bonallack's, amateur career even if they did remain amateur.

TEN MOST MEMORABLE LINES *from* *CADDYSHACK*

1. *You're a lot of woman, you know that? You want to make $14 the hard way?*

2. *"You should play with Dr. Beeper and myself. I mean, he's been club champion for three years running, and I'm no slouch myself."*

   "Don't sell yourself short, Judge. You're a tremendous slouch."

3. *I've sentenced boys younger than you to the gas chamber. I didn't want to do it. I felt I owed it to them.*

4. *I enjoy skinny-skiing . . . going to bullfights on acid . . .*

5. *I'm having a little party at the Yacht Club next Sunday. Christening my new sloop. Do you have any plans? How would you like to mow my lawn?*

6. *Let's pretend we're real human beings.*

7. *Hello, Mr. Gopher? It's me, Mr. Squirrel. Just a harmless squirrel. Not a plastic explosive or anything to worry about.*

8. *This calls for the old Billy Baroo.*

9. *"I tried calling, but they don't have a listing for Mr. Wonderful."*

   "What spelling did you use?"

10. *Did somebody step on a duck?*

SOME NAMES OF FEATURES ON THE OLD COURSE, ST. ANDREWS

Swilcan Burn: the stream running in front of the 1st green and 18th tee

Principal's Nose: a set of three bunkers located in the middle of the 16th fairway; playing to the left of them brings the greenside bunker into play, but playing to the right of them flirts with out-of-bounds

The Spectacles: two prominent bunkers that provide an aiming point for the tee shot on the 5th hole, but menace the landing area for the second shot

Shell Bunker: a large sand pit on the direct line from the 7th tee to its green—though taking the direct line is madness because of the considerable gorse that must be carried

Strath Bunker: a nasty little trap that eats into the 11th green; it was named for St. Andrean David Strath, a long hitter who was known to put his drives on the 7th hole into this distant bunker (the 11th hole shares a green with the 359-yard 7th)

Stroke Bunker: a wide trap placed in the exact middle of the 12th fairway, blind from the tee, at the two-hundred-yard mark; it can be carried, but two pot bunkers lurk thirty yards farther on

The Coffins: a group of bunkers on the 13th hole, two hundred yards from the tee

The Beardies: a series of bunkers to the left of the ideal line for the tee shot on 14, the Beardies also come into play on shots played too far left of the Spectacles on number 5

Hell Bunker: aptly named cavernous bunker that guards the second-shot landing area on the 14th hole; Jack Nicklaus took four shots to get out of it in the 1995 British Open, recording a 10 on the hole

Miss Grainger's Bosoms: two prominent humps that provide an aiming point from the 15th tee; named for Miss Agnes Grainger, a prominent local golfer who led the movement to create a Scottish Ladies Championship, first held in 1903 on the Old Course

Granny Clark's Wynd: the public road that runs across the 1st and 18th fairways

The Valley of Sin: grass depression at the front left of the 18th green; Costantino Rocca duffed a chip shot into the valley on the 72nd hole of the 1995 British Open, then holed a sixty-five-foot putt from there to force a playoff

WORLD GOLF HALL OF FAME

The World Golf Hall of Fame was dedicated in 1998 in St. Augustine, Florida. A prior incarnation that the PGA of America opened during the 1970s in Pinehurst, North Carolina, had failed to generate much interest. The PGA Tour, along with twenty-six international organizations including the Royal & Ancient Golf Club of St. Andrews and the Golf Course Superintendents Association of America, led to the creation of the World Golf Foundation and the World Golf Hall of Fame.

Here is the complete list of inductees, with their year of induction. (The LPGA has long maintained a separate Hall of Fame designation, with players qualifying by strict criteria involving wins and majors. For those players, marked with an asterisk, we are listing the year they qualified; their year of World Hall of Fame selection, if different, is listed on page 313.)

- Amy Alcott 1999*
- Willie Anderson 1975
- Isao Aoki 2004
- Tommy Armour 1976
- John Ball 1977
- Seve Ballesteros 1997
- Jim Barnes 1989
- Judy Bell 2001
- Deane Beman 2000
- Patty Berg 1951*
- Tommy Bolt 2002
- Michael Bonallack 2000
- Julius Boros 1982
- Pat Bradley 1991*
- James Braid 1976
- Jackie Burke Jr. 2000
- William C. Campbell 1990
- Donna Caponi 2001
- JoAnne Carner 1982*
- Billy Casper 1978
- Neil Coles 2000
- Harry Cooper 1992
- Fred Corcoran 1975
- Henry Cotton 1980

• Ben Crenshaw	2002
• Bing Crosby	1978
• Beth Daniel	1999*
• Bernard Darwin	2005
• Roberto de Vicenzo	1989
• Jimmy Demaret	1983
• Joe Dey	1975
• Leo Diegel	2003
• Chick Evans	1975
• Nick Faldo	1997
• Raymond Floyd	1989
• Herb Graffis	1977
• Ralph Guldahl	1981
• Walter Hagen	1974
• Marlene Bauer Hagge	2002
• Bob Harlow	1988
• Sandra Haynie	1977*
• Hisako "Chako" Higuchi	2003
• Harold Hilton	1978
• Ben Hogan	1974
• Bob Hope	1983
• Dorothy Campbell Hurd Howe	1978
• Juli Inkster	1999*
• Hale Irwin	1992
• Tony Jacklin	2002
• John Jacobs	2000
• Betty Jameson	1951*
• Bobby Jones	1974
• Robert Trent Jones Jr.	1987
• Betsy King	1995*
• Tom Kite	2004
• Bernhard Langer	2001
• Lawson Little	1980
• Gene Littler	1990
• Bobby Locke	1997
• Nancy Lopez	1987*
• Alister Mackenzie	2005
• Lloyd Mangrum	1998
• Carol Mann	1977*
• Cary Middlecoff	1986
• Johnny Miller	1996
• Tom Morris	1976
• Tom Morris Jr.	1975
• Byron Nelson	1974
• Larry Nelson	2006
• Jack Nicklaus	1974
• Greg Norman	2001
• Ayako Okamoto	2005
• Francis Ouimet	1974
• Arnold Palmer	1974
• Willie Park Sr.	2005
• Harvey Penick	2002
• Henry Picard	2006
• Gary Player	1974
• Nick Price	2003
• Judy Rankin	2000

Babe Didrikson Zaharias was Hall-of-Fame-worthy in every sport she tried.

• Betsy Rawls	1960*
• Clifford Roberts	1978
• Allan Robertson	2001
• Chi Chi Rodriguez	1992
• Donald Ross	1977
• Paul Runyan	1990
• Gene Sarazen	1974
• Patty Sheehan	1993*
• Dinah Shore	1994
• Charlie Sifford	2004
• Vijay Singh	2005
• Marilynn Smith	2006
• Horton Smith	1990
• Sam Snead	1974
• Karsten Solheim	2001
• Annika Sorenstam	2003*
• Payne Stewart	2001
• Marlene Stewart Streit	2004
• Louise Suggs	1951*
• John H. Taylor	1975
• Peter Thomson	1988
• Jerome Travers	1976
• Walter Travis	1979
• Lee Trevino	1981
• Richard Tufts	1992
• Harry Vardon	1974
• Glenna Collett Vare	1975
• Tom Watson	1988
• Karrie Webb	2005*
• Joyce Wethered	1975
• Kathy Whitworth	1975*
• Mickey Wright	1964*
• Babe Didrikson Zaharias	1951*

*Years of World Golf Hall of Fame induction: Berg, 1974; Carner, 1985; Lopez, 1989; Rawls, 1987; Whitworth, 1982; Wright, 1976; Zaharias, 1974.

MAJOR LONGEVITY

More than any other sport, golf measures its champions by their ability to reach the top and stay there. The following chart lists all the men and women who won major championships over a span of ten or more seasons from their first to their last. The top of the list is not surprising; what is surprising are some of the omissions. Where are Arnold Palmer, Tom Watson, and Ben Hogan?

MEN	SPAN IN YEARS	WOMEN
Jack Nicklaus 1962 U.S. Open–1986 Masters	24	
	21	Patty Berg 1937 Titleholders–1958 Western
John H. Taylor 1894 British–1913 British Gary Player 1959 British– 1978 Masters	19	
Harry Vardon 1896 British–1914 British	18	Betsy Rawls 1951 U.S. Open–1969 LPGA Juli Inkster 1984 LPGA/du Maurier– 2002 U.S. Open
Raymond Floyd 1969 PGA–1986 U.S. Open	17	Sandra Haynie 1965 LPGA–1982 du Maurier
Julius Boros 1952 U.S. Open–1968 PGA Lee Trevino 1968 U.S. Open–1984 PGA Hale Irwin 1974 U.S. Open–1990 U.S. Open	16	

MEN	SPAN IN YEARS	WOMEN
Willie Park 1860 British–1875 British Walter Hagen 1914 U.S. Open–1929 British	15	
Henry Cotton 1934 British–1948 British Open	14	Babe Didrikson Zaharias 1940 Titleholders–1954 U.S. Open
Gene Sarazen 1922 U.S. Open–1935 Masters	13	Louise Suggs 1946 Titleholders/Western–1959 Titleholders Patty Sheehan 1983 LPGA–1996 Kraft Nabisco Meg Mallon 1991 U.S. Open–2004 U.S. Open
Sam Snead 1942 PGA–1954 Masters	12	Betty Jameson 1942 Western–1954 Western Donna Caponi 1969 U.S. Open–1981 LPGA Amy Alcott 1979 du Maurier–1991 Kraft Nabisco
Peter Thomson 1954 British–1965 British Billy Casper 1959 U.S. Open–1970 Masters Ben Crenshaw 1984 Masters–1995 Masters	11	Nancy Lopez 1978 LPGA–1989 LPGA
Jimmy Demaret 1940 Masters–1950 Masters Payne Stewart 1989 PGA–1999 U.S. Open	10	Mary Mills 1963 U.S. Open–1973 LPGA Kathy Whitworth 1965 Titleholders–1975 LPGA Betsy King 1987 Kraft Nabisco–1997 Kraft Nabisco Annika Sorenstam 1995 U.S. Open–2005 Kraft Nabisco/LPGA

RULES DIFFERENCES BETWEEN MATCH PLAY AND STROKE PLAY

According to Rule 2: Match Play, "a match consists of one side playing against another in a stipulated round. . . . The game is played by holes . . . a hole is won by the side that holes its ball in the fewer strokes." Rule 3: Stroke Play indicates that "[t]he competitor who plays the stipulated round or rounds in the fewest strokes is the winner." This difference in objective—to defeat a particular opponent by winning the most holes, as opposed to shooting the lowest score against an entire field—leads to some interesting differences in the Rules themselves.

PRACTICING: Practicing on the course before a round is permitted in match play; in stroke play, a player practicing on the course on the day of a competition is disqualified. (Rationale: In a stroke-play competition, players teeing off late in the day would have an advantage over earlier players if they could practice on the course. In match play, your only relevant opponent has the same time you have to prepare for the round.)

ORDER OF PLAY: While the earliest known code of rules established that the ball lying farthest from the hole is to be played first, there is no penalty for playing out of turn in stroke play. In match play, a stroke played out of turn can be recalled and ordered to be replayed, at the discretion of the opponent. (Rationale: Do we really want all tournament golfers to wait before tapping in?)

TEEING OUTSIDE THE TEEING AREA: The penalty for teeing off from outside the teeing ground (bordered by the tee markers, and extending two club-lengths back) is two strokes in medal play. In match play, there is no penalty, though the opponent can demand that the stroke be replayed from within the proper area. (One player of our acquaintance, upon seeing people placing their tee a few inches ahead of the markers, likes to say, "I'll give you those two inches on the tee if you'll give them to me on the green.")

DISPUTES ABOUT PROCEDURES: In stroke play, if a player is unsure of how to proceed, he may drop a second ball, play out both balls, and report the situation to the governing authority before signing his scorecard; the ball played under the appropriate rule will count for his score. In match play, this option does not exist; the players must agree on procedure or get a ruling before going ahead, and an improper decision cannot be changed once they've started play on the next hole. (Rationale: In match play, you're entitled to know where you stand in your match at all times; in stroke play, your result doesn't affect your fellow competitors.)

GIVING ADVICE WHEN ASKED: In stroke play, if your fellow competitor (the technical term for the others in your group) asks you for advice and you give it, you are both penalized two strokes. In match play, if your opponent asks you for advice and you give it, the opponent loses the hole. (Rationale: The moment your opponent asked for advice, he was subject to a loss-of-hole penalty, so it makes no difference if you answer or not. In stroke play, however, you're both culpable in this circumstance.) Under the Decisions on the Rules of Golf that took effect in 2006, information about a player's distance to the hole is not considered "advice."

WRONG INFORMATION: In match play, if you give wrong information to an opponent about how many strokes you've taken on a hole, you lose the hole. There is no such provision in stroke play—even if you're in a sudden-death playoff. In other words, if you're lying four and your playoff opponent tells you he's just holed out for four, and you pick up your ball marker and go to shake his hand—and then he realizes he holed out for five—you're screwed, because there's no penalty for him, and you've just incurred a one-stroke penalty for removing your marker. (Rationale: In theory, in a stroke-play event, you're only concerned about your own result. As for the playoff scenario, it certainly does seem wrong for the Rule to work this way, but that's how it is.)

MOVING ANOTHER PLAYER'S BALL: If another player, his caddie, or his equipment moves a player's ball at rest, touches it, or causes it to move (at any time other than in a search for a possibly lost ball), the ball is to be replaced in its original position. In stroke play, there is no penalty for the person

Golfer (Richard H. Sikes) outnumbered by rules officials (Frank Hannigan and Joseph C. Dey Jr.) at the 1963 U.S. Amateur.

responsible for the movement; in match play, the opponent is penalized one stroke. (Rationale: In a match, the position of your opponent's ball is of material importance to you; in stroke play, it's not as significant.)

STOPPING OR DEFLECTING ANOTHER PLAYER'S BALL: In match play, if a player's ball is accidentally stopped or deflected by an opponent, the player may play the ball as it lies or he may replay the stroke without penalty. In stroke play, he must play it as it lies, unless the stroke began on the putting green, in which case it must be replayed. (Rationale: In match play, you and your opponent are the game, and it would be improper for the opponent to have an effect on your result without offering you a do-over. In stroke play, your fellow players are just another "outside agency," and whatever effect they have is just the rub of the green.)

STRIKING ANOTHER BALL ON THE GREEN: In match play, there is no penalty if your ball hits someone else's ball. In stroke play, there is a two-shot penalty if your ball collides with another ball in play and at rest, so long as your ball was on the putting green when you struck it. (Rationale: This is probably a vestige of the stymie, which existed only in match play for most of its history.)

BOB DYLAN: GOLFER?

Does Bob Dylan play golf?

Dylan has included references to golf in some of his music. Having visited the folksinger Woody Guthrie in a New Jersey hospital, Dylan wrote a song about the experience. The song is called "Last Thoughts on Woody Guthrie," and in it, Dylan writes about the search for truth.

"And it ain't in a cardboard-box house/Or down any movie star's blouse/And you can't buy it on the golf course," Dylan wrote. He also referred to golf in his song "I Shall Be Free No. 10."

"I'm gonna grow my hair down to my feet so strange/So I look like a walking mountain range/And I'm gonna ride into Omaha on a horse/Out to the country club and the golf course/ Carry *The New York Times*, shoot a few holes, blow their minds."

Much later, an interviewer asked Dylan his handicap.

"Seventeen," he answered. "I hit it as if it were a baseball bat."

Then there was the time Dylan told a shopworn joke during a concert in Oklahoma City on July 5, 2000, while introducing his drummer.

"He must have thought he was playing golf today, because he wore two shirts, in case he gets a hole in one," Dylan said.

Finally, there are the titles Dylan chooses for some of his songs. They must represent golf working on his mind. Who but a golfer could have used the title "Blowin' in the Wind" or "Tangled Up in Blue"? Surely, Dylan's a golfer.

FOOTNOTES TO HISTORY

Jim Simons, 1971 U.S. Open, Merion Golf Club, Ardmore, Pennsylvania

Jim Simons at Merion. Few young golfers are ready for the pressures that accumulate during the last round of a major.

Simons, a twenty-year-old amateur from Butler, a suburb of Pittsburgh, had been runner-up to Steve Melnyk in the British Amateur the week prior to the U.S. Open. He had also been on the American side that lost to Great Britain and Ireland in the Walker Cup two weeks before at the Old Course. A senior at Wake Forest University, Simons was clearly an accomplished player, but nobody expected him to lead the U.S. Open after three rounds. Simons opened with 71–71; playing the third round with Lee Trevino, he shot five-under par 65. That staked him to a two-shot lead over Jack Nicklaus starting the last round. "That kid can play a little bit," said Trevino, whose 69 left him tied for fourth, four shots back. "He's got a lot of good shots. He showed me something. He's solid."

But solid enough to win his national Open? Simons said before the last round, "I don't know if I've had the experience enough to win the Open, not with Jack Nicklaus breathing down my neck tomorrow."

Merion's baskets instead of flags make it tougher to gauge the wind.

Simons was nervous. He couldn't find his car for twenty minutes in the parking lot at his hotel. He put his sweater on backward in the locker room—fortunately, his Wake Forest teammate Lanny Wadkins advised him of his mistake. Still, he maintained a one-shot lead after nine holes. He was tied with Nicklaus and Trevino after bogeying the 10th hole, bogeying the 14th, and missing makeable birdie putts on the 15, 16, and 17. He needed a birdie to get into a playoff, but double-bogeyed the last hole after trying to reach the green from high rough with a three-wood.

Simons finished fifth while Trevino went on to win a playoff the next day over Nicklaus. He turned pro and won three PGA Tour events, including the 1978 Memorial Tournament in Dublin, Ohio. He eventually left the pro game because of shoulder problems and became a stockbroker. Simons died in December 2005.

QUOTATIONS OF CHAIRMAN MOE

Moe Norman (see page 60) occupies a unique niche in the world of golf, one of the few players who could be described as a cult figure. He had an unusual way of expressing himself: Never complicated, sometimes elliptical, he spoke in an almost singsong, often repetitive manner, frequently with great insight. Here are some of Moe's aphorisms:

Two things I believed in, good shoes and a good car. Alligator shoes and a Cadillac.

I did what I wanted to do. For twenty-eight years now I've done what I loved, chase a golf ball. I gave Moe Norman a chance in this world to prove to the world what he has. I think I've proven it.

Come on now, let's not be a ball beater, let's be a mind beater.

Long and low. Stretch it. Shake hands with the flagstick. I want the right arm bent and the left arm a rod at impact.

I still believe in mass. What do you want out of the rough, a matchstick?

There are no tight holes the Moe Norman way. The ball will fit the Moe Norman way. My way is the way to greatness.

Don't force it, finesse it. Stabilize, energize, contain, release.

A missed golf shot will never hurt my golf swing, only my vanity, and vanity is the luxury of fools.

Fairways look like deserts to me, even if they're only thirty yards wide.

You have to use smooth, centrifugal force. Everybody uses brute force, not smooth force.

The feeling I want is light and extremely powerful.

Hope and fear, hope and fear, that's what people see when they play golf. Not me, I see happiness.

Everybody swings around their body except for Hogan, Trevino, and me. We swing under our body.

Let your body memorize your swing.

Golf is hitting an object to a defined area with the least amount of effort and an alert attitude of indifference.

Imagination plus vividness equals reality in your mind.

Two things you have to finish in this game, your backswing and your follow-through.

I like my shoes outside my knees. I lose distance, but I'm dead straight.

If they had a tournament in the dark I'd be the only one who could play. I'd know where to walk to find my ball.

Golf is not a hitting action. It's a pulling action, and there's no work whatsoever, no work whatsoever.

Hogan and I play by the sound of the ball. We don't have to look for the ball.

I'm not ball oriented. I'm divot oriented. I swing past the ball.

I know that I have something people want, to hit the ball in a repetitious way. What a good feeling, even in countries that I've never been they've heard of this guy Moe Norman.

Artificial strokes for artificial folks. (Moe said this after trying to teach Mickey Rooney at the National Golf Club of Canada in the late 1970s. The pro Ben Kern finally asked Moe to leave. He kept saying it all the way to the parking lot.)

I never feel the game is against me. You have to go get it. You can't expect a dumb thing to come to you. The golf ball is dumb, the course is dumb, but golfers expect a dumb thing to come to them.

I never think of hazards. Oh no, never. They're not in my jurisdiction, not in my vocabulary.

I'm just a different type of golfer, fastest player in the world, take one look and whack. It doesn't look like I'm trying.

Being successful in this world is when you're doing something you love. I've got something people wanted, to hit the ball in a repetitive way. I can control my destiny from tee to green. I did it for thirty-five years and I'm still doing it. So how can I feel bad? Not when I've got something everybody in the world wants. No sirree, I feel good, I feel good.

THE ONE THAT GOT AWAY

Five male golfers have won the career Grand Slam: Gene Sarazen, Jack Nicklaus, Tiger Woods, Gary Player, and Ben Hogan. Here are the players who won three legs of the Slam and never got the fourth:

1. Sam Snead, U.S. Open. Snead's seven major victories are sometimes overshadowed by the one he never won. His close call in the 1939 U.S. Open, when he took an eight on the last hole needing only a par for victory, is one of the most famous last-hole disasters this side of Jean Van de Velde. He finished second or tied for second three times after that, losing a playoff in 1947 to Lew Worsham by one stroke.

2. Arnold Palmer, PGA Championship. Palmer finished tied for second in the PGA Championship three times. He lost by a stroke to Julius Boros in 1968 and by two to Dave Stockton in 1970. Had he managed to win in 1964, at Columbus (Ohio) Country Club, it would have been a kind of payback to hometown hero Jack Nicklaus, who defeated Palmer for his first professional win at Oakmont, in Palmer's western Pennsylvania backyard. Palmer's final-round 69 left him two shots behind Bobby Nichols and tied with Nicklaus, whose 64 was his lowest final eighteen in any major championship.

3. Tom Watson, PGA Championship. In 1978, Watson held the fifty-four-hole lead at Oakmont, and was in front of John Mahaffey by five shots and Jerry Pate by four with nine to play, but his ultimate 73 left him tied with those two at the finish. All three parred the first playoff hole, but after Watson missed a thirty-footer on the next, Mahaffey made his twelve-foot birdie putt for the win.

4. Byron Nelson, British Open. Nelson's only trip to the British Open in his prime years was in 1937, when he was over for the Ryder Cup. He finished tied for fifth, six shots behind winner Henry Cotton. He played in only one other Open, in 1955 at St. Andrews, making the cut and finishing in a tie for 32nd.

Walter Hagen, always dapper (but no green jacket).

5. Ray Floyd, British Open. Floyd's only four top-ten finishes in twenty Opens came between 1976 and 1981. His best performance was a four-way tie for second in 1978, two strokes behind Nicklaus at St. Andrews.

6. Walter Hagen, Masters. The Masters did not so much get away from Hagen as it started too late; he was forty-one when the first Augusta National Invitation Tournament was held in 1934, and his best finish was a tie for eleventh in 1936. That placement earned him his only Masters prize money: $100.

7. Lee Trevino, Masters. Trevino reportedly believed that the nature of both the golf course and the club were incompatible with his own. He never came close in Augusta, finishing tied for tenth twice in twenty tournaments.

8. Tommy Armour, Masters. As with Hagen, Armour had his best years before there was a Masters. He competed in seven of them, beginning in 1935, with his best finish an eighth in 1937. He is the only Masters competitor to have a grandson play in the Masters as well (Tommy Armour III, 1990).

Six women have won the LPGA's career Grand Slam: Louise Suggs, Mickey Wright, Pat Bradley, Juli Inkster, Karrie Webb, and Annika Sorenstam. (Wright's stretch of seven wins in twelve majors from 1962 through 1964 sets a bar that Tiger Woods can aim for; his best thus far is six majors from 2000 through 2002.) Here are the golfers who won three of four in their careers, with the one that got away (through 2005):

1. Patty Berg, LPGA Championship. Her closest call came in 1956, when she lost to Marlene Hagge in a sudden-death playoff; she also finished second, a stroke back of Betsy Rawls, in 1959.

2. Betsy Rawls, Titleholders. Rawls never won the Titleholders, which was a major for most of her career. She was twenty-three when she won her first U.S. Open, and forty-one when she won her second LPGA. In 1980 she became the first woman to serve as a rules official at the men's U.S. Open.

3. Betsy King, Weetabix/du Maurier. King had eight top-five finishes in the du Maurier Classic, with her heartbreaker coming in 1993, when she was stopped short of the career Grand Slam on the first playoff hole, losing to Brandie Burton.

4. Patty Sheehan, du Maurier. Sheehan's only top-three finish in Canada's major was as runner-up in 1990, when she entered the final round trailing Cathy Johnston-Forbes by four strokes and could make up only two.

5. Kathy Whitworth, U.S. Women's Open. Whitworth and Snead, the career victory leaders, have the same USGA hole in their otherwise perfect résumés. She finished T5-3-T4-2 in consecutive years from 1968 through 1971, and held the third-round lead in 1981 at age forty-one before a 74 left her in third behind Pat Bradley and Beth Daniel.

6. Amy Alcott, LPGA Championship. Alcott's near miss came in 1988, when she was tied for the lead going into the final round, but her 74 opened the door for Sherrie Turner to win by a stroke with a 67.

7. Laura Davies, Kraft Nabisco Championship. Davies missed making a big splash at the 1994 championship when her putt on the 72nd hole stayed out, leaving her a stroke behind Donna Andrews, whose 276 total is the fourth best in the history of the Dinah Shore/Colgate/Kraft Nabisco tournament.

8. Sandra Haynie, Kraft Nabisco/Titleholders/Western. Like other LPGA pros whose careers stretched from 1966 to 1983, Haynie actually competed in six different majors, winning 2 LPGAs, one U.S. Open, and one Peter Jackson Classic (later the du Maurier).

9. Se Ri Pak, Kraft Nabisco. The twenty-eight-year-old Pak has only one top-ten finish in the desert, tying for ninth in 2002.

10. Beverly Hanson, U.S. Women's Open. Hanson played in fifteen U.S. Opens between 1948 and 1964, and never finished closer than eight shots behind the winner.

11. Meg Mallon, Kraft Nabisco. In 1996, Mallon tied for second, one stroke behind winner Patty Sheehan, her only near miss.

12. Jan Stephenson, Kraft Nabisco. Golf's 1980s glamor girl could play; she won three majors in just over two years and had a second in the Nabisco Dinah Shore in 1985.

Jan Stephenson proved that pin-up photos can overshadow a world-class game.

WHY AMERICANS MIGHT NOT HAVE ENTERED THE BRITISH OPEN IN THE 1950s

Contemporary golf fans are always a bit surprised to learn that Ben Hogan competed in only one British Open and never played a single round at the Old Course at St. Andrews. In fact, it was somewhat unusual for an American to make the trip across the ocean in that era; Hogan was the only American to win the British Open between Sam Snead's victory in 1946 and Arnold Palmer's in 1961.

Whatever prestige was attached to the British Open in those days was mitigated by the economic realities. Players traveled by ocean liner, a slow and rather expensive way to go. They had to allow some days to adjust to the time change, then had to play qualifying rounds before entering the Open itself—there were no exemptions. An American pro had to figure on at least a week and a half of lodging and expenses, assuming he played well enough to make it into the Open field.

But surely this was worth it for the potential prize money, right? Well, no. The following details the money paid out at the Open Championship held in Carnoustie in 1953, the year of Ben Hogan's triumph:

- First place, Ben Hogan: $1,400
- Four tied for second, Dai Rees, Frank Stranahan, Antonio Cerda, Peter Thomson: $472 each ($0 for Stranahan, an amateur)
- Sixth place, Roberto de Vicenzo: $140
- Seventh through twenty-sixth place: $84 each
- Twenty-seventh through forty-ninth place: $70 each

THE GOLFER'S LIFE LIST

Play with a Handicapped Person

My brother-in-law Dan Kozak has Down syndrome. Whenever he visits us, we go out for a game of golf. I take Dan to a par-three or executive course, we strap a few clubs on our backs, and off we go. I never come away from the round less than exhilarated. Dan knows how to enjoy the game in ways I too often ignore, or forget. He bangs the ball along and loves the sound of the ball rattling into the tin of the cup. Score? What's that? Oh, he cares when he hits a lousy shot, but I've never seen somebody forget the last shot so quickly or get to the next one with so much enthusiasm. And when the ball comes off the clubface just so, with that sweet click we all like, well, there's no sound so joyous as when Dan, his club held high, yells, "Yeah!"

Zohar Sharon takes dead aim.

Most recently we teed it up at a short course just north of Toronto. Dan's compact swing whupped the ball 150 yards or so down the left side of the first fairway, and off we went. Later he did a little dance on one fairway after a particularly pleasing shot, and on another hole he took a bow after a good stroke. My twelve-year-old nephew Sam had come along, and he high-fived Dan after the round and said, "Great playing with you. Good job." It sure was.

Zohar and friends.

It wasn't long after a round with Dan that I played a few holes at the nearby Maple Downs Golf and Country Club with Zohar Sharon, a fifty-three-year-old Israeli veteran who had been blinded in a military accident. He took up golf and can really play. Zohar made an eagle two on the par-four fourth, where he holed out from 140 yards. He learned the game by swinging the club back and forth, back and forth, back and forth, practicing what he calls "golf dances and mental games." His daughter Yasmin told me golf gets her father up in the morning. He returned to Israel a week or so after we played, and later in the summer somebody e-mailed me an article from a newspaper there: Zohar had made a hole-in-one. An eagle and a hole-in-one inside of a couple of months: not bad, not bad at all.

I pretty much forgot that Dan has Down syndrome and that Zohar is blind while I played golf with them. That's what we did. We "played." Golf became a game, a simple recreation. I'm looking forward to playing with them again, and soon.

—*LR*

FAMOUS COLLAPSES IN MAJORS

At Pinehurst, Gore got goosed and Goosen got gored.

Retief Goosen and Jason Gore, 2005 U.S. Open, Pinehurst No. 2

Goosen, who had won the 2001 and 2004 U.S. Opens, took a three-shot lead into the final round at Shinnecock Hills. Everybody was ready to hand him the trophy. Goosen was playing in the final twosome with Jason Gore, the Cinderella story of the championship who had come in ranked 818th in the world. He was second behind Goosen, and people were wondering whether he would hold up. The only thing they wondered about Goosen was by how many shots the South African would win.

Gore shot 40 on the front nine on his way to an 84, while Goosen started missing fairways and greens and putts and shot 81. Both Gore and Goosen took their rounds in good humor. Walking to the 16th tee, Goosen asked Gore if he knew anything about cricket. Gore said he didn't, but Goosen informed him that scores in the game run into the hundreds, so they were having a good cricket match. Taking on the role of a Sunday duffer, Goosen suggested that he and Gore play the last three holes for five bucks. They did, and Goosen won the wager. After thirty-six putts and nine lipouts, he had at least won something. (No money was exchanged, in deference to Tour rules against gambling—or so they said later.)

Goosen's final round didn't do much damage to him. He came back to tie for fifth in the British Open and to win the International on the PGA Tour.

As for Gore, he regarded his experience in a positive manner, figuring he'd been right there with the best golfers in the world for three rounds. He soon won three straight tournaments on the Nationwide Tour and thus got a so-called battlefield promotion to the PGA Tour. He won the 84 Lumber Classic on the PGA Tour in September, having taken the advice of his great-uncle Henry Gore. Gore had been following him during the summer of 2005 and sent him a note that Jason received a week before the tournament. His great-uncle had written, "Dear Jason, I'm always watching you on TV and I'm proud of you. And next time when you play in the U.S. Open, try to win!" Gore said, "I thought that was pretty darn funny," and his first Tour win completed the Cinderella story of the year, even if the U.S. Open ending wasn't what he wanted.

THE GOLFING MACHINE

Homer Kelley was an engineer who worked for the U.S. Navy and Boeing Aircraft during World War II. He believed that the golf swing is subject to the laws of force and motion, and in 1941 he decided to study the subject. Kelley published his book *The Golfing Machine: Geometric Golf—The Computer Age Approach to Golfing Perfection,* with what would become its famous yellow cover streaked with illustrations of hinges, fulcrums, and levers, in 1969, under the imprint Star System Press. Kelley used that name because he had once come across the idea that a star was a vision of distant truth.

Kelley treated golf as an acronym for Geometrically Oriented Linear Force. He concluded that the golf swing comprised 24 components with 144 variations. The book attracted a devoted following that was willing to plumb its abstruse and arcane depths. One Kelley acolyte, the late golf professional Tommy Tomasello, offered a course in how to use the book, believing that Kelley was alone in understanding the movements that, permutated and combined, can generate a nearly endless variety of ways in which to swing.

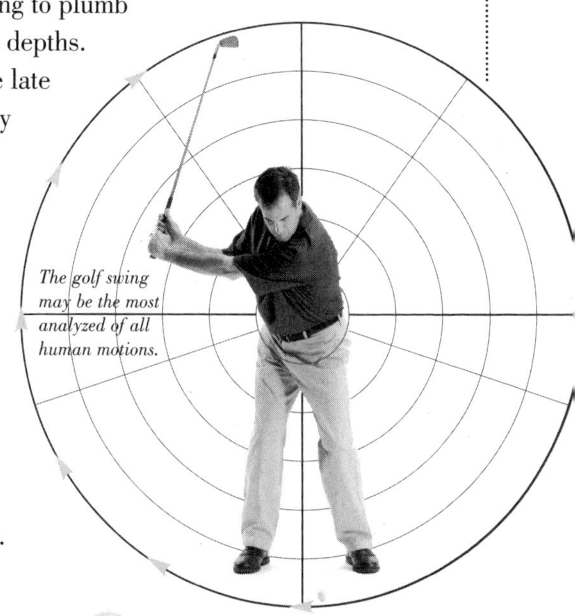

The golf swing may be the most analyzed of all human motions.

Another advocate refers to Kelley as "the Charles Darwin and Isaac Newton of golf."

Kelley died in February 1983 at the age of seventy-five, while giving a seminar to the Georgia PGA. The list below isn't meant as an instructional guide, but it does demonstrate how far some people will go in their quest to understand how to hit a golf ball.

THE TWENTY-FOUR COMPONENTS OF THE GOLFING MACHINE:

1. Grips—basic (the proximity of the hands to each other on the club shaft)

2. Grips—types

3. Strokes—basic (activity of the right elbow and arms)

4. Strokes—types and variations

5. Plane line (the direction and angle of the stroke)

6. Plane angle—basic

7. Plane angle—variations

8. Fix (correct impact positions)

9. Address (the position from which the backstroke is started)

10. Hinge actions (hand manipulation that controls clubface alignment)

11. Pressure point combinations (what drives the club through impact)

12. Pivot

13. Shoulder turn

14. Hip turn

15. Hip action

16. Knee action

17. Foot action

18. Left wrist action

19. Lag loading (the physics of both hitting and swinging)

20. Trigger types (the actions that initiate the release of the "power package assembly")

21. Power package assembly point (the positions selected as best able to supply the impact force as calculated for the situation)

22. Power package loading action

23. Power package delivery path

24. Power package release

GOLF HOLES THAT HAVE BECOME ARCHETYPES

You may not have heard of many of these holes, but you've undoubtedly played their descendants. Foundational examples of golf course design, they have inspired imitators and adaptors all over the world.

REDAN

A Redan hole is a rendition of the 15th hole at North Berwick, a half-hour east of Edinburgh, West Links, Scotland. The hole, on North Berwick's West links, is named after a fortress used during the Crimean War in the mid-nineteenth century, when the French and British were at war with the Russians. Geoff Shackelford in his book *Lines of Charm* writes that an officer playing the hole named it. He had returned from the war, and when he came upon the 15th he was reminded of a fortress that the British took from the Russians. The local term for it was "redan," and, as Shackelford points out, "Redan is now part of the English language, defined by the Oxford English Dictionary as a 'fort' that has two faces forming a salient towards the enemy."

C. B. Macdonald and Seth Raynor often copied this concept, most notably at the fourth hole at the National Golf Links of America in Southampton, Long Island. Macdonald actually improved upon the original concept at the National, eliminating the blind tee shot found at North Berwick. Macdonald probably described the Redan concept best when he wrote, "Take a narrow tableland, tilt it a little from right to left, dig a deep bunker on the front side, approach it diagonally, and you have the Redan."

Typically, a Redan is about 190 yards long, featuring a green set at a distinct, forty-five-degree right-to-left angle to the tee; it slopes in the same direction, right to left and also away from the line of play, falling away from the tee. This dictates a right to left tee shot that pitches short right of the putting surface, using the aforementioned slope of the approach area and green surface to funnel the ball to a back-left hole location. A high, soft, and precise shot is needed to go at the flag and hold the green.

BIARRITZ

Macdonald and Raynor frequently incorporated a Biarritz hole into their designs. It was one of four typical par-three concepts they consistently employed, along with the Redan, Short, and Eden. That said, Macdonald's National Golf Links of America does not feature a Biarritz.

The Biarritz is so called because the concept was taken from a Willie Dunn Jr.–designed hole (circa 1888), called "Chasm," at Biarritz, France. Dunn's dramatic hole, which no longer exists, played over a section of the Bay of Biscay to a massive green bisected by a deep swale that created three distinct sections of putting surface—two shelves at the front and rear, and the swale.

A Biarritz is typically long, more than two hundred yards. Apparently, the excitement in the old days came from landing the ball short of the green and watching it disappear into the swale, then reappear on the back shelf, near the flag. In most cases today, good players would simply fly the ball onto the back shelf when the hole is cut back there. The Biarritz is thus now a rather old-fashioned idea. However, it's still fun to run the ball through the swale on a Biarritz when the hole is cut on the rear portion of the green. Brian Silva, one of a small group of architects who do top-notch restoration work, made this shot possible when he restored the swale in the green at the 211-yard fifth hole at the Mountain Lake course in Lake Wales, Florida.

Usually, the big, rectangular green at a Biarritz is framed by a strip bunker on either side of the putting surface; in some cases, there is also a bunker well short of the green that's supposed to mimic the Bay of Biscay. Yale's dramatic Biarritz (Raynor, circa late 1920s), its ninth hole, is particularly appealing because of a pond that fronts the green and mimics the Bay as well.

It's interesting that many Biarritz holes left today do not feature the front shelf mowed as green; for some reason, the front shelf of green surface is mowed at fairway height. As interest in accurate restoration develops, though, more and more of these sections are being allowed to revert to Macdonald's and Raynor's original conception.

ALPS

The original Alps hole is the 17th at Prestwick Golf Club. Macdonald mimicked the Alps concept at the 3rd hole of the National Golf Links of America and elsewhere. The green at the National is thirty-five yards wide, so the golfer almost expects to find his ball on the green if he manages to carry the hill. Ran Morrissett, an aficionado of course architecture who with his brother founded the site www.golfclubatlas.com—a must-visit for anybody interested in the subject—considers the approach to the third at the National the finest blind shot in the game. The central, and essential, feature of an Alps is that the approach shot, usually the second because the hole is most often a par four, must carry a hill short of the green; the shot is therefore blind, no matter where one drives from the tee. The other significant feature is a large bunker just beyond the hill, in front of the green. A completely authentic Alps would have a free-standing hill short of the green rendering everything behind it blind, including any bunkers.

This type of hole in a new course would puzzle the contemporary golfer. Tom Doak called the 10th hole at High Pointe in northern Michigan an Alps because of the uphill second shot and the punchbowl green beyond the hill. The club cut away part of the hill on the left side of the landing area, allowing longer hitters to hit a driver over the first hill and down to the base of the hill in front of the green. Doak says that there was never much of a ridge short of the green, simply a big climb up and then a shallow bowl rising up off the back of the green. Still, the hole echoes the features at an Alps, and Doak clearly admires the original concept.

Eden

The Eden concept has been copied or mimicked more than any other theme for a hole. It's based on the famous 11th—High Hole In—at the Old Course at St. Andrews.

An Eden is typically a midlength par three, in the 160–170 yard range, featuring a relatively small green tilted severely from back to front à la the 11th at the Old Course. Three main bunkers dominate: "Hill," a deep pit left of the putting surface; "Strath" at the right; and, usually, a bunker behind the green that represents the Eden Estuary from which the hole, and that particular bunker, derive their name. John Low wrote in his book *Concerning Golf* that this bunker "is not very dreadful in itself, but sufficiently difficult, seeing that the recovery shot has to be played backward onto a downhill green."

Road

Here is one of golf's most notorious and feared holes. The golfer once had to drive over the Black Sheds, used for storing hickory, to a fairway that was blind from the tee. The fairway remains blind, but now the golfer drives over a sign that reads "Old Course Hotel." There's more room to the right than most golfers believe, which is why even tour players who have competed in the British Open here a few times must remind themselves in which wind they are to aim over which letter. In a gentle breeze, the line is usually over the *o* in "Course." The player who finds that line, and hits a slight draw, will be pleased to locate his ball in the middle of the fairway.

The green, running right to left, is protected by a pebbly road behind and a wall that separates the links from the town. The famous Road Bunker defends the far left side of the green. It appears about as big as the palm of a hand and as deep as a well from the fairway. Very few golfers will aim left of the bunker toward the 18th tee, but that's a reasonable place from which to putt, chip, or pitch back to the green and try to make par—a four, that is. Still, the more usual and probably more prudent play is to the front of the green, at the right side.

Four is always good at the Road Hole, because, as Louis Stanley wrote, the hole is the strongest in the British Open, always has been and, in his opinion, always will be, "for though revolutionary changes in clubs and balls have taken away many of its former terrors, it still remains one of the most feared holes in the world, and has ruined the chances of many prospective champions."

The Road Hole's concepts have been developed in a variety of settings. Holes that try to copy the Road Hole also exist, at such tribute courses as Jack Nicklaus's New Course at the Grand Cypress Resort in Orlando, and the Wooden Sticks course in Uxbridge, Ontario, northeast of Toronto.

Perhaps the 7th at the National Golf Links of America is the most successful attempt to apply the concept of the Road Hole. A Road Hole–like bunker seven feet deep defends the left front of the green, while an even deeper bunker behind the back right of the green stands in for the road itself. The 10th at Shoreacres Golf Club near Chicago also cleverly evokes the Road Hole. Like the Road Hole, there's an out-of-bounds down the right side, the brave line that will best open up the green. A ravine just big enough to scare the golfer also runs down that side, while a bunker protects the left third of the green. The road is represented by a long bunker behind the green.

SHORT

The story here is that Macdonald took this concept from the 128-yard fourth hole at Royal West Norfolk, also known as Brancaster, a lonely, remote links in an area of England called the Wash. Bird watchers visit here regularly, as do artists. It's a place to be inspired.

A Short is a par three, typically between 130 and 140 yards, almost surrounded by sand, creating an "island" effect. Sand encircles the 6th at Macdonald's National Golf Links of America. Curiously, the green at a Short hole is typically large, wider than it is deep, but featuring distinct sections separated by complex contours. The section becomes the target. Brancaster's Short hole features a serpentine "sleeper" bunker (faced with wooden railroad ties) across almost its entire front, and wrapping partly round the sides. The 10th at Pine Valley Golf Club evokes the concept. Maidstone Golf Club's 150-yard 14th achieves the same effect, with the green huddled among sand and scrub, and the Atlantic Ocean behind drawing one's eye to the horizon. The very short (107 yards) 7th hole at Pebble Beach and the 15th at Cypress Point, the latter surrounded by bunkers and cypress trees, also express the typical features of a Short hole, as does the 10th at Chicago Golf Club.

LONG

The Long hole, a take on the par-five 14th at St. Andrews, is usually the longest hole on the course—hence the name!

There's generally some kind of danger at right, to emulate the out-of-bounds at the Old Course, and of course, a rendition of the famous Hell bunker that influences decisions regarding the second shot. Today, however, decent players can usually carry Hell bunker after a good drive. This is a shame, because the idea of the Long hole, and the manner in which Hell bunker intrudes, was to compel the player to find a way to circumvent the hazard. The Old Course being so wide, it was possible to find a route. But more than anything, what Hell bunker did was introduce confusion into a player's mind. Contemporary architects, including Pete Dye, Tom Doak, and the partnership of Tom Mackenzie and Martin Ebert, use this idea to great effect on their courses. Long was never meant to be what John Low calls a "bee-line" hole, that is, one where the straight line is the correct line: "It is a mistake to suppose that because you hit a shot straight down the middle of the course and find it bunkered you are to fill up the offending hazard. Next time you will play on the true line, not on the bee-line, and all will be well." Michael Hurdzan and Dana Fry used this idea at the Devil's Paintbrush course in Caledon, Ontario. Bunkers are scattered seemingly at random around the course, including in the middle of the 10th and 17th holes. The bunker in the middle of the 17th fairway is also blind from the tee. The golfer wedded to "bee-line" golf will want to fill up these bunkers. But this golfer will miss the pleasures afforded by using his mind and finding a way round.

CAPE

This is by all accounts an original Macdonald concept, which he developed with the 14th hole at the National Golf Links of America. This hole was called Cape because its original green jutted into a water hazard at right. That green has since been replaced by a new putting surface farther back from the tee.

The Cape has since become known as a hole featuring a dramatic tee shot played over a diagonal water hazard. The most famous Cape hole is probably the par-four 5th at Macdonald's Mid Ocean Club in Bermuda. The 18th at the Leatherstocking course in Cooperstown, New York, is also a Cape hole, with an island tee. The golfer at a Cape hole is invited to cut off as much of the water hazard as he chooses.

Pete Dye loves this concept. The 18th at the TPC of Sawgrass that wraps around the lake to the left makes this obvious. Many of the holes he designs to close a round can be labeled Cape holes because the tee shot is very similar to the 5th at Mid Ocean—played over a diagonal water hazard, then into a green that all but falls off into water.

PUNCHBOWL

This word describes a hole where the green is set in a natural hollow, resembling a punchbowl. The 16th hole at National Golf Links of America is an example of this type of hole. A punchbowl green usually makes a golfer feel confident, because the ball will roll from the sides toward the middle. This is both an asset and a liability, according to Donald Ross. He wrote, "Punchbowl greens are attractive and one or two on a course are much in favor. However, they are not genuine testers of skill, as their sloping sides draw balls toward the center and offer equal advantage to both good and poorly played shots."

LEVEN

The 17th at National Golf Links of America is called Leven, and apparently was modeled after the 7th hole on the old Leven Links not far from St. Andrews. The original hole no longer exists.

Leven is a short par four, ranging from 330 to 360 yards. The strategy of the hole again involves a diagonal hazard off the tee. A more "heroic" line, usually over a large sandy waste area down the left side of the hole (à la the National Golf Links), leaves a wide-open approach to the green. The easier line to the right will avoid the demanding carry from the tee, but leave a semiblind approach over a convex bunker or sandy hill, played into the shallowest portion of the green; the green is angled so that the golfer who attempted to and was successful at making the longest carry off the tee plays down the length of the green.

RAYNOR'S PRIZED DOGLEG

Seth Raynor created this hole at the Lido course on Long Island, New York. Apparently he combined two concepts submitted to a design contest held by the British magazine *Country Life* into a single hole, the sixth at Lido, which alas no longer exists. The contest, which *Country Life* golf columnist Bernard Darwin started in 1914 after visiting Macdonald in the United States, invited readers to design a two-shot hole between 360 and 460 yards. Plans for eighty-one holes were submitted, of which more than fifty were doglegs.

Raynor used the concept several times, as a long par four—"a par four but bogey six," according to the architect. The hole is severely bunkered on the inside of the dogleg off the tee, with a green angled to favor those players who challenge the driving hazards. So, playing the tee shot away from bunkers leaves an awkward angle of approach and lengthens the hole considerably. A huge waste area (or some bunkers, usually set at an interesting diagonal) some sixty to one hundred yards short of the green presents a dilemma for those who drive left. Can you carry this hazard? Or should you lay up?

According to Macdonald's biographer, George Bahto (also a Raynor expert), none of these holes have survived in their original form.

Lion's Mouth

Raynor designed an intriguing Lion's Mouth hole, the par-four, 430-yard 16th at the Country Club of Charleston in South Carolina. The hole features a horseshoe-shaped green wrapped around a circular bunker that's seven feet deep. The bunker gives the hole its name; from the tee it's easy to imagine it swallowing one's ball.

Double Plateau

This is another typical Raynor hole. Its central themes are two distinct plateaus on the green, creating three distinct sections of the putting surface. It's as simple as that. The 1st hole at Mountain Lake, a Seth Raynor design in Lake Wales, Florida, presents a double plateau green. The 9th hole at Fisher's Island Club in New York and the 17th at Yale also offer double plateau greens.

According to George Bahto, Raynor sometimes used a Principal's Nose type feature, set some fifty to seventy yards short of the green, at his Double Plateau holes.

Bottle

The 8th at National Golf Links is the most well-known Bottle hole. This hole is apparently modeled after Willie Park Jr.'s original 12th hole at Sunningdale Old in London, which no longer exists.

The hole features a dramatic set of fairway bunkers set on a left to right diagonal to the tee, separating the fairway into two levels—usually low right and high left. High left is narrower and tougher to get to (a fade is also essential off the tee), but it affords the most advantageous angle into the green. Low right is the easier tee shot, but the approach is played uphill, over bunkers from a much more difficult angle.

The 2nd hole at Kinloch near Richmond, Virginia, and the 16th at Bandon Dunes are also Bottle holes.

HOG'S BACK

The fifth at the National Golf Links of America is probably the best example of this type of hole because of the crowned fairway that demands straight driving. Balls hit off line take the slopes on either side of the Hog's Back down into hollows or bunkers.

Some holes include not a hog's back fairway but a hog's back green. The fifth at the nine-hole Royal Worlington and Newmarket Golf Club, also known as Mildenhall, near Cambridge, England, is a textbook example. The par-three, 170-yard hole doesn't have a single bunker, nor is one required. Donald Steel compared the shape of the green to a "vaulting horse." The thin green falls off sharply on both sides of the horse. It's possible to go back and forth, back and forth. Many golfers have.

Pete Dye and Greg Norman designed the fourth green at Medalist Golf Club in Hobe Sound, Florida as a Hog's Back. The green was first set way up high, with a deep and long bunker in front wrapping around the left side of the green, which fell off precipitously behind and to the right into chipping areas. After the course was in play for a while, it was decided that the setting was too severe, so the green was brought down almost to the ground. It was later pitched back up, although not nearly at its first elevation.

KNOLL

Macdonald supposedly borrowed this concept from Scotscraig Golf Club near St. Andrews, which Old Tom Morris designed.

A Knoll hole is usually a short par four—some three hundred yards—whose green is perched atop a volcanolike hill (the fourth hole at Stanley Thompson's Highlands Links in Cape Breton Island, Nova Scotia, is a example). Macdonald and Raynor used this concept more than a few times. At such holes, the approach is usually blind due to the elevated nature of the putting surface. The green is frequently two-tiered (higher at the rear), with steep falloffs surrounding the putting surface. A Knoll green is also sometimes referred to as a High Hat green, particularly if it's relatively flat.

ISLAND

The most famous island green is on the par-three, 132-yard 17th at the Tournament Players Club of Sawgrass in Ponte Vedra Beach, Florida. The Pete Dye course hosts the annual Players Championship, and the hole is often the scene of one disaster after another, especially in windy conditions or when the green is firm.

Dye's wife Alice was the true architect of the hole. Here's how she tells the story: "It was the first Tournament Players Course and we had a very low budget, and so Pete was having a hard time finding sand for the greens. He found sand along the 18th where the lake is, and then back in the area where the seventeenth green is now, he found wonderful sand. He kept digging there and digging there and by the time I got out there, he said, Look, I don't have a 17th hole anymore. I just have this little lump that's left. So I said, 'Why don't you enlarge it, dig up all the sand around and just make an island green?' There's an island green at Ponte Vedra [the ninth hole at the Ponte Vedra Inn and Country Club] but I'd never seen it, and that green has a lot of area around it. Nobody had ever done one where it was just either-or [green or water]. Pete built it, and then he put the back end of the green in. He said, 'Well, this is such a short hole the pros will eat it up,' so he sloped it to the water behind. I looked at that and said, 'Pete, I can just see this on TV when the tournament's here, there will be a wind from the tee to the green and the TV guy will come on and say, "Ladies and gentlemen, it's two o'clock in the afternoon and we still have the first group on the seventeenth tee because no balls will stay on the green."' So Pete leveled out the back and put a bunker in the front, so they can play the hole now. But from the minute they tee off, they start thinking about that hole."

Not everybody is fond of an island green. Alister Mackenzie wrote, "Many people consider a complete island short hole a good one, but holes of this type can never be considered completely satisfying, as only one shot is required, the monotonous pitch."

Not many players, professional or amateur, find the shot to be just a "monotonous" pitch. Meanwhile, an island green has become all but de rigueur on new courses. The Coeur d'Alene Resort course in Idaho includes a floating green on its much-discussed par-three 14th hole, which can play from 100 to 175 yards; players must take what's called the Putter Boat to reach the green; the green does have flanking bunkers, so it's not all island. The 255-yard 6th hole on PGA West's Stadium course in Palm Springs, California, includes an all-but-island green, and asks the golfer to carry the tee shot 220 yards to reach it.

The problem with an island green is that it offers no options but to fly the ball into the green—the fear/anxiety/ terror that the golfer feels on the tee is based on this exclusion of other possibilities. The island golf hole represents penal golf at its most extreme.

THE WORD ON

The Old Course

Play it again, Sam—it is *a golf course.*

"St. Andrews? I feel like I'm back visiting an old grandmother. She's crotchety and eccentric but also elegant. Anyone who doesn't fall in love with her has no imagination."

—TONY LEMA

"Say! That looks like an old abandoned golf course. What did they call it?" —SAM SNEAD

"When it blows here, even the seagulls walk." —NICK FALDO

"You can play a damned good shot and find the ball in a damned bad place."

—GEORGE DUNCAN (who was in position to win the 1910 Open before a final-round 83)

"A British Open at the home of golf [is] the most intriguing and maybe the most demanding challenge in the entire game."

—JACK NICKLAUS

"The worst piece of mess I've ever played."

—SCOTT HOCH

"Perhaps Peter Thomson, of all the winners at St. Andrews, understood best the demands of the Old Course and how it must be played. . . . [During the final round of his Open win in 1955, he] was winning, but not by much, when he came to the Beardies, at the 14th, and had to play out backwards. He put his third into the bunkers by the green and had to play out backwards again. Then he reached the green and took two putts for his seven. Somehow that incident defines the essence of St. Andrews—a place where you play backwards twice on a hole because it is the smartest way to become Open Champion."

—GERALD MICKLEM

FOOTNOTES TO HISTORY

Mike Donald, 1990 U.S. Open, Medinah Country Club, Medinah, Illinois

Mike Donald and Hale Irwin were tied after regulation play. Irwin had made a sixty-foot birdie putt on the 72nd hole, after which he danced all the way around the green, slapping and high-fiving the outstretched hands of spectators. Donald still held a one-shot lead with three holes to play, but bogeyed the 16th hole. He parred the last two holes to get into the playoff.

"I don't know how you can be stoic after something like that," Irwin said after holing his monster putt on the 72nd hole. "In twenty-two years of golf, I've never made a putt like that to win or come close to winning. It was four times longer than any putt I made all week."

After Irwin's victory lap, Donald's dream came up just short.

Donald took a one-stroke lead to the last hole of the

next day's eighteen-hole playoff, but hooked his tee shot into the trees. His ball ricocheted off a spectator into the rough. Forced to play a low shot into the green because of intervening trees, he found the front bunker. Irwin's approach was within twenty-five feet of the hole. Donald's bunker shot came up twenty feet short, and he had that to win after Irwin hit his first putt to within tap-in distance. Donald missed, and he and Irwin went back to the par-four, 385-yard first hole, where Irwin made a ten-foot birdie putt to win.

Donald had birdied the first hole the three previous times he'd played it. His second shot came up thirty feet short, while Irwin's approach finished ten feet away. Donald putted to within a foot, marked his ball, and walked to the side looking like a beaten man. He sensed Irwin would make his birdie putt, and he did.

FROM THE SUGGESTION BOX, ROYAL WEST NORFOLK GOLF CLUB, 1899

Member: Why tee off the high tee at the third and so utterly destroy it forever?

Response: Trivial

Member: Is it necessary to place the tee for the 13th hole in the bunker, when there is plenty of good ground available?

Response: Yes

Member: Might the distance flags sometimes be placed in the line of the hole?

Response: Trivial

FOUR ACES

Only seventeen holes-in-one had been registered in the fifty-four U.S. Opens for which such records had been kept prior to the 1989 championship at the Oak Hill Country Club in Pittsford, New York. But four golfers made holes-in-one in a period of one hundred minutes during the second round at Oak Hill. Each player used a seven-iron on the 160-yard sixth hole. USGA officials had cut the hole in a trough, and just about every shot hit behind or to the left funneled toward it.

First up and in was Doug Weaver, who was playing in his first U.S. Open. The first player of the day to reach the hole, he made his ace at 8:35 A.M.. His ball landed eighteen feet behind the hole and trickled down and in. "It was a beautiful few moments, listening to the crowd getting more excited," Weaver said. "All of a sudden, it was just like lightning hit."

Mark Wiebe came through fifty minutes later. His shot hit the green eight feet left of the hole, rolled past and then spun back into the hole. Jerry Pate came through twenty-five minutes after Wiebe; he watched as his shot hit the green a foot to the right of the hole and eight feet beyond before spinning back in. His wife yelled from up by the green. Nick Price reached the tee at 10 A.M. and had a good look as his ball caught the green slightly to the right of the hole and then reversed course and spun into the hole.

The odds of four pros getting a hole-in-one on the same hole in one day were 8.7 million to one, according to the National Hole-in-One Association.

A footnote to the Four Aces' exploits: Sonny Savarino and Lars Hjalmquist, members of the Park Club in Buffalo, New

Weaver, Pate, Price, and Wiebe mark a foursome of aces.

York, worked as marshals at the hole. They also worked as marshals at the 190-yard eighth hole during the 1990 U.S. Open at the Medinah Country Club, when Jay Don Blake made a hole-in-one there.

THE LONG AND SHORT OF IT

PGA Tour's Longest Courses

1982	1992	2006
Colonial CC (South), Cordova, TN 7,249 yards	Castle Pines GC, Castle Rock, CO 7,759 yards	Castle Pines GC, Castle Rock, CO 7,619 yards
Colonial CC, Ft. Worth, TX 7,190 yards	Kapalua Resort (Plantation), Lahaina, Maui, HI 7,263 yards	Torrey Pines (South), La Jolla, CA 7,568 yards
Firestone CC (South), Akron, OH 7,173 yards	TPC at Summerlin, Las Vegas, NV 7,243 yards	Nemacolin Woodlands (Mystic Rock), Farmington, PA 7,550 yards
Walt Disney World (Magnolia), Lake Buena Vista, FL 7,170 yards	Las Vegas CC, Las Vegas, NV 7,162 yards	Walt Disney World (Magnolia), Lake Buena Vista, FL 7,516 yards
Fairway Oaks CC, Abilene, TX 7,166 yards	Firestone CC (South), Akron, OH 7,149 yards	Montreux G&CC, Reno, NV 7,472 yards
Inverrrary CC, Lauderhill, FL 7,129 yards	Tucson National, Tucson, AZ 7,148 yards	Redstone GC, Humble, TX 7,457 yards
Pleasant Valley CC, Sutton, MA 7,119 yards	Bellerive CC, St. Louis, MO 7,148 yards	Augusta National GC, Augusta, GA 7,445 yards
Muirfield Village, Dublin, OH 7,116 yards	English Turn CC, New Orleans, LA 7,116 yards	Quail Hollow CC, Charlotte, NC 7,442 yards
Congressional CC, Bethesda, MD 7,113 yards	Bay Hill Club, Orlando, FL 7,114 yards	TPC of Boston, Norton, MA 7,415 yards
Butler National GC, Oak Brook, IL 7,097 yards	Glen Abbey GC, Oakville, ON 7,112 yards	Kapalua Resort (Plantation), Lahaina, Maui, HI 7,411 yards

PGA Tour's Shortest Courses

1982	1992	2006
Westchester CC (West), Harrison, NY 6,329 yards	Hattiesburg CC, Hattiesburg, MS 6,280 yards	Pebble Beach GL, Pebble Beach, CA 6,737 yards
Indian Wells CC, Indian Wells, CA 6,455 yards	Indian Wells CC, Indian Well, CA 6,478 yards	Brown Deer Park GC, Milwaukee, WI 6,759 yards
Oakwood CC, Highlands, Coal Valley, IL 6,514 yards	Torrey Pines (North), La Jolla, CA 6,592 yards	TPC at River Cromwell, CT 6,820 yards
Oak Hills CC, San Antonio, TX 6,525 yards	Kapalua (Bay), Kapalua, HI 6,600 yards	Westchester CC (West), Harrison, NY 6,839 yards
Wethersfield CC, Wethersfield, CT 6,534 yards	Oak Hills CC, San Antonio, TX 6,650 yards	Torrey Pines (North), La Jolla, CA 6,874 yards
Hattiesburg CC, Hattiesburg, MS 6,594 yards	Harbour Town GL, Hilton Head, SC 6,657 yards	La Cantera GC (Resort), San Antonio, TX 6,881 yards
Walt Disney World (Lake BuenaVista), Lake Buena Vista, FL 6,642 yards	Westchester CC (West), Harrison, NY 6,779 yards	PGA West (Palmer), La Quinta, CA 6,930 yards
Torrey Pines (North), La Jolla, CA 6,667 yards	Kingsmill GC, Williamsburg, VA 6,790 yards	Bermuda Dunes CC, Palm Springs, CA 6,962 yards
Kingsmill GC, Williamsburg, VA 6,684 yards	Oakwood CC, Coal Valley, IL 6,796 yards	Harbour Town GL, Hilton Head, SC 6,973 yards
Phoenix CC, Phoenix, AZ 6,726 yards	Pebble Beach GL, Pebble Beach, CA 6,799 yards	Hamilton G&CC, Hamilton, ON 6,985 yards

THE STYMIE STORY

Of all golf's quaint and archaic past rules, none is as quizzical to the modern player as the stymie. Most living golfers have never played without marking their balls on the green, or at least doing so on request. 'Twas not always so.

Prior to the mid-twentieth century, the stymie was a maddening part of match play. If an opponent's ball lay in your line on the green and it was more than six inches away from yours, it would remain in place as you played and you had to find a way around or over it. (Scorecards often measured exactly six inches, to allow you to check the distance.) It was considered bad sportsmanship to deliberately "lay a stymie" on an opponent, but it was no doubt effective gamesmanship if your control was so precise.

Prior to 1952, it was illegal to concede an opponent's putt if you had not yet holed your own ball. A ball sitting in front of the hole could easily have you stymied. (This is why there is no penalty for striking an opponent's ball on the green in match play.) The USGA, showing great fairness or no sense of humor, passed a rule in 1938 that permitted lifting a ball that lay within six inches of the hole—the dreaded unnegotiable stymie. Thirteen years later, the USGA and R&A agreed to eliminate the stymie altogether.

The Oxford English Dictionary lists the term stymie as being of obscure origin, but we can guess at its derivation. The phrase "could not see a styme," meaning not to see at all (*styme* meant "faintest trace"), is first cited in the seventeenth century. Robert Burns wrote in *Epistle to John Goldie, in Kilmarnock*

(1785), "I've seen me dazed upon a time/I scarce could wink or see a styme." *Stymie* was a slang term for someone blind; it is easy to see how it could be picked up to describe a situation in which you cannot see the hole.

Bobby Jones, in his 1959 autobiography, *Golf Is My Game*, wrote an entire chapter calling for the return of the stymie; he considered dealing with them to be an essential feature of match play. Golf is not meant to be fair; the stymie, through its random inadvertence, extended "the rub of the green" to the green itself.

When Jones won his only British Amateur title in his Grand Slam year, he was aided by a 19th-hole stymie in his fourth-round match.

THE WORLD'S MOST UNDERRATED GOLF DESTINATIONS

A well-trodden path leads the global golfer from home to Scotland's Firth of Forth (Muirfield, North Berwick, Gullane to the south, Elie and Crail to the north, with St. Andrews and Kingsbarns further up the road), to the Monterey Peninsula (Pebble Beach, Spyglass, Spanish Bay), to the west of Ireland (Ballybunion, Lahinch, Waterville), to Florida and Arizona (courses, courses everywhere), and of late to Bandon, Oregon (one resort and three courses—but what a resort, and what courses!). But stirring golf can be found in concentrations in places you may not expect, whether you're traveling just for the golf or combining business with deductible pleasure. All courses mentioned allow visiting players; contact the clubs or courses for details.

1. Melbourne, Australia. Melbourne's Sandbelt, located south of the city and east of Port Phillip, contains ideal turf conditions for building outstanding courses. Royal Melbourne and Kingston Heath would be enough to make Melbourne a must, but the area throws in Metropolitan and Victoria, and down on the Mornington Peninsula adds Portsea, Sorrento, Rosebud, The National, and Moonah Links. An embarrassment of links riches.

2. London, England. Even the elite of the elite courses, such as Sunningdale Old, St. George's Hill, and Wentworth, are open to visitors on selected days. Plan a week-long visit to London, take in the restaurants and theater available in one of the world's most exciting cities, and combine this with golf. Play the aforementioned courses, perhaps. Try Woking, or the quirky J.F. Abercrombie–designed course called The Addington, or Walton Heath. Or all of these. And more.

3. San Francisco Bay Area, California. Ignore for a moment the proximity to Pebble Beach, and the contiguous classics Olympic and San Francisco GC (where a simple phone call will *not* get you a starting time). A visit that includes rounds at Harding Park, Metropolitan, and Half-Moon Bay, and jaunts to Pasatiempo, Coyote Creek, and Stevinson Ranch fully justifies lugging your clubs to the beautiful city by the bay. Consider a side trip to Napa that combines wine tasting with golf at Silverado or The Chardonnay Club.

4. Northern Michigan. Which states have the most public-access courses rated 4.5 or 5 stars (out of 5) by *Golf Digest*'s readers? You'd no doubt guess Florida and California as 1–2, and perhaps Myrtle Beach and Hilton Head would lead you to pick South Carolina third. But Michigan fourth, nearly even with the Grand Strand? The northern part of the state has embraced golf as a draw for tourists, and with such courses as Arcadia Bluffs, Forest Dunes, Black Lake, Bay Harbor, Red Hawk, and the Treetops Resort available, it's easy to see why golfers would respond.

5. Toronto, Canada. There are more than 100 courses within an hour's drive of Toronto. The Osprey Valley Resort northwest of the city includes three courses, named the Heathlands, and, for a bit of fun, Royal Hoot and Royal Toot—because train tracks are nearby. Each course is very good. Don Valley is an enjoyable municipal course near the bus and subway lines, and while it's been truncated over the years, it's still charming and a solid test. Among the other top public-access courses are Eagles Nest, Angus Glen, Bond Head, Willow Valley, Copetown Woods, Mystic, Woodington Lakes, Lakeview, Deer Creek, BraeBen, Royal Woodbine, Lionhead, Royal Ashburn, and Silver Lakes.

6. The Algarve, Portugal. This province along Portugal's southern coast has attracted European summer holidaymakers for a long time, and its comfortable year-round temperatures make it a natural destination for offseason golfers. Yet it's rarely considered by the Americans who jam Florida's roads and cartpaths every winter. The Algarve's first regulation golf course, Penina, was designed by Henry Cotton in the 1960s, and a building boom ensued. The region now boasts the top eight courses in Portugal according to *Golf Digest*: San Lorenzo, Vilamoura (Old and Millennium), Vale do Lobo (Ocean and Royal), Quinta do Lago (North and

The challenge of Royal County Down carries the world's golfers to Newcastle.

South), and Vila Sol. The main golf season runs from mid-autumn to mid-spring, which enables golfers to avoid the high prices of summer accommodations.

7. Northern Ireland. Royal County Down is one of the world's finest and most beautiful golf courses, and puts Newcastle on any serious golfer's itinerary. The rugged north coast of Northern Ireland has a craggy beauty reminiscent of the shoreline of Maine, and shows it to great advantage in the layouts of Royal Portrush, Portstewart, and Castle Rock. The nearby Bushmills distillery helps soothe any pre-round jitters or post-round regrets.

8. Northern New Zealand. Head north from the crowded roads of Auckland and see why the country has more golf courses per capita than any place but Scotland. Highlights include the spectacular luxury layout at Kauri Cliffs, the hillside charmer at Mangawhai, the seaside simplicity of Waipu, and the hidden links gem of Kaitaia at the foot of Ninety Mile Beach. Seasonal visitors escaping the northern hemisphere winters will find relief for soul and pocketbook at Kaitaia, where a season-long membership costs NZ$150—less than a quarter of the price of eighteen holes at Pebble Beach.

THE GOLFER'S LIFE LIST

Work with a Teacher for a Year (or at Least a Few Months)

The only way to improve is to take lessons with one teacher and to stick to the program he or she sets forth. Any other road is a detour. If you go from teacher to teacher you'll be in trouble from the start.

As a for-instance, look for a teacher who works on the "modern, big-muscle swing," if you have too much hand action and too little body involvement in your current swing. If this is your problem, by finding the right teacher you can work toward developing a more athletic swing. You'll be provided drills that will help remove excessive hand action. But you'll need to give yourself time, and with one teacher and one teacher only, to see improvement. You'll eventually hit many more solid shots, with a more efficient and easily repeated swing.

Tiger uses a teacher (here Butch Harmon). Are you good enough not to?

In fact, you'll likely be working toward a swing that you might even be able to explain in one sentence. Asked to do just that, Nick Faldo answered, "It's the turning of the upper body against the resistance of the lower body back and through." That's a stable swing, and one of the great pleasures of the game is in working steadily toward it.

THREE-HANKY GOLF

Remembering Payne

The golf world and all outside the game who knew him were shocked by the death of Payne Stewart on October 25, 1999, at the age of 42. Something went wrong in the Learjet 35 that was taking Stewart, business associates Robert Fraley and Van Arden, and golf course architect Bruce Borland from Orlando to a site visit in Dallas. Everybody on board the plane was killed, including pilot Michael Kling and copilot Stephanie Bellegarrigue. A sudden depressurization due to an oxygen leak was the suspected cause of the tragedy. The plane flew unguided until it ran out of fuel in South Dakota and crashed in a field.

Stewart seemed right out of an F. Scott Fitzgerald novel. He wore plus-fours and a peaked, Hogan-style cap when he played. There was more than a bit of swagger about him. His golf swing flowed long and smooth; there wasn't a hint of force in it. Stewart had won the 1989 PGA Championship, the 1991 U.S. Open, and then, only four and a half months before he died, the 1999 U.S. Open at Pinehurst No. 2 in North Carolina. A month before the plane crash, he'd been part of the U.S. team that won the Ryder Cup at the Country Club in Brookline, Massachusetts.

The week he died, he was supposed to be playing in the season-ending Tour Championship in Houston. Before the first round on Thursday, players and officials gathered at the first tee on a foggy morning, and a bagpiper played the traditional Scottish ballad "Going Home." Later, when it was Bob Estes's turn to tee off, he hit his opening "drive" with his putter, stroking it fifteen feet in tribute to the putt Stewart had made on the last hole to win the U.S. Open.

The 2000 U.S. Open was held at the Pebble Beach Golf Links, where Stewart was to have defended his title. A brief ceremony was held the day before the first round beside the 18th green. Stewart's wife Tracey spoke in front of some of Stewart's friends and colleagues, including his long-time instructor, Chuck Cook, and Phil Mickelson and his wife, Amy. Twenty-one golfers lined up and hit balls into the ocean. An image of Stewart swinging was displayed on the mast of a yacht.

When the U.S. Open returned to Pinehurst in 2005, Stewart was on everybody's mind. A bronze statue of Stewart in the pose he struck when he holed his winning putt had long been in place behind the 18th green. The statue, called *One Moment in Time,* shows Stewart with his right arm thrust forward as the ball drops. His right leg is well off the ground, and yet he's in balance.

The USGA held a ceremony on Tuesday evening of U.S. Open week. A bagpiper strode alone down the first fairway. Phil Mickelson described how Stewart, having holed the winning putt on the last green of the 1999 U.S. Open, had embraced him and reminded him that he was going to be a father soon, and how important that was. USGA president Fred Ridley gave Pinehurst Resort's president Don Padgett II a hole liner with Stewart's likeness on it and gave Stewart's mental coach Dr. Richard Coop, who was representing the family, the U.S. Open ring that was being made for Stewart when he died.

Five days later, New Zealander Michael Campbell holed a short putt to win the U.S. Open. An image of Stewart had been put on the flag at the 18th green, one last reminder of a life cut short in its prime.

THE CLASS OF '39

In 1939, *National Golf Review*—a short-lived American magazine with writers drawn from the recently-folded *Golf Illustrated* and *The American Golfer*—assembled a panel to select the top 100 golf courses in the world. The seventeen experts constitute as illustrious a group as has pondered the question: Bobby Jones; Walter Hagen; Gene Sarazen; Robert Trent Jones; Joyce Wethered; Glenna Collett Vare; Bernard Darwin; Edward, Duke of Windsor; Grantland Rice; William D. Richardson; Arnaud Massy; Percy Alliss; Joe Kirkwood; T. Simpson; C.H. Alison; D. Scott Chisholm; and Hans Samek.

Pine Valley's devilish short par-three 10th hole.

How much has the golf world changed in the nearly seven decades since their list was published? Twenty of today's top 25 appeared on the 1939 rankings (twenty-one if you includeTurnberry, which had to be rebuilt after World War II). The list is reproduced below; an asterisk indicates that the course was still ranked among the top 100 in the world in *Golf Magazine*'s 2005 list. (The number in parentheses after the course name gives the 2005 ranking.) The two selections that share the 100th slot were both nine-hole courses at the time; Royal Worlington still is.

1. *St. Andrews, Scotland. (3)

2. *Cypress Point, California. (2)

3. *Pine Valley, New Jersey. (1)

4. *Pebble Beach, California. (6)

5. *Sandwich, England. (32)

6. *National Golf Links, New York. (19)

7. *Hirono, Japan. (35)

8. Banff Springs, Canada.

9. *Royal Melbourne, Australia. (10)

Merion Golf Club has hosted five U.S. Amateurs and four U.S. Opens (so far).

10. Foulpointe, Madagascar.
11. *Augusta National, Georgia. (4)
12. Timber Point, New York.
13. *Oakmont, Pennsylvania. (14)
14. *Hoylake, England. (72)
15. *Newcastle Co. Down, Ireland. (9)
16. Westward Ho!, England.
17. *Merion, Pennsylvania. (11)
18. *Riviera, California. (37)
19. *Sunningdale, England. (46)
20. Bel-Air, California.
21. *Shinnecock Hills, New York. (5)
22. *Portrush, Ireland. (12)
23. Laksers, Illinois.
24. CC of Havana, Cuba.
25. Humewood, South Africa.
26. *Seminole, Florida. (22)
27. Rye, England.
28. Knocke, Belgium.
29. Yale, Connecticut.
30. Gleneagles, Scotland.
31. Le Touquet, France.
32. *Winged Foot, New York. (26)
33. Pasatiempo, California.
34. *Muirfield, Scotland. (7)
35. *Walton Heath, England. (92)
36. Jasper Park, Canada.
37. *Portmarnock, Ireland. (43)
38. *Pinehurst #2, North Carolina. (18)
39. Prestwick, Scotland.
40. *Birkdale, England. (31)
41. Lido, New York.
42. *Ganton, England. (68)
43. *Durban, South Africa. (81)
44. Oyster Harbors, Massachusetts.
45. Ponte Vedra, Florida.
46. North Berwick, Scotland.
47. *San Francisco, California. (24)
48. St. Georges Hill, England.
49. *Garden City, New York. (64)
50. Deal, England.
51. *Kawana, Japan. (80)
52. Engineers, New York.
53. Swinley Forest, England.
54. *Brookline, Massachusetts. (36)
55. Saunton, England.
56. *Bethpage, New York. (30)

Sod-walled bunkers made Hoylake (Royal Liverpool) a great course in 1939, and at the 2006 Open.

57. Addington, England.
58. Lakeside, California.
59. Hollywood, New Jersey.
60. Woking, England.
61. Wildhoeve, Holland.
62. *Royal York, Canada. (88)
63. *Oakland Hills, Michigan. (29)
64. *Morfontaine, France. (57)
65. Brancaster, England.
66. Pulborough, England.
67. Manoir Richelieu, Canada.
68. *Royal Adelaide, Australia. (54)
69. Hamburg-Falkenstein, Germany.
70. Olympia Fields #4, Illinois.
71. Chiberta, France.
72. Lawsonia, Wisconsin.
73. *Los Angeles, California. (51)
74. *Maidstone, New York. (63)
75. East London, South Africa.
76. *Carnoustie, Scotland. (21)
77. Burnham, England.
78. *Scioto, Ohio. (76)
79. Capilano, Canada.
80. Hot Springs, Virginia.
81. Nuwara Eliya, Ceylon.
82. *Ballybunion, Ireland. (16)
83. Porthcawl, Wales.
84. Liphook, England.
85. Knoll, New Jersey.
86. *Tokyo-Asaka, Japan. (94)
87. Maccauvlei, South Africa.
88. *Kingston Heath, Australia. (20)
89. *Chicago, Illinois. (33)
90. Sea Island, Georgia.
91. Alwoodley, England.
92. Eastward Ho, Massachusetts.
93. Mid Ocean, Bermuda.
94. Ville de Delat, Indo China.
95. Zandvoort, Holland.
96. Five Farms, Maryland.
97. *Turnberry, Scotland. (17)
98. Spa, Belgium.
99. *Fishers Island, New York. (28)
100a. Royal Worlington, England.
100b. *Prairie Dunes, Kansas. (25)

ROBERT HUNTER'S FACTORS TO CONSIDER WHEN ESTABLISHING A GOLF COURSE

Hunter was one of those golfers whose interest in architecture led him to study the subject as if for a doctorate, then a postdoctorate, then further. He wrote *The Links*, one of the few classics on course architecture, and became a friend and associate of architect Alister Mackenzie. Hunter died in 1942, aged sixty-eight. His common-sense advice still applies.

1. Select well-drained, slightly rolling land. Desirable contours are a valuable asset. They should consist of gentle upheavals in an area comparatively flat.

2. Avoid land with steep slopes and hills tiresome to climb. Territory broken up with deep ravines, streams of water, and outcroppings of rock is not desirable. Soils full of coarse gravel and timber lands are often difficult to put into shape for golf.

3. The most desirable soil is a well-drained, sandy loam, porous enough to dry quickly after heavy rains. Pure sand is very desirable, but it is nearly always necessary to mix other soils with it.

4. When the soil and the contours best suited to the game have been found, it is important to buy an acreage ample for all future needs.

5. A soil technologist should be employed to prepare a map of the soil resources on the property.

6. A surveyor should be employed to prepare a map of the contours. An aerial photograph will often be useful.

7. The architect should be selected with the greatest care, and only after seeing some of the work he has done. His superintendent of construction and his greenkeeper should be judged in the same manner.

WINNERS OF THE BOB JONES AWARD

This is the USGA's highest honor, presented annually by the United States Golf Association to a person recognized for distinguished sportsmanship in golf.

1955: FRANCIS OUIMET. Amateur who won 1913 U.S. Open at twenty years old in a playoff against Englishmen Harry Vardon and Ted Ray. Played in seven Walker Cups and was a prominent committee member of the USGA for many years. Elected captain of the Royal & Ancient Golf Club of St. Andrews in 1951. He was the first person who wasn't British to hold the office.

1956: WILLIAM C. CAMPBELL. Runner-up 1954 British Amateur, champion 1964 U.S. Amateur. Played on seven Walker Cup teams and was Walker Cup captain in 1955. On USGA executive committee 1962–65.

1957: MILDRED "BABE" DIDRIKSON ZAHARIAS. Won 1946 U.S. Women's Amateur and 1947 British Ladies Amateur. Won two gold medals in track and field in the 1932 Olympics.

1958: MARGARET CURTIS. Played with her sister Harriott and other Americans in an informal match against British women in 1905 at Royal Cromer course and got the idea of playing international matches regularly. This led eventually to the Curtis Cup, biennial matches between teams of American and British golfers.

1959: FINDLAY S. DOUGLAS. Scot who emigrated to the United States in 1896. Won 1898 U.S. Amateur. USGA president 1929–30.

1960: CHARLES (CHICK) EVANS JR. Winner of eight Western Amateurs between 1909 and 1923, and 1916 and 1920 U.S. Amateurs. Won 1916 U.S. Open. Former caddie who set up scholarship fund for caddies at Northwestern University near Chicago.

1961: JOSEPH B. CARR. Dubliner who won three British Amateurs. Played on ten Walker Cup teams and was twice captain.

1962: HORTON SMITH. Won first Masters in 1934, and won again in 1936. President of PGA of America in 1952.

1963: PATTY BERG. Won 1938 U.S. Women's Amateur and 1946 U.S. Women's Open. Turned professional in 1940 and was first president of LPGA. Leading LPGA money-winner in 1954, 1955, and 1957.

1964: CHARLIE COE. Won 1949 and 1958 U.S. Amateurs. Five-time Walker Cup member and captain in 1959.

1965: GLENNA COLLETT VARE. Six-time U.S. Women's Amateur champion. Played on four Curtis Cup teams and was captain on four occasions.

1966: GARY PLAYER.

1967: RICHARD S. TUFTS. Harvard graduate and grandson of the founder of Pinehurst. USGA president, 1956–57. Rules expert whose book *The Principles Behind the Rules of Golf* is a classic. Captain of U.S. Walker Cup team in 1963.

1968: BOB DICKSON. Won 1967 U.S. and British Amateurs. Walker Cup member in 1967.

1969: GERALD H. MICKLEM. Englishman who played on four Walker Cup teams and was twice captain. President of European Golf Association, 1967–69, and R&A captain, 1968–69.

1970: ROBERTO DE VICENZO. Winner of 1967 British Open, runner-up in 1968 Masters.

1971: ARNOLD PALMER.

1972: MICHAEL BONALLACK. Five-time British Amateur champion. Nine-time Walker Cup player, twice captain. Secretary to the R&A, 1983–2000.

1973: GENE LITTLER. 1953 U.S. Amateur champion, 1961 U.S. Open champion. Played on six U.S. Ryder Cup teams.

1974: BYRON NELSON.

1975: JACK NICKLAUS.

1976: BEN HOGAN.

1977: JOSEPH C. DEY, JR. Long-time USGA executive director. One of golf's outstanding administrators.

1978: BING CROSBY AND BOB HOPE. Golf-loving actors, hosts of popular PGA Tour events. Crosby, an accomplished amateur, played in the 1950 British Amateur at St. Andrews.

1979: TOM KITE.

1980: CHARLES YATES. Atlantan who won 1938 British Amateur. Walker Cup member in 1936 and 1938. Long-time member of the Augusta National Golf Club; worked with the media during the Masters.

1981: JoANNE CARNER. Five-time U.S. Women's Amateur champion, 1971 U.S. Women's Open champion. Four-time Curtis Cup player. LPGA Hall of Fame member.

JoAnne Carner, amateur and professional champion.

1982: BILLY JOE PATTON. Third as amateur in 1954 Masters. Low amateur 1954 and 1957 U.S. Opens. Five-time member of Walker Cup team and captain in 1969.

1983: MAUREEN RUTTLE GARRETT. First-class Englishwoman who captained 1960 Curtis Cup team. Signed up for land army in World War II, milking cows and working with land horses.

1984: JAY SIGEL. Won 1979 British Amateur; 1982 and 1983 U.S. Amateurs; 1983, 1985, and 1987 U.S. Mid-Amateurs.

1985: FUZZY ZOELLER. Winner of 1979 Masters and 1984 U.S. Open.

1986: JESS SWEETSER. 1922 U.S. Amateur champion, 1926 British Amateur champion. Played on five Walker Cup teams and was captain in 1967 and 1973.

1987: TOM WATSON.

1988: ISAAC B. GRAINGER. USGA president 1954–55. Co-chairman of USGA Rules Committee for many years.

1989: CHI CHI RODRIGUEZ. Fun-loving winner of eight PGA Tour events who started a foundation in Clearwater, Florida, for troubled and abused youngsters.

1990: PEGGY KIRK BELL. Founding member of LPGA. Won 1949 Titleholders Championship, then an LPGA major, and played on 1950 Curtis Cup team for the U.S. Renowned teacher. Family has owned Pine Needles Lodge and Golf Club in Southern Pines, North Carolina for more than fifty years.

1991: BEN CRENSHAW.

1992: GENE SARAZEN.

1993: P. J. BOATWRIGHT, JR. USGA Executive Director 1969–80. Rules expert who often cited what became known as the unofficial 35th rule of golf: "Don't play golf with a fool, idiot, or jerk."

1994: LEWIS OEHMIG. Won three U.S. Senior Amateur Championships and eight Tennessee State

Amateur Championships, his first in 1937 and his last in 1971. Captain of 1977 U.S. Walker Cup team.

1995: HERBERT WARREN WIND. Long-time golf writer for *The New Yorker.*

1996: BETSY RAWLS. LPGA founding member. Won fifty-five LPGA events, including eight majors. First woman to serve on U.S. Open rules committee.

1997: FRED BRAND, JR. Closely associated with Western Pennsylvania Golf Association for many years. Founding member of WPGA Scholarship Fund and instrumental in developing Caddie Welfare Movement in 1939, during a period when some 500,000 caddies were working in the United States, often under harsh conditions.

1998: NANCY LOPEZ.

1999: ED UPDEGRAFF. Iowa urologist who played on three Walker Cup teams and captained the U.S. team in 1975 at St. Andrews. Played in six Masters and won the U.S. Senior Amateur.

2000: BARBARA MCINTIRE. Won two U.S. Women's Amateurs. Played on six Curtis Cup teams, captaining squad in 1976 and 1998. Won British Ladies Amateur in 1960. Served on USGA Women's Committee 1985–96, and was its chair in 1995–96.

2001: THOMAS COUSINS. Atlanta developer and avid golfer who bought East Lake Golf Club in Atlanta when it was run down. Turned it into the centerpiece for urban renewal in a blighted area. Believes in using the sport to improve social conditions, what he calls "golf with a purpose."

2002: JUDY RANKIN. Won twenty-six LPGA events. Low amateur at age fifteen in 1959 U.S. Women's Open. Captain of 1996 and 1998 Solheim Cup teams. One of game's leading analysts on television.

2003: CAROL SEMPLE THOMPSON. Played in one hundred USGA championships. Won seven USGA championships. Played on twelve Curtis Cup teams. On USGA executive committee 1994–2000.

2004: JACKIE BURKE JR. Won 1956 Masters and PGA Championship. Cofounder with Jimmy Demaret of Champions Golf Club in Houston, which has hosted more USGA championships than any course in Texas. A much sought-after instructor.

2005: NICK PRICE.

SPLENDOR IN THE GRASSES

Turfgrasses are generally divided according to whether they thrive under cool or warm conditions. Cool-season grasses grow best when the temperature ranges between 55 and 85 degrees Fahrenheit. Warm-season grasses thrive when the temperature ranges between 75 and 95 degrees. In North America, cool-season grasses are usually bentgrasses, bluegrasses, or fescues. Warm-weather grasses are usually Bermuda grasses.

Cool-season grasses have thin blades and grow densely. They tolerate cold but not heat, which is why northern courses favor bentgrasses for greens. They can be closely mown, and often the pressure on greenkeepers today is to cut them as thin as possible to create extremely fast greens. Bentgrass is of a fine texture, and the ball rolls smoothly, seemingly on top of the turf rather than through the blades. Tour golfers and, increasingly, the average player, favor fast, bentgrass greens. The Augusta National Golf Club is hardly in a cool climate, but it went to bentgrass greens in 1981, employing an underground system to ensure that the greens remain at an appropriate temperature, no matter the heat above.

Cool-weather grasses include varieties such as colonial bentgrass, creeping bentgrass, Kentucky bluegrass (often used in fairways and roughs), perennial ryegrass (sometimes used to overseed warm-weather courses during the winter), fine fescue, and tall fescue.

Warm-season grasses have thicker blades than bentgrasses. The blades tend to stand up rather than lie down. There's also more grain in Bermuda grass. Golfers who grow up playing greens of Bermuda grass tend to learn to pop the ball off the face of the putter rather than to roll it. This is changing, because it's possible with modern equipment and chemical application to cut Bermuda greens closely and to make them smooth and fast—rarely as smooth and fast as bentgrass greens, however.

Fescues are often found in coastal areas and thus on links courses. Fescue is a hardy grass. It's sometimes used in North America for roughs, and some courses have fescue fairways. Tom Doak, wanting to replicate British playing conditions when he designed High Pointe in Michigan, convinced the owner to allow fescue fairways and even greens. Fescue allows for a less manicured appearance, producing a brand of golf seen more often in Britain and closer to the traditional game. Many courses that have bentgrasses also allow for traditional golf, but the temptation is always to overwater the grass.

Sadly, High Pointe's owners grew concerned that golfers wouldn't accept the look and playing characteristics of fescue fairways and greens, as originally planned by Doak. The entire course was overseeded with bent, and almost all of the fescue is gone.

Cultivation of fescue requires excellent drainage, low fertility, and light traffic. If it's too wet, fescue is easily outcompeted. Heavy cart usage also compromises fescue and makes it all but impossible for the turf to thrive. Architect Rod Whitman and his assistant Jeff Mingay considered fescue fairways at Edmonton's Blackhawk course, but the expected heavy traffic wouldn't allow for it. Fescue was used in the primary roughs, but the roughs are weak where carts exit from paths.

Sand Hills, the inspiring course that Bill Coore and Ben Crenshaw designed in Nebraska, began with fescue fairways, but these were later converted to bluegrass. There's a lot of cart use at Sand Hills, and the weather is very harsh—hot summers and cold winters with brutal wind that essentially burns the grass. The fescue wasn't hardy enough, requiring the switch.

Whistling Straits in Kohler, Wisconsin, where the 2004 PGA Championship was played, has fescue fairways; so do the highly regarded courses in Bandon, Oregon, that golfers know collectively as Bandon Dunes; and the Kingsley Club near Traverse City, Michigan. Carts aren't allowed at Whistling Straits or Bandon, and Kingsley has a very small membership with limited cart use, which helps in cultivating fescue fairways. The Bandon courses and Kingsley are also built on sandy, free-draining soils. Whistling Straits wasn't built on a sandy site, but the course was capped with tons of sand and enough subsurface pipe was installed to get the water off the course efficiently.

SEASHORE PASPALUM

This grass is native to warm-weather maritime environments and has become popular in recent years for courses exposed to brine and salinity. It grows well where the temperatures are warm and the days are long. It's found in the United States along coastal regions from Texas to Florida, and south from North Carolina. The turf—dense, bluish-green, and quite bright—offers an excellent playing surface for tees, fairways, and greens. Many courses in coastal areas have gone to paspalum in the last few years, and the results have usually been impressive. The texture is similar to that of Kentucky bluegrass.

Seashore paspalum arrived in the United States from Africa by boat. As the story goes, it was used as bedding in slave ships and thrown out onto the seashore after the ships arrived at port. There it grew, and there it stayed. Course architects and superintendents had been looking for a grass with paspalum's attributes for some time; it's the first new warm-weather grass to show as much promise in thirty years. Its salt-tolerant quality alone has made it a turf of choice both at many new courses and at others that have stripped their turf and replanted with it. Growing paspalum isn't free of challenges, but the results so far are encouraging. It grows low to the ground and so tolerates traffic and wear well. It can also be irrigated with salt water, an economic advantage, as water normally has to be desalinized to irrigate a course.

Some courses with paspalum

- Jupiter Dunes Golf Club, Jupiter, Florida (a par-three course only a few hundred yards from the Atlantic that converted to paspalum)

- Galveston Country Club, Galveston, Texas
- King's Crossing, Corpus Christi, Texas
- Ocean Course, Kiawah Island, South Carolina, tees and greens; fairways eventually
- Old Collier Golf Club, Naples, Florida
- Old Palm Golf and Country Club, Palm Beach Gardens, Florida

ZOYSIA

This grass thrives in mild to hot zones, generally below Michigan in North America, and coast to coast. It's suitable for tees, fairways, and rough and greens collars. Zoysia originated in Southeast Asia, China, and Japan, and is named after Karl von Zois zu Laubach, an eighteenth-century Austrian botanist.

Zoysia produces a dense, dark-green turf that handles traffic and tolerates shade well. It can cope with drought as well as inconsistent rainfall patterns. Zoysia is suitable for golf courses built in coastal areas with appropriate temperatures because it can handle salt spray. The ball sits up well on the broad-leafed, dark blades. Some zoysia blades can be prickly to the touch, but newer, softer varieties have been emerging; one example is GN-Z, from the Greg Norman Turf Company.

East Lake Golf Club in Atlanta has zoysia fairways, while the Dallas National Golf Club has zoysia tees and greens collars.

KIKUYUGRASS

Sound out this grass: *kick-oo-ya-grass*. Now here's a grass to reckon with. Most golfers know it as the grass that forms the rough at the Riviera Country Club in Pacific Palisades, California. Patrick Gross wrote in the USGA Green Section Record that it's the Rodney Dangerfield of grass, in that it gets no respect. Golfers want to stay out of it and, as the saying goes, one could lose a small child in the tangled, thick turf.

It's no surprise that kikuyugrass is featured at Riviera, because it landed on American shores in 1918 right in the neighborhood. The warm-season grass is native to the Kenyan highlands in Africa, as Gross points out, but it was imported to Pacific Palisades in 1918 for erosion control. The grass caught on at Riviera, where it's used in the fairways and, of course, cut short. It's when a ball is in the kikuyu rough that the description of it as "Bermuda grass on steroids" seems apt. It grows and grows and grows, which the folks at Riviera don't mind at all when the PGA Tour's Nissan Open stops there every year. In a classic understatement, Gross writes that the plant's "wide leaf blades tend to grab the club and make it difficult to extract the ball." Difficult, at a minimum.

WON MAJOR CHAMPIONSHIPS ON THE MOST COURSES

Jack Nicklaus	11*	(Oakmont, Augusta National, Dallas AC, Muirfield, Baltusrol, St. Andrews, PGA National, Pebble Beach, Canterbury, Firestone, Oak Hill)
Walter Hagen	10	(Midlothian, Brae Burn, Inwood, Royal St. George's, Hoylake, French Lick, Olympia Fields, Salisbury, Cedar Crest, Muirfield)
Ben Hogan	8	(Portland, Riviera, Norwood Hills, Merion, Augusta National, Oakland Hills, Oakmont, Carnoustie)
Gene Sarazen	7	(Skokie, Oakmont, Pelham, Fresh Meadow, Prince's, Blue Mound, Augusta National)
Gary Player	7	(Muirfield, Augusta National, Aronimink, Bellerive, Carnoustie, Oakland Hills, Royal Lytham)
Tom Watson	7	(Carnoustie, Augusta National, Turnberry, Muirfield, Pebble Beach, Royal Troon, Royal Birkdale)
Bobby Jones	7*	(Inwood, Scioto, Royal Lytham, St. Andrews, Winged Foot, Interlachen, Hoylake)
Tiger Woods	7*	(Augusta National, Medinah, Pebble Beach, Valhalla, St. Andrews, Bethpage, Hoylake)
Sam Snead	5	(Seaview, St. Andrews, Augusta National, Hermitage, Oakmont)
Lee Trevino	5	(Oak Hill, Merion, Royal Birkdale, Muirfield, Tanglewood)
Byron Nelson	4	(Philadelphia, Hershey, Augusta National, Morraine)
Arnold Palmer	4*	(Augusta National, Cherry Hills, Royal Birkdale, Troon)
Raymond Floyd	4	(NCR, Augusta National, Southern Hills, Shinnecock Hills)
John H. Taylor	4	(Royal St. George's, St. Andrews, Deal, Hoylake)
Harry Vardon	4	(Muirfield, Prestwick, Royal St. George's, Chicago)
Jim Barnes	4	(Siwanoy, Engineers, Columbia, Prestwick)
Bobby Locke	4	(Royal St. George's, Troon, Royal Lytham, St. Andrews)
Peter Thomson	4	(Royal Birkdale, St. Andrews, Hoylake, Royal Lytham)

*The golfers above also won major amateur championships (U.S. and British) on the following additional courses: Jones (Merion, Oakmont, Minikahda, Brae Burn); Palmer (CC of Detroit); Nicklaus (Broadmoor); Woods (TPC Sawgrass, Newport, Pumpkin Ridge)

YOU KNOW YOU'RE IN SCOTLAND WHEN

1. You can walk your dog on the course.

2. A golf "club" or "society" means a group of people who gather once or a few times a year to have at the game. The group might be taxi drivers, chefs, carpenters—anything goes.

3. The proprietor of a bed-and-breakfast is thrilled to see you walk in with your clubs and immediately takes one in his hands to have a brief waggle.

4. The proprietor of said bed-and-breakfast invites you for a game.

5. You are listed in the B and B's registry not by name, but as "golfer."

6. You're invited into the home of a fellow who has a vast collection of golf books, prints, clubs, and other artifacts.

7. A player allots a specific amount of time to play golf—for instance, between ten o'clock and one o'clock—and simply plays as many holes as the time allows.

8. You're invited to join a threesome comprising a son, father, and grandfather, while their wives walk along with a picnic basket at hand.

9. Postcards with golf themes are sold in the National Museum and also the National Library, and a golfer wearing his club's red coat leads a display of uniforms through the years.

10. You stop thinking about stopping for a drink and a sandwich after nine holes and soon lose the concept of a "halfway house."

11. You put your scorecard away because you're no longer into what the Scots call "card and pencil" golf. You're just hitting the ball along, perhaps engaged in a match.

12. You hole every putt and don't think of playing preferred lies.

13. You walk the course at nightfall without clubs.

14. It's possible to bring up a family on a caddie's income.

15. People walking on the beach next to a links stop as you play a shot.

16. Just about every town has a street called Golf Road, leading to the local course.

17. You begin to appreciate bagpipes and to insist on haggis at least once a week during dinner.

18. You start to question your way of life and imagine yourself living in a cottage beside the course at Lossiemouth, or Gullane—or anywhere in the country.

YOUR GOLFING ZODIAC

Know your stars, know your game, know yourself. What does your sign tell you about whether you should play to the fat of the green, or should try to clear the creek in two? Find your sign, and find your traits and role models (all characteristics taken from standard non-golfing astrological sources).

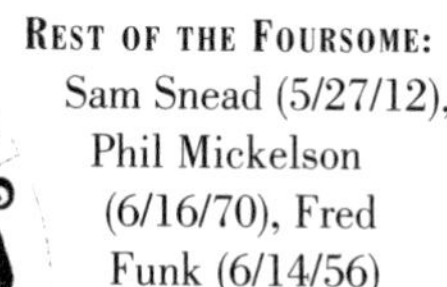

ARIES (MARCH 21–APRIL 19)

CHARACTERISTICS: Daring, risk-taker, energetic, careless.

REST OF THE FOURSOME: Seve Ballesteros (4/9/57), JoAnne Carner (4/4/39), Roberto de Vicenzo (4/14/23)

TAURUS (APRIL 20–MAY 20)

CHARACTERISTICS: Stable, cautious, deliberate, comfort-seeker, stubborn, resistant to change.

REST OF THE FOURSOME: Jim Furyk (5/12/70), Mike Weir (5/12/70), Johnny Miller (4/29/47)

STAR-CROSSED: John Daly (4/28/66)

GEMINI (MAY 21–JUNE 21)

CHARACTERISTICS: Alert, adaptable, friendly, curious, original, creative, talkative.

REST OF THE FOURSOME: Sam Snead (5/27/12), Phil Mickelson (6/16/70), Fred Funk (6/14/56)

CANCER (JUNE 22–JULY 22)

CHARACTERISTICS: Moody, sensitive, nurturing, shy, family-oriented.

REST OF THE FOURSOME: Billy Casper (6/24/31), Juli Inkster (6/24/60), Colin Montgomerie (6/23/63)

ON THE RANGE: Moe Norman (7/10/29)

STAR-CROSSED: Babe Didrikson Zaharias (6/26/14)

LEO (JULY 23–AUGUST 22)

CHARACTERISTICS: Proud, dignified, confident, superabundant willpower.

REST OF THE FOURSOME: Ben Hogan (8/13/12), Robert Trent Jones Jr. (7/24/39), Paula Creamer (8/5/86)

VIRGO
(AUGUST 23–SEPTEMBER 22)

CHARACTERISTICS: Perfectionist, analytical, skeptical, finicky.

REST OF THE FOURSOME: Ray Floyd (9/4/42), Bernhard Langer (8/27/57), Tom Watson (9/4/49)

STAR-CROSSED: Arnold Palmer (9/10/29)

LIBRA
(SEPTEMBER 23–OCTOBER 22)

CHARACTERISTICS: Charming, gracious, diplomatic, organized.

REST OF THE FOURSOME: Fred Couples (10/3/59), Ernie Els (10/17/69), Annika Sorenstam (10/9/70)

GATE-CRASHING: Michelle Wie (10/11/89)

SCORPIO
(OCTOBER 23–NOVEMBER 21)

CHARACTERISTICS: Strong-willed, secretive, possessive, investigator.

REST OF THE FOURSOME: Gary Player (11/1/35), David Duval (11/1/71), Ian Baker-Finch (10/24/60)

STAR-CROSSED: Chi Chi Rodriguez (10/23/35), Fuzzy Zoeller (11/11/51)

SAGITTARIUS
(NOVEMBER 22–DECEMBER 21)

CHARACTERISTICS: Independent, traveler, talkative, theatrical.

REST OF THE FOURSOME: Walter Hagen (12/21/92), Lee Trevino (12/1/39), Lanny Wadkins (12/5/49)

STAR-CROSSED: Tom Kite (12/9/49)

CAPRICORN
(DECEMBER 22–JANUARY 19)

CHARACTERISTICS: Mature, ambitious, purposeful, goal-seeker.

REST OF THE FOURSOME: Tiger Woods (12/30/75), Nancy Lopez (1/6/57), Ben Crenshaw (1/11/52)

STAR-CROSSED: Sergio Garcia (1/9/80)

AQUARIUS
(JANUARY 20–FEBRUARY 18)

CHARACTERISTICS: Stubborn, societal, mentally poised, opinionated, unconventional.

REST OF THE FOURSOME: Greg Norman (2/10/55), Payne Stewart (1/30/57), Curtis Strange (1/30/55)

PICK ANY POSITIVE ADJECTIVE AND IT'LL WORK: Jack Nicklaus (1/21/40)

PISCES
(FEBRUARY 19–MARCH 20)

CHARACTERISTICS: Vulnerable, shy, compassionate, theatrical, risk-taker, self-pitying

REST OF THE FOURSOME: Bobby Jones (3/17/02), Gene Sarazen (2/27/02), Vijay Singh (2/22/63)

WILL YE NO COME BACK AGAIN?

On October 9, 1958, Bobby Jones was given the Freedom of the City and the Royal Burgh of St. Andrews. He was the first American since Benjamin Franklin, in 1759, to be honored in this way. The ceremony took place in Younger Hall at the University of St. Andrews. Jones was crippled by syringomyelia, the disease that would take his life on December 18, 1971, but managed to address the gathering after Provost Robert Leonard made his introductory remarks.

Here are Jones's remarks in front of the 1,700 people who filled the auditorium:

"*The Provost has given me permission to tell you that, lacking a middle initial of his own, he will, in future, be known as Robert T. Leonard. I consider that the greatest triumph I have ever won in Scotland.*

"*People of St. Andrews, I know that you are doing me a very high honor and I want you to know that I am very grateful for it. I appreciate the fact that my good friend, the Provost, has glossed over my first encounter with the Old Course, but I would like you to know that I did not say a lot of things that were put out that I said. But I could not play the course, and I did not think anyone else could. I ask you to remember, of course, that at the time I had attained the ripe old age of nineteen years, and I did not know much about golf.*

"*Actually, that first time, we got along pretty good, the Old Course and me, for two rounds. I scored 151—of course there was no wind. My boys here this week will admit that ain't bad.*

"But I started off in the third round and the wind was blowing right in my face. That day it was really blowing! I reached the turn in 43, and when I was playing the 7th, 8th, and 9th, I thought, 'Well, that's fine, I'll be blowing home with the wind.' Well, as I stood on the tenth tee it turned right round and it blew home all the way against me. I got a six at the 10th, and then, at the 11th, I put my shot into Hill Bunker, not Strath, as they said. They also say that when I got out of that bunker I hit my ball into the Eden. That's not so, for I never did get the ball out of Hill Bunker. [However, Jones, in his autobiography *Down the Fairway*, wrote that he did get his ball out of Hill Bunker and onto the green, where he had a short putt left "for a horrid six." He picked up his ball, tore up his card, and continued to play, although he couldn't post a score. "I have some sterling regrets in golf," Jones wrote. "This is the principal regret—that ever I quit in a competition."]

"I came back to the Old Course in 1926 to practice for the Walker Cup, but before that I had a lot of thinking and talking to a lot of transplanted Scots who knew St. Andrews. I set about studying it and I pretty soon found out that local knowledge is a real important thing if you want to play that golf course. You have to study it, and the more you study the more you learn; the more you learn the more you study it. I have this to say of the Old Course, that after my chastisement she seemed to be satisfied for she never let me lose another contest. When I say that, I mean what she did to the other fellow.

"But you people of St. Andrews have a sensitivity and an ability to extend cordiality in an ingenious way. When I won the Amateur in 1930 and got back home, I rêceived, through the post, a perfect miniature of the Amateur Championship Trophy. It was an exquisite thing, perfect in every detail, down to the

names inscribed on it. There was an inscription on it, which, at this moment, I could not trust myself to repeat. That miniature came to me with the simple message that it was from fellow-members of the R&A. It has remained my prized possession.

"Then I have another great memory. In 1936 I set out with my wife to go to the Olympic Games in Berlin. Of course, I took my clubs along with me because in those days they were very necessary impedimenta. We met some friends and planned to spend two days at Gleneagles. Well, we played two rounds there. Then I told my friends I could not be this close to St. Andrews without making a pilgrimage to it. We got there before noon and had lunch. I had been playing perfectly dreadful golf, too, I can tell you. Anyhow, we finished lunch and walked to the first tee—and there were waiting about 2,000 people!

"I said to myself, 'This is an awful thing to do to my friends if they have come to see me golf with the dreadful stuff I am playing.' Anyway, Willie Auchterlonie and Gordon Lockhart started off with me, but Gordon stopped after two holes. By that time the crowd was about 4,000. Such a spontaneous show of warmth and affection I have never known in my life. It was such a splendid welcome you people gave me that I played the best golf I had played for four years, and certainly never since. I had a three at the second—I'm not bragging. Then I got to the sixth—in those days we were playing the old tee and I still think it's the better tee. I say so for this reason, that the second shot you have to play then is the old St. Andrews run-up shot. I said to myself, 'Look, Jones, these people are all expecting you to play that run-up, so don't you funk it.'

"I can tell you it was with considerable misgivings that I played the shot, but that ball ran up and on the green and it finished six feet from the flag. I holed it for a three. That, and

my score, were just nothing [but] the inspiration of playing St. Andrews. I went out in 32 and had a two at the 8th. I was so happy and in a transport almost when I reached the 11th I went over Strath going for the green and landed in a bunker that no longer exists. It was fifteen feet from the hole and I went out looking for that bunker the other day and the greenkeeper told me it had never been there. I said to him, 'You can't tell me that, because I played two shots in it in 1936.'

"That was a great day for me—and now I have this. I could take out of my life everything except my experiences at St. Andrews and I would still have had a rich and full life.

"There are two very important words in the English language that are very much mis-used and abused. They are 'friend' and 'friendship.' When I say to a person, 'I am your friend,' I have said about the ultimate. When I say, 'You are my friend,' I am assuming too much, for it is a possibility that you do not want to accept my friendship. When I have said as much about you and you have done so much for me, I think that when I say, 'You are my friend,' under these circumstances, I am, at the same time, affirming my affection and regard for you and expressing my complete faith in you and my trust in the sincerity of your friendship.

"Therefore, when I say now to you, 'Greetings, my friends at St. Andrews,' I know I am not presuming because of what has passed between us.

"I hope I have not been too sentimental on this theme of friendship, but it is one that is so important at this time. It is another element of the sensitivity that you people have—a wonderful, warm relationship. Friendship should be the great note of this world golf meeting, because not only people, but nations, need friends. Let us hope that this meeting will sow seeds

which will germinate and grow into important friendships among nations later on.

"I just want to say to you that this is the finest thing that has ever happened to me. Whereas that little cup was first in my heart, now this occasion at St. Andrews will take first place always. I like to think about it this way that, now I officially have the right to feel at home in St. Andrews as much as I, in fact, always have done."

Herbert Warren Wind attended the ceremony, and wrote in *The New Yorker* of what transpired following Jones's speech.

"At the end of his talk he was helped from the stage to his electric golf cart, and as he directed it down the center aisle toward the door the whole hall suddenly burst into the old Scottish song 'Will Ye No Come Back Again?,' and it came pouring out with all the wild, overwhelming emotion of a pibroch wailed in some lonesome glen."

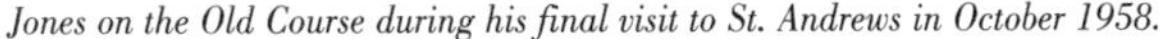

Jones on the Old Course during his final visit to St. Andrews in October 1958.

ACKNOWLEDGMENTS

Ideas seem to come out of nowhere, but they usually take root somewhere. Jeff Neuman and I were returning from a golf game when he broached the subject of working on this book together. We started firing bits and pieces about golf at one another, and presto, the roots took hold. The only problem was that now we had to get to work.

Categories kept coming to us, and we kept sending them back and forth. (Thank you, e-mail.) Doug Pepper at McClelland & Stewart in Toronto loved the idea, as did Peter Workman at Workman Publishing in New York. My agents Bruce Westwood and Natasha Daneman were enthusiastic from the start, and I record my thanks also to Jeff's agent, Faith Hamlin of Sanford J. Greenburger in New York. My wife Nell and I have become close friends with Faith and her husband Greg, a wonderful and unexpected consequence of the work on this book. To Nell I record my appreciation for her willingness to put up with the disorderly way I filled rooms in our home with research material. Nell doesn't play golf, but I can't imagine a better sport.

Thanks also to Ruth Waterman, who read the manuscript at various stages and made perceptive suggestions; to Jeff Mingay, Tom Doak, John Companiotte, Dan King, Catherine Lewis, John Marshall and Don Thom for help along the way with various categories in which they have particular knowledge; to Jennifer Griffin, Cassie Murdoch, and Richard Rosen at Workman and Greg Midland for their editing skills and advice. To Brad Klein and Harvey Freedenberg I record a special thanks for their friendship on and off the course and on the printed page and in many conversations about writing and golf, for sharing MTLTG (more to life than golf) days with me, and for helping bring order to my thinking about this disorderly compendium.

—*Lorne Rubenstein*

In the modern age, any honest author must first and foremost thank Google, without which this book would be impossible.

Our disorderly endeavor got started thanks to an act of friendship by a literary agent—not my literary agent—who thought I might enjoy taking a shot at writing a very miscellaneous kind of golf book. Because he made this suggestion while having nothing to gain from my efforts, I will not mention his name here, lest he be shunned by his peers. The idea percolated, and then I shared it with Lorne Rubenstein, as he notes above. I had worked with Lorne on his wonderful book *A Season in Dornoch,* and I thought it would be fun to put this together with him. I was right.

My next stroke of good fortune came when the proposal caught the eye of Peter Workman. Through my years as an editor, I had always admired the creativity and sensibility of the books from Workman Publishing. My regard for Peter's instincts is such that when he indicated he wanted a volume that would be three times as long as the one we were proposing, I leapt at the chance to take on the work. I have never had the slightest regret about that decision.

Many friends have been forced to listen to my enthusiasm for obscure facts and odd juxtapositions in the course of the research; to Bill Hohauser, Alan Spatrick, Paul Zanis, Carol Trefethern, Jon Malki, Doug Grad, and John Chuhran, my thanks. I am grateful to those who made suggestions and answered strange queries ("Was Tommy Aaron wearing glasses when he won the Masters?"), and were generous with their thoughts and knowledge: Craig Brass, Bill Carle, Kevin Costello, Mark Cubbedge, Jane Fader, David Griffith, Mary Hirdt, Jill Maxwell, Valerie Melvin, Greg Miles, Laura Neal, Craig Smith, Frank Thomas, Ron Whitten. Steve Goodwin and George Peper read an early draft, and were kind enough to tell me what they thought, or at least something encouraging.

Oh, what the hell. The agent was David Black. Thanks, David.

My agent—and my friend, my protector, my confidante, and my default movie companion—is Faith Hamlin, and I'm happy that she's finally getting some financial windfall out of our twenty-plus years of talk and laughter. On Workman Publishing's behalf, our phalanx of editors included Jennifer Griffin, Cassie Murdoch, Richard Rosen, Randy Lotowycz, Melanie Bennitt, and Greg Midland.

Laura Sherman signed on for this journey after it was well under way, and has proved to be an endless source of encouragement, inspiration, and joy. My life is infinitely better because she is in it, and it wasn't so bad to begin with.

Finally, I'd like to express my appreciation to two people who played a vital and unknowing role in my personal evolution. I had the good fortune to work with many fine people in the golf world during my days as an acquiring book editor, but Bo Links and Jim Finegan taught me the most important lesson of all: that it is possible to be a mature, productive, worldly, and engaging adult, while still being absolutely batty about the game of golf. I am grateful for their example, and hope they like what I've done with the torch they passed me.

—*Jeff Neuman*

ABOUT THE AUTHORS

JEFF NEUMAN's fascination with golf probably began at age eight when he tried to wrap a putter around his older brother's neck. He has played the game during a partial solar eclipse; on the fairways of New York City; through a herd of grazing sheep; and in a ninesome with Willie Nelson. He has worked on golf books with Harvey Penick, Davis Love III, Butch Harmon, Jack Nicklaus, Raymond Floyd, David Owen, and Alan Shipnuck. He has written about Pete Rose for *The New York Times*, about the golf courses of New Zealand and Australia for *Links Magazine*, and about Pinehurst for *Private Clubs*. He lives in New York City.

LORNE RUBENSTEIN took up golf after watching older folks hit all sorts of weird shots while he caddied for them at a Toronto course. Now he's older than most of the golfers for whom he caddied, and he's the one hitting the weird shots. He's spent a summer in Dornoch, Scotland, evenings putting by the lights of passing cars at his local club, Don Valley in Toronto, and taken lessons and advice from David Leadbetter, Rick Smith, Hank Haney, Manuel de la Torre, Tiger Woods, Nick Price, and Mike Weir, not to mention people he meets in pubs, cafes, and on the subway. He's written eight books and contributes a twice-weekly column to *The Globe and Mail*, Canada's national newspaper. He lives with his wife Nell in Toronto and Jupiter, Florida.

PHOTO CREDITS

AP/Wide World Photos: 5, 19, 20, 21, 28, 34, 37, 38, 39, 45, 47, 51, 58, 61, 65, 70, 77, 78, 80, 83, 91, 94, 101, 102, 103, 105, 119, 121, 127, 136, 138, 142, 148 both, 150, 153, 160, 167, 175, 178, 187, 190, 194, 202, 212, 219, 221, 224, 241, 246, 257, 265, 266, 268, 275 bottom, 275 top, 279, 284, 291, 294, 301, 313, 319, 320, 325, 326 bottom, 328, 329, 330, 346, 351, 355, 360, 370, 378; **Corbis:** 159, 215; **Evan Schiller:** 67; **Getty Images/Hulton Archive:** 131; **Globe Photos:** 111; **Harry Snyder:** 323; **Historic Golf Photos:** 25; **Larry Lambrecht:** 12, 14, 15, 22, 23, 28, 354, 359; **Library of Congress Prints and Photographs Division:** 9, 33, 73, 238; **Mary Evans Picture Library:** 92, 183, 195; **Phil Sheldon Golf Picture Library:** 72, 193, 228, 308; **Photofest:** 249; **Robin Nelson Golf Course Architect:** 171; **The Granger Collection:** 247; **Tony Roberts Photography:** 6, 48, 84, 141, 166, 192, 217, 237, 273, 321, 343, 344, 358; **USGA Golf-House:** 318, 356.

SELECTED INDEX

NOTE: Page numbers in *italics* indicate photographs and illustrations.

A

B

C

T

U